Hewing to Experience

SHERMAN PAUL

Hewing to Experience

Essays and Reviews on Recent American Poetry and Poetics, Nature and Culture

University of Iowa Press Iowa City

University of Iowa Press, Iowa City 52242

Printed in the United States of America
First edition, 1989

Design by Richard Hendel
Typesetting by G&S Typesetters, Austin, Texas
Printing and binding by Thomson-Shore, Dexter, Michigan

Library of Congress Cataloging-in-Publication Data
Paul, Sherman.
Hewing to experience: essays and reviews on recent American poetry and poetics, nature and culture/by Sherman Paul.—1st ed.
p. cm.
ISBN 0-87745-247-4
1. American poetry—20th century—History and criticism. 2. Poetics. I. Title.
PS323.5.P29 1989 89-32349
811'.509—dc20 CIP

Drawings from "The Scribe" *alfarda* and the Temple of the Inscriptions, Palenque, Yucatán, by Linda Schele

for George F. Butterick

Contents

Introduction

It is fitting, I suppose, that I am writing this in the woods, where, after all these years, I find myself, as Charles Olson said of himself at Gloucester, "physically [at] home." Rereading the work of twenty years gathered here—yes, gathered here and some of it written here—I see the special fitness of having written about recent poetry because this poetry confirmed my desire and taught me how to "Love the World—and stay inside it." Again I cite Olson, who knew the large work the generation of poets associated with him had done—knew, on daily evidence of ecological spoliation, the odds of living "in a world on an Earth like this one we / few American poets have / carved out of Nature and of God."

This is the exigent issue, the issue of most critical importance to me, and almost all of the poets who claimed my attention—initiating sallies of inquiry and steady keeping-up—have engaged it. Having written a new poetry, they have also proposed a new poetics, a requisite poetics of *descendentalism, ambulation,* and *worlding* that helps us enter the field, live processually in our experience, and find ourselves at home *here/now,* to use the title of a journal I once wrote here in the practice of this discipline.

Descendentalism, ambulation, worlding. These somewhat heavy words will be lightened, I hope, by subsequent explication, and perhaps all that is needed now is to note their respective polar terms—*transcendentalism, saltation, world alienation*—and to see in the movement from them a shift as radical as (indeed, consequent with) that from philosophical idealism to pragmatism or, as Whitehead puts it, from Kant to his own philosophy. "For Kant," Whitehead says in *Process and Reality,* "the world emerges from the subject; for the philosophy of organism, the subject emerges from the world." Whitehead, the patron modern philosopher of poets to whom process is reality—the pre-Socratic philosopher is Heraclitus—also brings us home by putting mind, the sovereign power of idealists, in its place; and much of what the new poetics addresses in behalf of stance toward the world and obedience to it is succinctly stated in a sentence I take to be Whitehead's: "An experiencing subject is one occasion of a sensitive reaction to an actual world." Now, randomly opening Robert Creeley's *A Quick Graph,* I find underlined an injunction equally succinct and to the point: "At no moment may one step aside—to think *about* the world, rather than *in* it or *of* it or *as* it." This is to say that in our attentions and the work at hand—writing notably—we must *hew to experience,* "find ways," Olson says in "Human Universe," "to hew to experience as it is."

We come to "an actual earth of value" (Olson once more) by means of poetry, for *poesis* is making/creation, and poetry has always been the human agency of this homecoming. Poetry mediates the primary contradiction of nature and culture, the ultimate ground of myth. When we speak now of the need to recover some of the vital elements of nature-related cultures, we are, in effect, repudiating the idealizing, and concomitant aestheticizing, by which cultures become Culture, nothing particular and local so much as transcendent and universal, a realm where the mind in its supremacy may enjoy the rationality and beauty of its Ideas—and, as Ortega said in opposing it, its bigotry. The task of restoring the vital reason to which Ortega called the first generation of moderns—it was, he said, the modern theme—remains the task of postmodern poets who would bring poetry back (and down) to life and make it once again, as Tristan Tzara said in thinking of "primitive peoples," "a way of life rather than a subsidiary manifestation of intelligence and will." Do we need to recall Pound's lines on "a botched civilization" or the dilemma of Eliot's Prufrock to realize the strength of the alliance of poetry (Poetry) and Culture and that, in America, poetry has not often answered to a culture in the American grain and to what Dennis and Barbara Tedlock call "teachings from the American earth"? American criticism from Emerson's time to the present, as the work of canon-making shows, turns on this issue, and what Pound told Creeley in 1950 might have been said by Emerson to Whitman a century earlier (when there was another *Dial,* the progenitor of the magazine with which Pound dates the modern era): ". . . isn't time for Creel's generation to revolt against the dead hand, dating from Dial or before / backwash of aestheticism?"

Aestheticism is what Pound knew in England before he took new bearings: the religion of Art that Culture, defined by Arnold, had become; the Genteel Tradition in America that William James "broke," as Santayana said—broke by insisting on *ambulation,* the finding of ideas in experience (not Ideas above it, as in *saltation*) and their employment in ongoing experience. *Ambulation:* a good word for walkers *in* the world; a word, with *saltation,* I owe to Richard A. Hocks' *Henry James and Pragmatistic Thought,* where these terms from William James' letters guide the study of two great writers who had learned that "knowing as it exists concretely" is processual, an open-ended activity, "a continual event."

These admittedly brief formulations should make it clear where I place the New Criticism (Tory Formalism, according to Grant Webster) in which I was trained at Iowa in 1938–41, and why *Understanding Poetry,* which I studied in the first edition, often serves in what I have written as a signpost to mark a point of turning, a road no longer taken. This is not to say that I owe nothing to the New Criticism—I am especially indebted for the discipline of close reading and the respect I feel for the literary "object" and the literal work of words. And because I entered the conversation in the study of the New Criticism, I joined the issue, the fundamental issue of my work. Some poets, more aware, more needful, had also come to this turning (see the installments on the Olson/Creeley correspondence), but even though our paths crossed at this time I did not find them on the way until later, perhaps because I was not yet as concerned with poetics and was chiefly concerned with the neglect of history and the avoidance of American literature in New Critical teaching.

The collection of essays with which I think to place the present collection is called *Repossessing and Renewing: Essays in the Green American Tradition* (1976). It represents the cultural criticism I had undertaken, some twenty-five years' work that began with a study of the Emerson whom neither the New Humanists nor the New Critics honored. It overlaps *Hewing to Experience* by virtue of essays on William Carlos Williams and Gary Snyder and because the Emerson who moves it is the poet of experience and the proponent of unclosed genres and an aesthetics of liberation. The present collection could no more omit Emerson, who speaks for resurgence, than it could Whitman, more often acknowledged by recent generations of poets, the agenda of the "new American poetry" (Donald Allen's title) read out of Whitman by Creeley in the introduction to his *Whitman*. The overlapping, inevitably, works both ways because the poetics with which the present collection is concerned is not narrowly construed—is searched out in its cultural, historical, political, and philosophical bearings. And the collections go together in hewing to my experience, in helping me track my life in the very work of scholarship and criticism. I see in them, so to speak, how things add up, and think of them as serial criticism, after the serial poem, the poem, as Louis Zukofsky said, that poets both live with and for, and write all of their lives.

Both collections are the result of day-to-day work, of writing, or preparing to write, book-length studies. They are not ancillary, because work that claims full attention is not subordinate. It would be truer to the case to say that the essays and reviews in *Hewing to Experience* accompany other work, specifically *The Music of Survival* (on William Carlos Williams), *Hart's Bridge* (on Crane), *Olson's Push* (on Olson), *The Lost America of Love* (on Robert Creeley, Edward Dorn, and Robert Duncan), *In Search of the Primitive* (on David Antin, Jerome Rothenberg, and Gary Snyder), and *In Love with the Gratuitous* (on Armand Schwerner). Merely to name the poets treated in these books is to chart a tradition of lively and pertinent experiment, of "advance," as Williams said. It is also to suggest the extent to which the headings of the collection follow the trajectory of the books, why the essays and reviews cluster as they do, and to give notice, in what is often advocacy, of poets not named in the headings who nevertheless are prominent in the discussion because of my stake in them. The books themselves follow the course of an attempt to engage in criticism openly, that is, after the fashion of open poetry, and the meditative proceeding of the last three books is represented here by this introduction and the most recent long meditation, on Barry Lopez. This meditative practice of encounter-and-dialogue accounts, I think, for the personal register of work coincident with it—the installments on the Olson/Creeley correspondence, for example, and the essays on Snyder and Berry.

Still, in being occasional—in being prompted by occasions, the publication of books and other events of intellectual life—the critical work here is essentially open, and all the more so because of "the specificity of the response," which, as Raymond Williams says, "is not a judgment but a practice, in active and complex relations with the situation and conditions of the practice and, necessarily, with all other practices." This is reason enough for including reviews, which are current and always engage me at the edge of thought, and are not brief notices but, as I learned from F. O. Matthiessen, in *The Responsibilities of the Critic,* "short piece[s] of criticism." The exception to this may be the single paragraph devoted to Robert Coles' book on Williams, written, I recall, during a long wait at the hospital. I include it for the record in order to show how the critic, by attending to new work, keeps record. This, too, is a responsibility of the critic, as is *evaluation,* to use a less harsh word that explains the process of *judgment.* In his minimal prescription, Matthiessen says that a review "should furnish exposition and description . . . enable you to feel concretely what is being described . . . and give you in the process an evaluation." He has in mind the reviewing of works of literature, but what he says—and goes on to say: that one should place the work, tell what it adds, and consider principles of art—applies to works of scholarship and criticism.

I am most stringent, I find, when scholarship is thin and critical practice is inappropriate to the interpretation and assessment of radically new writing. To put this another way, I am critical of those who have not sufficiently prepared themselves and those, sometimes as a consequence of this, whose practice is *saltatory,* who use schema, an a priori procedure that both privileges the mind and forecloses full response. It seems to me, even as I give order to my own work here, that criticism is not so much the business of putting things in boxes as of finding them and finding out about them—and of encountering them, in Buber's sense, in the expectation of changing one's mind. This is why what I have done is exploratory, the work a *periplus,* a description of coasts, unknown to me, that, sometimes at sea, I have been fortunate to come on—aided, I should add, by the similar charting of others. And this is why I am most adamant and partisan when the "other practices" Raymond Williams speaks of are those of established critics ("Establishment" critics) who are reluctant, or do not know how, to give new poets a hearing.

The gathering together of these essays and reviews makes a book of more than usual range, one, I think, with an integrity of its own. The essays and reviews in each section are ordered chronologically to show how I made my way from one thing to another and how literary history, respected in the order of the sections, depends initially on what one chooses to attend. The first section is prefatorial and sets out the contexts of poetry and the insistences (not themes, because they emerged in encounter) that I discuss: "open" as against the judgmental practice of criticism, the crisis of criticism at the present time, the poetics of "projective verse," the ideogram and the serial poem, poetry and old age, ethnopoetics, the gift exchange of the imagination, canon-making, and nature poetry. Rereading this section now, the essays and reviews seem to me to belong to a single discussion in which criticism is (re)aligned with the "American" tradition that runs from Emerson and Whitman to Williams and Olson. This tradition may be said to be "American" because it accords primacy to experience, the "original relation" that Emerson called for in *Nature* and the "nakedness" that Olson called for in *The Maximus Poems*. Openness covers both, and nothing is so essential, as Olson told Creeley early on, as "this open man, staying open in there. . . ."

The formal means I employ—essay, review, position paper, lecture, letter, and meditation—also answer to the need for openness.

The subsequent sections require little explanation. Some, those on Williams and Crane, for example, survey scholarly and critical studies. The reviews of Williams follow my own early book and an early essay on *Kora in Hell,* and comment on the ever-widening discussion of his work; the reviews of Crane both precede and follow my own book and are chiefly concerned with contesting the New Critics' assessment and placement of Crane. With contemporary poets—Olson, Creeley, Snyder, Lopez—most of the critical engagement is with the poets' work and, of necessity, is of the pioneering kind (probably the most gratifying) that helps to open the field. To my knowledge there is no other considered commentary on all the published volumes of the Olson/Creeley correspondence, a measure, surely, of what is called "the situation in poetry." This commentary, which provided me a second-take on two major poets and an opportunity to treat in detail the emergence of a new generation of poets and the evolution of a new poetics, now refocuses the book. The concluding sections on Snyder, Berry, and Lopez address the relationship of poetry and ecology.

I put the epigraphs last. I take them from serial poems.

> pulling things together as they happen
> and getting them altogether occasionally
> —Stuart MacKinnon, *The Intervals*

> the precision of openness
> is not a vagueness
> it is an accumulation
> —bp Nichol, *The Martyrology*, Book IV

Wolf Lake
September 1988 S.P.

PART I
Insistences

Open(ing) Criticism

1. Let's begin with an Englishman whose work immediately speaks to the issue. "*Criticism,*" Raymond Williams says in *Keywords,* "has become a very difficult word, because although its predominant general sense is of fault-finding, it has an underlying sense of judgment and a very confusing specialized sense, in relation to art and literature, which depends on assumptions that may now be breaking down." That's the initial sentence of a long entry. Much of it is available to us simply by inspecting the associations that *criticism* calls up in our minds. *Criticism* derives from *kritos,* Greek, a judge. Fault-finding, negative judgment, is its persistent primary meaning. And so it's the closing phrase of Williams' sentence, already quick with his animus as a critic, that arouses us: "assumptions that may now be breaking down"—yes, assumptions that he himself is breaking down.

Criticism, Williams observes, was early associated with "learned or 'informed' ability" and "still often tries to retain this sense." It acquires the weight of *Culture* and *discrimination* and marks the separation (difference) between critic and reader—*consumer,* as Williams reminds us. What this separation involves is the "social development of personal impressions and responses, to the point where they could be represented as STANDARDS of *judgment.*" The retrospective account tells. "The notion," he continues, "that response was judgment depended, of course [of course! as we now know], on the social confidence of a class and later a profession. The confidence was variously specified, originally as *learning* or scholarship, later as *cultivation* and *taste,* later still as SENSIBILITY."

Now, though forms of this confidence have broken down, other bases for judgment have been found; and "what has not been questioned," Williams says, "is the assumption of 'judgment.'" This questioning, necessary to an open criticism, is the burden of his work.

Let me cite a substantial portion of his argument:

> What is at issue is not only the association between *criticism* and fault-finding but the more basic association between *criticism* and judgment as apparently general and natural processes. As a term for the social or professional generalization of the processes of reception of any but especially the more formal kinds of COMMUNICATION . . . , *criticism* is ideological not only in the sense that it assumes the position of the *consumer* but also in the sense that it masks this position by a succession of abstractions of its real terms of response (as *judgment, taste, cultivation; disinterested, qualified, rigorous* and so on). This then actively prevents that understanding of response which does not assume the habit (or right or duty) of judgment. The continuing sense of *criticism* as fault-finding is the most useful linguistic influence against the confidence of this habit, but there are also signs, in the occasional rejection of *criticism* as a definition of conscious response, of a more significant rejection of the habit itself. The point would then be, not to find some other term to replace it, while continuing the same kind of activity, but to get rid of the habit, which depends, fundamentally, on the abstraction of response from its real situation and circumstances: the elevation to judgment, and to an apparently general process, when what always needs to be understood is the specificity of the response, which is not a judgment but a practice, in active and complex relations with the situation and conditions of the practice, and, necessarily, with all other practices.

2. To get rid of the habit of judgment is a total project, essentially transvaluative, requiring nothing less than a revolution in thought. For the habit of judgment depends on deeply established dualistic and hierarchical modes of thought, and these must be abdicated. Not only is it requisite to replace judgmental with admirative criticism ("admire first," Gaston Bachelard counsels, "then you will understand"), it is necessary to enter a universe, in actuality as well as of discourse, where this is possible—where we do not find ourselves separated from either art-object or reader but immediately related to them as elements of our "occasion" in the "field." The model of open criticism, as "occasion" and "field" suggest, might well be the open poetics brought forward so vigorously in our time, a poetics dependent in its turn on the conception of an open universe such as Alfred North Whitehead proposes in *Process and Reality.*

An open universe is a process universe. Both "open" and "process" tell us that it is a universe of risk (and possibility), of chaos (and creativity). To enter such a world we must yield the ego and its imposing rationality for the enabling condition of responsiveness Keats so fittingly called Negative Capability. We must become "capable of being [yes: capable of being] in uncertainties, mysteries, doubts, without any irritable reaching after fact and reason. . . ." With William Carlos Williams we must prize the "unbound thinking" that this permits us, and not out of fear—"the tidy fear chaos," Charles Olson said of T. S. Eliot—set boundaries to and close off the field. In fact, we must give over the rules (the *a priori* conditions of order, form, perfection, finality) for modes of action and discourse that exemplify our situation in the field and adequately tell the multidimensionality, the very phenomenology, of experience. We must not impose idea on act because "ideas," as Olson reminds us, "are not what we act to, however much we do see afterwards. . . ."

We are familiar with the conventional rules of verse and with the free verse that challenged them, that demanded open rather than closed forms, forms more responsive to process and less intent on product. D. H. Lawrence called such open verse the "poetry of the present" because it addressed the present, the immediate occasion, and was not moved by reminiscence. Such verse is never "finished" (in two senses); it has "no static perfection, none of that finality which we find so satisfying because we are so frightened." We may feel, with Robert Frost, that verse-making of this kind is comparable to playing tennis with the net down. But in Robert Duncan's rejoinder—as applicable to the practice of criticism as to the practice of poetry—we see that it is an activity of a different kind: "For those who see life as something other than a tennis game, without bounds, and who seek in their sciences and arts to come into that life, into an imagination of that life, the thought comes that the counterpart of free verse may be free thought and free movement. The explorer displays the meaning of physical excellence in a way different from that displayed by the tennis player."

3. Both William Carlos Williams and Charles Olson make conspicuous use of the explorer because the activity of discovery accords with an open poetics as well as with the insistence in criticism on an American point of view. For them criticism is finding, not fault-finding. It is, as in poetry, that "New effort of attention," which, Lawrence observed, "'discovers' a

new world. . . ." An explorer is not a judge, a guardian of the rules. As Williams said, fully aware of the difference, he belongs with the *out-laws,* the brigands who live in the open, outside the walled cities. He is moved by the desire to find something new, or fresh: that moment, Williams says, in which we truly live; that nakedness, that original relation to the universe, the mandate of our art, announced by Emerson. He is moved by the desire to move beyond the boundaries of previous (past) experience, to open or extend the field, the territory of possibility.

This idea has always been an attractive element of the myth of "America," and many writers from the time of Emerson and Whitman, with their concern for what Emerson called "unclosed genres," have endorsed it. It stands, for example, behind Duncan's statement that "the inspiration of Reason was to close off consciousness in an area that was civilized, European, superior in race, practical and Christian"—a statement that names some of the limitations an open poetics and criticism questions.

The poet takes the risk of entering the field, of standing exposed in his occasion. So does the critic, who now encounters art-objects as part of his occasion ("in active and complex relation with the situation and conditions of the practice"). He may be said to discover them in the way an explorer discovers a coast, enters a new terrain, and with the intent of telling this and opening it to us. His practice is one of participation not domination ("coercive criticism"). Necessarily tentative, he reports only what he himself experiences in the encounter. He does not raise his "personal impressions and responses" to judgment, giving them authority by mediating them—and distancing them—in terms of universals. He does not, to cite Raymond Williams again, abstract his response "from its real [immediate] situation and circumstances. . . ." Nor does he consider the reader, who also belongs to (shares) the occasion, a consumer whose responses may profitably be intermitted by superior judgment. Instead, in being open, the critic acknowledges relationship, is generous and generative. He transfers his energy and the energy of the work, a fact easily recognized in our response and notably, especially, in his voice, which is never magisterial.

In belonging to its occasion, criticism of this kind belongs to a specific place. For Americans, who have necessarily had to consider "Europe" in forging their criticism, it belongs to America and represents an American point of view. "Criticism," William Carlos Williams insisted in *Contact,* "must be first in contact with the world for which it is intended." He objected to "appreciative articles . . . being written at [him] from Europe."

If the American genius in practical matters has been the result of "paying naked attention first to the thing itself," why should such "discovery and invention" be any less successful in the arts? in criticism?

4. Williams' appeal is clearly indebted to the functional demands of our organic tradition. *Form follows function:* forms answer living needs, and so must criticism. In speaking up for an original relationship to the universe, Emerson also asks, "Why should not we have a poetry and philosophy of insight and not of tradition. . . ?" Why shouldn't we attend our experience? follow, as George Santayana says Emerson did, the transcendental ("critical") method and not the transcendental system? Or, as Santayana suggests in his famous essay on the Genteel Tradition, why not turn to "the daily discipline of contact with things, so different from the verbal discipline of the schools"?

The issue here is a long-standing one—long-standing because of the tenacity of Tradition or "the mind of Europe," as Eliot defines it in "Tradition and the Individual Talent." Santayana accounted for it by noting that "America is a young country with an old mentality," or rather, as he amends this, "a country of two mentalities, one a survival of the beliefs and standards of the fathers [the "hereditary philosophy"], the other an expression of the instincts, practice, and discoveries of the younger generations." Open criticism, obviously, belongs with the latter, is the legatee of the organic-functional tradition in American thought, a tradition, early and late, opposed to the Genteel Tradition.

Two mentalities: two habits of thought and two traditions. We have known them as paleface and redskin and most recently as involving a "poetics of domesticity" and a "poetics of adventure." Our concern with the map vs. the garden also names them; and they are the voices, literary and vernacular, that we often hear in the dialogue (*dialectic*) of American literature.

Eliot identifies them in the title of his most influential essay, "Tradition and the Individual Talent" (1919). For convenience we might cluster their associations in the following way:

Tradition	is to	*Talent*	as
Europe (mind of)		America (energy of)	
Culture		(a) culture	
past		present	

universal	particular
symbol	image
idea	act
judgment	discovery
frame	experience (unbounded)
closed	open
time (history?)	space

5. In considering examples of critical practice we might turn first to another essay of Eliot's, that on William Blake, published in the year following "Tradition and the Individual Talent" and demonstrating its thesis. In this essay, so wonderfully accommodating yet dismissive, Eliot speaks with all the authority of "the mind of Europe" and in its defense. He acknowledges that Blake is a genius and is honest "in a world too frightened to be honest." He notes—introducing terms his later judgments will recall—that Blake was not "a naïf, a wild man. . . ." Up to the age of twenty, Blake, he says, was "traditional"; his beginnings were "normal." This Blake is not troublesome, but rather the "naked man" he became: the poet who "saw man naked, and from the center of his own crystal," the poet with his "naked vision" and his "naked philosophy." (Eliot is not fond of nakedness, the divestiture and attendant exposure that are conditions of open poetry.) The trouble with the naked man is that "his philosophy, like his visions, like his insight, like his technique [are] his own." The naked man is the individual talent *in extremis;* he himself does everything, submits to nothing traditional, discards all previous framing devices. Consequently, Eliot says, Blake became "eccentric" and was "inclined to formlessness."

Though eccentricity, for Eliot, is inevitably the result of making one's personality central, it is formlessness that especially concerns him here. He addresses it when he speaks of the necessary "structure" of long poems. He says, categorically, that "you cannot create a very large poem without introducing a more impersonal point of view, or splitting it up into various personalities." This statement covers his and, perhaps, Ezra Pound's practice, but not Blake's (nor Whitman's, the poet who, for Lawrence, exemplifies "the poetry of the present") because what he means by structure is "a framework of accepted and traditional ideas. . . ." Blake, we now learn, is only a genius where Dante is a classic because Blake felt

that "he must needs create a philosophy as well as a poetry." He indulged himself. His genius was not "controlled by a respect for impersonal reason, for common sense, for the objectivity of science. . . ." He refused to order and validate his experience by using the "accepted" frame, that is, "the mind of Europe," of which Dante is a preeminent representative. And so Eliot, aware of the danger of following the example of Blake, admonishes us by reminding us that "we are not really so remote from the Continent, or from our own past, as to be deprived of the advantages of culture [Culture] if we wish them." Should we refuse these advantages, our work, like Blake's in Eliot's summary judgment, would exhibit "a certain meanness of culture [Culture]," the "crankiness," the "eccentricity, which frequently affects writers outside of the Latin traditions. . . ."

(At this very time, in announcing the "modern theme," Ortega proposed that we restore the vital basis of ideas by challenging the "bigotry of Culture.")

6. Eliot restored the confidence of a generation of critics, themselves often poets, in a particular framework of accepted and traditional ideas. He taught them that such a framework, already at hand, was necessary (necessary, as Allen Tate recently said of the "poetic order" given by "formal versification," to assure both reader and poet that "the poet is in control of the disorder . . . outside him and within his own mind"). And Eliot himself became their model of critical authority and judgment.

The best example, because the most important, is the critical reception (rejection) of Hart Crane's *The Bridge,* in its time, and subsequently, the test poem of American poetry. Here, in the hands of such distinguished critics as Allen Tate, Yvor Winters, and R. P. Blackmur, criticism (as I think in Eliot's essay on Blake) becomes an instrument of judgment that forecloses the possibility of reading (entering) the poem openly, responsively. The framework of accepted and traditional ideas necessary to the long poem is also necessary to critical authority. It provides the critical perspective and the framework of judgment, and allows the critic to put the poem (and as often the poet) in its place.

Tate had admonished Crane for his previous work, remarking that the fault it shares with the work of Baudelaire and Blake "appears whenever the existing poetic order no longer supports the imagination"—by which he means not so much that the existing order has itself eroded as that the individual talent has strained it by pushing beyond it. So now, with the publication of *The Bridge,* Tate and the others scold Crane for not knowing enough, for immaturity, for hysterical, even publicly dangerous, work. All remark the absence of an accepted framework, the poetic order, system, ideational background needed for control, and needed, incidentally, by the critics who, in their distance from the poem, have no other means of understanding it. Some stress a correlative issue, that Crane, with the advantages of Culture available to him, had gone to the "wrong masters" and had submitted to the bankrupt inspiration of Whitman. Crane was reproved, then, because he questioned the framework of accepted and traditional ideas—because in his concern for possibilities other than those expressed in Eliot's work he chose to write an "American," an open poem.

7. Twenty years later, Crane is still being dismissed as "a pitiable anarch," for in that time the New Criticism, which owes so much to Eliot, established its authority in the schools. I take the phrase from Grover Smith, an explicator of Eliot's work, who used it in an omnibus review that included Crane's *Letters* and the first critical study of William Carlos Williams. Representative of much criticism at this time, Smith's review may be considered the critical counterpart of the kind of academic poetry that by this time had come to be recognized as "New Critical" poetry. I mention it because Charles Olson's letter in reply to this review is a landmark in our critical dialogue as significant as "Projective Verse."

Olson meets Smith "on the premises of the systematic by which he . . . judges, out of hand, the work of Hart Crane and W. C. Williams." He addresses Smith's "strictures" on their disorder and randomness—and the "cultural colonialism," the "Reaction," that supports such judgments. Smith's beliefs, that form to be form at all "must be shaped in *rational patterns of discourse*" and that the desideratum of form is the *"union between general and particular,"* focus the issue for Olson. Smith demands an *a priori* framework of ideas (universals); the rational patterns he asks for might be called, in view of the last-ditch stand made by Tate and others for formal versification, the Rime of Reason. He believes that ideas precede and control act, and dismisses Williams' dictum, "No ideas but in things"—that is, that ideas emerge in the response to an actual occasion.

Olson recognizes that Smith's standards have been the measure by which poetry has been tried since Eliot's "Tradition and the Individual Talent" and pursues the issue in terms of "symbol" and "image." Smith, he says, insists that images should "emerge as 'symbols' in order that there be an objective vision." An image becomes a symbol when it is placed in a framework that works this metamorphic transformation, universalizing the particular, validating it, giving it "meaning." Symbols—the evidence of transcendent order—are requisite in a New Critical poem. But the new poetry, with its insistence that prosody again answer to experience and that a new discourse be found to "cover . . . the real," forswears symbols. Here images are only images, the verbal equivalents of things, and poetry is not enclosed by framing devices.

8. We may understand better now Tate's statement that "formal versification is the primary structure of poetic order, the assurance to the reader and to the poet himself that the poet is in control of the disorder both outside him and within his own mind." In telling us why the framework is necessary Tate also tells us the preferred content of the New Critical poem. It is the *maladie moderne,* the traditionalist's distress in the modern world where all is chaotic because the old order has collapsed. Poetry of this kind is a discipline/ritual of ordering and controlling. It teaches those who read it a way of containing experience. This is the primary lesson of understanding poetry, to borrow the title of the most influential New Critical textbook.

And this, in turn, may help us understand the fear of experience and unearned maturity Norman Podhoretz observed in the younger generation of the 1950s, whose sensibility to a great extent had been shaped by the New Criticism. These young people, he said, were so intent on quickly appropriating "meaning" because they felt that "everything must be understood before it gets out of control."

9. Have you practis'd so long to learn to read?
Have you felt so proud to get at the meaning of poems?

Stop this day and night with me, and you
shall possess the origin of all poems;
You shall possess the good of the earth
and sun. . . .
You shall no longer take things at second or
third hand, nor look through the
eyes of the dead, nor feed on
the spectres in books;
You shall not look through my eyes either,
nor take things from me;
You shall listen to all sides, and filter
them from yourself.

Here the stance is open. Whitman speaks to us, with only his personal authority. He welcomes us ("Stop . . . with me") and is generous, delivering us from whatever it is that, in mediating our experience, denies us an original relation to the universe. His commands are imperatives of liberation, and what he proposes is prospective, in the process (the reality) that for him, as for Whitehead, has no beginning or end. He addresses our individual talent and replaces the tradition with which Eliot would circumscribe it with the cosmos, the nurturer, the origin of all poems.

I have spelled out this passage in "Song of Myself" because it is also important to remember that open poetry is not without "standards"—that "standards," as Robert Creeley says, "are only interesting in relation to the possibilities they recognize." Following this observation Creeley recalls that "in the forties I felt them [standards] arbitrarily restrictive and dominated by the practice of criticism apart from the practice of poetry itself."

10. *The practice of criticism and the practice of poetry.* Creeley's own examples of literary *criticism* become literary *opinion* ("literary criticism is just an exchange of opinion and has no authority in relation to the activities it criticizes") may be found in *A Quick Graph,* the work of a "[man] active in the arts making notes. . . ." Here the value of criticism is the result of the generous attention that, to cite one of Creeley's insistences, opens possibility.

Another example of this double practice is David Antin's *talking at the boundaries.* Antin sees "all poetry as some kind of talking which is some kind of thinking" and considers the texts collected in this book "the notations or scores of oral poems"—"talk poems," he calls them. I am not (yet) as certain as he is that these remarkable improvised lectures are poetry, but I am certain that they are criticism, and criticism as responsive to the conditions of open poetry as we have had it.

Antin not only talks at the boundaries, making us aware of the crucial differences between oral and literate culture, speech and writing. ("The word forms / on the left: you must / stand in line. Speech / is as swift as synapse"—lesson one of Olson's "ABCs.") He also talks against boundaries of all kinds. The scores of his talks are printed in lowercase type; they are unpunctuated; the breath-phrase units that compose them are set off by the space between them; and the margins of the page are not justified. Talk flows, in response to the occasion. It liberates the vernacular and is physically close to the speaker, its only imperative the imperative of speech, "speaking straight ahead," as William Carlos Williams says.

("Not after the establishment, but speaking straight ahead. I would gladly have traded what I have tried to say, for what came off my tongue, naturally. . . .")

Though the speaker is central he is as inconspicuous as the lowercase i which does not control the flow but lets it carry him onward in the work of thought and self-definition. The occasion is public but the mode is meditative: "i come here with my private thing so to speak   and i tell you im here to define myself and im telling you who i am and what im doing it for[.]" It is possible to write a language alone but not, Antin finds, "to speak a language alone." And since his whole being clamors to talk he has come out of the writing-closet into a public place. He has come "with a kind of private occasion to a public place"—his definition of the work of poets—and he asks us to "come in   come in   this is nothing terribly formal and what poem there is here will be built around whatever happens. . . ." Pontificating does not accord with such informal, open occasions, and Antin, with all his brilliance—he is a profound critic of contemporary life—is wonderfully comic in ways that suggest Whitman in "Song of Myself," Kenneth Burke, with his direct dialectical both/and mind, Olson in "Reading at Berkeley," and stand-up comedians.

11. no occasion in which you speak in any sense at all turns out to be a
private occasion   in fact the idea of a private occasion in the act of
talking is somehow   almost a contradiction in terms   you come
into a situation   prepared to externalize or prepared   i try not to
be too prepared   i mean in aiming not to be prepared   so that i
can do what i dont expect to do   in terms of something i want to
say   and which is what one means by improvisation   to do
something you want to do in a way you didn't know you were going to
do it   which is to do something new and what you mean by
improvisation is coming out and saying something you dont
know   perhaps discovering something you dont know and in doing
that you circle around the things you do know looking for an opening
between what you know and what you dont know   and before you
take your move into what you dont know you go over in a sort of
family way and pat the things you know on the head nicely things i
know about improvisation   namely that improvisation needs a sort
of warmup   you kind of warm yourself up to the situation and
pretend youre talking to yourself   but im not really talking to myself
i wanted to talk not to myself and that's why i came
out   out?   what was i in that i came out of?

12. We may not wish to practice criticism in quite this way, but the occasional risk and liberation it involves would help us rid ourselves of many habits, perhaps even the habit of judgment.

Antin, who observes in one of his poems that "a door without a wall is ridiculous," says that "as soon as you take a position very forcefully youre immediately at the boundary of that position." Louis Sullivan knew that his flowing ornament depended on the resistance of rigid geometrical axes, and Whitman did not forget the framework of accepted and traditional ideas:

> Creeds and schools in abeyance,
> Retiring back a while sufficed at what they are,
> but never forgotten,
> I harbor for good or bad, I permit to
> speak at every hazard,
> Nature without check with original energy.

In "Projective Verse," where speech and energy are again conspicuous considerations, Olson acknowledges closed verse—how much "each of us owes to the non-projective, and will continue to owe, as both go alongside each other. . . ."

In recognizing the considerable uncovering therapy of open practice, we may realize that being open is preferable to being closed, but that being closed is most often our condition. And even so, we may remain closed because, as Lawrence reminds us, opening is a "naiveté" and the requisite act of attention is difficult. Yet, in criticism as in poetry, we want the fullest awareness, the "essential act of attention," the "essential poetic and vital act," which, Lawrence claims, comes only of being open.

Clinging to the Advance: Some Remarks on "Projective Verse"

It is now September, and I am writing in response to the conference on literary criticism held in July. (The previous essay was the keynote paper at this conference at the University of North Dakota.) So much of the discussion then turned on "breath": on Olson's "Projective Verse" and his conception of open poetry as a useful model for criticism. But very little was said—certainly neither enough to explain nor convince—about the assumptions of his (and a generation of poets') poetics. I'd like to address this now, not have the last word but a few words on a very important subject.

"Ignorant men of genius," Pound remarks in *ABC of Reading,* "are constantly rediscovering 'laws' of art which academics had mislaid or hidden." Charles Olson, who knew Pound, shares his disdain for academics, and, like Pound, for the reason that he rediscovered some "laws" of art, may be considered an ignorant man of genius. Both were eminent teachers as well as poets, and both concerned themselves with just those matters that were necessary if art were to "advance"—that is, remain adequate to human experience in an ever-changing world of things, ideas, and feelings—"cover the real," as Olson said. William Carlos Williams, who was also involved in this major revisionary enterprise, reminds us of the difficulty: "How easy to slip / into the old mold, how hard to / cling firmly to the advance."

"Projective Verse" (1950) is Olson's most famous essay, a directive for the advance, one of those declarations poets make not only to rally other poets but to urge themselves to make the necessary demonstration. It is not the final word about poetry; the "laws" it announces are not "Laws." It is best seen in the context of its occasion, as a document prompted by a poet's awareness of his particular moment in history and the history of verse. As those who denigrate it remind us, its matter is not especially new, though to a new generation of poets and at the time of its publication it had the force of something new—and needed. Were it as new as ignorant academics think (but why tar only them? there are ignorant poets too), it would probably have been less effective than it has been.

Cover the real. Let me go back to this requisite of art. Every recovery of "experience" is accompanied by reconsiderations of language. Behind Olson's essay is the push of many modern poets (the most important theorists were themselves poets) who tried to recover means that had been mislaid or hidden. Consider some of them: quantitative, not accentual, verse; spoken, not written, verse (song, not "literature," as Pound says of the Provencal poets with whom he begins our reeducation), verse as flexible as the voice that utters it, impossible to score with the old measures, and once again responsive to the body, itself an action of the body; verse whose form is not imposed but generated in the act of speech, the movement of ongoing speech, a dance; a verse of attention and precision, claiming again the physical world (a real world), attending to particular things and immediate feelings and ways of being in it, presenting them (in images), not describing them (in symbols and metaphors).

Free verse, Imagism, Vorticism, Objectivism—these movements, beginning in the first decade of the twentieth century, are sallies of advance, having behind them the advances in the nineteenth century made, among others, by Coleridge, Emerson, and Whitman. Now the movement of these movements accords with the genuinely "modern" spirit of the age: with the rejection of limiting systems (absolutes, abstraction, idealism) and the rejection of dualisms (there is a new physics, a real physical world); with the restoration of feeling (there is a new psychology) and the reliance, in a universe of process, on the human power of imagination (a more humble power than the shaping imagination of symbolism: a power of attention and letting-be) to make momentary coherences and vital stabilities (there is a new philosophy of "event").

All of this stands behind Olson's essay. The conspicuous early directives are those of Fenollosa and Lawrence, then those of Pound, Williams, Crane, and Cummings. All except Lawrence are acknowledged in the essay. Robert Creeley, whose education in these and other poets is one of the impressive things of *A Quick Graph,* cites the essential texts and gives us the critical touchstones. This remarkable book provides a vital context for Olson's essay, and the more recent *The Poetics of the New American Poetry,* though not as complete as it might be, provides many of the texts to which the serious reader of Olson's essay will want to turn. And return: texts of this kind do not lose their generative power.

Creeley also reminds us, as does almost every poet of his generation who responded to Olson, that the impact of "Projective Verse" owed much to the very state of poetry from which it was intended to arouse us. The time, remember, is 1950. Speaking of the preceding decade, he says: "The forties were a hostile time for the writers here included [young writers of his generation, the third generation since that of the elders, Eliot, Pound, and Williams, the generation between the wars in tutelage to Eliot and Auden having been the second]. The colleges and universities were dominant in their insistence upon an *idea* of form extrinsic to the given instance." And that idea of extrinsic form, I'm sure you recall from our discussion, is the correlative of what Eliot in his essay on Blake called a "framework of accepted and traditional ideas." Moreover, as Creeley goes on to say—and some of us will vouch for the accuracy of what he says—"there was so much talk *about* the poem, about levels of meaning, ambiguities, symbols, allusions. It was even felt that criticism itself would prove the most significant literary activity of the time." In *Poetry and the Age* (1953), Randall Jarrell spoke of an "age of criticism," not having to add that the criticism in question was "new," and that by now it had become a new formalism, a new classicism. During the 1940s, Williams tried repeatedly to state clearly his notion of a new measure (the "variable foot," recognizing the necessity Pound had mentioned in *ABC of Reading:* "a fixed element and a variable"); in 1948, at Seattle, he admitted that "that project itself [a new world, made new by a new physics, requires a new prosody] . . . is not yet raised to consciousness, to a clear statement of purpose, is our fault," and he may have printed part of "Projective Verse" in his *Autobiography* (1951) by way of acknowledging that Olson had succeeded better than he had in doing this. In his essay Olson himself notes the "reaction now afoot to return verse to inherited forms of cadence and rime." And Robert Duncan recognized its basis in fear, remarking that poets who had "once had dreams and epiphanies, now admit only to devices and ornament. . . . Taste, reason, rationality rule, and rule must be absolute . . . because beyond lies the chiaroscuro

. . . the darkness of possibilities that controls cannot manage." Reaction is desperate; and in the 1940s and 1950s the attempt to strengthen a declining authority and shut out the complexity of experience the New Criticism itself had once claimed for poetry was desperate. "Projective Verse" did not clear the field so much as raise up resistance—and it may still be felt in the careless jibes of detractors (who dismiss it as a trivial avant-garde proposal of the 1950s and belittle it by considering it a simple-minded system that enables any undergraduate, unthinkingly, to write poetry) and in the necessarily sharp edge of David Antin's analysis of the limitations of the "new critical" poem.

It took more than Olson's essay to open the field—by which I mean open a space for the practice of open poetry. What *angered* Olson in Grover Smith's review of Hart Crane and Williams was the ease with which Smith overlooked the forty years' *work* of Olson's predecessors—Pound, Williams, Crane. So if I move on it is not because I fail to recognize the *work* of the 1940s that made possible an anthology like Donald Allen's *The New American Poetry* (1960). I want to turn to this anthology because in it Olson has an eminent position. Not unwittingly, Allen opened the anthology with a section on the Black Mountain poets (a designation too limiting yet probably made in awareness of the importance of *Origin* and the *Black Mountain Review*) and opened this section with a substantial selection of Olson's work. Similarly, in the statements on poetics gathered at the back of the book, he reprinted "Projective Verse" and "Letter to Elaine Feinstein" in the opening position, having already pointed out in the preface that they "present the dominant new double concept: 'composition by field' and the poet's 'stance toward reality.'" Anthologies such as Allen's bring us abreast of the times, in this case marking not the emergence but the establishment of a new generation of poets. And Allen brought Olson forward. Hitherto without the kind of public recognition accorded Ginsberg for *Howl,* Olson, who at this time also published the first volume of *The Maximus Poems* and a collection of verse, *The Distances,* took his deserved place as a major theorist and practitioner.

Why didn't Olson call his essay "Open Verse"? What does *projective* convey? The sense of push, of thrust forward, also conveyed by the prefix of *projectile* and *prospective.* Olson is a poet of forwarding, and a poet of resistance. As he told the Gloucester poet Vincent Ferrini, poetry for him was a way of making evident his resistance—resistance because his own vital imperative was to stand forth, feeling as he did, literally to the point of suffocation, the pressure of the world upon him. That is the message told in his appropriation of Fenollosa's etymological observations on the copula *is:* "Is comes from the Aryan root, *as,* to breath [Fenollosa also says that *exist* means to 'stand forth']. . . . Be is from *bhu,* to grow." To breathe, accordingly, is to stand forth and to grow; it is the primary self-act. So like his daughter, mentioned in one of the *Maximus* poems, Olson "sings / as best [he] can, and loudly, / back. . . ." To mock his concern with breath is to mock the root of being, vital impulse itself, a root deeper than the mind, that source, as he says at the end of the essay, where "breath comes from" and "all act springs." *Projective,* then, as he told Ferrini, evokes *propellant:* "I think of man as his own muzzle—and charge." It calls attention to the *self-action* involved in open poetry—the energy, the speech-force, that enables it, and also the stance, since, by way of the allusion to Keats' criticism of the "Egotistical Sublime," it speaks for "negative capability," the projection of self outward to things that is the condition of being open to them, openness itself the condition insisted on as privilege by D. H. Lawrence. Open poetry requires that risk, the self-action by which one moves oneself, "puts himself in the open."

Of *projective* in the psychological and formal senses, Creeley's remarks to Corman provide the best gloss. In a letter (like Olson's letter to Ferrini published in the earliest issues of *Origin*) Creeley addresses the long-standing creative problem of inside-outside, self-and-world, and explores the implications of his own statement, incorporated in "Projective Verse," that form is the extension of content. "The materials of poetry or of prose (materials: the externals, the phenomena outside the given man, around him, OBJECTS)"—the materials, he says, "are that which the content IN the man uses to declare itself—that this declaration, this COMING OUT by means of materials, MAKES the form. . . ." Art is a projective act, a declaration of the self; form is the extension of one's *inner* content. We think, perhaps, of Emerson's and Thoreau's practice of correspondences and of Whitman's praise of the faithful solids and fluids, the necessary film, the beautiful ministers of the soul. And there is that appreciation of the "external" world and its uses just as there is (as Duncan first pointed out) a direct connection—a continuing tradition—with Emerson's energetic conception of art. But the correspondence to the world is no longer correspondential: the Idealism that underwrites symbolism is absent, the imagination abdicates its sovereignty, and symbolic meaning as an end yields to the making, to the formal object that enables the artist (as Williams said) to turn himself inside out.

Projectile covers Olson's notion that the poem, an energy-construct, transfers the energy that the poet brings to it to the reader. Olson was indebted to Pound for the conception of the poem as energy-construct and indebted to Fenollosa for the idea of transference of energy, but the idea that the poem does this (essentially ecological) work is his own. Taking Fenollosa's model of the sentence (agent/act/object::subject/verb/object) Olson replaced the grammatical terms with poet/poem/reader. In this way he expressed his belief in poetic activity, in the actual work a poem does, and in a trajectory of communication that includes (requires) a reader/listener. As Creeley says, this notion of the poem "breaks the line of aesthetics, or that outcrop of a general division of knowledge." To employ the title of Dewey's relevant book, art is experience. In this insistence—as also in the insistence on organism-in-environment—we begin to see the indebtedness to pragmatism that Olson acknowledged later.

Prospective speaks for another kind of openness best glossed by Olson's Whiteheadean sense of process. The absolute resides neither in an Ideal nor in a past condition but in the never-to-be-completed future; it is actualizing but not actualized. As Duncan puts it, "we're at the point of genesis and . . . the end of things is back of us." As Whitman said, "Urge and urge and urge, / always the procreant urge of the world." Like Whitman, Olson gives us vista.

As for *percussive,* another term in the title's cluster, it is not exclusively Olson's, derived from his own rhythmic necessities, the need—expressed percussively—to "get on with it, keep moving, keep in, speed, the nerves, their speed, their perceptions, theirs, the acts, the split second acts, the whole business, keep it moving as fast as you can. . . ." That need is a general requirement of energized verse—as it is of such allied kinetic arts as jazz, action painting, and "modern" dance.

Olson also defines "projective verse" against "closed verse," the apposition here being especially important: "that verse which print bred." Closed verse is connected with "literature" and with the eye, which scans the lines. Open verse is oral (and aural), and recalls us (as Olson in other ways recalls us) to oral traditions (and knowledges) antedating "history." I cannot here spell out the vast significance of this repossession; I refer you to the spring 1975 issue of *Boundary 2,* devoted to the oral impulse, and to the 1976 issue of *Alcheringa,* devoted to the First International Symposium on Ethnopoetics. It is probably enough now to mention Pound's and Williams' contribution to open verse. According to Louis Zukofsky, himself an important poet of the advance, Pound reminded us of "quantity" and instructed us to "LISTEN to the sound that it makes." As for Williams, consider the preface to *The Wedge* (1944), the book that awakened (released) Creeley. Here Williams says that the physical movement of verse "is distinguished in each case by the character of the speech from which it arises . . . each speech having its own character the poetry it engenders will be peculiar to that speech also in its own intrinsic form." The idea of intrinsic form is a legacy of Romanticism, but the primacy now is speech; it is not the argument (idea) of Emerson's "meter-making argument," it is the speech-act that is generative. With these minimal consequences: that we now begin to listen to the poet's voice—begin to hear poems—and begin to realize, as Frank O'Hara observed, that the fixed form or format of a poem is only its design, and its true form is its intrinsic movement. We see the spatial and hear the temporal.

Open verse is also defined as "composition by field," opposed, Olson says, "to inherited line, stanza, over-all form." To come into the open, to write such verse, is not to impugn order, for order may be vital, organic, intrinsic, but an order that is external to the event and imposed on it. Open verse (in its respect for the "field" of the poem) advances free verse, which Williams, in an article in the *Princeton Encyclopedia of Poetry and Poetics,* traces from Whitman to the Imagists. "In England and America," he says, "it has been argued (especially by Pound and Williams) that conventional meters . . . deform the natural speech. . . . It is the refusal of English (especially American English) to conform to standard prosody which has given rise to free verse." Open verse claims the freedom of free verse but goes beyond it in seeking forms not only adequate to natural speech but to natural thought: occasion, event. As *composition* in "composition by field" tells us, something is composed—composed within the field of the poem, the field created in its very making. Open verse is a most careful and attentive art (act) in which all the elements of verse, in the very process of the making, are made to cohere, to create, in their relationships, the tension of an "energy construct." *Field,* here, calls up an electromagnetic field, the "patterned energies" Hugh Kenner has so expertly treated in the work of the poets of the Pound era. Another equally important analogue is collage, that kind of visual, "paratactical" composition. But finally what is most important in considering *field* is its philosophical significance, the fact that it replaces the correspondential with a coherence notion of truth. Truth (or meaning) is no longer a matter of validation in respect to something external to the field; truth (now lowercase "truth") is a matter of relationships within the field. And as Olson said of any thing, so we may now say of the poem: that to exist through itself constitutes meaning.

Fenollosa (I have been speaking of his remarkable little book, *The Chinese Written Character as a Medium for Poetry*) not only taught Olson the related ideas of a process universe and the wholly verbal character of language, but another idea of profound ethical importance for his poetics. Fenollosa says that "will is the foundation of our speech," a remark that evokes Olson's "actual willful man" ("Man is, He acts"). This is the chief concern of *The Special View of History,* where he proceeds, he says, "on the level of history and of a concept of man with the dynamic first proposed in *Projective Verse*." Now what needs to be noted here is Olson's distinction, in Keatsian terms, between a will to power and a will to achievement, and that the latter, a positive and beneficent use of the will, is the virtue of "negative capability," which in turn is the stance he insists on in his poetics. We recall his recollection of Keats' comments on the "Egotistical Sublime" at the beginning of "Projective Verse" when he says of the will to power that the self is "as ego and sublime." And we better appreciate his concern with stance (how we stand toward reality, the very condition of writing open poetry) when we realize that the "ego and sublime" must be abandoned for the "self as center and circumference."

Open poetry is itself a way of responding to an open universe. That the universe is open is one of the "new recognitions" involved in it. In such a universe—in the "field," in the process—the self, itself only a thing among things, is a center of relationships. Its circumference is merely the space that bends around it and constitutes its particular field. Of most importance is the fact that the self is *in* the field (involved in an occasion, or an event), that the situation is ongoing, not to be described but presented or enacted. For the poet who, as Olson says, now *ventures* into the field has indeed put himself in the open, has given over whatever mediates experience to confront experience directly—nakedly, freshly, firstly. "From the moment he ventures into FIELD COMPOSITION—puts himself in the open—he can go by no track other than the one the poem under hand declares. . . . he has to *behave,* and *be,* instant by instant, aware of some several forces just now beginning to be examined" (my italics). He must, Olson says, listen to the objects that share with him the secrets of the universe (this is less mystical than it seems, in nature comparable with Williams' ability to attend to and dance with objects). He must not only go "by ear," as Pound insisted, but play it by ear.

The poets Creeley admires are "saints of this exposure." And one suspects that it is not so much the element of breath as the element of risk that disturbs those who most furiously denounce open verse. Contrary to opinion, poetry of this kind requires incredible discipline. Galway Kinnell says that "it is easier to write in rhyme and meter than to write without them," that the latter presents psychic difficulties of releasing the self (*descent* is Williams' term). "It is hard to let the poem flow from oneself or move into the open that way"; it is hard to *wander* (Gertrude Stein's great image), give over "external guides." The imagery here is fittingly that of journeying. This is a poetry of movement; Creeley's favorite image of it is driving a car. And Kinnell mentions Whitman, who journeyed in this way on the open road of experience and says that the burden of such journeys is to exegete the self. *Incredible discipline.* No overstatement when one considers the acts of attention requisite to being present at one's own life, to knowing and daring to know, as Williams said in *Spring and All,* "what he is at the exact moment that he is." To attend one's *life*—"life tracking life" is Creeley's phrase—is the work open poetry proposes.

The form of such poems, according to Olson's brief statement, is merely the extension of content. This tells us that form is neither imposed on nor separable from content, that form (as "the going energy of content toward its form" suggests) occurs in completed movement, and perhaps that form is inherent in this activity, as Allen Ginsberg believes it is when he declares that "Mind is shapely." Ginsberg says this in his notes on prosody in *Indian Journals,* where, without acknowledging Olson, he tells us how to score or graph the movement of thought on the page—"the arrangement of the lines on the page *spread out* to be a rhythmic scoring of the accelerations, pauses & trailings-off of thoughts in their verbal forms as mouth-speech." Ginsberg's recent *Ginsberg's Improvised*

Poetics (1971), which fully considers these formal matters, is dedicated "To Charles Olson, prosodist."

Of course, what Olson says about ear/syllable and breath/line addresses these formal matters obliquely. I say "obliquely" because at this point Olson's chief concern is to return poetry, as Creeley says, to its "*physiological* condition." Open poetry originates in a physical response to a physical (real) universe; it is a vital bodily action; and breathing is its inspiriting and expressive energy. The importance of bodily being in this poetry is best glossed by Kenneth Burke's account of Sir Richard Paget's theory of gesture speech. This theory seeks the roots of language and takes us back to our primary contact with and response to things—to our "neuromuscular knowledge" (Kenner's phrase). Like Dante's *Of Vulgar Eloquence,* the greatest poetics of sound according to Burke, it grounds language on "a *biological* or *naturalistic* base." As for the significance of breath, consider the following:

> 'Psyche' or 'animus' is breath. . . . Breathing is a physiological function, yet its period of requiring the environment is so frequent, and indeed continuous, that it is always on the verge of becoming aware, a kind of contact. . . . In breathing one sees par excellence that the animal is a field, the environment is inside, or essentially pervading at every moment. And so any anxiety, the disturbance of breathing, accompanies any disturbance of self-function. . . . (Paul Goodman, *Gestalt Therapy*)

> Rhythm [the characteristic principle of vital action] is the setting up of new tensions by the resolution of former ones. . . . Breathing is the most perfect exhibit of physiological rhythm. (Susanne Langer, *Feeling and Form*)

These are a sufficient foundation for what some might consider the recondite or far-fetched oriental notions of breath notably treated by Gary Snyder and Allen Ginsberg.

The foregoing makes it unnecessary to give a close account of ear/syllable and breath/line. All that needs to be said is that both are aural/oral concerns that have formal value and that the head and heart involved in them are one, that intelligence is single, as Olson explains in "A Syllabary for a Dancer," the dance-equivalent of "Projective Verse." Also that speech, the instrumentality of this verse, can now be scored exactly, that the typewriter can be used to register precisely both the course of thought—its logic, its waywardness, its many dimensions—and the accompanying intervals of breath. We can now see what we hear, how verse says. And lest one think that using a typewriter to such ends is frivolous (even, as some have it, the *reductio ad absurdum* of this poetics), let me cite a rebuttal as strong as the demonstrations of the best poets who have followed this practice: Robert Duncan's great defense of both the practice and the liberty it affords. See his Preface to *MAPS #6* (1974).

Tory Formalists and New York Intellectuals

The important book *The Republic of Letters,* by Grant Webster, had its inception in the recognition, among other things, of a fact anyone who lives long enough on the critical scene knows: that generations displace each other with great rapidity—from five to fifteen years in America—and, in consequence, there are discontinuities in criticism that make it all but impossible for a critic to survive, to maintain authority throughout a lifetime of work. Grant Webster began this study of the most prominent recent critical groups, the Tory Formalists, as he renames the New Critics, and the New York Intellectuals, in 1963, when, by his accounting and that of others, they had already been superseded, were obsolete, their critics superannuated. Unlike this reviewer, he belongs to a generation that came of age too late to share in the intellectual excitement of the vital years. My teachers were Austin Warren and René Wellek, but Webster came of age in the "Age of the Theorists"—their work was mostly of the 1950s—which signaled the end. This may explain the distance, the objective view, and the dismissive, sometimes rancorous assessment of the work of an entire generation or two of critics.

Whatever it intends—and there is evidence of this in Wellek's review of Webster's book in *The Georgia Review*–this account of literary "opinion" since World War I will make many people uncomfortable. Its total impact is to wipe the slate clean. A curious history that chronicles the past so that it can be put in its place and better forgotten; that for the most part prompts us not to read or reread the work of these critics but gladly give them over (the exceptions are Eliot, Wilson, Blackmur, perhaps Trilling); that severs us from them, increasing the very discontinuity it claims in any case is inevitable! Webster works in the spirit of science more than that of art—science, he cites Thomas Kuhn as saying, "destroys its past." This does not disturb him, not even enough to say, "Rest in peace." It is clear that a new generation of writers unlike those who considered the past "usable" and wrote the New History, has a spokesman for whom the things that matter are obsolescence and replacement. It is to be noted, however, that Webster, this charter of charters, is himself charterless, or that his charter is not literary-critical but historical.

The Republic of Letters is a work of history whose methodological departure—not just methodological razor—is of first importance and, again, upsetting, as Wellek testifies by entitling his rejoinder "An End to Criticism?" Webster adopts Thomas Kuhn's notions of intellectual revolutions and paradigms (from *The Structure of Scientific Revolutions*, published in 1962), replacing *paradigm* with, what for his study is certainly more useful, the idea of *charter*. His work, I think, is neither an end to criticism, nor only an end to the history of criticism as an autonomous literary discipline. He does for the history of criticism, for the history of charters, what a new generation has begun to do again for literary works—locate them in the primary context of history and culture as well as in respect to the lives of writers who wrote them. He repudiates the separation of art and life on which the claim of the transcendent value of art depends. So a charter is only of historical moment and has a stage-by-stage development from inception to obsolescence (usually fifty years), when a new historical occasion, a crisis in history, gives rise to a new charter. So critics, rallying to a charter, do not outlast its authority. What is to be judged, then, is relative to history—the originality and influence of a charter (hence the two charters delineated here and the judgment that neither is first-rate and counts for much, finally, in the repository called the history of criticism). And what figures most is the filling out of a charter's course, a detailed account of its emergence and fostering and the careers bound up with it. This involves a history of magazines and critical communities (for example, *Kenyon Review* and *Partisan Review*) and critical portraits of critics (eight Tory Formalists, six New York Intellectuals) as well as "profiles" of the lives and works of eighteen critics, most of them also treated in the text. One does not have to agree with Webster's methodology or judgments to appreciate his "career analyses" and his sociology of letters in our time. His book anatomizes the literary profession, which since the 1950s has found its home in universities, and therefore has much to say to anyone who undertakes critical work and follows that career.

Webster's accounts of the charters of the Tory Formalists and New York Intellectuals are coherent and cogent—"generally acceptable," to use a phrase of a question he asks of me in a letter. To call the New Critics Tory Formalists may not help much in identifying Kenneth Burke but it answers well to the New Critics' politics and aesthetics—extrudes them, as it were, so that we see that for them as well as the New York Intellectuals the failure of politics (actually the crisis of civilization of World War I) had much to do with the purposes they ask aesthetics to serve. The term, moreover, acknowledges the fact that the charter takes its authority from T. S. Eliot (who, it may be noted, understood and accepted its passing). As for "New York Intellectuals," that term is clear enough, and loaded, too, if one remembers that to be an *intellectual* invites the fate of becoming a member of the *intelligentsia,* a fate suggested in the oppositions of the elaborating phrase, "The Bourgeois Avant-Garde." And what of his accounts of individual critics? Wellek says that they are "often scurrilous and harshly satirical," which they may be. Webster warns us that he has followed Dr. Johnson in bringing critics to public judgment. But though I think the portraits of Austin Warren and Kenneth Burke merely sketches, hardly definitive of their work, there is too much truth (if ungenerosity) in some of the others—of Tate, Winters, Irving Howe—to deny them. Webster simply remarks what more polite people do not. Retrospect without having been involved may invite this; or maybe only his sometimes sharply funny style of mind (the editorial staff-listing of *Partisan Review* is likened to "a partridge in a pear tree"; the way the New York Intellectuals use *we* calls up "a gaggle of twenty or thirty friends"; *Dissent* is said to be "a living memorial" to Howe's socialist youth; Podhoretz is said to have "the rhetorical trick of sounding like fifty"; Trilling is identified as "a critic without a cause"—superannuated by rebels with a cause?; critics are fortunate because of "Dilsey's law of cultural reward").

Webster's treatment of the Tory Formalists is more extensive and thorough than that of the New York Intellectuals. Having for its authority figure the only critic of eponymous stature, having also the support of imaginative work and institutional prestige, it is the more important of the two, or the group with the more notable career and lasting influence. The New York Intellectuals, mostly journalists not professors and journalists even when professors, are not so easily codified and seem to be in disarray. Of its Men of Letters only Trilling is substantially treated. Under the heading "Howe, Rahv, Kazin," Steven Marcus is more fully treated and praised than those named: Howe gets three paragraphs, Kazin less than one. And what is most curious, Edmund Wilson, whom Webster considers the authority figure of this group, closes rather than opens the account and is treated at greater length than all the rest combined. Webster writes well of Wilson (his understanding of the later years is more appreciative than, say, Kriegel's) and concludes the book with him. This, I think, has something to do with the title of the book, which ostensibly parallels Polanyi's "The Republic of Science" and thus endorses the relativity and collective search for truth of the scientific enterprise, but resonates with Wilson's Old Republicanism and literary service to the Republic—with those "old fashioned" ideals and with the reminder that the Republic has had to be saved over and over again and that this, finally, is a work of letters.

Had Webster heeded this resonance and entitled his study *Letters in the Republic,* he might have recognized the major issue of American criticism and the essential continuity within it. Wellek is right to question a model that makes discontinuity complete, to adduce Eliot's antecedents in New Humanism, and to note that the gulf between the Tory Formalists and the New York Intellectuals is not as wide as Webster assumes. These groups share a great deal, as we shall see, but most of all the fact that between them they rehearse once more in terms of their historical moment the allegiances that have polarized cultural debate since the beginning of the Republic and Emerson's summons to intellectual work in its behalf in "The American Scholar." The antecedents of the Tory Formalists are easily discernible in the New Humanism (with its rejection of the liberalizing forces of democracy and science and its concern with tradition) and in the Genteel Tradition that preceded it. In Santayana's terms it is one of the two mentalities of American culture, already in the nineteenth century defending itself from loss, the dispossession of religious faith and social leadership. What Webster charts so well in showing how their aesthetics culminates in "The Sacred Word" is, if seen as a stage in this defense, a consummate intellectual achievement. The New York Intellectuals represent a stage of radical, democratic insurgency that has its source in the Emersonian-Whitmanian tradition and has for its immediate antecedent the group that Van Wyck Brooks called to letters and leadership during the years of World War I. The dualism of Trilling's imagination vs. reality is another (more sophisticated) version of Brooks's highbrow vs. lowbrow, creative vs. acquisitive life. No one saw this so clearly as Richard Chase, who, regrettably, is not seriously attended to by Webster. Chase's last book, *The Democratic Vista* (1958), names and discusses the tradition and tries, too late perhaps, to restore the tension of the cultural dialectic and move Trilling and his associates off-center, from the stasis and conservatism that made *The Liberal Imagination* (1950), the terms of its title less a matter of tension than of concession, such a singular critical success (with both groups), a charter, actually, for capitulation. How could this book, published so late, be the charter for a group whose obsolescence is almost at hand? Even Wilson's *Axel's Castle* (1931) does not provide its charter. Brooks's *America's Coming-of-Age* (1915) does, which is why Chase's attempt to rename and realign the terms of the dialectic Brooks began with such polemical vigor and to nullify the accommodation of the middle term to which he aspired must be included in a just account.

Webster does not concern himself sufficiently with what these groups have in common. Both have their origin in the crisis of civilization and in failed political hopes which they displace on literature. Both are dualist and value the idea of tension. In the high regard they have for mind, imagination, ideas, both may be said to be Idealist. Both are elitist, think literature a high calling, and its agency, whether social or spiritual, redemptive. Though the New York Intellectuals are more concerned with American literature, neither finds its measure there. Both—it is one of the attractions of their subscription to complexity—are moralist(s). By the 1950s both are securely established in the universities, and neither responds generously to the subsequent rise of a counterculture, which is to say that by failing to respond, by being incapable of it, both miss the moment and become obsolescent. And if they are not deserving of a high place in the history of criticism, is it not because they represent in so many ways the nineteenth-century "mind" not fully abreast of the twentieth century?

The notion of a charter lends itself nicely to schematism and to the ready identification of critical movements past and present. So it is with some wonder that I do not note in a book so much concerned with obsolescence any recognition of a movement, emerging from a more recent crisis of civilization (World War II) and grounded in radical literary practice, that fills out all the stages in the development of a charter: the ideological period, the critical revolution, normal criticism, and so forth. I am thinking, of course, of the group with whom postmodernism is most often associated and of *Boundary 2*, which represents normal criticism in its behalf; thinking too of Paul Bové, an associate editor of this periodical, whose *Destructive Poetics*, in its incisive deconstruction of the work of Cleanth Brooks, supports Webster's account of Tory Formalism. I also mention this university-sponsored periodical because it is a very active force at Webster's own university and his acknowledgements do not include any of its personnel. Can it be, as he thinks, that schools of critics are mutually exclusive? And, finally, I mention it for the sake of those who are now critically displaced or otherwise doomed to superannuation.

But perhaps Webster intends to include this movement under *hermeneutics* in the subsequent volume he promises on recent charters. I look forward to that because in writing this challenging book he has—to cite his scheme for the making of critical careers—unquestionably done his journeyman work, found his voice, made his name.

Poetry and Old Age

The title—*At Last, the Real Distinguished Thing*—is choice, especially fitting in regard to the achievement of the late work of Eliot, Pound, Stevens, and Williams treated by Kathleen Woodward. Yet James, who provides it in his last words, may not have been commenting on art but on death, granting death superiority over art in terms of art, and this may gainsay the striving of artists who in their old age confront death with art, even gainsay the striving of art, the lifelong ambition involved in making distinguished things. The title, then, may be a touchstone of the wisdom accorded age—a theme with which this book is much concerned, that is, with aging and poetry, with endings, and with the accommodation that for the poet, and those who follow, will suffice.

Woodward's study focuses on four relatively old poets and four meditative late poems: Eliot's *Four Quartets,* Pound's *Pisan Cantos,* Stevens' *The Rock,* and Williams' *Paterson V.* The interest of her work derives from the characteristics she ascribes to these poems (they involve the "still point" and the wise old man as hero, a new meditative mode and dedication to tradition and creative act); the questions with which she interrogates them (did old age bring poetic fulfillment and do they offer insights into aging and its satisfactions?); the way in which she reads them; and the rank, the merit, she allows them.

The order in which she discusses them (as above) is not the order of their importance to her. Did she begin with Eliot because, old before his time, he is, she feels, the least truly wise? Because he insisted on loss, on physical decay, and sinned, as Leavis says, against the principle of life? (Yet why not respect this as consonant with his entire work, with his deflection of eros from the beginning? Why not recall this when considering the measure of eros in Williams' work?) Pound, interestingly, is treated with the most sympathy and is most wholly approved, the quality of his mind and thought never questioned. He is appreciated for resacralizing the landscape, for integrating the masculine and the feminine, culture and nature, for relying on the "feminine principle" (as did Williams), and for never forgetting the claims of the social order—these things defining what Woodward believes are needed now in the crisis of our culture. *Senesco sed amo* wisely sums it up. (But does the wisdom read out of the *Pisan Cantos,* those remarkable poems, carry over to the Pound at St. Elizabeths depicted by Olson and Williams? Humility? Did this wisdom prove satisfactory to Pound himself? Or is it, that for him, as for many artists, he was wiser in his art than in his life?)

Stevens lacks the necessary concern for community found in Eliot, Pound, and Williams, but moves, successfully, from an overvalued imagination to the real, gives over willing for receptivity, and replaces the supreme fiction with "Self"—learns, that is, to get out of the mind and into the world (a lesson perhaps of old age, yet one taken to heart by a new younger generation of poets, more, it seems, a matter of understanding the nature of the case than of age). As for Williams, he is diminished, most wholly persona non grata, a matter I will look into but not before noting that in Woodward's final assessment he is said to have been the most ambitious and hence a "great" failure:

> For each poet, what had to be given up and what embraced are different, conditioned by private obsessions. It is as if they intuitively understood that they had work which could only be finished by an act of balancing. In the *Four Quartets* Eliot did what he could to reach beyond the impersonality of the poet. . . . Stevens had to silence the meta-poetry of the mind, abandon the supreme fiction, and accept the thing itself. . . . In the *Pisan Cantos* Pound moved beyond the elite sphere of "literary" history and into the world of outcast men, and magnificently united the two. And Williams made the most ambitious effort of the four. For Williams the natural object had always been both necessary and sufficient, but in the whole of *Paterson* he abandoned imagism for allegory and abstraction, and in the fifth book he exchanged the industrial ground of the United States for the European tradition of art. He was wise to do this, although the radical difference between the two histories was too great for him to bridge.

What is paradigmatic here is the need to give up or *exchange* one thing for another, or perhaps only the need to yield it to something superior, and to *balance, bridge,* or *unite* them. It is clear that impersonality is not as valuable as the personal, the idea as the thing itself, the elite as the outcast community (*communitas* is nonhierarchical), and the local culture of immediate references as the European tradition of art (how does this square with Pound's choice?). The paradigm seems to follow Jung's union of opposites, with wisdom accorded to what, in one's development, was hitherto excluded. The paradigm is also binary, and the binary way of thought informs Woodward's thinking. Though she subscribes to Erikson's view of the life cycle, she does not consider the continuity of its ever-successive accumulative development, so that integrity, the virtue of old age, cannot be achieved by a binary switch but only by fidelity to every stage of the sequence. This sequential development reminds me that art (and life?) may have what Burke calls an entelechial motive: things seek their perfections (the ripeness Thoreau acknowledged in autumnal fruits); the artist works ever to bring his terms to their termistic conclusion, to the end of the line, so that at the end there is the real distinguished thing. Development of this kind requires memory, which Woodward (curiously?) disparages—Mnemosyne, the very mother of the Muses! But this is less disturbing, I find, than her categorical assurance of what wisdom is or involves, which is why she can treat such wholly different lives and careers as if they were commensurate. I suspect that the one thing one should not be an *expert* on is old age and its requisite wisdom—save us, I say for my constituency, from that. As I write this, having read Erikson, Jung, and the others, I think that *perhaps* fidelity to one's own life is the only wisdom, and certainly a useful guide for a critic assessing the life value of the work of poets.

Now consider Williams, Woodward's extreme case. The following covers her account of *Paterson V* as much as "Asphodel": "I do not wish to beat an old man's poem to death, but 'Asphodel' raises a serious poetic problem." I'd say that the problem is not Williams' but hers, and that it involves both the serious misreading of Williams' late poems and the unhappy choice of *Paterson V* as his exemplary last poem. I have never felt that *Paterson* was especially successful or Williams' great achievement; the finest *long* poems of his old age, I think, and the most instructive to a new generation of poets, are "The Desert Music" and "Asphodel." Both poems, incidentally, are meditative and resumptive of Williams' entire career, the one making possible his survival as a poet, the other affirming his lifelong, correlative journey to love. "The Desert Music," as I have argued elsewhere, had its occasion in the "closure" Williams felt on concluding *Paterson I–IV,* on seeing his collected works published, and on suffering a crippling stroke. Only by willful reading, by attending to one's scheme and not the poem, can it be read as "glorif[ying] the city," as his "last muscular, masculine poem" (whatever that is: are we to pick up the echo of Whitman's phallic argument? to bring to Williams' "sexual poetics" an understanding she does not?), and as "not a poem of reminiscence, of an agony of descent, or of memory." And by not reading it attentively (picking up the reference to Casals, which Williams associated with his excursions to the Cloisters in the 1920s) one misses or misconstrues the significance of the unicorn tapestries in *Paterson V.*

Woodward reads *Paterson V* in terms of the rubric (nicely ironical, coming from Eliot) of individual talent and tradition; that is, as a volte-face in which individual talent yields to tradition, the dream of sex to the dream of art, the real to the imaginary—and, most important, the city to the museum. Hence Williams' failure, his betrayal, his running for cover. Now if one can read "Asphodel" as "a rather flaccid amble down an associational memory lane," one can, I suppose, read *Paterson V* in this way. But first consider the following: that Williams had employed myth as early as *Kora in Hell;* that he had always been attentive to art, especially painting; that for him art and eros were inseparable; and that what he is endorsing, confirming for himself, is not tradition (a word Woodward uses loosely) but the high imaginative work of artists, which in the context of the poem is synonymous with his admonition to Paterson to "keep your pecker up / whatever the detail!" What he found affirming in this poetic work was twofold: the breaking of the closure of *Paterson I–IV,* so that *Paterson* became an open serial poem as admissive as the *Cantos,* and the redintegration of his earliest and latest poetic self. The lines on the *uroboros* Woodward insists on actually rehearse his baptism as a poet in "The Wanderer." Both poems, then, are equivalents in affirmation of "The Desert Music" ("I *am* a poet! I / am. I am") and justify the powers of imagination—its power over death, that is, its creative force—demonstrated here and in "Asphodel," the latter at one time intended to be a part of *Paterson.* In view of this recovery of creative force, which in Woodward's account is what he lost when he presumably lost *sexual* touch with the "supplying female" (his term), do not these poems exemplify the persistence about which he also wrote, persistence itself one of the life values? But what of the unicorn in those emblematic tapestries? Is it not the fabulous beast that fabled Williams' pursuit from the beginning; an imaginary beast representing the imagination which Williams always thought of in relation to *love,* to eros: the wonderful beast (as wonderful as the imagination) that, Rilke said, feeds on the possibilities of being?

After such readings, which put those of the other poets under suspicion, I find myself unable to extend the title to the book itself. It is not the last in any sense—in fact, it is distinguished by being one of the first such studies; and it is much too tenuous and contentious, too young and willful, lacking in the very openness and receptivity, the meditativeness, of the old, to be the real distinguished thing. It lacks the generosity that moves me in Ronald Blythe's *A View from Winter*—Blythe is a great student of *loss.* And it does not convey the vital usefulness of the courageous old poets in the exigent way Robert Duncan does in the *H.D. Book*. Duncan's is the best study I know on Woodward's theme, or themes, since it also concerns modernism as it opens into postmodernism, a book (of fugitive installments, to be sure) regrettably omitted here, reminding us also of the significant omission of H.D. Yet Woodward's book is important: ambitious, large in scope (it addresses a fundamental imbalance in our civilization), and, above all, rich in provocation.

Serial Poems from Canada

I hesitated purchasing *The Long Poem Anthology* (sight unseen: you order it from a distributor of small press books such as Writers & Books, 892 South Clinton Avenue, Rochester, N.Y. 14620) because I was troubled by its title. I suppose I should have trusted its editor, but I didn't know Canadian literature (to speak of), and though I had Frank Davey's *From There to Here: A Guide to English-Canadian Literature Since 1960* (I purchased it at the Winnipeg Airport in 1975) I didn't turn to it for the entry on Michael Ondaatje. He has, I find, written long poems, but includes none of his own, which is more self-effacing than either necessary or wise in an anthology that so admirably serves to introduce the avant-garde in Canadian poetry. And that's why *long* in the title troubled me: avant-garde poets write poems of length but these poems, though long, are better characterized as *serial,* which, in fact, is what Ondaatje defines so well in his introduction. Turning to it now, I note with approval his remark: "the most interesting writing being done by poets today can be found within the structure of the long poem"—a statement also applicable to poets in the United States, who have not yet found an Ondaatje to anthologize them.

I read *interesting* in Ondaatje's sentence in David Antin's sense. Interesting writers are usually avant-garde writers—writers who push beyond the limitations of previous forms. This, in fact, is what the writers in this anthology do, not *within the structure of the long poem* but by abandoning the structure of the long poem. This may explain my insistence on *serial* over *long*. In my own effort to define the difference between *long* and *serial* (I come to *The Long Poem Anthology* in the closing weeks of a semester during which I have been teaching contemporary long and serial poems: one reason, certainly, I find this book such a find), I employ *long* to cover poems of length that have a structure that encloses them, frames them, guides them. Poems of this kind have a framework external to them—a "framework of accepted and traditional ideas," as Eliot said in his essay on Blake, or variously, to cite the Eliot-inspired detractors of Crane's *The Bridge,* "poetic order" (Allen Tate), "system" (Gorham Munson), "adequate ideational background" (Yvor Winters). This structure both encloses and closes the poem: the *long* poem, as I define it, is a closed poem. And since it is enclosed by ideas, that is, validated by something other than its own literal activity and prosodic coherence, it is, philosophically speaking, Idealist. The reality it represents (I'm thinking of Wittgenstein: "A picture is a model of reality") is that represented by philosophical idealism. This is why *Understanding Poetry,* perhaps the most formative textbook of poetry in our time, correctly names the project of the closed poem in its title.

Serial poems represent another reality. As Ondaatje says, they are "involved with process"—are processual not procedural, to use Robert Kelly's terms. What's important now is the "movement of the mind and language," language as the act of the instant, as Charles Olson said; language itself one with/part of the act of attention, so that, as Ondaatje notes of the poems in this anthology, the poems "show a process of knowledge, of discovery during the actual writing of the poem." The poet trusts the language in the act of using it, does not defer to *a priori* thought to guide (structure) his attentions. The form of the poem is no longer conventional, a form we recognize as form, a form familiar to us. Instead it follows function: the profound movement of impulse, one's total being (the whole soul in activity), in its engagement with the immediate occasion. The poem, in the words of Robert Duncan, to whom these poets are indebted, "derives from impulse not from plan." And it requires of us not so much an act of mind intent on deriving meaning from the poem—the theme of its structure—as participation in its very activity, *that* kind of experience of poetry.

With the exception of Robin Blaser and Robert Kroetsch, both born in the mid-1920s, the poets in this anthology belong to a later generation, that of the 1940s, a generation that emerged in literature in the 1960s, and, it would seem, with the fostering of *Tish,* a Vancouver poetry newsletter begun in 1961 in response to what Keith Richardson, in *Poetry and the Colonized Mind: Tish,* calls the "Black Mountain poetics and politics." The importance of *Tish* in *opening* Canadian poetry is evident in Richardson's intemperate polemical book, and it is evident in *The Long*

Poem Anthology, which, to those favorably disposed to open forms, amply justifies its existence. Incidentally, of the poets included here, Frank Davey and George Bowering were founding members of *Tish,* and others, Robin Blaser, Daphne Marlatt, Roy Kiyooka, and bpNichol were/are in some way connected with Vancouver.

In speaking of the serial poem, Ondaatje gives prominence to Jack Spicer, who in turn mentions Robert Duncan. Neither Olson nor Robert Creeley (with Duncan composing the Black Mountain triumvirate) is mentioned, which I suspect may be out of deference to Richardson's book—or may be deference to Blaser, who has done so much to keep us mindful of Spicer, a poet worthy of such devotion, and who himself follows Spicer's practice. Spicer's notion of the serial poem was prompted by Duncan's *Medieval Scenes,* written in 1947, before Olson's poetics and practice of "field composition" were known. But in talking about the serial poem in his "Vancouver Lectures," Spicer connects his practice with that of Olson, Creeley, Allen Ginsberg, Duncan, and the William Carlos Williams of "The Desert Music." In many respects what he says of the serial poem tallies with what I have already said, but Ondaatje points up Spicer's insistence, not on dictation, which is one of the distinguishing aspects of his and Blaser's work, but on the fact that "a poem is never by itself alone." Spicer said of the serial poem that the book, not the poem, was the unit. Or, in Duncan's formulation of the open way of poetry: a book is more than a poem, a life is more than a book.

Another thing, evident here in Blaser's "The Moth Poem," itself an installment of the unfinished *The Holy Forest,* is the conjunction of *serial* with *narrative.* In the endnote on his work, Blaser speaks of a *serial narrative:* "The serial poem is not simply a sequence. It is meant to be a narrative that transfigures time. . . ." This description is perhaps too limiting, covering the early work of Duncan in *Medieval Scenes,* Spicer's practice, and Blaser's own practice in "The Moth Poem," early work, too, written in 1964. Other poems here may be said to tell stories in a fragmented, disjunctive way and thereby transfigure time, though not in any exalted or spiritual way. Accordingly, both the theory and practice of "The Moth Poem" may be used to measure the diversity of serial or open forms as we find them in the practice of other poets collected here. Ondaatje calls attention to the fact that anything (everything) can now enter the poem and that there are two characteristics of these poems that he especially prizes: their sometimes documentary quality and the relaxed mode that seems to him to accord with storytelling (yes, as both the probing of present situations and the story join, say, in Antin's talk poems, serial poems of still another kind not represented here).

The distinction between the long and serial poem shouldn't put anyone off. It is a necessary way into the poems, poems that I want very much to call to the attention of others because I have been exhilarated by them. I am pleased by their formal diversity and range of attentions, and by the way some of them become metapoems, their very making a concern of the making, as in Williams' "The Desert Music" (or *Kora in Hell* and *Spring and All,* earlier examples of the kinds of poems poets are now writing). Which is to say, if another distinction is needed, that these poets are postmodern. They know what Olson meant when he declared in "La Préface," "The closed parenthesis reads: the dead bury the dead, and it's not very interesting." They demonstrate, in Duncan's words, that there has been an "end of masterpieces" and a "beginning of testimony." These poems not only lack the finish we are accustomed to in well-wrought poems, they lack the persona, have come into the authenticity of the poet's own speech.

It strikes me now as I turn to the poems themselves—I thought to begin with Blaser's "The Moth Poem," the earliest and perhaps purest example of the serial poem—that Ondaatje's ordering isn't chronological but clearly designed to lead us in, not so much by moving from the simple to the complex as from the readily accessible (open in that sense) and immediately pleasurable. In fact, my excitement over the initial poems, Robert Kroetsch's "Seed Catalogue" and Stuart MacKinnon's "The Intervals," carried me through the book, which is not to say that the subsequent poems aren't exciting. There are nine poems, each between thirty and forty pages in length, in the collection, turning at midpoint on Blaser's poem. Those that precede it offer no "difficulty," but this isn't as important as the fact that Ondaatje says characterizes many of the poems: that in them the poets "look at themselves and their landscapes."

1. Kroetsch's "Seed Catalogue" concerns the home place, growing up on a farm "one and a half miles west of Heisler, Alberta," or, to be exact, "N.E. 17-42-16 W 4th Meridian." The *seed* is double-referring, and so is the *catalogue,* and of interest, too, is the fact, noted by Kroetsch, that "the seed catalogue is a shared book in our society" and prompted him "to write a poetic equivalent to [its] 'speech'. . . ." He has succeeded in

doing this, and in many ways has given us a representative serial poem, one still in progress, open and extensive with his own life. It is representative, too, in form: a collage of various kinds of statement spatially deployed to follow the wayward searching course of his thought. The poem begins with found poetry, an item on Copenhagen Market Cabbage from a seed catalogue, and for this reason as well as the fact that seeds concern matters of growth (and hope, as Thoreau reminds us) it may be endlessly resumed. If it is collage in the visual sense, it is meditative associative cluster in another: in the first section, for example, an ideogram of beginning, of making the garden, of childhood recollections, mediated/meditated moreover by the writer, now, from the perspective of the present. This section ends with the memory of his mother's funeral, and its lovely acceptant elegiac tone (hasn't he assimilated Whitman in the concluding words, "my mother whispered"?) pervades the rest of the poem, this "lifelost poem," this poem of "origins," as he calls it. This poem of growth, punctuated by italicized questions on how to grow a gardener, a lover, a prairie town, a poet, a garden, is more profoundly Whitmanian than Wordsworthian because it is concerned with love and death and a specific task: *"Poet, teach us / how to love our dying."* It is poetic, according to Kroetsch, by virtue of the way the mind working here transforms narrative into myth, that is, gives us the "imagined real" rather than the "actual" and thereby rises above the realistic fiction of the kind we may be familiar with in the depiction of our own homesteading history.

2. There is a different kind of narrative in Stuart MacKinnon's "The Intervals." Its movement is wavelike, made up, as he says in the poem, of "a succession of / calm and movement / that made intervals." It is set down in visually discrete yet connected sections, so that each act of speech emerges from an interval of silence. The poem, moreover, explores an interval in his life, a space between events, that involves the profoundest self-transformation. This change proposes social change because the new self requires a new society, one that sees in change not a danger to be ordered or controlled but rather the essential condition of life itself. The poem warrants reading this self-transformation in terms of the remaking of the mind that characterizes postmodernism. It puts the poet, in his initial isolation and self-preoccupation very much a Prufock, against Olson, or in need of learning, as Olson said in "The Kingfishers," that "What does not change / is the will to change." MacKinnon says in an endnote

that "Heraclitos is chosen over Plato, dialectics over idealism, and political action over passive contemplation," and the poem does indeed realize these changes, these requisites of survival.

The setting is an interval (intervale), a public park on the lake at Kingston, Ontario, bounded by a hospital and a penitentiary. In the course of the poet's meditative investigation of what the opening lines, with their appropriate Roethkean echo, declare,

> In the long silence of the heart
> longer than the wave reaching this shore
> how did I come to this sad voice
> how did I enter this dead space

he finds a voice for suppressed rage and the needed examples of resistance and defiance in the Doukhobor women on hunger strike and the prisoners who riot, or as he says in a letter, tear "the shit out of it [the jail]." As for form, the lines cited earlier are samples of the unpunctuated (flowing) free verse that is normative in the poem. This meditative poem contains found material and sometimes is set down spatially, fittingly in one instance where Olson and Eliot enter it. Verse of this kind represents a mind that is transforming itself and enacts what it says:

> pulling things together as they happen
> and getting them all together occasionally

In this remarkable poem, it is fully adequate to dream and reality ("reality"), dementia and sanity.

The poems by Kroetsch and MacKinnon have more in common with each other than with the subsequent pair by Daphne Marlatt and Don McKay. They are more meditative and in their way less concerned with their specific geographies, geographies such as those named by Marlatt's "Steveston" and McKay's "Long Sault." What Kroetsch, Marlatt, and McKay share is a sense of loss, and what MacKinnon and McKay share is a sense of urgency. MacKinnon's poem seems to me to be involved in a decision to act—to be that act—in the way Olson's "In Cold Hell, In Thicket" is. McKay's poem is also an act, not merely of attention to the foreclosed, to a past that is irretrievable, as in Marlatt's poem, but an act, prompted by outrage with the spoliation of a natural wonder (correlative with his childhood and young manhood), an act that gives voice to the sault itself, to its irrepressible natural/folk element.

3. This may also describe Marlatt's "Steveston," or what I may be missing there because her prose-poetry, though certainly accessible, is, I find, too exquisite and lapidary and, curiously, keeps me outside. I say "curiously" because this is both the most documentary of the poems and in its method (style) the most phenomenological. Steveston, a decaying "onetime cannery boomtown" at the mouth of the Fraser River in British Columbia, is a place Marlatt *names* by imaginatively working-up its history, a place not unlike Olson's Gloucester, though not for her a natal place, a place to re-found. Are her places places for the exercise of consciousness? I think of her *Zócalo,* which I had read because its place is Yucatan (Olson, again) and I had been there. Marlatt's prose-poetry is "poetic." It is evocative: everything she reports has the impress of her consciousness. Her engagement, finally, is not with place so much as with writing, the verbal space in which consciousness and place come together. The writing is foregrounded: it is *her* writing, and this accounts for her presence. However true and fine in its way, I do not think it will do to say "the marsh grass . . . stutters out of silt" or the "fire dusking deeper & deeper tongues of scarlet purple grey. . . ." Such writing strikes me as "affected" and "literary," and when it sweeps on with large rhythmic movements, swirling around parentheses and eddying in word-play, I recall, however wide the analogue and unfair, the polyphonic prose of Amy Lowell. Consciousness has become too conscious, too deliberate, and this destroys the openness and risk of a serial poem.

4. McKay's "Long Sault" seems to be formally ordered. It is in four parts, each with five or six poems, and all, parts and poems, have titles. But this is the extent of its order, not that there is disorder—hardly—so much as a rich variety of voices and forms, especially so in the last part where the blues and the vernacular and a devastating parodic speech (reminding me of Ed Dorn's "The World Box-score Cup") come together. This brings this "tale full of endings"—it tells of the harnessing of the sault by a power dam and subsequent "developments"—to an exuberant close. *Long Sault* are the last words, and the sault has the last word. It also has the *last laughs,* to cite the title of part two, and speaks in the spirit of an earlier, and still present, unregenerate Canada: "And only the Long Sault is laughing: / Fuck your renaissance, get me a beer."

5. Now, what of Blaser's "The Moth Poem," the pivot of the collection? His own description of it in an endnote is accurate: "It is a small poem full of grace notes," which is why I think the pretentious explana-

tion in the endnote (of which he is aware: "What a trip to lay on *The Moth Poem*!") explodes its pretentions. The poem is composed, as George Bowering says of such serial poems, of discrete but symbiotic sections. Each poem is struck from silence and wavers back to silence, but the series is not, as with George Oppen, discrete, and what Bowering calls *symbiotic* might be called *symbolic*. For all of its modernist surface, "The Moth Poem" is an extended Symbolist poem. The moth—literally trapped in a piano, its fluttering creating a "marvelous tentative music" and commanding the poem—becomes the poet's "master," an emblem of his spirit as it moves in and out of the occasions of the poems. The narrative that concerns Blaser involves friendship and poetry, but it is elusive because of the poem's allusiveness, its oblique presentation. The moth is assimilated to *"fantomes / de sentiments,"* a spectral consciousness with a predilection for the occult, and when Blaser takes it as master he follows H.D., to whom the series is dedicated. This is not to impugn H.D. nor those who have learned valuable lessons from her. Rather it is to question a practice less disciplined, perhaps less genuine, than hers—to question poems, which, unlike hers, do not certify themselves, which do indeed accord with Blaser's offhand reference to "god and man in terms of this century's questions." He may include the Pythagorean scale (a wonderful visual effect), but I am not convinced that he hears the music of the spheres. I prefer to take his word when he says, "there is nothing here but an intense [?], / interior monologue with moments of color. . . ." Reading his poems recalls the strictures of Olson's "Against Wisdom as Such," addressed to Duncan, who took them to heart, and still useful to poets who, as Olson says, court religion.

6. Frank Davey's "King of Swords" follows Blaser's poem probably because its title, taken from the Tarot, readily links it with the occult. The King of Swords equates with King Arthur and Arthurian materials, which in turn equate with Davey's personal history. This history, told in forty brief poems, involves an education in sexual roles—"lances chasing grails" is part of it—the breakup of his first marriage and the prospect of another marriage. Davey says that the material in terms of which he tells his story operates phenomenologically; it is not symbol but the present furnishing of his mind. Still we must consider this material symbolical because we must discover its meaning in order to appreciate the relevance of its presence here. The texture of the poem is much too allusive, and when we trouble to read *through* it, we find it heavy-handed, even unnecessary,

or necessary only to furbish an otherwise commonplace and uninteresting contemporary event. Davey has done much as a critic, editor, and publisher to foster avant-garde writing, but he has, I think, written the least satisfactory poem here, one, however, that may be used to demonstrate how difficult it is to bring the mind to bear in poetry of an open, serial kind.

7. This is what George Bowering does exceedingly well, with virtuosity. The title of his poem may arouse suspicion. But he explains "Allophanes" quite simply and truly: "Allo means all. Phanes means appearances." For which, I suppose, we should be grateful to an "egg-ziled" god. All is appearance, or transitory, and that's what concerns him, even his poem, which, were it not printed, would melt away in its making. The moth of his poem, presented in the first line, is a sentence he says he heard in his head in the voice of Jack Spicer: "The snowball appears in Hell / every morning at seven." This sentence generates a poem whose "subject" is (to repeat) its own making and melting, or Bowering's hostility to "unmelting literature," to history-as-description over against language as action, to art as phony lastingness. In keeping with the process-nature of things and the "fine étude of man," he would "build . . . with snow," as he does here in this poem of snowballs. Or, in another figure, he would have us hear *compost* in *composition.*

Now this is consonant with the project of postmodern poetics, and of all the poems collected here his is the most tuned into, or most conspicuously employs, its vocabulary. It is not just because its twenty-six sections are one shy of those in *Kora in Hell* that I think of Williams' poem. Sometimes there are interpretative glosses, as in *Kora in Hell,* but, more important, the poem is improvisatory and dialogic, concerned with writing as a present activity and questioning it as it goes. In part and whole it is disjunctive, its frequent declarative sentences, its aphorisms, its every piece, discrete, giving the writing a brisk staccato movement and a pleasant caustic tone in keeping with its genuinely ludic quality. This poem refuses to take its seriousness seriously—just serially. Its use of myth, alchemy, and Kabbalah is measured by vernacular skepticism (*"Do you believe all this stuff?"*). It is, moreover, a *Kora in Hell* that has gone to school to Pound and Olson, is ideogrammic and set out over the entire page, in this respect less restrained (fittingly) than "Seed Catalogue."

8. Roy Kiyooka's "The Fontainebleau Dream Machine" is also playful, but in surrealist fashion. I do not know Kiyooka's work but suspect

that his mixed-media poem—18 frames/collages composed of illustrations and verse-texts—is an example of what he calls "mind graffiti." The balloons that figure in each etching represent a kind of dream speech which the verse may be said to explain. The frames have a similar design: an illustration, an introductory line of verse separated from but running into the body of verse and, again following a separation, a concluding comment, sometimes mystifying, sometimes deflationary, etc. Illustration and text, of course, call up Blake, but perhaps a more helpful analogue would be Rimbaud, a master of indeterminacy. Besides, in Kiyooka's poem I find myself seeing what is heard and hearing what is seen. So it is not, I think, a poem readily "explained," and the author's endnote is as rich in implication as his poem: "F.D.M. incurs within the body of its own forebodings, the notion that Language-as-Rhetorick is, itself a terrifying dream, the F.D.M. is, among other things, my oftimes bemused Homage to the whole domain of European Art. . . ." Among other things, its imaginative fertility is liberating. After all, it is a dream machine.

9. The concluding poem, "The Martyrology Book IV," by bpNichol, not only comments on its own making but on the poems that precede it and the project of postmodern poetry. It is, in the poet's words, a "journal journey," a meditative poem involving its own "unwinding," evolving "in and around the writing." All here is lowercase and without punctuation, spoken language, the dialogue of the writer with himself: enacted on the page, a "w   rite of consciousness," a literal reweaving of the world by the closest attention to the letters with which we spell it out. The poem, as if restricted to a set of words, begins with a trickle and accumulates, its purpose proposed by the following:

> the precision of openness
> is not a vagueness
> it is an accumulation
> cumulous

Nichol wants—is seeking—"the absolute precision / of fluid definition." His attention, indebted to his work in concrete poetry, is on words, on the letters that compose them, the sounds they make, and the transformational fluidity that fragmenting them and punning them permits. In the course of discovering his stance he realizes what he has in fact been attending to: "what's immediate is / the word in front of me." He realizes that the new beginning he wants ("The Martyrology" is part of a lifelong poem) is to be found

> amid the sensory sensation of
> speech
>   these words
> the arch
> ark
>   IO
> logical
>   invocation of
> the change

His regard for letters is almost kabbalistic and opens the poem to myth, to the long human past as well as his own immediate past, to origin and being. And because he senses the return of the glacier and the coming night, his concern with language becomes a concern with healing and making whole: "art is to bring together // join."

Nichol's poem makes a good ending because it treats the most important considerations of poetry in our time, those set forth, for example, by Olson in "Projective Verse," which opened again the possibility of poems of "size." He himself suggests Olson when he puns on "compo / sition," or composition by field, and speaks of "the present activity of the writing." And his need to work out in the poem a stance and a poetics that enable him to meet the complex occasions of his life is Olsonian. "All knowledge," he finds,

> is to know the ledge you stand on
> half way between earth & sky
> where the clouds slide
> form & dissolve around you)
> a way of moving in the fluid surely
> . . . .
> to teach them
> the stupidity
> of rigid category

He knows, too, that the ego must diminish itself, that "i centre is a tease / no centre ring at all," that it is better when

> the i dies finally
> merges with the land's scape
> scope increases

—the pun here asking us to recall Olson's great poem of being-in-the-world, "Out Over the Land Skope View." Nichol's poem also remembers Olson in not forgetting Canada, in not forgetting place.

I don't know if Ondaatje put this poem at the end as an example of the most advanced or the most summary and hence conclusive. It certainly bears on all the work published here, work, I might add, that denies Poe's dictum on the impossibility of poems of length. Each of these poems can be read, and I find is best read, in a single sitting. The only requisite is an open mind and a magnifying glass to bring out the detail of Kiyooka's etchings.

Ideogram

An 8th century form . . . means *in some measure the whole conceptual world of the 8th century which invented it and to which it is fitted, whereas a 20th century form should embody . . . something of the astrophysical, chemical, sociological make-up of its day.*
William Carlos Williams

And we've both of us, got Grandpa [Ezra Pound] to thank for our way station of the ideogram.
Robert Duncan to Charles Olson

2.12 A picture is a model of reality.
2.151 Pictorial form is the possibility that things are related to one another in the same way as the elements of the picture.
Wittgenstein, Tractatus Logico-Philosophicus

Not an especially good ideogram: just a clustering of statements about it that Laszlo Géfin fully develops in *Ideogram.* This excellent book, in addition to being a history of a modernist mode of composition, is a manual of its exemplary practice and eloquent advocacy of its significance in a time of "reactionary, antimodernist" literary consciousness. It reminds us of Pound's great methodological contribution to our way of composing and thinking, and pays tribute to Pound in sketching the ideogrammic tradition created by those who endorsed his practice. Williams, Zukofsky, Oppen, Reznikoff, Olson, Creeley, Duncan, Ginsberg, Snyder: merely to name the poets treated here is to recall Imagism, Vorticism, Objectivism, "Projective Verse," the movements by means of which poets were able, in Williams' telling phrase, to cling to the advance, and to remember that the ideogram, this "new logic of depiction," belongs to open form and field composition.

The ideogrammic method, which Pound found in Fenollosa, is also familiar to us in collage, montage, and mobiles, and it should be more than *parti pris* to be reminded that its significance derives from the fact that literary techniques are validated, finally, by the extent to which they "cover the real" (Olson's phrase). The paratactic, particularist mode of the ideogram is not simply archaic, but belongs to the modernists' search for the primitive—that is, for primary ways of enacting in language the recovered sense of a universe of process. It belongs to our awareness of being in the field, a thing among things, not above them, able to measure (and have measures) only by participating in the transference of energies. It restores us to vital creation, but not as sovereign, and this is the significance of Pound's repudiation of symbol, his concern with "language beyond metaphor." For what is repudiated here is philosophical idealism, our inherited, long-established way of depicting reality.

The first third of *Ideogram* treats Pound's early work and disposition to find his own concerns in Fenollosa's *The Chinese Written Character as a Medium for Poetry.* Géfin goes back to the manuscript and discusses Pound's "fruitful misunderstanding" and examines the ideogrammic form of "In a Station of the Metro" and the more complex developments of *The Cantos* and *Guide to Kulchur.* His account of Pound's poetics uses but does not supersede Herbert Schneidau's in *Ezra Pound: The Image and the Real.* Readers of Géfin will want to turn to this definitive study and will also want to consider the epic aspects of *The Cantos,* considerably simplified by Géfin's reference to Eric Havelock's description of *The Iliad,* in the light of Michael Bernstein's *The Tale of the Tribe.* Bernstein, moreover, is valuable for noting the failures of ideogrammic method, something Géfin never calls to our attention.

Brevity as well as partisanship may be the reason for this, and in a book so useful I hesitate to question Géfin's method. It is not itself ideogrammic but, as we say, soundly academic. His procedure with each poet is to set out the poetics and demonstrate its application in carefully selected examples. Touchstones. The repetition of ideas inevitable in the former serves the purpose of advocacy, but the later, despite perceptive readings, always begs the questions raised by the larger work. To name the major poems employing the ideogrammic method—*The Cantos, Discrete Series, "A", Testimony, Paterson, Maximus Poems, Passages, Pieces, The Fall of America, Myths & Texts*—is to realize that the method has made possible a new kind of long poem and that its success must be judged in terms of the whole, not merely suggested by the compositional brilliance of a part. It is not enough to mention Pound's cumulative practice or Zukofsky's fugal composition—though the later is a notable example of the adaptability of the method. Nor is it enough to quote Olson's approval of Pound's "RAGBAG" and forget his reservations about Pound's "ego-system" ("so much of Ez, is, the 19th century stance").

The discussion of Williams' *Paterson* is an instance of what I have in mind. Géfin's reading of parts of Book II is excellent as is his understanding of Williams' stated intentions. Yet *Paterson* does not fulfill them—or only does so if we overlook, as Géfin does, the closed, imposed form of Books I–IV. Another instance is *Maximus*, considered here in the simplest examples of ideogrammic form in Volume One, omitting almost entirely the formal departures of the subsequent volumes. Still another instance is Creeley's *Pieces*, of which it is not exact to say that "echoes and references to previous images or perceptions are absent."

It is to Géfin's credit (and acumen) that he recognizes Ginsberg, "the artistry and serious theoretical foundation of his work," and acknowledges here a connection between surrealism and the ideogrammic method. Later on, he situates this method between closed composition and surrealist-associational writing, but had he followed up his earlier insight he would have found that the "deep imagists" deserve a place in the tradition, and all the more so when the measure of value, as his seems to be, is the archaic. Géfin's highest praise is for Ginsberg ("with [his] poetics and oral-elliptical method the ancient art of poetry comes full circle") and for Snyder (he "has not only adopted and revitalized archaic modes of expression, but refashioned his thinking and lifestyle to such an extent that they all but exclude *in toto* the values and achievements of Western civilization").

Ginsberg and Snyder. With this pairing and high ranking Géfin concludes his book. This reminds me of Charles Altieri's *Enlarging the Temple,* where the pairings and rankings, in the service of other values, are different. Ginsberg is omitted, Snyder is paired with Duncan, and Creeley and Merwin take highest honors. Ranking (good) poets is probably an idle game, and my quarrel with Géfin's ranking, especially of Snyder, is that it is based on something besides what Snyder accomplishes as a poet. It is not so much that he has not rejected Western civilization as absolutely as Géfin claims, as that there is not enough evidence in Géfin's treatment to support his claims. Even *Myths & Texts,* a formally closed work from which he takes his examples, is slighted, and *Mountains and Rivers without End,* the most open work, is not mentioned. With greater justice, on the evidence supplied, he might have cited Duncan, who said of Pound what might well be said of himself—that "in the art at large [he was] the creator of a mode, projecting beyond his work new considerations of the meaning of form." As Géfin says of this poet of co-inherence, "Duncan's collage ideograms are not strictly cumulative, contrastive, fugal, or overlapping, though they contain traces and elements of each. They are cyclical or rather *spherical,* each point within the global field faintly or strongly connected to every other."

It should be added that the ideogram of Duncan's work is still open, and open to new formal departures. This is why *history* in the subtitle of Géfin's book seems ill-advised and *tradition* would have been been better, suggesting, as it does, the continuing work and not the completed accomplishment of this method. Shouldn't there be, at least, a hint of present activity? Is this a manual only of established practice? What, then, of advocacy? Closing the book with Pound rounds it thematically, but ends it by putting ideogrammic practice under suspicion. Géfin affirms the coherence of *The Cantos* because he believes that the ideogram is a representation of a coherent universe ("the entire universe cohere[s]"). I share his faith in the coherence of the universe but not his assurance that the ideogrammic method is foolproof. Coherence is the assumption on which this method rests, but sometimes, even after patient, serious study, poems do not cohere. This is not necessarily because they are badly made (it is not a matter of imposing a form, making it cohere, as Géfin rightly argues) but because the poet, in availing himself of a conspicuously modernist method, may not in fact have entered the field, put himself into relation with the process. This stance, as Olson knew, is *the* requisite of the method, and this is why poets who are unwilling to risk this way of being often impugn it.

Eros and Logos

Gift exchange stands to market exchange as *eros* stands to *logos,* as *imagination* stands to *will,* as "*female*" stands to "*male.*" This, of course, does not exhaust the ramifications of these binary terms, for, as Marcel Mauss tells us in *The Gift: Forms and Functions of Exchange in Archaic Societies* (1925), gift exchange is a total phenomenon, that is, inextricably part of the social and cultural fabric. For this reason it is also an admirable object of study for a sociologist who, like Mauss, is aware of contemporary society and wants to bring to it from the past some relevant moral conclusions (feedback). Mauss' sociology is cultural criticism, and so is Lewis Hyde's, whose *The Gift: Imagination and the Erotic Life of Property* acknowledges Mauss in its title and its extension of Mauss' classic work in its subtitle. It might even be said to be cultural criticism with a vengeance because, with Mauss' work at hand, Hyde takes over the idea of gift exchange as one of the "opposed catchwords," to use Van Wyck Brooks' term for such pairs, and enjoys the excitement Brooks enjoyed when "fighting for . . . some clearly seen and deeply felt good against some greatly scorned evil."

There is no question of where Hyde stands, any more than there is with Mauss. But neither, like Brooks, is combative or melodramatic, and in Hyde's case the work itself bestows on him an ameliorative grace. What began as *either/or* becomes *both/and,* as assuredly it reasonably must when the central question addressed in the book is what can a young man do (the phrase belongs to Brooks' time and recalls the expatriation of the artist) when he possesses gifts and bears gifts and finds no other exchange for them than that of the market. The impetus of Hyde's book is personal: gift exchange vs. market exchange is his way of telling us how it is with him—and with us—in the world. These remarkable terms are kindred to Brooks' *creative life* and *acquisitive life,* and they resume the primary critical debate that Brooks began and deepen it because they ask us to consider not merely what Brooks thought was the contradiction of American culture—the consequence of Puritanism (and the rise of capitalism)—but the very dilemma of civilization itself.

Gift exchange belongs to an economy and *ecos* of creativity and spirit, which is to say that it respects generativity and generosity and is a circular way that represents a reality that is circular, processual, interrelated—yes, natural and sacred. As Mauss' study tells us, it is notably the economy of archaic societies. Mauss studied it because his work, like Hyde's, was prompted by one of the central intellectual undertakings of our time, the search for the primitive, as Stanley Diamond calls it. For them, and for so many who take up the "primitive," its evocation is a way, according to Kenneth Burke, of "temporalizing the essence," that is, of making things of first importance first in time and thereby reminding us that we have lost something inalienable. At the end of his essay, Mauss asks us to "return to the old and elemental," to "motives of action" still within memory, to ways more generous and joyful, to find a place in our dehumanized economy for the eminently human gift of giving, for the *eros* without which exchange loses its highest value. Gift exchange—itself one of the definitions of love—is an *econ* become an *ecos* by virtue of *eros;* for the gift, identified with the person, is the person, and the exchange, as endless as the transferences of energy in nature, is of the very self, what Whitman called the *me myself.* The gift economy exists to exchange something besides commodities. As much as the round dance, another representation of reality that it recalls, it is a practice of love, as love may be practiced in a social form.

To point out that Hyde is more "at ease with emotion [with *eros*] as a social force" than Mauss and more concerned with the erotic life of property than with the obligations gift-giving imposes is to suggest, I think, how much Hyde's book owes to the cultural debate of the 1960s—how much *The Gift* is a sixties book. Indeed in reading it I was reminded of nothing so much as the legacy of that unusual time when "fundamental questions" were asked "as if the answers mattered . . . [and] as if the nation's politics and ways of life were fluid enough to flow in new directions" (I quote from "The Talk of the Town," *The New Yorker,* 1 August 1983). Hyde's book is a labor of gratitude for the thought and example of such writers as Paul Goodman, Erik Erikson, and Ivan Illich; it is a gift of the period when the Party of Eros flourished, and it continues its work, its concern with anarchist politics and small-group life, which favor the gift economy. It is also a sixties book in other ways: in its moral vocabulary, its unashamed didacticism and homiletical urging. Its mode is vernacular and personal, though in some respects still academic, and the essential element is the anecdote—folk tale, myth, Emily Post directive—which secures the discussion, grounds it. Hyde's way of using "The Shoemaker and the Elves," for example, reminds me of Brother Blue, another storyteller in Boston; and perhaps by mentioning Brother Blue I can suggest the relation of teacher to child that Hyde so often assumes, as if he forgot that those who read his book will probably not need elementary instruction. Though less elegant than Paul Goodman's work, Hyde's is most like it in offering psychological explanations that address the discipline of the creative spirit—*Kafka's Prayer,* where we learn that we may eat of the tree of life, is a special instance of its kind because for Goodman it is so exclusively literary criticism. But so is the second half of Hyde's book, devoted as it is to Whitman and Pound, to case histories of the creative gift that again recall Van Wyck Brooks, our first psychologically disposed critic and a writer, as Hyde is here, of exemplary (Whitman) and cautionary (Pound) tales.

In its use of anthropology, the most frequently adduced evidence of the first part of the book, *The Gift* is very much in keeping with recent literary studies. This is true as well of its Jungian psychology, which makes it easy to employ words such as *soul* ("A gift revives the soul"). This psychology mediates both parts of the book (i.e., the Jew is Pound's "shadow"), though the last chapter of the first part, a long history of usury, may be said to bridge them. Even so the coherence of the book derives from its pervasive concern with the binary oppositions mentioned at the outset, and these, especially *eros* vs. *logos,* put it in the company of some of the most significant work of our time, work that in this instance, since Hyde himself is a poet, is curiously ignored. For what Hyde argues in behalf of gift exchange, another poet-pedagogue, Charles Olson, argued for in terms of a "human universe." No one was more relentlessly a critic of *logos* (which stands to *eros* as *mind* to *body, concept* to *image, universal* to *particular*) than Olson, nor so convinced that *myth,* which opposes *logos* as preliterate opposes literate culture, was concerned chiefly with *eros.* When considered in this light, Olson's insistence on an oral art answers to more than the fact, noted by Hyde, that "the oral tradition . . . keeps the gift of speech alive." It is a way of defending the kind of culture and cultural values that thrived in archaic societies, and it summons, as readers of Havelock's *Preface to Plato* know, the crisis of *paideia* that was concurrent in Greece with the rise of civilization. It may even be said to be a way of defending an oral matrifocal culture, which values bestowing and nurturance, against an anal patriarchal culture, which hoards and possesses its "filthy lucre," a defense, that is, of the gift economy. None of these concerns, of course, is unique with Olson; they characterize the intellectual climate of our time. But I cite Olson because he was involved with them as a poet and "scholar without institution," just as Hyde is, and because in speaking of barter, voluntary poverty, and polis, he addressed the very things Hyde does—how artists survive in our culture. And besides, Olson, who knew Pound and generously sustained him at St. Elizabeth's, indicted him, pretty much as Hyde does, by saying that Pound became a *jongleur* when he served the State instead of his art.

Gift exchange is the subject of this book for many of the reasons suggested above, but it is also the subject, I think, because as metaphor or conceit it enables the discussion of values that matter most to Hyde and because a culture acknowledging these values would be an optimum one for the artist, the man (or woman) of gifts. Like Brooks, Hyde reminds us that the artist's vocation is spiritual—"the true commerce of art is a gift exchange" and commoditization jeopardizes it—and that the artist, the representative of the spirit, is the best measure of what is truly valuable in a culture. This may be put in binary terms: where "logic is the money of the mind" (as Marx said), imagination is its gift. Hyde also begins where Brooks began, with the fact that in our culture the (true) artist is a failure. He cites Bellow's Charlie Citrine, "So poets are loved, but loved because they just can't make it here."

Now this is the real subject of the book, and explains why the transformation of opposites to contraries is interesting. Hyde not only speaks up for *eros* and imagination but seeks ways in which to accommodate his binary terms, ways in which to live in a market economy. If he begins with *either/or,* it is because that was the uncompromising way in which he considered his situation in the 1960s. Now, however, he is less resistant and recalcitrant because he realizes—if I may borrow the title of a Goodman novel—that he must make do, that though elements of the gift economy survive, ours is not a gift economy.

This, the most important part of the book, is the least satisfactory because the treatment is skimpy, the solutions offered needlessly limited, and the conclusion acquiescent. Hyde suggests three solutions to the problem of livelihood: to take a second job, find a patron, or support oneself by marketing one's work. All involve the double economy of markets and gifts, and the only guide in this difficult public and private commerce is "the conversion of market wealth to gift wealth." "Fidelity to one's gift" is the requisite thing; integrity, we used to say. Then, voluntary poverty, which, protestation to the contrary, Hyde romanticizes—or maybe it's only that his examples are of young artists committed to art but not yet encumbered by marriage and family. I find it strange that he does not consider the most frequent source of support, that of the universities. If he considers this patronage, it is patronage of a different kind and merits investigating. This is also true of governmental support, which he himself has had, and which, in Canada, to cite an example of generous subsidy, has contributed to vigorous cultural expression, a remarkable bestowing of gifts. And what of writers' cooperatives and what might be called the double culture, the culture of the avant garde, of little magazines, small presses, marginal people, in many ways our most vital culture? Does he neglect this because it was the option of the 1960s, and for the same reason give over what truly attracts him, the small-group life that accords with gift exchange? Finally, since the market economy will not accommodate us (*us,* because in the course of the book we have given our allegiance to the economy of spirit and have identified with the artist), we must accommodate ourselves by realizing that our interior lives are more rewarding than our exterior lives, that the actual poverty of the latter does not limit the wealth of spirit of the former. Brooks believed this too, but did not practice what he preached. I don't know many artists who gladly do, and not because they have been corrupted but because the binary terms *interior/exterior* and *spirit/wealth* belong to the philosophical idealism we owe to *logos* and foster the very aestheticizing of life that the *eros* of gift exchange denies. The solutions Hyde offers are private, acceptable to him because he assumes that gifts nurtured in this way still do the necessary spiritual work, as Brooks used to say, of leavening society. I do not deny this, but, having been given the gift of this imagination of the gift exchange and the accordant psychology of healing and wholing, I find such solutions unworthy of our gifts.

Ethnopoetics: An "Other" Tradition

The land! don't you feel it?
doesn't it make you want to go out
and lift dead Indians tenderly from
their graves, to steal from them . . .
some authenticity. . . .
William Carlos Williams, In the American Grain *(1925)*

I have no doubt, say, that the
American will more and more repossess
himself of the Indian past. . . .
Charles Olson, Mayan Letters *(1953)*

Some of the young men
Have become aware of the Indian
George Oppen, This Is Which *(1965)*

Michael Castro, who wrote a poem called *The Kokopilau Cycle* published in 1975 by the Blue Cloud Quarterly Press of Marvin, South Dakota, is one of the young men to whom Oppen alludes; one who "finds the Indian," as Oppen says, by recovering a holistic way of life that is healing and wholing, and may even appreciate the Indian, as Oppen does, because they were "a people in danger" and "feared . . . the thing might end." Castro insists less on an ending than Oppen does, but his search for the "primitive" (*primitive:* first, primary, fully human) is surely prompted by the beginning that the sense of an ending asks us to resume. "Return," Oppen writes in § 10 of "A Narrative," from which I've been citing, "the return of the sun," intending us to recall the conclusion of Lawrence's

Apocalypse (1931): "What we want is to destroy our false, inorganic connections, especially those related to money [see Marcel Mauss, *The Gift: Forms and Functions of Exchange in Archaic Societies* (1925) and Lewis Hyde, *The Gift: Imagination and the Erotic Life of Property* (1983), the basic studies of a first economy, an *ecos* other than that of the marketplace] and re-establish the living organic connections, with the cosmos, the sun and earth, with mankind and nation and family. Start with the sun, and the rest will slowly, slowly happen."

Kókopilau, the humpbacked flute player of the Hopi, is the locust *máhu* who wins for his people the privilege of living on the eagle's land. Song, which in the Hopi view accords with the vibration of the earth's axis and is essentially healing, secures his victory. So Kókopilau is readily adopted by poets—poets like Gary Snyder, who defines his own work by assimilating the poet to the shaman, to masters of healing like Kókopilau, Coyote, and Buddha (see "The Blue Sky" and "The Hump-Backed Flute Player" in *Mountains and Rivers Without End,* an endless poem, as the title says in nominating nature, but also because poets who plant seeds, as Kókopilau does, are culture-heroes who ensure rebirth). Castro, too, has adopted Kókopilau, not only in *The Kokopilau Cycle* but in an introductory scholarly-critical study recently published, *Interpreting the Indian: Twentieth-Century Poets and the Native American.* The petroglyph of Kókopilau that greets us on the title page is the visible sign of the book's meaning, of the belief, reiterated in advocacy, that in our time of alienation, fractured spirit, and incomplete humanity, "the red man has come to teach the white." Castro says of Kókopilau, "For us he can become an image of the New Man in the New World that American poets attracted to the Indian have ultimately sought to create."

Castro's book, and the spirit in which it is written, owes much to the counterculture of the 1960s. He came to the Indian by way of oral poetry and the performance-practice of that time. Oppen refers to this in *Of Being Numerous* (1968) when he notes the "art of the young in cities"—the art of his young friends, Jerome Rothenberg among them—and dismisses it as "Dithyrambic, audience-as-artists!" Castro also came to the Indian by way of opposition to civilization as represented by the war in Viet Nam, and because Jerome Rothenberg's *Technicians of the Sacred* (1968)—Eliade's phrase defines the shaman—and *Shaking the Pumpkin:*

Traditional Poetry of the Indian North Americas (1972) pointed up the convergence of modern and primitive *poesis*.

Though Castro reminds us of the stereotypes of brutish and noble savage that for much of our history inform our awareness of the Indian, his account centers on the twentieth century and the effort to understand and assimilate Indian ways—what Dennis Tedlock calls "Teaching from the American Earth." He begins with early translators of Indian poetry; translation is initial in ethnopoetics, a primary work in which anthropology and poetry join, and "total translation," which finds ways of reconstructing both the literal verse and the fullness of its occasion, is of special concern to it. Perhaps the most notable of the early translators is Mary Hunter Austin (1868–1934) whose work of "reexpression" culminates in *The American Rhythm* (1923). This polemical work belongs with Constance Rourke's *American Humor* (1931) because it does for Indian poetry what Rourke does for our "native," indigenous vernacular art. Both books attend to arts little noticed by the literary establishment, the official culture (what George Quasha, in speaking of marginal arts and other traditions, calls the consensus), arts that cannot be neglected in any account of the "American character" and, once noticed, are impossible to neglect. This revisionist work, so much the work of women, is not adventitious, and should remind us that in the search for the primitive, which to a considerable extent is a search for the feminine, women should not be left out of account, that the "New Man in the New World" that Castro proposes does not represent the fullness of the ethnopoetic undertaking even though Mary Austin claims that "poetry is a man's game." Castro considers only Leslie Silko in the subsequent discussion of poets and then chiefly for her defense of Indian literary territory. Even Diane and Jerome Rothenberg in their new reader in ethnopoetics (*Symposium of the Whole: A Range of Discourse Toward an Ethnopoetics*) do not include many women poets, only Maria Sabina (a shaman) and Diane Di Prima, which may cause us to wonder whether ethnopoetics, concerned as it is with what patriarchal civilization has excluded, is itself, as presently presented (perhaps necessarily?), patriarchal. Or perhaps a better question might be, if this lack of interest is the case, why is it so?

The American Rhythm and *American Humor* were expressions of the renewed cultural nationalism of the first decades of the century, the period of America's coming-of-age, to borrow the title of Van Wyck Brooks' stirring critical summons of 1915. Both books belong with William Carlos Williams' *In the American Grain* (1925), especially Austin's book, which made so much of the need to contact the aboriginal ground, to come into the genius of place and take up the Indian as part of the American identity—not, imperially, to take over the Indian, but, as Williams says of Daniel Boone, "to be *himself* in the new world, Indian-like." Sometimes, in ignorance, we overlook the concurrence of such books and the fact that their occurrence depended on a rewakening—commensurate with the decline of the Indian—that went back to the American Renaissance of the mid-nineteenth century. One testimony of renewed interest is the February 1917 issue of *Poetry* magazine devoted to "aboriginal poetry," which reminds us that at this time, not just in the 1960s, Indian poetry was brought forward in connection with "the concerns and practices of poetic modernism." Sandburg, one of Austin's exemplars of an American rhythm, humorously remarked at the time that "the red man . . . committed direct plagiarism on our modern imagists and vorticists," and Louis Untermeyer, defending the establishment in *The Dial* (1919), denounced both: "the harsh aborigine can commit poetry as trite and banal as many an overcivilized paleface."

Vachel Lindsay, Hart Crane, and William Carlos Williams, whom Castro subsequently treats, are part of this awakening, not translators, however, but poets in whose work the Indian figures. The chapter devoted to them is followed by others on Lew Sarett and John G. Neihardt, Charles Olson, Jerome Rothenberg, Gary Snyder, and, finally, some contemporary Indian writers who, for the most part, are unhappy with the non-Indian appropriation of Indian art-forms and consciousness. This history, sketchy and brief as it is, is useful, especially so in reminding us of antecedents, of a "usable past." But, except for the study of Neihardt and the composition of *Black Elk Speaks* (an unquestionable national treasure) and the criticism of early translations of Indian poetry and poetry like Lindsay's and Sarett's, it is superficial, often reductive, mistaken in details, and curiously omissive.

To misdate Williams' *Spring and All* (1923), from which Castro quotes the concluding poem on the Black-eyed Susan, is of little consequence. To gloss over the poem is another matter, for what matters to Williams—the very import of this important book—is both the emergence of Kora from Hell and her transformation as a native wild flower, a "dark woman," and the descendental work of the imagination (*poesis*) that opens this redemptive possibility. Like Hart Crane, who mythicized Pocahontas (and, more than has been sufficiently acknowledged, saw the poet's vocation in terms of the shaman and under the necessity of restoring "the tribal dawn"), Williams mythicized the flower. Both discovered American great goddesses of the Demeter-Kore kind, testifying to the fact that their search for the primitive was indeed a search for the feminine. (As Rothenberg says of Robert Graves' *The White Goddess* [1948], "The 'return of the goddess' is one of the central events of a poetics of recovery. . . .") Troublesome also is the confusion over the order of events in "The Desert Music," and even more so are readings of texts like Olson's "The Kingfishers," which seem to be skewed in order to foreground the evidence Castro wishes to present. I doubt that "The Kingfishers" was intended to be chanted, that in it Olson himself uses words magically, and that a poem so essentially personal—preparatory and programmatic—was addressed to other poets. Why, I wonder, is *Mayan Letters* (1953), which did awaken other poets, given only a page or so, and why is nothing said of Olson's interest in other early cultures, Sumer, for example, or in still earlier cultures, as shown in *Olson #10,* the issue devoted to the human sciences? Similarly, with Snyder, I wonder at the failure to mention Buddhism, an influence in his life and thought as great as Amerindian lore; the failure, even, to mention Snyder's use of Kókopilau, to treat such central works as *He Who Hunted Birds in His Father's Village: The Dimensions of a Haida Myth* (1951; 1974) and *Myths and Texts* (1960), and to show, what especially needs showing, that to be himself Indian-like in Turtle Island was an accomplishment far from easy, making it possible for him to approach the condition he proposes for ethnopoeticists, that of becoming an informant, "that old man sitting in the sand house telling his story. . . ." With Rothenberg, too, whose centrality Castro recognizes, how is it he fails to see that ethnopoetics (an undertaking Rothenberg named in 1968) is ecumenical, concerned with all cultures? How is it he omits *A Seneca Journal,* the most evident Indian work, companion to the equally ethnopoetic *Poland/1931,* and, in treating the important goal of "total translation," overlooks the essential work of Dell Hymes and Dennis Tedlock and such scholarly articles as H. S. McAllister's "'The Language of Shamans': Jerome Rothenberg's Contribution to American Indian Literature" (1975/76)? Finally, what of other poets, poets like Ed Dorn, whose *The Shoshoneans* (with Leroy Lucas), *The Poet, The People, The Spirit,* and *Recollections of Gran Apachería* merit a place in a chronicle of this kind, and all the more so because they remind us that "a poetry which is associated with American Indian culture," as Fredric Jameson insists in the issue of *Alcheringa* devoted to the first international symposium on ethnopoetics (1975), "can scarcely forget [the] relationship between a politics of nature [best defined, I suggest, in the work of Stanley Diamond] and a politics which aims at the basic imperializing mechanisms of our socio-economic system"?

As for the protests against cooption represented here by Geary Hobson and Leslie Silko, Castro is surely right to quote the measured good sense of the medicine man in Silko's *Ceremony:* "You don't write off all the white people, just like you don't trust all Indians." Perhaps such protests are necessary on ideological grounds, but, like the similar protests of other minorities, the exclusive claim to ethnic, racial, sexual, or gender territory denies all common sense and the symposium of the whole that ethnopoetics ultimately serves. Castro's advocacy is not limited in this way but rather by the fact of his limited awareness of the scope of ethnopoetics. It seems that he failed to see that other of Rothenberg's anthologies—*America a Prophecy* (with George Quasha, 1973), *Revolution of the Word* (1974), and *A Big Jewish Book* (with Harris Lenowitz and Charles Doria, 1978)—prepare for what may be the summary gathering of his and his wife's latest book.

The subtitle of the Rothenbergs' book—"A Range of Discourse Toward an Ethnopoetics"—does not deny their advocacy so much as enlist it in an ongoing, open, marginal endeavor. This is often spoken of as a poetry of changes and, considering Jerome Rothenberg's restoration of Dada, may be defined by Tristan Tzara's proposal to follow "primitive peoples" by making "poetry a way of life rather than a subsidiary manifestation of intelligence and will." From the start, in the early 1960s, when Rothenberg championed the "deep image," of greatest importance to him was the issue Tzara said was foremost for Dada: "to recover from the depths of consciousness the exalted source of the poetic function." Ethnopoetics may be said to begin with this "freeing-up of the imagination," with the recognition of *poesis* as fundamentally creative of self and world, with the return to what Vico said was the "poetic nature of these first men."

As for *discourse,* it tells us that the Rothenbergs are concerned with transmission (and transformation). Accordingly, in keeping with the ethnopoetic interest in oral, preliterate cultures, the printed pieces collected here should, where possible, be read with the ear, heard as voices, the entire work constituting a conversation. I hear much of it in this way, pleased with the brief entry, now and then, of the editors' voice in the headnotes—the only apparatus other than a bibliography in this simply organized book. It may be that after all Jerome Rothenberg had done in his previous work, the Rothenbergs could let the siftings of twenty-five years of scholarship speak for themselves without the commentaries or such ideogrammic complexity as one finds in *America a Prophecy,* where juxtaposition challenges a traditional sense of American literature. Everything collected here is choice—readers of Rothenberg will recall that he had chosen or alluded to some of these essays in other collections—and now (by now) many are classic; there are also essays hitherto unpublished by J. Stephen Lansing and Simon J. Ortiz. Were it not for the fact that it is not in the nature of ethnopoetic inquiry, this consolidation as well as opening of the field might, as George Quasha said of the symposium in 1975, find itself "absorbed back into the consensus." Ethnopoetics brings scholars and poets, academic and avant garde, together, but it is quite another matter to make ethnopoetics an academic field. This book—in so many ways a textbook, published by a university press and likely to remain in print—will surely move others, as it moves me, to offer a course in this "subject." But I suspect that the Rothenbergs pondered this and took the risk. The symposium in *Alcheringa* was prefaced by Jerome Rothenberg's rejoinder to Donald Davie's "attack" on the "range" of poetries set out in *America a Prophecy,* and though Harold Bloom is not mentioned in *Symposium of the Whole,* Rothenberg's rejoinder to him in *Sulfur* 2 (1981) should be read by way of explaining the present move. The academy, after all, has become an arena of criticisms and perhaps the time has come (finally?) for it to become an arena of poetries.

This large book is in five sections. The first, "Preliminary Moves," traverses the temporal scope of the book by beginning in the eighteenth century with such early spokesmen as Vico ("the first gentile peoples . . . were poets who spoke in poetic characters") and Herder ("Savage, uncivilized peoples? I can hardly subscribe to your point of view") and coming forward by way of more familiar recent writers—Rimbaud, Fenollosa, Pound, Lorca, for example—to the present. Here, the important statements, comprising a significant cluster, are Charles Olson's "Human Universe," Stanley Diamond's "Plato and the Definition of the Primitive," Gary Snyder's "Poetry and the Primitive," and Rothenberg's "Pre-Face to *Technicians of the Sacred*." In this way, the first connects with the last section, "Contemporary Moves," where some of these writers appear again along with their associates in poetry and anthropology. The intervening sections, much of them given to anthropological work, are called "Workings," "Meanings," and "Doings," the participles according with "Moves," not so much because of the importance of the processual in ethnopoetics as because *moves,* in the course of the book, acquires a strategic meaning. This is especially the case in the way section four, ending with Richard Schechner's account of "efficacious theatre," carries over into the fifth section headed by Robert Duncan's "Rites of Participation" and Victor Turner's review of the international symposium issue of *Alcheringa*. This gives *contemporary,* in "Contemporary Moves," the insistence of *now*.

Symposium also picks up on conversation, which in this instance is about the whole—and the healing that comes of wholing. In its entirety the title establishes the large work that has made the Rothenbergs—one a poet, the other an anthropologist—advocates of ethnopoetics and, it should be said, has made ethnopoetics *the* name for the project of the most significant and radically interesting poetry of our time. The Rothenbergs recognize this by taking the title from a phrase in Robert Duncan's "Rites of Participation" that, once before, in prefacing the symposium in *Alcheringa,* had been used to define the ethnopoetic undertaking. In this essay, a chapter of *The H.D. Book,* Duncan declares that "the drama of our time is the coming of all men [and women] into one fate," this being the case because we now realize that this fate is "'the dream of everyone, everywhere.'" Accordingly, we, too, not just the Australian aborigine, must attend "the eternal ones of the dream," as *alcheringa,* so defined, tells us. (Rothenberg said in *Poems from the Floating World,* his first magazine, that "the world as it existed for the first man still exists. It taunts us and breaks into our dreams.") Then, in the course of explaining why our *arête* is not Plato's, Duncan explicitly sets out the nature of the inclusivity ethnopoetics seeks: "To compose such a symposium of the whole, such a totality, all the old excluded orders must be included. The female, the proletariat, the foreign; the animal and vegetative; the unconscious and the unknown; the criminal and failure—all that has been outcast and vagabond must return to be admitted in the creation of what we consider we are."

In recognizing the other and not excluding it, ethnopoetics challenges Plato, that is, renews the long-standing quarrel of the poets with the philosopher who cast them out. What Victor Turner said of the symposium issue of *Alcheringa,* which is still the liveliest introduction to ethnopoetics, holds for the present symposium: "this counter-Platonic Symposium." Stanley Diamond's essay, part of his landmark book, *In Search of the Primitive: A Critique of Civilization* (1974), is the basic statement, so much so it is surprising that the Rothenbergs failed to mention Eric Havelock's equally important *Preface to Plato* (1963), an investigation of Plato's hostility to the *paideia* of preliterate Homeric culture that supports what Diamond says of "modes of thinking [that] are substantially concrete, existential and nominalistic, within a personalistic context"—modes of thinking, Charles Olson claims, that "cover the real" and "hew to experience," that relocate us in the world and overcome the world-alienation of philosophical idealism.

Ethnopoetics would restore the outcast poet-trickster-shaman and the full range of communal uses that oral poetry had in preliterate cultures. (Incidentally, as the previous reference to *paideia* suggests, this would include its epic didactic task and thus account for some of the long poems of our time.) In reoralizing poetry it would also restore the performative, "event"-ful aspect of poetry, take poetry off the page and bring it to life. And in its respect for rites it would restore our rights of participation. The extent to which it represents another tradition—the tradition of the other—is easily seen. Its politics—its connection with ecological awareness and the destruction of diversity, human and otherwise—is clear enough, though the most notable statement, Gary Snyder's "The Politics of Ethnopoetics," in the symposium issue of *Alcheringa,* is regrettably not included. Nor is George Quasha's "The Age of the Open Secret," in the same issue, a remarkable meditation on the word *ethnopoetics* that, among other things, brings this poetics to bear on critical practice and opens a way to do criticism openly.

Canon-Making

The large ambition of this book is not the obvious one announced by its title. There is no attempt in *American Poetry and Culture 1945–1980* to suggest, let alone chart, this vast territory or probe the problematical relation of poetry and culture. The latter is what I had hoped for because nothing, it seems to me, has been so difficult to sort out: anything written within a culture is inescapably of cultural significance but very little of this writing claims importance, that is, directly concerns itself with the culture and, since it counts for Robert von Hallberg, with Culture. The ambition of this book is not fulfilled in survey—to read it without prior knowledge of the field will surely mislead one. It is fulfilled instead in the imperial design whereby the title is limited to the poets he selects, poets who are said to accommodate rather than oppose the culture and who may be said to be centrist. It is limited to select poets of the "mainstream" of the culture, itself imperial, when the most culturally significant as well as interesting American poetry, like the rest of American literature, has been, as always, of the margins, informed (to use a Veblenesque measure) by perspectives both within and outside of the culture. The title, then, like much of the weighty argument of the book, is mostly cover for canon-making, though the canon appropriates some poets better placed elsewhere and may be nothing more, finally, than buttress for writing about poets von Hallberg likes: Robert Creeley, John Ashbery, James Merrill, Robert Lowell, Edward Dorn, Mona Van Duyn, Robert Pinsky, James McMichael, John Hollander, and Elizabeth Bishop.

Von Hallberg's argument is well stated in "Conclusion: Suburbs," the chapter title tellingly right because the suburbs spurned by the poets in the 1950s (even poets like Richard Wilbur) have become the places of their accommodation—their audience, university-bred and -fed, and centrist in acceptance of imperium. Here's the argument:

> I have tried to show that many of the best poets of the last forty years have written with fascination for the ideas, experience, and even institutions that seemed central to the country. The notion that literature should judge and condemn the mainstream culture is not helpful in understanding the shape of recent literary history. Where poets have been most intent upon playing adversary to the dominant culture (and many of the poets I have overlooked are content with that role) the poetry has been blunt, rhetorical, and misleading. Much of what I take as the best recent poetry has not been written from an adversary perspective, and one of its distinguishing characteristics is a tendency to register fine distinctions where other poets and people see none. The poetry I admire from this period has been one of accommodation rather than opposition.

There is much to question here—the proposition of the second sentence, the attribution of playing roles, the immunity declared in *mainstream culture* and *dominant culture,* the easy strokes of *seemed central, blunt* and *fine,* and so on—and even more to question when the passage is juxtaposed to the following:

> . . . canon formation has a particular function in an empire. When critics have as an objective the formation of a canon . . . they tacitly presume or deliberately construct a culture with a strong authoritative center. . . . A canon demonstrates not only the quality of a culture but also its coherence. The nations that most need to demonstrate coherence are those most open to diverse influences and are yet striving to assert hegemony, which is the situation of a colonizer.

Von Hallberg has deliberately constructed a culture with a center—and the Culture of the center. He does this in the chapters "Audience, Canon," "Tourists," " Politics," and "Pop Culture." These chapters, in their way a sociology of literature, alternate with readings, respectively, of Robert Creeley and John Ashbery, James Merrill, Robert Lowell, and Edward Dorn. This procedure is attractive, but much in the sociohistorical chapters is flashy rather than sound—the evidence is thin, more often declared than proved—and the perspectives provided by these chapters are sometimes limited and fail to do justice to some focal writers.

Take, for example, von Hallberg's insistence on consensus. Consensus strengthens the centrist position, but consensus in the 1950s was supposition, the claim of Daniel Bell in *The End of Ideology* (1960) at the very beginning of the decade that made it clear that whatever center had been assumed was far from vital and could not hold. Von Hallberg says that "in the 1950s American intellectuals had every reason to feel a part of the national culture" because "they had attached themselves to the upper-middle class that then seemed to be setting standards for the rest of the culture." This addresses a notable fact of many *established* intellectuals at this time: their *embourgeoisement*. And this helps to explain the closer relations of New York Intellectuals and Tory Formalists (see Grant Webster, *The Republic of Letters*) and their common cause against the writers of the Beat generation. Even so, the intellectuals did not put aside ideological concerns—how could they in the decade of Senator McCarthy and the defeat of Stevenson by Eisenhower, a decade that von Hallberg admits "was no time for poets to repatriate"? And neither did the emerging writers whose radical literary experimentation in the 1950s challenged the literary establishment and, as Quentin Anderson complained in *The Imperial Self*, threatened established culture (Culture) itself.

Von Hallberg says nothing of the open forms initiated by these writers but approvingly notes that many of the writers he discusses have written in conventional forms. He omits the very thing literary history should remark: this "poetry of changes" (the phrase is Jerome Rothenberg's) and a poetic task involving the "will to change" (the phrase is Olson's) that made the work of poetry both cultural and political in significance. The task of poetry in these and subsequent years had been, and continues to be, to open the openable and encourage the "symposium of the whole" (the phrase is Duncan's)—not to encourage consensus but all the voices excluded by it. This inclusivity characterizes the poetry of the last forty years: this *panharmonicon,* which Emerson said abrogated "stiff conventions" and, admitting everything, abandoned the "tame," the "ineffectual," and the "decorous." It is simply not true that "beginning in 1960 the poetic avant-garde has been drawn into the mainstream of American literary life." Nor is it true that "civic virtues are not the responsibility of the avant-garde," for what is striking is the extent to which this avant-garde demonstrates, if not "civic virtues," a more primary civic concern for the "great household" (Duncan's phrase) and for the *polis* (Olson's as well as Hannah Arendt's term)—in sum, a concern for what Olson spoke of as "the initiation of another kind of nation."

Von Hallberg's notion of systems, as this derives from cybernetics, is also questionable, and Creeley and Ashbery, his representatives, are, to my mind, poor examples. They are not well served by his use of them, and the reader who finds them diminished here (Creeley's relation to Olson is not brought forward, nor Ashbery's to O'Hara, whose verse von Hallberg doesn't approve) might benefit from their pairing in Stephen Fredman's *Poet's Prose* and the pairing of Creeley with Merwin in Charles Altieri's *Enlarging the Temple.* To reduce systems to manners ("systematic behavior") is to have overlooked the importance of feedback and the reason that poets like Olson and Snyder are most conspicuously cultural when they insist on *loops* and *lore,* feed back into our system much needed information. It is also to have forgotten that the open processual procedure of finding ideas in experience and feeding them back into subsequent experience—William James called this *ambulation*—is closer to the spirit of cybernetics than the examples of Creeley and Ashbery presented here. But then, to use *system* and *systematic* in von Hallberg's sense, he himself is a systematic critic who has a system and, accordingly, doesn't recognize that the poets he categorizes as having systems (Olson, Duncan, Ginsberg) have repudiated systems, have shunned the *a priori* for the difficult work of hewing to experience. The learning of these poets shouldn't be confused with system.

And learning, which Ginsberg says belongs more to the avant-garde than the academic poets, should be emphasized because it bears on the discussion of travel in the chapter "Tourists." Von Hallberg begins this chapter by noting that Olson went to Yucatan when many of his contemporaries went to Europe. (He might also have noted that Snyder went to Japan.) But this clue is not followed up. Olson wasn't "about half-typical," as he says, and his example of digging in a place (recorded in *Mayan Letters,* the most remarkable travel book of this period) might have served as a foil for the *tourists* whose lineage goes back to Irving and whose postwar adventures in Europe, in kind if not in extent, recall the earlier cultural imperialism of the British and the Germans. The homelessness of poets abroad might have led, by way of the homelessness at home that John Bentley Mays and Ralph Ellison consider our gravest cultural problem, to the poetry in these years of finding-and-making-place, of inhabiting, a repossession of America, as in bioregionalism, of political importance. Readers of this chapter would be advised to read the fifth poem of Pound's *Mauberley,* Olson's "To Gerhardt, There, Among Europe's Things . . . ," and Pynchon's *Gravity's Rainbow;* recall, too, what Olson said about staying inside the "Western Box." But maybe their own good sense in reading of Merrill, the tourist par excellence whom von Hallberg commends for "pure style without content" and for the aristocracy of taste this playfulness assumes, is enough. They will wonder, where von Hallberg hasn't, at a literary situation in which a coterie poet wins all the prizes (is this how the center holds?) and more than wonder at the claim that Merrill is "perhaps the best [love poet] of this era."

Politics should be a central matter in a book of this kind. But von Hallberg's pertinent observation—"political poetry is now thought of too narrowly as protest poetry"—restricts rather than widens his attention. More might have been done to evoke the period when poets protested (Mersmann's *Out of the Vietnam Vortex* treats only a sector of the field) and, more important, other kinds of political concern than "political watching" might have been noted. To characterize political poetry as "voguish" is dismissive and weakens one of the strongest claims a writer has on culture. Von Hallberg's example of political watching is Robert Lowell's *History,* which for the first time provides him a subject he can treat with focus and point. Dorn's work, chiefly *Slinger,* is equally attractive to him and is treated in terms of popular culture (justly: Dorn is "perhaps the most astute observer of popular culture"). Yet Dorn, always a poet of the margins and as far from the center as any poet in America, might have figured also as a political poet not only on the testimony of such books as *The Shoshoneans, Recollections of Gran Apachería,* and *Our Word: Guerrilla Poems from Latin America,* but because his watching is watchful, that of a *vagrant,* to use Raymond Williams' term for someone whose complete lack of social commitment is resistant as well as contemptuous of mainstream culture. Von Hallberg's treatment of Dorn, like that of the other poets, is partial (in two senses), and even his good account of Dorn's recent career is marred by his subscription to wit. The poet so accurately described in the following is not exemplary: "His trick is to write in a manner that makes his readers feel like insiders at the same time as their sacred cows are rendered a little swinish."

The *Culture* of the title of this book is Arnoldian, and Arnold—not the Arnold of "Wragg is in custody"—is von Hallberg's tutelary critic. His critical concerns are Arnold's, derived perhaps from the New Humanists and the New Critics. When he writes of class distinctions and taste that "Merrill and Lowell would agree that canons of taste measure humaneness more accurately than egalitarianism," I think of Paul Elmer More, who said that the dollar is more than the man. Von Hallberg's book, it seems to me, denies criticism by the closure of its point of view. It is nothing so much as genteel, and what it asks of those who endorse it is equivalent to having been asked to read Longfellow and James Russell Lowell when Whitman was there to be read. This book serves the considerable academic poetry of our time. Eliot Weinberger, I find, is closer to the truth of recent poetry when he says, in *Sulfur 13*, that "the road to a new poetry will start out from ethnopoetics, which seems to be the most fruitful and interesting configuration in American poetry in the last 20 years."

Nature and Poetry

The argument and scope of *Imagining the Earth* are so well set out by John Elder in the "Introduction" that these few pages, printed in full, might be its review. They would explain the excitement with which I took up the book, the concern awakened by his threefold study of the relation between attentiveness to nature (*wilderness*) and alienation from tradition (*culture*), the interdependence of inner and outer landscapes (the role of *imagination*), and the assimilation of science in poetic vision. Without hesitation I wished to follow his account of the "imaginative passage from estrangement to transformation and reintegration" by means of which poets "enact a circuit of healing," and all the more so because his own *Excursions* (after Thoreau?)—nature essays that divide the sections and conclude the book—promised the authentication of personal experience.

In these essays Elder tries to represent himself as present within a natural landscape. Yet he never gets out of himself, out of the "mind's terrain," in the way he appreciates in the work of Gary Snyder; never forsakes the literary appropriation of nature that characterizes so much nature writing. Like confessional poetry, much of this writing is sentimental—as, for example, Annie Dillard's, which he approves—sentimental because of what Charles Olson called "the lyrical interference of the individual as ego." I mention Olson, who followed Keats in questioning the Wordsworthian "Egotistical Sublime," the better to place Elder, for whom Wordsworth is the presiding poet, his work almost always the touchstone of the others he treats—Jeffers, Eliot, Snyder, Berry, Ammons, Basho, Levertov, Everson, Dillard, Peter Matthiessen, and Robert Pack. Elder is conversant with natural science and ecology, Whitehead's philosophy of organism and Zen Buddhism. His book addresses the largest issues of Western culture, but from a point-in-time, the nineteenth century, when *world alienation* and *worlding* (to use Richard Pevear's terms) could still be talked about as a matter of *reconciliation,* as if in respect to the duality of mind and nature, mind itself was the reconciler and could do the needful work, a correspondential work of symbol-making that assimilated nature to mind, aggrandizing mind, and poetry, too.

Elder himself is not so much an adept at nature writing as a student of literature who has found in nature writing a model for literary excursions. (*Walking* is one of his primary metaphors, lacking, however, the resonance of Williams' injunction to "WALK in the world.") The scheme set out in the "Introduction" does not indicate the considerable walking he does within its boundaries and the metaphors, taken from nature and poetry (*decay, fertility, circuit,* and so forth), that exfoliate within his mind and do the work of argument. Given his associative way of thinking, he can make connections denied to closer thought. For example, because of their "cultural despair," he connects Jeffers and Eliot, when, in any meaningful sense, Eliot is the least of nature poets, turning elsewhere for amelioration; or, to cite another connection made in terms of "tradition," that between Eliot and Snyder, when the European tradition affirmed as an order by Eliot is incommensurable with the inclusivity and diversity of culture Snyder figures in an ecologically mature climax-culture. As for the poets whose work provides the focal points of Elder's excursion, he no more participates in their work than he does in the natural landscape. He studies none largely, yielding himself to their imaginations, and his close reading of a few poems adds little to previous interpretive and prosodic criticism.

The walker of this book is belated. His walking, to use William James' terms, involves *saltation* rather than *ambulation.* He leaps above experience on the strength of Ideas; he does not find ideas in experience and feed them back as he goes on his way. He is still a philosophical idealist for whom the mind is sovereign, and in spite of his respect for Whitehead's philosophy and Snyder's selfless art, has not discovered the metaphysical basis of poetry in our time. (Whitehead: "For Kant, the world emerges from the subject; for the philosophy of organism, the subject emerges from the world.") Among other things, he overlooks Fenollosa, Pound on the Image, the Objectivism of Zukofksy and Oppen, and Olson's projective verse, all of them either corroborating or indebted to Whitehead. He doesn't consider *reinhabiting* in the sense given the term by Peter Berg, nor realize that nature-related cultures are necessarily small, "primitive" and tribal, that their art, fostered now by ethnopoetics, is performative and sacred, and that bioregionalism, working to this *deep* ecological end, proposes a similarly close life—eco-centrism not egocentrism. Nor does he see that the work of building and cultivating that Snyder does at Kitkitdizze (was he ever a hunter and gatherer?) is poetic in itself and need not be fulfilled in the landscape of a poem. Elder is still a humanist. In his account, poetry will do nicely for nature, for we can get "nature" in the spaces of the poem, be reconciled there. He is content with imagining the earth, with a mediated way of being, itself of primary value, which gives us a vision of nature. But what of the need to resist the passivity this view fosters? And what of the happiness reported by Oppen when the mind rises into "what is there," when it discovers *this in which?* What of the counsel of Shunryu Suzuki (whom Elder has read)—"When you are there, everything else is there"—this corroborated by Maritain when he says, "We awake in the same moment to ourselves and to things"?

PART II

Emerson

Emerson's Poetic Legacy

"In spite of much literature on the subject," Stephen Whicher noted in 1957, "an adequate account of Emerson's theory and practice of poetry remains to be published." The concluding phrase undoubtedly exempts the pioneer studies of Carl Strauch, a lifework already well known at the time. But Whicher states the case, as does Hyatt Waggoner's review of Emerson's achievement as a poet (*Emerson as Poet,* 1974), that makes the publication of *Emerson and the Orphic Poet in America,* by R. A. Yoder, and *Emerson and Literary Change,* by David Porter, so significant. Probably because even in a work as recent as Waggoner's Emerson's achievement as a poet is considered modest—consensus of a century of criticism, the poetry not to be compared with the high achievement of the prose—the poetry has not been engaged for what it so obviously is in view of Emerson's belief in the primacy of the Imagination: the focal, deepest ground of his life. Poetry always is for a poet, and Emerson, as he claimed, was a poet whose work *as a poet,* both Yoder and Porter demonstrate, is as central to American poetry as his work as a thinker (culture hero) has always been believed to be in respect to American thought. Yoder and Porter depict different Emersons—at best, complementary Emersons—but they agree on his centrality as a poet and on the continuing centrality of just those issues (for a poetics inevitably expresses religious, philosophical, epistemological, and ethical concerns) that Emerson probed in his poetry. It would be enough to say in praise of Yoder and Porter that by revivifying Emerson's poetry in their readings of the drama of its deep allegories of Imagination they compel us to reread it. (And on this reading I find in it more excellences than they allow.) But as an Emersonian and as one of the "anonymous scholars" Yoder mentions, I also wish to say that these books are noteworthy because they acknowledge their foundations in earlier work and renew in terms of perspectives scholarship and criticism have since brought forward the inquiries that in our time have established Emerson as "central man." Not since Bishop's *Emerson on the Soul* have we had work of such importance.

What matters here is not an upward reassessment of the poetry but an appreciation of Emerson's profound commitment to poetry (Imagination) and its central place as the generative source of his work. Emerson himself spoke the critical consensus (and as Porter shows, the very thing that pressed him to liberate the Imagination in prose) when he said, "I am born a poet, of a low class without doubt yet a poet." He knew—and we know—that his "singing" was "'husky.'" Even so he insisted that it was his "nature & vocation" to be a poet, and in the high sense of "perceiver & dear lover of the harmonies that are in the soul & in matter, & specially of the correspondences between these & those." Here *perceiver* speaks for the Imagination, and *correspondences* for the metaphysical faith that early in Emerson's career assured him of "harmonies"—the spiritual vision, the transcendence represented by the binary structure and conversion plot of his poems, the vision soon enough challenged by his experience. Both Yoder and Porter begin here, with the recognition, as Yoder says, that the initial design of Emerson's poems is "founded in the order of correspondence" and that this design "implies the easy victory of imaginative insight over ordinary, mundane powers." And beginning here, both follow the development charted by Whicher—the descent from imaginative heights and assurance to the midworld of skepticism and endless accommodation—to arrive, however, at different conclusions and different Emersonian traditions in poetry.

Yoder tells this story of transcendence and descendence in terms of the Orphic poet-figure so conspicuous in Emerson's work, and though the second part of his book is devoted to the poems he tells the story chiefly in terms of ideas, as an intellectual historian. He does not approach the poems as closely as Porter. Their literal activity does not concern him as much as the influences on them (for example, George Herbert on the early poems) and the legacy they bequeathed to American poets. Telling the story twice, first in an account of the development of Emerson's Orphic mind, he recalls for us a great tradition and the more immediate context of European romanticism that nurtured Emerson's Orphic aspiration and subsequently sustained his Orphic compromise.

Emerson's Orphic career is the story of the Poet-hero (the American Scholar, as Porter shows, for the fable is everywhere in Emerson's work) who believes in the "conversion of the world." He believes, as Emerson says in "The American Scholar," that "as the world was plastic and fluid in the hands of God, so is it ever," and the poet, the godlike man, may give it "his signet and form." He is Orphic by virtue of being possessed by this "heroic passion," the passion to conform things to his thought, to invest "dust and stones with humanity, and [make] them words of Reason." And he is Orphic, too, by virtue of his belief in the sovereign power of the Imagination. In the conclusion to the paragraph in *Nature* (1836) from which the previous quotations are taken, Emerson says, "The Imagination may be defined to be the use which the Reason makes of the material world."

Now the Emerson who believed this is clearly a Promethean figure serving revolutionary ends. He is the exalted early Emerson who, under stress experience (a word underlined by the essay of that name), yielded revolution for revelation (song), external for internal apocalypse, spiritual summits for the mundane midworld. The later Emerson, who accepts the "titmouse dimension," is the faithful skeptic who conforms to nature and seeks the answers to her riddles. He has yielded the vertical ascent, and his humbler task is to reconcile or balance the polarities of the horizontal, the actual prudential world. Orpheus-Prometheus, Osman, Saadi, the Plato of *Representative Men,* Merlin—the sequence of these figures in Emerson's work tells of the descent of Orpheus, of Emerson's defeat by nature.

This defeat, according to Yoder, is the Emersonian legacy, and in a compensatory way he sees it as a victory, hence as a *valuable* legacy. He explains:

> Because America has always had great expectations of a sublime and philosophical literature, its poets have accepted the tradition that Orpheus, the first poet, was the Whole or Universal Man, and they have tried to live up to Emerson's magnificent fable of the Orphic poet that promises freedom, revolution, and transcendence. But fable meets fact, and in the meeting progeny discover the severer limitations of their kind. The key to Emerson's prolific fatherhood is that, having made impossible demands on poets, he does not abandon them when they cannot do what he asks; his own example offers the ideal of a lesser Orpheus, who understands "the precise fact of our condition. . . ."

And so Yoder gives us an Emersonian tradition of poetry of the dark, at the edge; a poetry of qualified idealism and limitation whose chief practitioners are Dickinson, Stephen Crane, Robinson, Frost, Stevens, and Ammons. He puts in eclipse the brighter Orphic Emersonian tradition of Whitman, Pound, Williams, Stevens (in others' reckoning), Hart Crane, and (I would add with qualifications in regard to idealism) Olson and Duncan.

And Porter? In giving us the fullest account we have had of Emerson's poetics and the struggle for "aesthetic liberation" it involved, he traverses a similar course from transcendence to descendence only to find in Emerson's *descendentalism* values wholly overlooked by Yoder. Where Yoder's work may be said to support the literary establishment, Porter's may be said to subvert it. And this is in keeping with his fresh view of Emerson as preeminently an *artist* concerned with formal matters. As artist, Emerson subverted the literary establishment of his time out of vital imaginative necessity. He had to shatter the formal constraints of his own poems—those converting mechanisms, with their upward, transcending, abstracting plots—and discover for himself the imaginative possibilities of the spaciousness of prose.

No one has told so exactly the faults of Emerson's poetry and showed why we so much appreciate his prose, the *poetry* of the prose, to cite a chapter title in Waggoner's book, where Waggoner acknowledges that Emerson's prose is "more imaginative" than his verse. Yes, *more imaginative*. For even when the poems enact the correspondential vision and do the necessary Emersonian work of turning "adversity to advantage," they warp away from life, life leaks out. I borrow Porter's phrases and his measure of poetry—the very measure that finally moved Emerson to liberate his imagination (lowercase: no longer in the service of Reason), to turn it back/down from its translation of life into ideas, to life. (In this context, consider Williams' insistence on *descent* and *no ideas but in things*, and the Pound-Olson insistence on image over symbol.) Liberation is in this descent, and if descent is the defeat of one kind of aspiration it is also the victory of another. The extremity that proposed this redirection is evident in the polarity of ascent-descent and in the view that poetry is higher than prose, the one a vehicle of higher Truth, the other the vehicle of mundane truths. Emerson himself believed this "genteel" view—that poetry is limited to "poetic" subjects—and so in moving from it he rehearsed the continuing struggle between the genteel-spiritual and liberated-experiential traditions that for Porter represent the *discontinuity* of American poetry.

Experience is the crux. Nothing shows better Emerson's vocation as poet than his determination to liberate the Imagination in its behalf, to fasten it, as he said of words, to visible things, to give over the vertical (the correspondence of lower to higher) for the horizontal (the correspondence of language and thing, function and form), to forego remembering and mental deliverance for an active exploration of experience, to find imaginative means—among them, speech, the open form of the essay—equal to both the present activity of thought and the richness of the actual world. Where once Emerson dreamed the dream of consciousness that informs his early poetry—he would eat the apple of the world, swallow it—now he would marry it, possess its energy and life by coupling with it.

Porter speaks of this achievement as "a breakthrough into spaciousness," and so his alignment of Emerson and Charles Olson is not unexpected. Some may find it—and the reassessment of Emerson that makes it possible—shocking, but it is just: "Olson and Emerson a century apart called for a new reconciliation of the world and the language in which it is to be experienced." And with Olson as a touchstone, we know that Porter's version of the Emersonian legacy will diverge from Yoder's. It does, but with qualification. For open form, he believes, led to a disturbing "atomization":

> The great irony is that, in opening up poetic space, [Emerson] intended to demonstrate "the cheerful hint" in all things "of the immortality of our essence." . . . With the disappearance of that faith, what remained was an open form crowded with intractable experience, manifesting more clearly than ever the multitudiness of experience and the failure of the idealistic philosophy. The form was capable of a great gathering of life without any certain way to understand it.

The failure of the idealistic philosophy is indeed the issue. But Porter is himself not yet liberated from its assumptions. That he finds in the open form of Emerson's work "the first glimpses of the wasteland" and feels compelled to *understand* (to put experience in a certain framework, as in *Understanding Poetry*) indicates this. He is right to choose Olson as a gauge of the poetic enterprise, but he has yet to fully appreciate the open universe poets like Olson inhabit and the extent to which this has liberated the imagination and permitted what Williams called "unbound thinking." If Porter's interpretation is sound, and I think it is, then Emerson would have approved Hart Crane's concern with only the absolute nature of experience and preferred to *understanding* Williams' concern with *thinking with the poem* and in the writing living in the moment that he truly lives. Had Porter carried his study, as Kenneth Burke would say, to the end of the line, he would have had to consider texts like Whitehead's *Process and Reality* which underwrite postmodern open poetics and provide a post-wasteland generation of poets with another definition and assurance of *meaning*. Which is to say, as Hart Crane said, that we need not succumb to the "wasteland" nor give privileged status to a poetry of despair, of the dark, of the edge.

It does not detract from the merit of these studies to note their incompleteness. How is it neither Yoder nor Porter treats Fenollosa, who brought so much of Emerson's poetics over into significant use in the modern era? Again, how is it Robert Duncan is omitted, this poet of liberated imagination whose Orphic determination is as conspicuous as Emerson's and whose work, founded on other assumptions, has not become that of a "lesser Orpheus"? And how is it a scholar so thorough as Yoder has not considered a book so much to his purpose and to the Orphic revitalization of language, Gerald Bruns' *Modern Poetry and the Idea of Language*?

But who isn't incomplete? It is only fair to add that these excellent studies may provoke the poets of the open tradition to recognize Emerson as the father of the "libertarian aesthetics," and every bit as important to them as Whitman. Perhaps the next edition of *The Poetics of the New American Poetry* will include Emerson.

PART III

William Carlos Williams

A Sketchbook of the Artist in His Thirty-Fourth Year: William Carlos Williams' Kora in Hell: Improvisations

Perhaps he is modern. He addresses himself to the imagination.
Marianne Moore on Williams (1927)

This book . . . is probably the most important in the development of Williams' poetry. In order to compose the Improvisations *he has asked himself all the artistic questions of the day, and in writing them he has most intimately come into contact with his gifts.*
René Taupin on Williams (1929)[1]

I

Sometimes the explanations that William Carlos Williams gives of his own work explain very little. In his *Autobiography,* where he misplaces *Kora in Hell* (1920) in the sequence of his development, he tells us that the title represents the rout by the war of springtime, his own creative beginning and the resurgence of American letters with which he identified it. He does not mention the war—the First World War—in the fuller account of the book in *I Wanted to Write a Poem,* the autobiographical bibliography of his work; and the war, except perhaps as a pressure of the time leaving an indefinable imprint on the book, is not a part of it. He may have remembered (rewriting his own past, as so many writers do, from the evidence of others) that Gorham Munson had said of the book, in *Destinations,* that "Williams, suffering from the ghastly business of war, could yet try to reconstruct a springtime." Even then he may have remembered only the first and not the second phrase, which is closer to the spirit of the book as he delightedly recovers its intention in *I Wanted to Write a Poem.* Here he provides other and better clues. "I was feeling fresh," he remarks in reference to the cover design, an ovum, surrounded by spermatozoa, in the act of accepting one and being impregnated—a "beginning of life" that he thought a "beautiful thing" and wanted the world to see. And he himself was "Springtime," the Kora of the title his friend Ezra Pound had prompted: "I felt I was on my way to Hell (but I didn't go very far). This was what the Improvisations were trying to say."[2]

In this account of the book he also replaces the war of these war-years with a literary war closer to him. (The "Prologue" to *Kora in Hell,* published first in two installments in the *Little Review,* to which Pound had introduced the work of Joyce, Yeats, Eliot, Ford, and others, was one of Williams' heavy salvos.) For in these years, seven years before *The Waste Land* arrived to alter the literary landscape with what Williams always referred to as its atomic force, Eliot published "Prufrock." Williams confuses this poem with the title of Eliot's first book, *Prufrock and Other Observations,* which appeared in 1917, the year in which his own third book of poems, *Al Que Quiere!,* was published. He remembers this accurately enough: "When I was halfway through the Prologue, 'Prufrock' appeared." And the violence of his response, the sense of the betrayal of his hope for the enterprise of modern art, was just as accurately remembered.[3]

The reason for this deep and enduring memory is not a petty one of recognition but a traumatic one of confirmation. *Prufrock and Other Observations* was noticed almost immediately in *Poetry* by Ezra Pound in a long unstinting review; this book was a major event, "the best thing in poetry since . . . ," Pound said, and he meant it. But *Al Que Quiere!,* an equally impressive work of force and originality showing clearly that Williams had found his way, was not so enthusiastically praised when it was reviewed by Dorothy Dudley in the same magazine in the following year. Williams was said to have the conscience but not yet the ease of a great artist (and in some poems this was true), and his task was perceptively identified with (and prefigured in) "Chicory and Daisies," a poem upon which he pointedly commented later in the "Prologue." Williams' arrival was not proclaimed, where Eliot's was, and this, not the publication and reception of *The Waste Land,* which only reminded him that his place in the galaxy of poets was still uncertain, stirred his deep, not wholly aesthetic, antipathy to Eliot.[4]

It is interesting to note that Williams did not take issue with "Prufrock" when the poem first appeared in *Poetry* in June, 1915. Five poems of his own, under the covering title of "Root Buds," had been published there the previous month, among them "Sub Terra," the call for a new poetry with which he introduced *Al Que Quiere!*. He was aware of his humble emergence, but also confident, and even aggressive—the title of this book of poems means "To Him Who Wants It." But now, in 1917, Eliot's advent and Pound's annunciation of it (Williams assured Marianne Moore in 1918 of Pound's "unswerving intelligence in the detection of literary quality") shook his confidence and established the pattern of declaration and demonstration that ever afterward showed him to be hurt irreparably. Eliot did not destroy the root buds—did not touch the vital source of Williams' creativity. But because of Eliot he would, it seems, like the chicory, have over and over to lift his flowers "on bitter stems" out of the scorched ground.[5]

II

The composition of *Kora in Hell* immediately followed the publication of *Al Que Quiere!* and carried forward its themes and exuberant creativity. ("The Wanderer," placed at the end of the volume, was a summons to further creation.) The title suggests a downward turning of spirit, a descent, a phase of the rhythm of ascent-descent that marks the inner movement of Williams' work; and since every complete act of creation passes through these phases, the title suggests a descent of greater importance and profundity—descent as a conscious intention of the poet. Usually one turns in this direction in search of self-recovery and transcendence, because of defeat or creative impasse; it is the way of abandonment, of falling back on the deepest, the unconscious resources of the self, and on chaos, and hopefully a fertile one. It is the way of growth that Emerson enthusiastically endorsed in "Circles": "The way of life is wonderful; it is by abandonment." When Williams speaks of the "he and she of it"—what Emerson called intellect constructive and intellect receptive—"she" represents the phase of descent, the guardian spirit of formlessness and darkness, of creative night. Or passing beyond metaphor, "she" is the very "mother stuff," the ovum of the cover design; and here, as Williams wrote of it later in *A Voyage to Pagany*, he always retreated when he was beaten, to lie and breed with himself. Clearly the Kora he pursues in Hell is his own creative self, his feminine secret nature, the Beautiful Thing that the constructive or inventive work of art, by turning "the mind inside out," restores to the world. Nothing less than this generative passion, this dream of love and desire to release the self, moves him, an author who, Pound recognized, was primarily "concerned with his own insides." Where "The Wanderer," a ritual narrative of the realization of poetic vocation, celebrates the discovery of the female principle of his art, *Kora in Hell* celebrates his willing pursuit and the mating with himself that may account for his sense of the book's uniqueness and his remark that "it reveals myself to me."[6]

This is but one aspect of Williams' awareness of the profound processes of the imagination, an awareness justifying René Taupin's opinion that "Williams knows more about the work of the poetic imagination than any American poet today." In terms of the situation in poetry at the time, especially the conformity Williams derided, one of the most needed lessons provided by *Kora in Hell* is that nurture may be found in the ground of the self as well as in tradition. The poet shows how one might follow the directives of "Sub Terra" and "Ballet." His program, as Vivienne Koch says, translates the Emersonian ethic of self-reliance to the aesthetic sphere, though the actual descent into the self, the nurturing of self-reliance, owes little, I think, to Emerson and much to Whitman—and most, in this immediate instance, to Kandinsky. But *Kora in Hell* is not concerned solely with the "she" of it, though the title and subtitle suggest that it is. It also follows the compositional advice given in "To a Solitary Disciple" and brilliantly exemplifies the "he" of it, the constructive or formal means by which the self is again revealed and conformity again denied. For after the abandon of writing, Williams says, "one goes forward carefully." What descent discovers is made good in art, first by the intelligent acceptance of "the new and the extraordinary," and then by the invention of an appropriate form. *Kora in Hell* exhibits this double work. Its improvisations are not improvised.[7]

This may explain what Williams meant when he said that he was on his way to Hell but didn't go very far. Williams may have begun the book in a postpartum mood, as a loosening-up exercise following the difficult ascent of his recently completed book of poems. His prose experiments, especially *The Great American Novel,* the early prose portions of *Spring and All,* "Notes in Diary Form," and *A Novelette,* seem to have a function similar to that of *Kora in Hell,* which, Vivienne Koch says, was "preparation for a new poetic modus in his work." In *Spring and All* (1923), where he admits the faults of judgment in the "Prologue," he gives another account of *Kora in Hell* that merits quotation here:

> The Improvisations—coming at a time when I was trying to remain firm at great cost—I had recourse to the expedient of letting life go completely in order to live in the world of my choice.[8]
>
> I let the imagination have its own way to see if it could save itself. Something very definite came of it. I found myself alleviated but most important I began there and then to revalue experience, to understand what I was at—
>
> The virtue of the improvisations is their placement in a world of new values—[9]

Williams let the imagination go in a conscious attempt to test the organic theory of art set forth by Wassily Kandinsky in *Concerning the Spiritual in Art,* especially the notion of inner necessity that he later held up to "Ezra and Eliot" in the "Prologue." He let the imagination have its own way by writing down daily whatever came to mind, an automatic procedure that Kandinsky had suggested in his definition of an improvisation: "A largely unconscious, spontaneous expression of inner character. . . . This I call an 'Improvisation.'" There was nothing especially unusual in this procedure of expressionism except Williams' adoption of it—his willingness to experiment, not in a time of ebb or defeat, and in full awareness of the risk.[10]

What risk? The risk, as he puts it in the *Autobiography,* of "the longest leap, the most unmitigated daring, the longest chances"—the risk of discovering his "perfection," his inner necessity. In "The Basis of Faith in Art," he recalls that the first thing he learned as a writer was "that it isn't so easy to let yourself go." If conformity ("stereotype") hedged him on one side, chaos threatened him on the other: "If I ducked out of that I ran into chaos." Yet chaos was the only way, necessary, whatever the risk, to the creative sally; only that fluid condition, the occasion of so much terror in his work, released the mind. And so—to borrow words he would use in respect to Whitman—he set out "to discover . . . by headlong composition . . . what we can do."[11]

Marianne Moore remembered his recklessness and admired him for it he had once written to her of his need to free himself by "violent methods." But Else von Freytag-Loringhoven, in a review of *Kora in Hell* that is a literary curiosity of the time, thought otherwise of Williams, whose favorite theme, acknowledged in a description of the hero of the autobiographical fiction, *A Voyage to Pagany,* was "the abandon of life and the—check," and whose choice of vocation and way of life, for all the benefit it conferred on his writing, was not, admittedly, a risky one. Still, as an act of the imagination, as a conscious pursuit of his imagination, his self—the pursuit of the imagination by the imagination, his great lifelong endeavor and theme—*Kora in Hell* represents a considerable risk. In it, Williams descended as far as he had ever gone into chaos, a fact corroborated, I think, by the compensatory nature, the check, of the composition. This book is the largest, most carefully realized formal achievement of these early years, the work in which he both hazarded most and discovered the saving virtue—and liberation—of form. The imagination, he found, was not only the substance and energy of the self (one of its erotic forces) but a plane of the self's existence upon which (or where) the self freely disposed itself. Kandinsky had defined for him both the imperative to improvisation and the conscious compositional aspect of imagination that he followed. The virtue of the improvisations was their placement in this world of new values, the world of his choice, the world of art in which the artist, Kandinsky said, was free.[12]

III

This aspect of the book has been obscured by the tendency to see in *Kora in Hell* a derivative example of literary modernism. Williams, it is true, knew French well and, like most of the poets who shared with him the experimental work of *Others,* knew the current movements of the avant-garde. He was familiar with the writing of the Symbolists and with Dada, which Marcel Duchamp, one of his many artist friends in New York, had introduced there in 1916. The literary magazines to which he contributed, especially *Poetry* and the *Little Review,* having Ezra Pound for their foreign editor, were the most effective schools of writing and literature of the time; and chiefly because of Pound's insistent teaching, René Taupin could say without exaggeration in *L'Influence du Symbolisme Français* (1929) that "poetry in America today speaks French." In this important early study of the American poets of his generation, Williams was recognized as a poet to be considered seriously along with Eliot and Pound. But the price of this recognition was Taupin's opinion, arrived at by comparing the Rimbaud of the *Illuminations* with the Williams of the *Improvisations* (a comparison endlessly perpetuated), that Williams was in the mainstream of French influence.[13]

In response to Pound's letter about his book, Williams himself had publicized the comparison in *The Great American Novel* (1923), a work published in France and of some consequence there. Employing Pound's comment, he writes in Chapter Three, "Take the improvisations: What the French reader would say is: *oui, ça; j'ai déjà vu ça; ça c'est de Rimbaud.* Finis." But in the context of this exploratory work, the passage denies Pound's assertion, an assertion denied again in *A Novelette,* another exploratory work: "Kindly note that all I have ever done has been the one thing. Pound will say that the improvisations are—etc. etc. twenty, forty years late. On the contrary he's all wet. Their excellence is, in major part, the shifting of category. It is the disjointing process." [14]

Pound was not entirely wet, as the persistent denial perhaps indicates, but too much concerned with literary influence, which was not, as Williams tried to point out, the significant influence in this work. It may be true, as Taupin says, that Williams is very much like Rimbaud in gifts, intelligence, and spirit; that, like Rimbaud, he has a talent for irony, an eye for minute detail, a predilection for the commonplace and vulgar, even a profound concern for the dance of the imagination. But likeness is not necessarily influence, and in the most important element of Taupin's comparison he is not like Rimbaud at all—in uniting the power to contact things with the freest and most visionary imagination.[15]

Williams is not a visionary poet. He is not a seer but the buzzard he mentions in *Kora in Hell* whose eyes are of "a power equal to that of the eagle's" and whose vision is not given to transcendental flight but to earthy things. Williams is aware that the mind itself is sufficiently visionary (his mother was a medium at spiritualistic séances) and, in the passage Taupin cites as evidence of his visionary concern, wishes to be rid of the "*floating visions of unknown purport*" that obstruct his sight:

> In the mind there is a continual play of obscure images which coming between the eyes and their prey seem pictures on the screen at the movies. Somewhere there appears to be a mal-adjustment. The wish would be to see not floating visions of unknown purport but the imaginative qualities of the actual things being perceived accompany their gross vision in a slow dance, interpreting as they go.

Like the modern artists he admires most, Williams is a realist, rigorous and intellectual—scientific, like the doctors he praises in *A Voyage to*

Pagany—in his search for truth. He wishes to sharpen but not to derange the senses, for he wants the actual things that the senses give him. "I want all my reactions," he declared at this time in an autobiographical study which depicts a pure young man (Thoreauvian, but hardly Rimbaldian) whose only passion is the desire to write. "I want to write," he says. "It does not drug my senses, it sharpens them. It is the holy ghost of that trinity: The Senses, Action, Composition." Williams is a poet of the actual, whose large freedom belongs to the inventive powers of the imagination, the power to dispose things on its own plane and thereby make an art-object, a new, real thing. Here, in turning from the artist as seer (the visionary imagination) to the artist as maker (the constructive imagination), is the shifting of category of which he speaks in *A Novelette.*[16]

The comparisons of *Kora in Hell* and the *Illuminations,* like Pound's attribution of "opacity" to Williams' work, a quality Taupin believed to be "essentially a virtue of modern French poetry," are either superficial or misleading. They belong to a criticism that praises by association, and makes association almost everything; this is even true of Kenneth Rexroth's instructive essay, "The Influence of French Poetry on American." Nearly everyone who has written about *Kora in Hell*—Williams, too, in the preface of the recent City Lights reprint, where he admits familiarity but denies influence—refers to the precedents, usually French, of prose poetry. Karl Shapiro, for example, lists *Aucassin and Nicolette,* Baudelaire's *Small Poems in Prose,* the *Illuminations*—and "the abortive prose experiments of Eliot." He might have added, with, I think, as little usefulness, Stuart Merrill's translations of French prose poems, *Pastels in Prose,* or the work that Williams might have seen in the literary magazines—that, say, of Jean de Bosschère, John Rodker, Rabindranath Tagore, and Sherwood Anderson. Judging from Williams' writing, none of this work contributed in an essential way to his book. Even the "official precedent," as Shapiro calls *Varie Poesie* (Venice, 1795), the work of Pietro Metastasio that Pound left behind, perhaps for Williams' edification, only suggested how, by drawing a line between prose elements, he might arrange them.[17]

A work, however, from whose experiments he might have benefitted but may not have known at this time, was Gertrude Stein's *Tender Buttons* (1914), which faced "the problem . . . of a thing existing in itself, of an absolute and absolutely present literary work." This cubist work was in the spirit of contemporary French painting, the new art Williams had already seen at the Armory Show and at the gallery of Alfred Stieglitz. As the "Prologue" to *Kora in Hell* with its references to Walter Arensberg and to such painters as Duchamp, Gleizes, Man Ray, and Demuth indicates, this was an influence to which Williams enthusiastically responded.[18]

IV

Although Williams employs the method of automatic writing associated with the surrealists, his work is not surrealist because it exists primarily for the writing itself. What he does in *Kora in Hell* is well characterized in Donald Sutherland's comment on Gertrude Stein's procedure: "Anything inside or outside that 'happens to come' is as it were waylaid by the consciousness of the writer, and just as it is, with the writer's feeling about it and his angle of vision, it forms a composition in itself." The daily effort is made not so much for purposes of psychological investigation as for compositional experiment—imaginative exercise. Williams is not interested, to use Kenneth Burke's words of adverse criticism, in "the usual modern data of mental tests"; much of what he uncovered by automatic writing is familiar to us from *Al Que Quiere!,* and he himself rejected the "pure nonsense." If, in one respect, the result of his year's work is a diary of the unconscious, in another and more important respect, it is a diary of the imagination (what Robert McAlmon called "a portrait of Williams' consciousness"). It might be thought of as a sketchbook of free but carefully composed drawings comprising a composite portrait of the author—a good likeness if we accept as an essential feature of Williams' modernist awareness the criticism by Wallace Stevens of *Al Que Quiere!* that Williams countered in the "Prologue": "To fidget with points of view leads always to new beginnings and incessant new beginnings to sterility."[19]

The work is not prose poetry, not, at least, the usual kind whose effect depends on the heavy rhythms of poetry. Its rhythmic quality is achieved by using direct speech and the cadences and contours of the phrase (in a humorous Steinesque example: "When beldams dig clams their fat hams . . ."). The foundation of rhythm in speech is clearly visualized in the spaces between phrases that guide one's reading, a kind of punctuation and notation that may have been suggested by Pound, whose "In a Station of the Metro" first appeared in *Poetry* with three widely spaced phrasal units to the line, a prefigurement perhaps of Williams' triadic line, and by the poetry of Mina Loy and Robert Alden Sanborn in *Others*. We take this prose for poetry, I think, because it makes us intensely aware of language rather than rhythm (as in Amy Lowell's "polyphonic prose"); it has the nonexpository presentational directness that modern painting and poetry have taught us to prize. This is the "poetry" of the prose that, along with compositional design, establishes its existence as art; this is the "opacity," the solidity of language, that presents to eyes unaccustomed to seeing words for what they are, an impenetrable surface. Once seen, the work, though not always explicable, is intelligible.[20]

The book is composed of blocks of prose, not single words, which Williams said later were too much the object of attention of those influenced by the "disintegrationists," Joyce and Stein. He was more concerned with the synthetic than with the analytic phase of cubism (his prosody, for example, as Shapiro says, involves the "total form"; his touchstone among cubist painters is Juan Gris). In speaking of *Kora in Hell* he recalled that the frontispiece, "an impressionistic view of the simultaneous" by Stuart Davis, "was, graphically, exactly what I was trying to do in words, put the Improvisations down as a unit on the page." In the larger format of the original edition—the largest and most impressive work he had yet published—one more readily appreciates the distinctive constructivist quality of the visible form.[21]

Williams' description of this form as following the "A.B.A. formula" and his example of it in *I Wanted to Write a Poem* do not adequately represent the complexity of the work. Variations on a form by Metastasio more accurately describes it. There are twenty-seven chapters (or sketches), each composed of at least three improvisations and one interpretation, the latter set in italics and divided from the former by a line. More than half of the sketches are original designs, and even those that repeat the number and the relation of parts vary in respect to the size of the parts and their functions. Some are very complex, Chapter Four, for example, which is composed of the following: Part One—an improvisation, an interpretation followed by an improvisation, and another interpretation; Part Two—a two-paragraph improvisation; and Part Three—an improvisation and interpretation (without a dividing line). Sometimes a coda is added, and seldom is the interpretation, which itself exemplifies the fact that the presented improvisation cannot be reduced to a statement, simply interpretative. The numbering of chapters and sections is an essential visual element, formalizing the work and giving it a tidy appearance. It is also, curiously, an intrinsic formal agency, for although sequences can be made out, the serial or absolute order of the numbers is not significant—or only to the extent that, failing to help us keep order, they indicate a new relative order, the order of the imagination.[22]

This seemingly decorous form—compare its quiet visual order to the visual disorder of Williams' later experiments—allows anything to enter the world of imagination. It supports Williams' contention that "a poem can be made of anything" if only the imagination lifts it "out of the ruck." Like the Stuart Davis frontispiece, it presents, in the very act of lifting, in a dance of the imagination, the common everyday objects of the artist's world. The Hell of *Kora in Hell* is simply this ordinary world untouched (unexplored) by the imagination, a ruck similar to the American environment of *The Great American Novel, Life Along the Passaic River,* and *Paterson,* a place from which Kora may be rescued and that world saved (discovered and emotionally enjoyed) by the poet's art. This is a major theme that the book propounds and demonstrates as it discloses the full range of themes developed in Williams' lifetime. Among these, for example, are the important themes of the dream of love, which seems to have possessed him at this time, and of the discovery of America, which he mythicizes here, somewhat after the fashion of "The Wanderer," in terms of American "presences." These themes, as well as their presentation, may be considered in Chapter Sixteen.[23]

In the first improvisation of this chapter, the poet meditates on the writing of a "happy poem" and imagines, as an actual present living experience, a "bare, upstanding fellow" swimming a river and breaking through thickets in chase of "a white flash over against the oak stems!" The interpretation that follows succinctly states the "meaning" and mythicizes it: *The poet transforms himself into a satyr and goes in pursuit of a white skinned dryad. The gaiety of his mood full of lustihood, even so, turns back with a mocking jibe.* The poet has become a sort of Pan and the dryad he pursues but never possesses is Beautiful Thing, the Diana of his imagination, the Kora of this book, which the dissolute Jacob Louslinger of Chapter One had already glimpsed while "bumming around the meadows": "Meadow flower! ha, mallow! at last I have you." The satyr-poet begins to learn what Williams expressed at the end of his life in *Paterson V,* where the satyrs and their tragic dance are invoked, that "The dream / is in pursuit."[24]

The second improvisation, the "'fallen' Olympiad" whose importance to *Paterson* was first recognized by Vivienne Koch, works downward, into the present, against but with the help of the mythicizing activity of the previous interpretation:

> Giants in the dirt. The gods, the Greek gods, smothered in filth and ignorance. The race is scattered over the world. Where is its home? Find it if you've the genius. Here Hebe with a sick jaw and a cruel husband,—her mother left no place for a brain to grow. Herakles rowing boats on Berry's Creek! Zeus is a country doctor without a taste for coin jingling. Supper is of a bastard nectar   on rare nights   for they will come—the rare nights! The ground lifts and out sally the heroes of Sophocles, of Aeschylus. They go seeping down into our hearts, they rain upon us and in the bog they sink again down through the white roots, down—to a saloon back of the railroad switch where they have that girl, you know, the one that should have been Venus by the lust that's in her. They've got her down there among the railroad men. A crusade couldn't rescue her. Up to jail—or call it down to Limbo—the Chief of Police our Pluto. It's all of the gods, there's nothing else worth writing of. They are the same men they always were—but fallen. Do they dance now, they that danced beside Helicon? They dance much as they did then, only, few have an eye for it, through the dirt and fumes.

Flexibility, movement, control—all are evident in the writing of this brilliant passage. Williams thereby restrains his passion, so easily sentimentalized, for things Greek, and transforms this passion, both by the careful composition of the passage itself and by what is juxtaposed to it, into a passion for the local. The significant glosses on this passage are his criticism of Hellenism in his reply to Hilda Doolittle in the "Prologue"; an early poem, "An After Song," in which the sudden splendor of Apollo seems "strange" to him "in the modern twilight," a response developed in one direction by Eliot, and the letter to Kay Boyle in which he says that "the classic lives now just as it did then—or not at all." This epistolary essay shows us the close connection between Williams' concern for the local and for formal invention and, in conjunction with the doctor's outburst in *A Dream of Love* ("There's something in our day, common to them [the Greeks], that we can't even talk about!"), helps us understand his lifelong quest for Beautiful Thing, the ultimate "presence," the perfect realization of place.[25]

Following the intense present thought of this improvisation is a passage of flat, straightforward prose in the past tense. The common narrative style of this interpretation is easily recognized—the interpretation, in fact, is the anecdotal situation of a short story about the Venus of the improvisation and exemplifies one way in which a writer now might embody her presence. To this end the interpretation purposely demythicizes. But the weakminded girl with the lust in her is still, for those with "quick eyes," the *Juana la Loca,* the queen, the Beautiful Thing, to whom the poet earlier sings his song.[26]

The third improvisation, about Homer in a butcher's shop, presents the poet's antipathy to the misuse of the classics. He will go his own way, please himself, as he also announces in the "Prologue." He will do what he has just done. To Ezra Pound's admonitions, represented in the interior dialogue by "Reading shows, you say," he replies, "Yes, reading shows reading." Homer's individual talent did not suffer for want of tradition. The literature of the past, conformed to, used for its "associational or sentimental value," is a "carcass" (the butcher's shop is a library) and, as the flip interpretation suggests, has only the stink of death.[27]

V

Only close attention of this kind serves a text of the richness and complexity of *Kora in Hell.* As might be expected, the poet continues to treat recent themes, the themes of emergence, anti-success, and the common and the low that figured so prominently in *Al Que Quiere!*. He is the fool of the opening improvisation: "Fools have big wombs. For the rest?—here is pennyroyal if one knows to use it. But time is only another liar, so go along the wall a little further: if blackberries prove bitter there'll be mushrooms, fairy-ring mushrooms, in the grass, sweetest of all fungi." Here the assertion of the fertility of the irrational is followed by the natural things, the improvisations themselves, his leaves of grass. Some, like the pennyroyal, may be used as carminatives; others, for their sweetness (the doctor-poet knows folk medicine—and the natural is itself tonic). Such a "fool" is Jacob Louslinger, who, like the poet of "Pastoral," rejects middle-class security and order ("I would rather feed pigs in Moonachie and chew calamus root") and has gone afield to be rewarded by beauty ("the great pink mallow stand[ing] singly in the wet"). His physical descent, like Boone's in *In the*

American Grain, is lateral, a matter of space and freedom from conformity; but release may be found, as the juxtapositions in the terminal paragraphs of this unit also indicate, by going downward, through the surface of respectable tidiness to the dark disorder and vitality of things.[25]

This is the difficult poetic way Williams chooses, difficult because he must first overcome the "secret arrogance" of his own gentility. The conventional tunes that impede him in Chapter Two are associated with success, with the treetops (with the robin of "Ballet" whom he had implored to "come down"). Yet he himself is beset by "*jumping devils,*" the "*images which he has invented out of his mind,*" which work against his desire for success and invite him "*to rest and disport himself according to hidden reasons.*" This conflict ("You think you can leap up from your gross caresses of these creatures and at a gesture fling it all off and step out in silver to my fingertips")—this conflict is resolved temporarily when the spirit of gentility, the "lady" of this book, abandons him:

> Hark! it is the music! Whence does it come? What! Out of the ground? Is it this that you have been preparing for me? Ha, goodbye. . . .—and I? must dance with the wind, make my own snow flakes, whistle a contrapuntal melody to my own fugue! Huzza then, this is the dance of the blue moss bank! Huzza then, this is the mazurka of the hollow log! Huzza then, this is the dance of rain in the cold trees.[29]

These examples, so tightly knit, sometimes dramatic and sometimes serial in their development, represent the structure of the book. They begin the enactment of its theme: that imagination and desire, the quickest energies of being, cannot be restrained, not even by the natural seasons, the conditioning circumstances of life. "*There is neither beginning nor end to the imagination,*" we learn in Chapter Three, "*but it delights in its own seasons reversing the usual order at will.*" White-haired Jacob Louslinger pursues a flower ("age's lust loose!") and Amundsen, in the anecdote of Chapter Three, runs off with the girl at supper—both instances of the "violent refreshing of the idea" that Williams, in the "Prologue," says is necessary to "love and good writing. . . ." When "wiser and older," he too—or rather the narrator of *The Great American Novel*—runs off with Nettie Vogelman, another notation of the incident treated in *A Dream of Love.* And now, in Chapter Four, he promises to be wiser: "Mamselle Day, Mamselle Day, come back again! Slip your clothes off!—

the jingling of those little shell ornaments so deftly fastened—! The streets are turning in their covers. They smile with shut eyes. I have been twice to the moon since supper but she has nothing to tell me. Mamselle come back! I will be wiser this time."

This lovely passage is Williams' equivalent of Emerson's "Days." In it, the poet relinquishes the genteel symbolist imagination of his Keatsian youth for an imagination of naked everyday reality—an imagination of great power ("the streets are turning in their covers" links it with the comparable forces in "St. Francis Einstein of the Daffodils") and an imagination of the new world (the shell ornaments may link it with Pocahontas or the Indian spirit of place). In any case, day has fled—Kora is in Hell—because the poet has been inattentive or looking elsewhere. But now, in a passage indebted to the fifth section of Whitman's "Song of Myself," he possesses her: "If one should catch me in this state! —wings would go at a bargain. But ah to hold the world in the hand then—Here's a brutal jumble. And if you move the stones, see the ants scurry. But it's queen's eggs they take first, tax their jaws most. Burrow, burrow, burrow! there's sky that way too if the pit's deep enough—so the stars tell us." By descending, touching, burrowing, attending to the particular things in the "brutal jumble" of the world, the poet uses the imagination to seize the day. For Kora is not captive to the seasons (much of the book is autumnal) but only to the poetic self that has not yet learned what the closing interpretation of the book again affirms—that *"The true seasons blossom or wilt not in fixed order"* but according to the imagination itself, by whose agency an autumn day may have *"perfect fullness"* and be *"its own summer."*[30]

VI

When Williams wrote *Kora in Hell* he was about the same age and at about the same stage in his career as Whitman in "Song of Myself." In Chapter Twelve, he records his awareness of radical change: "The browned trees are singing for my thirty-fourth birthday [September 17, 1917]. Leaves are beginning to fall upon the long grass. Their cold perfume raises the anticipation of sensational revolutions in my unsettled life. Violence has begotten peace, peace has fluttered away in agitation. A bewildered change has turned among the roots." This change, the emergence of the poet's authentic self, is what *Kora in Hell* signifies as a literary gesture. In this, and in other ways, it is, I think, the modern work most closely related to "Song of Myself."[31]

In *Kora in Hell,* the poet had the luck he mentions in Chapter Twenty-three, the *"luck that gets the mind turned inside out in a work of art";* in it, he found a form for his *"phallus-like argument."* Marianne Moore was one of the few critics to read the book in the requisite psycho-biographical way and to appreciate it as the work of a profound poet. She described it well when she spoke later of the "pressure configured" in Williams' work. For this is what the imagination of his literary gesture discloses—an urgent need for release and for the free yet ordered space of the imagination. He wishes, as he said later in *Spring and All,* "To enter a new world, and have there freedom of movement and newness." This accounts for his otherwise curious identification with the visionary Poe, as well as for his identification with Whitman—poets, according to Williams, who had "to come from under." But he also wishes to create a new world, a new reality complete in itself. In another section of *Spring and All,* where the argument includes Juan Gris and his own desire to overcome "the fragmentary nature of his understanding of his own life," he writes of Whitman: "Whitman's proposals are of the same piece with the modern trend toward imaginative understanding of life. The largeness which he interprets as his identity with the least and the greatest about him, his 'democracy' represents the vigor of his imaginative life." Here, I think, we begin to see one of the most significant ways in which Williams, a romantic formalist, appropriated Whitman.[32]

Of course the most apparent indebtedness to Whitman is the "Prologue," which originally introduced *Kora in Hell* and was chosen later to begin the *Selected Essays.* Williams wrote it after he had completed the composition of the book and first published it with a subtitle that announced the book's achievement: "The Return of the Sun." He used it, as Whitman had the 1855 Preface to *Leaves of Grass,* to survey the literary situation and proclaim the departure of his own literary work—the "defiance advancing from new free forms." Although different in style, the essay has a similar declarative force (it belongs with such deliverances as "Belly Music" and the editorials of *Contact*). In it, Williams provides a modern version of the imagination that complements the imagination of the modern in *Kora in Hell.*[33]

This is why he repudiates the work of Eliot and Pound, "men content with the connotations of their masters," and ridicules Edgar Jepson, the English critic who considered Prufrock, "a New World type." Not Prufrock, but Williams himself, the poet of these improvisations, is the New World type. For *Kora in Hell* shows that he has fully understood the liberation from all absolutes that constitutes the essential nature of modernism and that for him the New World man is the poet-discoverer who possesses an imagination of this new world.[34]

Notes

1. Moore, "A Poet of the Quattrocento," *Dial,* LXXXII (March, 1927), 215; Taupin, *L'Influence du Symbolisme Français sur la Poésie Américaine* (Paris, 1929), 284.

2. *The Autobiography of William Carlos Williams* (New York, 1951), 158; *I Wanted to Write a Poem,* ed. Edith Heal (Boston, 1958), 26–31; Munson, *Destinations* (New York, 1928), 112. In his *Autobiography,* Williams mistakenly recalls that a "dark" spermatozoon was accepted, a mistake in favor of his conception of the Beautiful Thing in *Paterson.*

3. "Prologue," *Little Review,* V (April, 1919), 1–10, and VI (May, 1919), 74–80; *I Wanted to Write a Poem,* 30.

4. Pound, "T. S. Eliot," *Poetry,* X (August, 1917), 264–71; Dudley, "To Whom It May Concern," *Poetry,* XII (April, 1918), 38–43; "Prologue to *Kora in Hell,*" *Selected Essays of William Carlos Williams* (New York, 1954), 17. Conrad Aiken, in reviewing Williams' *Collected Poems* in 1934, not only set Williams, the poet and the theoretician, squarely against Eliot, but praised *Al Que Quiere!* and *Kora in Hell,* books "obscurely published and poorly circulated," as his best, his "finest and sharpest" work. How consoling this may have been may be gathered from his well-meant praise of Williams as "still, at the age of fifty, a promising poet" and from Williams' very late poem "The Pink Locust," in *Journey to Love.* Aiken, *A Reviewer's ABC* (New York, 1958), 380–83.

5. Williams, "Root Buds," *Poetry,* VI (May, 1915), 62–66; *The Selected Letters of William Carlos Williams,* ed. John C. Thirlwall (New York, 1957), 42. For his remarks on his "inner security," see *Selected letters,* 147.

6. Emerson, "Circles," *The Complete Works of Ralph Waldo Emerson* (Boston and New York, 1903), II, 321; Williams, "How to Write," in Linda W. Wagner, *The Poems of William Carlos Williams* (Middletown, 1964), 147; "Night," *A Voyage to Pagany* (New York, 1928), 122–27, 277; *Kora in Hell* (San Francisco, 1957), 72; *Autobiography,* 288–89, where, in speaking of the "secret gardens of the self," he returns to the conceptions of "perfections" and "presence" first used in *Kora in Hell;* "Dr. Williams' Position," *The Literary Essays of Ezra Pound,* ed. Eliot (London, 1954), 398; *I Wanted to Write a Poem,* 26. See also

"Revelation," *Selected Essays,* 268–71. In the manuscript of *Paterson IV,* now in the Yale University Library, Williams writes: "His other self, himself his woman"; he begins the "Prologue" by characterizing his imagination in terms of his mother's.

7. Taupin, *L'Influence du Symbolisme Français,* 286; Koch, *William Carlos Williams* (Norfolk, Conn., 1950), 31; Wagner, *The Poems of William Carlos Williams,* 146–47. The poems from *Al Que Quiere!* are in Williams, *Collected Earlier Poems* (Norfolk, Conn., 1951), 117–18, 169–70, 167–68.

8. Richard A. Macksey gives a valuable account of the tension of the book in "'A Certainty of Music': Williams' Changes," in *William Carlos Williams,* ed. J. Hillis Miller (Englewood Cliffs, N.J., 1966), 142–43. See Koch, *William Carlos Williams,* 33. See also *Selected Letters,* 52, and "The Black Winds," *Collected Earlier Poems,* 246: "How easy to slip / into the old mode, how hard to / cling firmly to the advance—."

9. *Spring and All* (Dijon, 1923), 43–44.

10. Kandinsky, *Uber das Geistige in der Kunst* was published in Germany in 1912, translated under the title *The Art of Spiritual Harmony* and published in London and Boston in 1914. The edition cited in this essay is *Concerning the Spiritual in Art* (New York, 1947). The formulation quoted by Williams is on p. 52 and is followed by Kandinsky's belief that "all means [forms] are sacred which are called for by internal necessity." Kandinsky's definition is on p. 77. Williams may have learned of Kandinsky from Marsden Hartley, who met the Blue Rider group in 1912, or from Pound's *Gaudier-Brzeska* (London, 1916). By 1923, he was critical of Kandinsky's Expressionism, calling it the "apotheosis of relief." See Williams, *The Great American Novel* in *American Short Novels,* ed. R. P. Blackmur (New York, 1960), 315.

11. *Autobiography,* 288; *Selected Essays,* 177; Wagner, *The Poems of William Carlos Williams,* 145; *Selected Essays,* 230. In *Paterson,* which in one respect is an autobiographical rehearsal of his poetic career, he writes: "Why have I not / but for imagined beauty where there is none / or none available, long since / put myself deliberately in the way of death?" *Paterson* (New York, 1963), 30.

12. "Interview with Donald Hall," *A Marianne Moore Reader* (New York, 1965), 273; *Selected Letters,* 52; Else von Freytag-Loringhoven, "Thee I call 'Hamlet of Wedding-Ring,'" *Little Review,* VII (January-March, 1921), 48–55, and (Autumn, 1921), 108–11; *A Voyage to Pagany,* 211; Williams, "Three Professional Studies," *Little Review,* V (February-March, 1919), 36–44; Kandinsky, *Concerning the Spiritual in Art,* 77, 75.

13. Taupin, *L'Influence du Symbolisme Français,* 288.

14. *The Great American Novel,* 312; *The Letters of Ezra Pound,* 1907–1941, ed. D. D. Paige (New York, 1950), 160; *A Novelette and Other Prose* (Toulon, 1932), 25; Pound, *Literary Essays,* 393. The citation in *A Novelette* is, significantly, in a chapter entitled "Juan Gris."

15. Taupin, *L'Influence du Symbolisme Français,* 281–84. Munson, *Destinations,* 111–12, taking up the references to Rimbaud, considers *Kora in Hell* a deviation in Williams' development. This, I think, is not the case, though the following comment of Munson's is crucial and correct: "Rimbaud was an altogether different type, a prodigy who came to an end of skepticism and saw no way to make an affirmation."

16. *Kora in Hell,* 75, 59–60. On the importance of the senses, see Kandinsky, *Concerning the Spiritual in Art,* 23n.; "Three Professional Studies," 36–39. "Professional," here, relates to both medicine and poetry. For Williams' theory of the emotional basis of poetry and knowledge see "Notes from a Talk on Poetry," *Poetry,* XIV (July, 1919), 211–16.

17. Pound's comment on "opacity," *The Letters of Ezra Pound,* 124, was printed by Williams in the "Prologue," where Taupin, *L'Influence du Symbolisme Français,* 284, picked it up. What Pound had in mind was probably a quality countervailing the sentimentalism of American verse, the "Soft mushy edges" he mentions in his *Letters,* 90. Marianne Moore thought Williams' "exactness" and the "crisp exterior" of his work were like the French. See her review of *Kora in Hell* in *Contact* (Summer, 1921), 5–8. Williams' own comment in *The Great American Novel,* 312, is: "It [this novel] is Joyce with a difference. The difference being greater opacity, less erudition, reduced power of perception." For Shapiro, see "The True Contemporary," James E. Miller, Jr., Karl Shapiro, and Bernice Slote, *Start with the Sun* (Lincoln, Neb., 1960), 218.

18. Donald Sutherland, *Gertrude Stein: A Biography of Her Work* (New Haven, 1951), 100. According to Kenneth Rexroth, Stein and Arensberg were the pioneer literary cubists and *Others* was the most advanced modernist magazine. See "The Influence of French Poetry on American," *Assays* (Norfolk, Conn., 1961), 154–55. Williams acknowledges his debt to the cubists in "Tribute to the Painters," *Pictures from Brueghel and Other Poems* (Norfolk, Conn., 1962), 135–37, and to painters in the Preface to *Selected Essays.* Williams does not speak of Arensberg's poetry, from which I think he could have learned little, but of his "sumptuous studio" and of the famous painting by Duchamp that was a nucleus of Arensberg's great collection of modern art. See *Twentieth Century Art,* the catalog of the Louise and Walter Arensberg Collection, The Art Institute of Chicago, 1949. He might also have found instruction in the new art in *Camera Work,* Stieglitz's magazine, which published Gertrude Stein.

19. See "Prologue," *Selected Essays,* 12, for Williams' awareness of a method adequate to the speed and freshness of the emotions; Sutherland, *Gertrude Stein,* 88; Burke, "Heaven's First Law," *Dial,* LXXII (February, 1922), 198; this method contributed to an unfavorable opacity according to Munson, *Destinations,* 110–11; *I Wanted to Write a Poem,* 27; "Prologue," *Selected Essays,* 11–13; McAlmon, "Concerning 'Kora in Hell,'" *Poetry,* XVIII (April, 1921), 57–58.

20. *Kora in Hell,* 37; Pound, "In a Station of the Metro," *Poetry,* II (April,

1913), 12. Mina Loy is praised for "freshness of presentation, novelty, freedom, break with banality" in the "Prologue," *Selected Essays,* 7.

21. *Selected Letters,* 131; Shapiro, *Start with the Sun,* 211–13; *I Wanted to Write a Poem,* 29; *Kora in Hell* was published by the Four Seas Company, Boston, 1920.

22. *Selected Essays,* 26; *I Wanted to Write a Poem,* 28.

23. *Kora in Hell,* 65, 11; *Selected Letters,* 130ff. The dream of love is treated in "The Ideal Quarrel," "Prose About Love," and "Love Song," *Little Review,* V (December, 1918), 39–40, and VI [*sic*] (June, 1918), 5–11.

24. There are echoes here of the poetic impulse of his earliest work, an imitation of Keats's *Endymion; Paterson,* 259.

25. Koch, *William Carlos Williams,* 35. For Hebe, see *Paterson,* 168; for Zeus, see "Old Doc Rivers," *The Farmers' Daughters: The Collected Stories of William Carlos Williams* (New York, 1961), 77–105; "Prologue," *Selected Essays,* 9–11; *Collected Earlier Poems,* 22; *Selected Letters,* 130ff.; *A Dream of Love,* in *Many Loves and Other Plays* (Norfolk, Conn., 1961), 218.

26. *Kora in Hell,* 45–46.

27. "Prologue," *Selected Essays,* 10, 11. There is nothing picturesque in Williams' sketchbook. His view recalls that of Horatio Greenough, who advocated "Greek principles, not Greek things." Williams' statement that "the 'Greek' is just as much in Preakness as it was in Athens" seems to echo Greenough's statement that "the men who have reduced locomotion to its simplest elements, in the trotting wagon . . . , are nearer Athens at this moment, etc. . . ." See *Selected Letters,* 130, and *Form and Function,* ed. H. A. Small (Berkeley and Los Angeles, 1947), 22.

28. *Collected Earlier Poems,* 121. It is possible to see in Jacob Louslinger a disguised Whitman, the bard whom respectable people considered a tramp. His search for beauty represents the kind of heroism Williams admired in Columbus and Boone.

29. The spirit of these passages is intensely Whitmanian; they provide a condensed version of the opening sections of "Song of Myself." See Williams on Whitman in *I Wanted to Write a Poem,* 5.

30. *Selected Essays,* 20; *The Great American Novel,* 338. See also *Autobiography,* 289; for "St. Francis Einstein . . ." see *Collected Earlier Poems,* 379–80. The two passages cited were printed without interpretations in *Little Review,* where a third passage completed the unit: "Lullaby! Lulla-by! the world's pardon writ in letters six feet high! So sleep, baby, sleep!" The second passage suggests "Sub Terra" and this passage "The Shadow," the poem closely following it. *Little Review,* IV (January, 1918), 4.

31. Robert McAlmon used Whitman as the measure of his extravagant but nonetheless significant judgment that "*Kora in Hell* is immeasurably the most important book of poetry that America has produced." "Concerning 'Kora in Hell,'" *Poetry,* XVIII (April, 1921), 58.

32. Moore, "Kora in Hell," *Contact* (Summer, 1921), 5–8; Moore, "Things Others Never Notice," *Poetry*, XLIV (May, 1934), 103; *Kora in Hell*, 56: *"The act is disclosed by the imagination of it"; Spring and All*, 68, 36; *In the American Grain* (New York, 1956), 213. Another aspect of his identification with Poe is his quest of Beautiful Thing; *Spring and All*, 38; *Selected Letters*, 40; Williams wanted to suggest the democracy of *Al Que Quiere!* by calling it "THE PLEASURES OF DEMOCRACY."

33. For "defiance . . . forms," see Whitman, 1855 Preface to *Leaves of Grass;* Williams, "Belly Music," *Others*, V (July, 1919), 25–32.

34. "Prologue," *Selected Essays*, 21–22. See Jepson, "The Western School," *Little Review*, V (September, 1918), 4–9.

Stieglitz, Williams, and Cubism

Two needed, inevitable studies are compacted in Bram Dijkstra's *The Hieroglyphics of a New Speech:* a study of Alfred Stieglitz and a study of the decisive influence of the visual arts on William Carlos Williams. Neither has been wholly neglected, but neither has been thoroughly or well done. The difficulty in treating Stieglitz has been the vested interest of adulators and the nonverbal character of his work. (We are tired of slim memorial volumes of photographs; a full-scale biography of this genius is overdue.) The difficulty in treating Williams, until recently, has been the general unfamiliarity with his work and the lack of adequate studies to provide the context for narrower scrutiny. Mr. Dijkstra has overcome the first difficulty and also established the background for treating Williams' early poems by discussing Stieglitz in terms of the cultural movements to which he contributed and in the words and work of the remarkable group of critics and artists who explained and extended his ideas. To a large extent he chronicles the milieu of "291" and *The Seven Arts* in order to show Williams' heavy indebtedness for his "original" ideas, and to a still larger extent he celebrates Stieglitz, the sovereign force within it. One takes up his book expecting to find Williams at its center and instead finds Stieglitz. But this is salutary: by way of its interest in Williams, a new generation may come to know Stieglitz and his formative role in American art and letters.

Mr. Dijkstra focuses on the period 1910–30, and on two movements within it. During the early years of this period cubism had its revolutionary impact on America not only because of the Armory Show (1913) but because Stieglitz, in his magazine *Camera Work* (1903–17) and at his gallery "291," had already prepared for it and his associates had promoted it—Marius de Zayas and Agnes Meyer in *291* (1915–16), Waldo Frank and Paul Rosenfeld in *The Seven Arts* (1916–17), and Alfred

Kreymborg and Walter Arensberg in *Others* (1915–19), the magazine that Williams said had saved his life as a writer. Cubism taught a generation of painters and writers to "make it new," to see the work of art as object or construction, and as a nonrepresentational or nonmetaphorical imaginative investigation of objects. But Stieglitz taught them—once the revolution had been assimilated and the new and less fruitful directions of abstraction and Dada had been tested—to use the lessons of European art to the end of creating the first truly independent American art. What he taught them we all know, having probably learned of the aesthetic of the "American Moment" from Williams: the theories of contact and place (of attention to the objects of one's immediate environment) and of objective "equivalents" for the double encounter of self and world. Or we may have learned it from Stieglitz's "evangelists," from Waldo Frank in *Our America,* Marsden Hartley in *Adventures in the Arts,* and, most notably, Paul Rosenfeld in *Port of New York.*

As Rosenfeld knew—he devoted a chapter of his book to Williams—no writer had learned these lessons as well as Williams. They transformed his art. By the time of *Al Que Quiere!* (1917) he had relinquished literary models and had succeeded in making poetry a visual art; he had learned to treat the poem as a canvas and, as the title of one poem tells us, to make "metric figures." Mr. Dijkstra traces this transformation and Williams' subsequent *artistic* development in descriptive, well-illustrated chapters devoted chiefly to *Al Que Quiere!, Kora in Hell, Sour Grapes, Spring and All,* and *The Descent of Winter.* But even here, where so much is useful, he seems to be preoccupied with scoring against Williams the influences and indebtednesses he established to Kandinsky for so much of the early work, to Hartley and Rosenfeld for *Spring and All,* to Rosenfeld for *In the American Grain,* and to Stieglitz, Hartley, Marin, Sheeler, and Demuth, whose works were sometimes the sources, the very objects, of the poet's still lifes.

This prejudice of originality mars this book in several ways. It accounts for Mr. Dijkstra's defensive tone and his insistence on his own originality. He would have us believe that his work is a pioneer study when it isn't—the very thing he is so concerned to show up in Williams' case. Others have seen the relationship between Williams and the Stieglitz group (Williams himself acknowledged Stieglitz in the foreword to his *Autobiography* and not, as Mr. Dijkstra claims, as an afterthought but in a profoundly memorable context, and he wrote "The American Background," one of his most brilliant essays, as a tribute to Stieglitz). And others have seen the relationship between painting and poetry. It is not necessary to Mr. Dijkstra's thesis to insist, as he does, on a radical divergence in sources between the pre- and post-World War I literary generations, the former turning to painting, the latter to literature. The cubist revolution didn't end that suddenly, and other writers, Hart Crane for example, found inspiration in it as well as in the work of Stieglitz and his associates. (Crane acknowledged the cubist revolution in "Modern Poetry"; like Williams, he sometimes painted and derived much of his aesthetic education from painters.)

This prejudice also accounts for the unpleasantness in Mr. Dijkstra's treatment of Williams. It appears most often when Williams' debts are in question, and it appears because Mr. Dijkstra believes that Williams purposely failed to acknowledge them. Sometimes it is gratuitous and defamatory, as when he says that "Williams mutilates Cravan's name" and when, without considering the complexities of lifelong friendships, he impugns Williams' loyalty to Pound and accuses Williams ("some of his best friends were Jews"!) of anti-Semitic feelings toward Stieglitz. The case against Williams cannot be made on the evidence supplied, and certainly not without considering the doubts we are told that Stieglitz had, where Rosenfeld hadn't, about Williams' poetry and the fact that he never published Williams in his magazines. But is it necessary to exalt Stieglitz by needlessly diminishing Williams?

We learn from Mr. Dijkstra to admire Williams' Stieglitzian-inspired accomplishment but not to understand the radical originality of it. The most serious omission in Mr. Dijkstra's study, especially in light of the double nature of the created object, is the failure to treat the subjective importance, the personal or imaginative significance of Williams' designs, or, since it is related to it, to consider the reason that Williams, unlike other poets of his generation, found so much in the new art. Surely he responded to cubism not merely because he was at heart a painter but because he found in the revolution in art (in perception) an ally for his own rebelliousness, his resistance to Procrustean order, and because "make it new" was for him (as he shows in "St. Francis Einstein of the Daffodils") the correlative of a willingness to be changed by change, to accept the open condition of life created by modernism and the morality of attention that contributed to its finest art.

Williams' Background

The pleasure and excitement of reading Mike Weaver's *William Carlos Williams: The American Background* recalls for me that of reading—yes, reading!—Emily Mitchell Wallace's *A Bibliography of William Carlos Williams*. Both attend to primary matters that immeasurably help the literary critic and often clarify his work, and both elicit confidence because the authors themselves are critics who are familiar with all that Williams wrote and much—*so much*—that relates to him. Their books are enterprises successfully accomplished, clearly excellent.

Though Mr. Weaver's book is not large, its effect is. His ability to search out the facts is matched by his ability to use them representatively. He is essentially an intellectual historian concerned with "the formation of Williams' thought," not only that referred to in the subtitle by "American background" but that of England and Europe as well. He organizes his materials chronologically, that is, biographically. New themes are introduced at those stages in Williams' life when they were new or especially prominent, and their treatment is developmental. His work is significantly biographical, becoming emphatically so as the book reaches the 1930s, ending in fact with an excellent psychological sketch of Williams ("The Core of the Man") in his last years. At the same time he also considers those materials that elucidate *Paterson*. At the end of the first chapter on Williams' family background, early literary influence, and nineteenth-century poems on the Passaic River by Washington Irving and Thomas Ward, he observes: "The materials of *Paterson* were already to hand, the perch of the tradition of the regional poem established; it remained Williams' life-long task to evolve an indigenous method by which he could build a new bridge over the Passaic." (The appendices include a thirty-five page selection from Ward's *Passaic*, which relates the incidents of Sam Patch and Mrs. Cumming, and eighteen pages of notes on *Paterson*.) Intellectual history, accordingly, is at the service of life and work, which, as Weaver shows, are themselves inseparable.

When Weaver says Williams did not acknowledge that *Paterson* "belonged to a tradition of poems on the Passaic region," he declares his own intention: to make available to us the sources, acknowledged or not, in tradition and cultural-critical situation that nurtured Williams' work. His assumption—necessary to the intellectual historian—is that nothing comes from nothing. The "provincial" poet is not on that account outside the intellectual currents of the age; he may be, as Williams was, very much in them. We find, for example, that the erotic element so notable in and necessary to Williams' art was liberated by his engagement to Flossie—"the engagement itself," Weaver perceptively notes, "was his first act of daring and resolution"—and that this deliberate act had been prompted by reading Otto Weininger's *Sex and Character,* from which he had learned, among other things, that "man is genial [able to develop genius] and woman material [to be formed]." And Weininger, along with Max Stirner, was a basic text of Dora Marsden, editor of *The New Freewoman* (later renamed *The Egoist*), with whom Williams, at the time of his emergence as a poet, discussed such fundamental issues as feminism and egoism and male and female psychology.

The richness of Weaver's account—a matter of a few close, well-written pages—is not easily conveyed. But having acknowledged this, perhaps it is only necessary for purposes of review to indicate the range and importance of the intellectual episodes that comprise the book. When Weaver turns next to *Contact,* which had been Robert McAlmon's idea, the focus of his treatment is McAlmon's writing in *Ace,* a magazine of aviation, his reading in John Dewey, and his concern with functional education ("contact with experience, and with life"). His discussion of the impact of the new art on Williams' poetry is, in respect to the influence of Stieglitz, sketchy (perhaps because I compare it with the book-length study by Bram Dijkstra). But in respect to Kandinksy, his discussion is the fullest I know. And it opens into a major contribution—Williams' reading of Whitehead's *Science and the Modern World* ("Finished reading it at sea, Sept. 26, 1927—A milestone surely in my career") and his correspondence with John Riordan, a young engineer with scientific and mathematical interests, over Steinmetz's *Four Lectures on Relativity and Space* and his own essay on Williams' poetry, "The Theory and Practice of Precision Poetry" (1926). Anticipated here are Williams' concern with "objectivist" poetry and the "variable foot"; and there is ample support here, and later, for Weaver's claim that "Williams' analogies for invention in poetry in the late twenties were drawn from physics rather than from linguistics."

Weaver treats these central matters of objectivity and movement in poetry in subsequent chapters, one on Williams' relations to Zukofsky, Stieglitz, and Charles Sheeler, another on the musical contributions of Zukofsky and Antheil (prompted by Pound's book, *Antheil and the Treatise on Harmony*) and on the impact of classical jazz, in the 1940s, by way of Fred R. Miller. Miller was the editor of *Blast* (the American magazine), who introduced Williams to Bunk Johnson and with whom he collaborated on *Man Orchid,* an unfinished novel. Also treated here is Williams' lifelong interest in prosody and the American idiom: an early essay entitled "Speech Rhythm" (1913), his criticism of *The American Language* and correspondence with Mencken, and the employment in the later work of the "triadic foot."

Much of what follows also involves the 1930s and 1940s, the period especially fertile for *Paterson.* A chapter on Williams' politics tells of the attack on him by Mrs. Virginia Cummins of *The Lyric* that lost him an appointment, in 1952, as consultant in poetry in the Library of Congress (one wonders what he would have proposed or done in this position), of his attendance, in the 1930s, at the Third Writers' Congress and his connection with the Writers' Project in New Jersey (it produced a state guidebook), and his involvement in the American Social Credit Movement that Gorham Munson did so much to promote (a movement of consequence to Williams if only because James Laughlin's *New Directions* had its inception in *New Democracy,* the Social Credit review). Another chapter traces the development of Williams' "epic documentary style," a style owing much to photography and film and the efflorescence of documentary art in the 1930s (Alfred Kazin explores this more fully in *On Native Grounds*) as well as to the concern with original documents Williams had shown as early as *In the American Grain.* Such documents were readily available in Herbert A. Fisher's manuscript, "Legends of the Passaic," and Williams was encouraged to use them by Mrs. Kathleen Hoagland, a Rutherford writer who, in the 1940s, was writing a novel based on local historical materials (she also typed the first three books of *Paterson*). As for Williams' method of disposing them in the stream of his poem, he was most immediately indebted to another local resident, David

Lyle, a communications engineer, whose letters provide him instructive models (an example addressed to "Noah"—Williams—and signed "Faitoute"—Lyle—is included).

Lyle, Weaver says, "turned Williams' attention to the news, and the conception of a poem as the truth of contemporary events." But equally important to *Paterson* and of *deeper* significance, as Weaver shows in the penultimate chapter, is all that Williams had learned of Dada and surrealism and was learning now about the fantastic and monstrous, the magical, occult, and alchemical from *View,* the paintings of Pavel Tchelitchew, and the writing (including correspondence) of Robert Motherwell and Nicolas Calas. Much that had been of profound concern to Williams—the violence of emotion, the beauty of the monstrous, the mind's release, the dialectical relationship of the sexes, an open renewable world and the relation of the self to it—was now resumed because of the urgency of his poem and advanced by intellectual encounter. Relationship with Tchelitchew, whose masterwork *Phenomena* and anthropomorphic landscape *Fata Morgana* (reproduced here) influenced *Paterson,* confirmed his wish to create "a mythology of contemporary life consisting of the strata of events both external in the objective world and internal in the subjective world." And relationship with Calas—he and Calas had proposed the magazine *Midas*—opened to him the alchemical conception of the artist's work, which, in Jung's words, expressed his deepest intention: "the alchemistic *opus* is the labour of man the redeemer in the cause of the divine world-soul that sleeps in matter and awaits redemption."

Weaver's analysis of some of the alchemical imagery of Williams' *opus* suggests to me that he himself should undertake a fuller study of this kind. Or if not that, then perhaps he should—since he has the skills and commands the manuscript resources—undertake a biography of Williams (hopefully with a more detailed index than in the present book and as many or more illustrations). And should he do either or both of these necessary studies, he should also do, by the way, what his own work shows is very much needed—new editions of Williams' letters and essays.

The Later Poems

Writing about a poet's later poems, as Jerome Mazzaro does in *William Carlos Williams: The Later Poems,* is not an exclusive task. It requires that one write about the earlier poems—about all the preceding poems—and the relationships between them; it requires—and this makes it so rewarding for both writer and reader—that one follow the course of an imagination and, finally, see it whole. One may consider this pursuit, as Mazzaro does, a study of poetics. But poetics, again, is not exclusive, and widened (and deepened) as it has been by interest in the developing imagination, it reaches into profoundly psychological ground, into self and way-of-being-in-the-world, into the very sources and sustenance of poetic activity.

Mazzaro's study is of this larger kind. There is as much in it about the earlier poems as there is about the later poems (*Paterson* I-IV, V, "Asphodel, That Greeny Flower," and *Pictures from Brueghel*). It treats not only such formal matters as imitation vs. copying, the "variable foot," and the appropriation in verse of cubism, but psychological matters, such things as—to cite a chapter title—"Sex and the Williams Poem." Its guiding purpose is large: "To link the phenomenal world of the older poet with the dreams he had in his youth."

I respect Mazzaro's endeavor and his scholarly virtue; he does his "homework," as Austin Warren would say. My reservations about his book do not include lack of seriousness but the fact that his seriousness does not give me intellectual pleasure. His work leaves me confused, uncertain about its accomplishment and the merit of its ideas.

The basic difficulty, I think, is the inability to conduct an argument, with all that this implies about lack of clarity. Mr. Mazzaro is not a good writer. He has no felicity. He usually makes a book, not its author, the subject of an assertion ("Earlier, *Spring and All* . . . had insisted that 'the word . . .'"); he clots his prose with references; he quotes too much, often using quotations to advance an argument that would be better and more quickly moved by a clear statement of his own. This sample is characteristic:

> More practically, the dual, natural and imaginative lives of a poem permitted Williams within the "stasis" of his general technique to shift his developing perception from direct observation to an extended, often fortuitous "parallel between contemporaneity and antiquity" and achieve, as Robert Lowell's "William Carlos Williams" (1963) asserts, an idiom that "comes from many sources, from speech and reading, both of various kinds."

Nor is he a helpful and careful thinker. Where it matters most, where ideas are initially presented, he doesn't consider them in the poems, secure them in the artwork. His concern with poetics might be said to be speculative rather than practical; he talks too much about, demonstrates too little. Too few poems are closely and thoroughly treated, not even the major later poems. "Asphodel" and *Pictures from Brueghel* receive the most attention—in the latter the comparison of the poems with Brueghel's paintings is especially valuable. But the treatment is still insufficient and inconclusive, chiefly for the want of interest in symbolic action, the very thing that must be considered in an account of the deepest motives and continuities of Williams' work.

The pivotal early work for Mazzaro is *Kora in Hell.* For him it is an example of descent that, with Jung's interpretation of Orphean descent, becomes archetypal, the mythic pattern of rescue that is most consummately and consciously realized, he believes, in the great later poems. Jung's interpretation is useful—how useful James Olney has recently shown in *Metaphors of Self,* a study of autobiography—and this interpretation is not in question so much as Mazzaro's meager use of it and his way of using it not as the basis of an ever-deepening explanation but as reference-point or motif. He does not, for example, sufficiently examine *Kora in Hell,* an exceedingly rich and difficult work, and so his argument is not well founded. Nor does he see around it: he does not make enough of the fact that the pattern of descent-ascent is the *process* of the creative act and that every poem involves it, and in treating it he creates divisions between art and life that do not hold for Williams. Mr. Mazarro pays too little attention to *Spring and All,* the text that would have helped him most in clarifying the issues in Williams' early work; misreads several poems, among them "To a Solitary Disciple," and muddies our understanding of Williams' relation to cubism; and does not discuss love in the survey of sex in Williams' poems. These are serious faults; I think they damage his book.

The Embodiment of Knowledge

There is nothing overwhelmingly new in this new work by William Carlos Williams. It does not alter the configuration of his thought: it confirms it, adds new evidence to it, and helps one place it more securely in its obvious American tradition.

The Embodiment of Knowledge is the title Williams gave to the notes, fragments, short essays that he wrote during the years 1928–30. It does not designate a book, and the reader who takes it up (and pays exorbitantly to do so) should be warned that it offers little of the intellectual excitement of *Spring and All,* with which it is sometimes visually comparable, that it is extremely repetitive, much of it fits and starts, and that, often failing to engage the attention as Williams' best prose does, it is tedious. The measure of its disorganization—but, then, Williams didn't choose to publish it!—is *Five Philosophical Essays,* a coherently argued work of youthful moral earnestness, probably of his apprentice years, that has been appended to it. And not unreasonably: the former is a defense of poetry, the latter is the argument in which Williams reached the conclusion that he could most fully serve the wonder of the world by choosing one vocation—and though he had two vocations, he meant the overriding vocation of poetry.

The best thing about *The Embodiment of Knowledge* is the title, a richly constitutive metaphor that Ron Loewinsohn, who edited the text, treats perceptively in his introduction. Williams literally wants us to assimilate what we know, to take it into our bodies and thereby into our activity. Knowledge is not abstraction (disembodied knowledge, as we say), and it is not an end in itself; it is instrumental, essential to "the practice of human life," and because it is he seeks the "humanization of knowledge." The argument goes back to Emerson and to Williams' contemporary John Dewey; it owes something to Whitehead, whom Williams had recently read; and it points ahead to Charles Olson. For Williams is concerned, as Olson is, with stance toward reality, with how to use knowledge in a world where all is process. In Olson's terms (perhaps originally Williams', addressed more fully by Olson), it might be said that Williams changes fields of knowledge to *field:* he destroys the boundaries, the compartments and specialties, by introducing the reality in which we find ourselves, in which knowledge is not only a matter of what we know but of how we know, a life-activity, our very way of being in the world. He assaults the arrogance and aristocracy of "knowledge" by reminding us of the concrete human condition, of the life-knowledge, the experience, all of us, however lowly or ignorant, have—and his own text is most alive when he introduces examples of this ("I won't get a divorce. I'm not going to spoil my kids' names just for his lousy pleasure").

What is at issue here, of course, is a modern theme (to cite Ortega's phrase), the restoration of our life in a physical universe. "The first difficulty of modern life," Williams writes, "is a difficulty of thought; not emphatically of philosophy nor of philosophic thinking—but of thought, of the imagination of the world, the immediate." And what is especially interesting is the extent to which Williams, in treating this theme, anticipates Olson: in the insistence on negative capability ("risk"), on freshness, contact, "nakedness" (Olson's term), on the Socratic misuse of mind and the betrayal of what Olson calls the old discourse ("By false direction," Williams says, "stretching back two thousand years by the varnishers, the thinkers who have degraded and disarmed us"), on decentralization, the actuality of place, over against the centralization and uniformity such thought has fostered. Like Williams, therefore, Olson was concerned with (re)education, was in fact an educator who, in planning the reorganization of Black Mountain College, strengthened the already central place of the arts in the curriculum and proposed that Williams serve on the advisory council. One reason, undoubtedly, was his realization at this time that Williams, as he said, "looms as answering more of the difficult questions (those which arise from reality) than the above gr-eat poeat [Pound]"; another, their profound disregard for boundaries and their endorsement of "unbound thinking" (the poet who thinks in this way is, in Williams' example, a brigand, living in the open, outside the walled cities; or, recalling Joseph Louslinger in *Kora in Hell,* one of those men who "keep the real and are called vagrants").

As a defense of poetry, *The Embodiment of Knowledge* is defensive in stance but not without equanimity. This may be explained by the fact that Williams, a doctor, was himself a scientist (scientists have a favorable, prominent place in *A Voyage to Pagany* and *Paterson*) and that here he was arguing philosophically; even better, it may be explained by his awareness of the complementary nature of the scientific-philosophical and the poetic ways of thought. Nevertheless, given the larger context of the book—during these years when the ascendancy of science was critically noticed, Krutch wrote *The Modern Temper,* a New Humanist assessment Williams' work recalls but with which it disagrees—and given Williams' sense of the diminished place of poetry in modern society, the argument turns on oppositions. These conveniently indicate the range of the argument and how much, for Williams, the defense of poetry entailed: science and philosophy vs. poetry (art); abstract thought vs. concrete and "objective" thought; authority, aristocracy vs. individualism, pluralism, democracy; old vs. new, youth; order vs. vital disorder; bound vs. "unbound"; utilitarian language vs. writing-as-writing; Bacon vs. Shakespeare; Europe, tradition vs. America, place. The argument, of course, is assailable; and much of it is familiar to us from Williams' work and the work of his contemporaries and others. That on youth, for example, calls up Randolph Bourne: "Youth is right when it attacks those who would lead it and have lost the direction. When we must go by instinct, failing leadership, trust youth." Much—the defense of art as a humanizing agent in a technological world, the consideration of art in its widest contexts and as "natural thinking," and the confrontation with the thought of Henry Adams—recalls Louis Sullivan, whose *Kindergarten Chats,* a primer, merits comparison with Williams' primary text. And much recalls Emerson's argument in "The American Scholar," not only the delegation of whole-man-thinking to the poet but the following insistence on the centrality of present individual experience: "The conviction that fills the whole body of a man is nearer to him than all the books that have ever been written." And this reminds us that the conviction that fills these jottings is one of the most important things about them. "All my life one thing," Williams says, "—to break through to a more comprehensive basis away from rule"; "—a luminous conviction that . . . by the removal of impediments, arrive at renewals." Williams himself is the individual—would be the individual—he speaks of in the epigraph when he says that "an entire generation [owes] its outward freedom to the inner freedom of one individual." He knew what Emerson meant by a silent revolution of thought.

To be of greater use *The Embodiment of Knowledge* requires more editing than Mr. Loewinsohn provides. His notes are chiefly textual, and there is no index. The text is not sufficiently placed in the context of Williams' life and works. No use is made of such helpful books as Mike Weaver's study of Williams' American background; clues, like the mention of "The Descent of Winter," are not followed up; and people mentioned in the text, especially contemporaries like Harold Stearns, whose contribution to current intellectual life we may have forgotten, are not identified. Nor are the topics treated here related to other texts. Williams had written about Shakespeare elsewhere, though not so fully as he does here; he also addresses modern writers (Joyce, Stein, Yeats, Eliot, Pound) and modern painters (especially Gris) elsewhere, and this should be brought to the reader's attention. Oversights on Williams' part, such as the omission of John Quinn in his comments on the lack of patronage, might have been noted, or such interesting things as the fact that he appreciated *Finnegans Wake* where Pound did not and attributed to Shakespeare the "opacity" Pound attributed to him. But perhaps the most conspicuous omission, either in the introduction or the notes, is a gloss on "clarity," one of Williams' essential terms and in all of his work most conspicuously present here.

"Clarity" means many things to Williams—bodily thinking, "wholeness"-thinking, the "revelation in the speech that he uses" stressed in the introduction to *The Wedge*. But the fundamental meaning established by *The Embodiment of Knowledge* and *Five Philosophical Essays* involves the very thing Williams finds lacking in contemporary education: the placement of specialized knowledge in the context of all knowledge; the kind of ordered knowledge the Church once provided; a "comprehensive basis." His thought, for all that it is "unbounded," seeks such an order (ordering, placement), perhaps the correlative of form in his work. And what is striking here is the extent to which he is moved by the need to find this ground. Because of this—and its necessity in his emergence as a poet—*Five Philosophical Essays* stands in the same relation to his career that *Nature* stands to Emerson's. And it is a text well worth recovering, in spirit much like Emerson's, glowing with wonder and acceptance of life ("So life, then, is to do where I am, to the fullest of my powers, with clear eyes. . . . I must be ready to go anywhere at any time, faithfully, at the command of the true, but when I am bidden there will be little doubt as to the direction, the call is as distinct as birth"). *Five Philosophical Essays* tells us that for Williams the choice of vocation was, as Emerson had told the young men at Dartmouth, the crisis of his life.

The Early Poems

Emergence is the theme of Rod Townley's short (easy-flowing, easily read: quick) study, *The Early Poetry of William Carlos Williams.* He traces, and distinguishes between, the phases of Williams' early development, charts the process of release and the accommodation of allegiances this involved. The movement is necessarily from *Poems* (1909) to *Spring and All* (1923), with other chapters treating *The Tempers* (1913) and *Al Que Quiere!* (1917), *Kora in Hell* (1920), and *Sour Grapes* (1921), and with an "Afterword: Prologue" treating "The Descent of Winter" (1928). He employs both biographical-psychological description and close, often comparative, textual reading. The former, especially where the evidence is thin, leads to conjecture, a risk Townley acknowledges and accepts ("The real theme of the poem ["A Tragedy"] is not love but obedience. It is of course dangerous to try to extract biographical meanings from a poem whose incidents are entirely conventional and whose diction is derivative, but . . ."); the latter, usually perceptive and useful, is selective, and often, it seems, determined not so much by what is central to the text as by the desire to use materials come upon in the vast store of Williams' manuscripts.

The biographical-psychological foundation on which Townley builds is sound enough, and familiar, and my only regret is that a new study, especially of the early work, does not add more, and more solidly, to it. The dualities with which Williams struggled aesthetically in respect to Keats and Whitman have (or may have) extensive counterparts in his hostility to his father and devotion to his mother, in his genteel, idealist, spiritual Victorianism (often protested, however, in letters to his mother) and his sensual and bodily being, in his early devotion to "Poetry" and the practice of medicine, in the erotic conflict (complicated by cultural notions of Europe and America) represented by Charlotte and Flossie Herman, and so on. According to Townley the Whitman side, questionable and "secret," was the true, or deepest, correlative of Williams' self. This is the self the poetry tries to release, the self whose spontaneous voice engages the controlled voice of the other self, as Townley notably points out in the formal arrangements of *Kora in Hell, Spring and All,* "The Descent of Winter"—engages, and I would add, does not silence the other self, for that self, as we hear it, say, in *Five Philosophical Essays,* is not always in conflict with it, is actually necessary to it, as much so as in Emerson's paradigm of the soul. And it is the self, Townley claims, that Williams had in fact released at the start, when at the age of ten he wrote "Tree," a paragraph, later rearranged in free verse and published in *The Dial.* Townley's conclusion, that "Williams was capable of writing excellently at ten and execrably at thirty," determines his view of Williams' development: for example, his view that Williams "conceived of the book [*Poems,* 1909] as an ending rather than a beginning, an epitaph to his youth and to a wrongly directed apprenticeship" (Townley notes the resemblance to gravestone art in the floral design of the title page *and* also the similarity to the design on the cover of the first edition of *Leaves of Grass*); that *The Tempers* is "a naughty book," a "secret" book expressing inhibited sensuality (it is dedicated to the Carlos-Dionysius self); that *Al Que Quiere!,* which he had once entitled *Pagan Promises,* is characterized by violence, energy, sexuality, rankness—views that might have been developed also in relation to *Kora in Hell* and *Spring and All,* in terms of the ways in which they are companion books and the way the later asserts Williams' emergence, not only in the first poem but in the victory of the black-eyed Susan in the last.

Of all the books, Townley treats *Poems* most thoroughly, that is, gives us a sense of the complete text. "The Wanderer," he says, enables us to "witness Keats being reborn as Whitman," but he does not inspect this important poem for us. And all the subsequent texts, even when a chapter is devoted to one of them, are sketchily treated. This is not to say that they are without value but that their value is limited—that the weakness of this study is not so much in what it does as in what it does not do. In treating Williams' early attempts at playwriting, for instance, I miss the connection that might have been made with the later plays, specifically *A Dream of Love;* and in the chapter on *Kora in Hell,* which Townley says is "a major American work," Williams' "first work of genius" and the sourcebook of his later writing, I miss the proof of these assertions and especially an account of the last. Context is missing, sometimes at the expense of judgment: it is not enough to cite Bram Dijkstra on the importance of cubism in Williams' development (liberation), to pass on the questionable opinion that Williams insufficiently acknowledged his debt to Alfred Stieglitz, or, even, to characterize *Camera Work* as "notorious." Williams' emergence, to say the least, was concurrent with the advent of cubism (so was the battle for free verse), which is why general reference to such an important movement (revolution), in little more than a page, is not enough. And it may be that this secondhand knowledge explains what seems to me the misplaced emphasis on cubism in Williams' career; that is, in respect to *Spring and All* instead of *Kora in Hell,* a work of that heady time. Or it may be that Townley found Kandinsky's definitions of impression, improvisation, and composition a tidy way of ordering the development in *Kora in Hell, Sour Grapes,* and *Spring and All,* and withheld the discussion of Kandinsky's *Concerning the Spiritual in Art,* which Williams knew at the time he was composing *Kora in Hell,* until he turned to *Spring and All.* (Here, Townley also considers the thought of Juan Gris and Pierre Reverdy; his source is Kahnweiler's study of Gris, to which I would add, for Reverdy, *The Poetic Theory of Pierre Reverdy,* an excellent monograph by Robert W. Greene.)

In what way is the "Afterword" a prologue? It contributes to openendedness, points beyond to other phases (renewals) of Williams' career—but it is not needed and impairs the structure of the book. It is also a deferred or second introduction introducing an animus, absent in the first, toward critics like Hyatt Waggoner and Randall Jarrell, who do not appreciate Williams' aesthetics and intelligence. And this, too, is needless, since the work of several critics has already answered them, and in a preferable way, by making, what Townley might have made, a more complete or fuller study of Williams' art and thought. But, then, Townley is ambivalent about "critics," and, although he himself is a critic, speaks as a poet, one of that increasing number for whom Williams is "what Whitman was to him: a father, a fellow conspirator, a rich source of liberating attitudes and techniques, an endless pleasure."

Coles on Williams

These lectures, delivered by Robert Coles at Rutgers University in 1974, and subsequently published in *William Carlos Williams: The Knack of Survival in America,* are not compulsory reading. There is very little that is new to be learned from them. They have the often loose, expansive, repetitive character of lectures. They are marked by commonplace observations on Williams and on the difference between art and social psychology. Though they were probably pleasant to hear, they are dull to read. Essentially testimonial—Coles, a physician like Williams concerned with children and with the working class, has found his "identity theme"—they are not critical. They are too general, not close enough to the object, which is not sufficiently or significantly charted in respect to literary history or in respect to the large body of Williams' work; in respect to scholarship and criticism, they are underfurnished. Coles does little more than comment on a few texts—on "A Face of Stone" and "Jean Beicke" in *Life along the Passaic River,* and on *White Mule,* the novel of the Stecher trilogy he finds most interesting. His criticism-by-commentary has the value of recalling us to these texts but it does not appreciably improve our understanding of Williams' prose fiction.

Whittemore's Biography

Every literary figure permits the biography he gets, but it is not necessarily the one he deserves. In this first biography of Williams, *William Carlos Williams: Poet from Jersey,* by Reed Whittemore, we see Williams' vulnerability, the lack of esteem, the unwillingness to accord him what a biographer of James or Eliot, Joyce or Pound, would accord them. On the testimony of this book Williams is unquestionably "the doctor-hick from the country," a confused, self-divided, unstable, deluded, even paranoid person who, fortunately, was saved from himself by the steadying influence of his wife and the middle-class life they lived together at 9 Ridge Road, Rutherford, New Jersey. Whittemore dedicates his book to Florence Herman Williams not because it is in any way an official biography but because it is a tribute to her and all the "normalcies" she stands for. This is not regrettable but simply the fact that Whittemore's treatment of Williams is mocking and confirms the prejudiced in their prejudices. His biography of Williams is a work of ridicule informed by hostility to the movements to which Williams largely contributed: modernism (and the anti-puritanism of the American insurgents) and postmodernism (especially the movement of poetry from the time of Williams' greatest recognition in the late 1940s and 1950s to the present).

This is not to say that only those who are partisan should be allowed to write about Williams. Rather, that in writing about him Whittemore might have exhibited the primary virtue of the position he defends: rationality above all scrupulous in its concern for truth and sound judgment. This is wanting in almost every aspect of his book, from its scholarship to its style.

His scholarship, for example, is measured by the unconcern he attributes to other scholars, by lack of thoroughness in respect to the critical literature and to what he calls "school treatises" (that is, dissertations—which are sometimes excellent: the best work on Williams' stories is an unpublished dissertation, and there is a brilliant dissertation on *Paterson;* and Whittemore, a defender of the university from detractors like Williams, should not dismiss them). This neglect impairs his book because he derives much of his biographical material from Williams' literary work—and it is not compensated for by the heavy investment in search and research of the kind one finds in Blotner's biography of Faulkner or Unterecker's biography of Crane or, for that matter, in Mike Weaver's pioneer work on Williams. Moreover, this neglect is not so egregious as the way in which he treats intellectual movements: without clearly and fully presenting them (biography is a work of reconstructing, reconstituting), in an offhand way that discredits them and makes them appear frivolous, that vulgarizes history and depreciates human effort.

None of the literary figures whose presence is necessary to Williams' life is present (evoked), and most appear foolish; Pound, for instance, an easy target whose work deserves more respect than it gets, or Olson, whom Whittemore treats as a "wild theorist" whose essay on projective verse "became a basic alienated-student text on how verse was to be written." (For Pound, and especially for clarification of Pound's poetics and understanding of the profound significance of Imagism, consult Herbert Schneidau's *Ezra Pound: The Image and the Real;* for Olson, compare his understanding of the technical issues involved in *The Cantos* and *Paterson,* in *Mayan Letters* and *Letters for Origin,* with Whittemore's.) And none of the literary movements is treated any better than that of the 1950s in this characteristic passage: "The aesthetic talk of the fifties was wild and woolly and sometimes full of the flavor of mad scientism, but it was at the center a rather sharply focused wildness with the aestheticians reaching for their peyote but also meditating solemnly on ways of changing the verse line." Or consider: "Much of the rebellious modernism in art has always, especially to the young, had such a base, which is why so many students who ought to be taking Bonehead English are to be found instead doing Cummingsy-Williamsy things (and Ginsbergy-Snydery-Olseny [sic] things) in Creative Writing. WCW must have himself had some of that fierce need to convert weakness to strength by a trick, by changing the game rules."

Now Whittemore's posture and style enable such ridicule. He is almost always distant from and superior to what he treats. (Exceptions: his accounts of Williams' mistreatment in the Library of Congress affair—Whittemore himself was later a consultant there—and of Williams' illnesses.) And his clever style—breezy, loose, wordy, full of clichés—makes him the ever-present subject of the work. Some of its touchstones are "boy-days" (for boyhood or youth), "*nuevo mundo* females," and "pen-pal society" (for the correspondence by which literary movements sometimes come into being and continue to exist). Such an unhappy choice of style! Was it deliberately chosen to make it impossible to render Williams—or to *render* him? What audience—unless an incredibly ignorant one, a popular audience, as we say—did Whittemore have in mind?

That Williams is reduced to his initials (WCW) is the least of the diminishments he suffers in this book. Not much of his work survives in this account, none of the short poems early or late, none of the plays, none of the experimental books (*Kora in Hell, Spring and All, The Great American Novel,* and so forth), neither *In the American Grain, A Voyage to Pagany,* nor *Paterson*—only the "social" writing of the 1930s, the stories in *Life along the Passaic River* and *The Knife of the Times,* and *White Mule,* the first novel in the Stecher trilogy. And Williams himself hardly survives the inexpert psychologizing and the dubious reports of his infidelities and drunkenness (dubious because never verified, but fully alleged then briefly retracted, as in the instance of several pages on "stealings" that reach the conclusion that "some of the stealings were not even real, that is, were not stealings with real women but with dreams of women. He was out in his car in the night with a dark second life that sometimes added up to women and sometimes poems. And the connection between them was itself murky").

At least Williams is spared this book. It lends credence to the reasons for many of his resentments. Having more than the knack of survival he will of course survive it. There are many things, as he reminds us, that have to be done all over again.

Williams and the Other Arts

One of the virtues of these books on William Carlos Williams' relationship to the arts of painting and photography is the recognition that the practice of any art involves relationship—*contact,* Williams might have said—with the other arts, that his literary art, in particular, is not an isolated affair. Literary criticism has been long in catching up with Williams and even longer in catching up with the importance of the visual arts to his work. Only with the studies in the late 1960s and early 1970s by James Guimond, Mike Weaver, Bram Dijkstra, and Dickran Tashjian has this aspect of his work been given the consideration it deserves. In consequence we have these new books, *A Recognizable Image,* a collection of Williams' published and unpublished writings on art and artists expertly prepared by Bram Dijkstra, and *William Carlos Williams and the American Scene, 1920–1940,* the lavish catalog prepared, again expertly, by Dickran Tashjian for the exhibition gathered under this title at the Whitney Museum of American Art in the winter of 1978–79.

So Williams has at last been recognized as a literary figure sufficiently at home in the arts to provide the nexus for an exhibition that is virtually the art history of the period 1920–1940. And here are the visual milieu and, what is perhaps of more significance, the social milieu in which Williams moved and had so much of his being.

I emphasize the social milieu because what I find of most interest in both books—central to Dijkstra's, peripheral to Tashjian's but perhaps only because he chose to moderate Dijkstra's views—is the concern with Williams' politics. Again, and only recently, have (most) literary critics seen fit to attend to such matters, and the long neglect may explain Dijkstra's determination to use the occasion of prefacing Williams' writing on art to give us the most extensive and stringent examination of Williams' political views we have. If one of the things we learn from

Williams is that almost always the study of a poet leads us to the other arts, another is that art is inextricably connected with politics—yes, even when purity is claimed for it. (And isn't it interesting that the résumé of this book on the dust-jacket does not mention Dijkstra's important contribution? The book might well have been titled *Williams' Views on Art, Politics, Race, and Women.*) We can only be grateful that Dijkstra has done this critic's job of work.

Which is not to say that *his* views necessarily merit wholesale endorsement. But first, what has he done? He has brought together and arranged in a fairly chronological way some thirty-one or so writings on art and artists from 1915 to 1960. He has restored the original versions of many essays—literally reconstructed them and thereby demonstrated how much other of Williams' published essays need such restoration—and has valuable things to say about Williams' impulsive way of composing and responding to criticism. He has included forty-eight illustrations, placed conveniently to accompany one's reading. In sum: he has done a scholar's job of work, marred only by the lack of an index (which, in these days of high-priced books, may be a publisher's ridiculous economy). *And* he has supplied a substantial introduction and note on the text (fifty-four pages).

There is nothing in the introduction about the way in which Williams appropriated the visual arts to his art of words. Dijkstra treated this in *The Hieroglyphics of a New Speech* and others have also treated it. Instead, the introduction treats art *and* politics, or art-and-politics, and reprimands as naïve and irresponsible the view of art vs. politics that Williams insistently upheld. One might, simply out of exasperation with much of the writing collected here, score Williams; it is seldom his most vigorous or intelligent work. But Dijkstra does so from the vantage of our recent education in the ideological nature of perception and from what I suspect is a Marxian view of the relation of art to society. He finds Williams politically conservative (backward?) and condemns his politics as narrowly conceived and founded on the social (cultural) efficacy of art, an art too privileged (pure) and even, residually, genteel (the imagination raises up, art heals). Of Williams' political statements he says: "They are most interesting, and can best be read, as statements of Williams' *aesthetic* preoccupations, as reflections upon the *transcendent magic* of art. For it is to the theme of art as a *haven* from the high seas of everyday experience, to the theme of art as an *oasis* of insight in a desert of human mutual misunderstanding, that Williams returns time and again—to that, and to the theme of the glory of the lone individual, of the magnificent inventions of the artist . . ." (my italics). Dijkstra is not inaccurate here, no more than in his statement that Williams' "political" (his quotation marks) writings of the 1930s, on Social Credit, for example, "give no greater indication of political perspicacity than Pound's." And when he goes on to consider Williams' "destructive traits"—his anti-Semitism and depreciation of women—it is clear that he is less concerned with differentiating Williams from Pound than with fixing an identification with one of the most publicly recognized, politically miscreant artists of our time.

If not inaccurate, these strictures are unfair, unjust, because they are insufficiently understanding of the very milieu that gave rise to such views. Take Williams' insistence on the independence of the artist: this was not so much a vestige of art for art's sake as partisanship in behalf of the great victory of modern art, which Meyer Schapiro, a Marxian, in an essay on the Armory Show, says involved the "progressive emancipation of the individual from authority, and the increasing depth of self-knowledge and creativeness through art." When Charles Olson, an immigrant worker's son, assessed Pound's "treason" in the 1940s, it was in just such terms: "He was false . . . when he subordinated his critical intelligence to the objects of authority in others." And it was in just such terms that many writers of more political perspicacity than Pound and Williams refused the inducements of doctrine and ideology—criticism at the poles, Kazin called it, in defining the conflict of allegiance between New Humanist/New Critic and Marxists in the 1930s. As for the accompanying social view of art, its utility is this very independence, the independence claimed by the avant-garde (the very designation an appropriation of a military term). And this has a long American lineage, coming down from Emerson's "American Scholar" and Whitman's "Divine Literatus" to such contemporaries of Williams as Stieglitz and Van Wyck Brooks, the latter having in his quarrel with Croly put art over politics as the redemptive agency in (of) American culture. To pit the "creative life" against the "acquisitive life" (and these are in fact the Brooksian terms of Williams' respect for Stieglitz) is to promote art vs. politics rather than art *and* politics. Now this alignment of terms, with what it says about American idealism, is worth exploring, for it may explain not only Williams' "narrow" views of politics but ours, the general American view: politics as solely the business of political parties and pragmatic politicians, not an aspect of all life but a mere sector of it. And it may explain the difficulty we have in defining and determining the politics of artists, until, in desperation, our extremity will finally force us to accept imprisonment as conclusive proof. The section "Poetry and Politics" in a recent issue of *Parnassus* does little to clarify these complex matters; it reflects our current thought. Dijkstra raises important issues that are far from settled.

There is always the suspicion that in explaining such matters as Williams' sexism and racism one is explaining them away. Not so. They are deplorable. To say that Otto Weininger's *Sex and Character* made a deep impression on others (and other artists, e.g., Sullivan) is not to excuse Williams' lifelong adherence to Weininger's misogyny. Rather it is to ask how this thought, perhaps grasped quickly out of convenience as Dijkstra notes of other appropriations, comports with the unbound thinking, the profounder thought/thinking of the poems. And his racism? Dijkstra treats only "What of Alfred Stieglitz," a hitherto unpublished eulogy in which Williams certainly vented his feelings of irritation with the "God" of "291," Stieglitz in "his little shitty hole of an office building." It is true he names him "Jew" and associates the Jew with money and power even as, in the concluding assessment, he claims him as "a profound prophet of real values as opposed to the murderous falsity of cash over everything else." What to make of this? That the context merits closer attention, and that Dijkstra does not mention the fact, brought forward by Tashjian in treating the same essay, that Williams himself was partly Jewish and had the difficulties of identity of immigrants (and, I would add, of many Jews, who at this time were trying to enter the cultural "mainstream"). Again, this is not to exonerate Williams. Recall Olson on Pound: "No man can attack a race and remain useful to anyone as an artist." Rather it is to ask that matters of such importance be presented fully, in their complexity. It is not fair, for example, to cite Williams' view, via a *persona,* that Van Gogh's "Potato Eaters" is "very bad" because it does not portray peasants as the happy people they are, and to omit a later reference to this picture in which he appreciates the way in which it expresses the deep troubled feelings of the artist. Nor following on this is it fair to say that the remark about the peasants "helps to explain the absence of portrayals of serious poverty and economic depression in Williams' poetry." For this statement is too extreme, not, as I now summon my impressions, in accord with the evidence of my reading of the work or with the evidence, for example, of Robert Coles in *William Carlos Williams: The Knack of Survival in America,* who reminds us that "Williams wrote about the working people who live near the Passaic River at a time when sociological studies had yet to gain the dominance they now have."

It is salutary to read these books together because Tashjian provides much of the background (or is it foreground?) that Dijkstra could not afford. His primary concern is the story of the American assimilation of European avant-garde art—how the modernist forms and techniques of cubism, Dada, surrealism were adapted to the American scene, to American experience. His focus is Williams and the artists he knew well—Hartley, Stieglitz, Sheeler, Demuth—and Williams' idea of contact. His account is often familiar (after all, he told some of this story in *Skyscraper Primitives*), generally sound (without nuance), frequently anecdotal. For those unacquainted with the art history of this period his canvass is helpfully introductory.

What is most curious to me in his account, however, is the relegation of Stieglitz to the end of the book when from the beginning Stieglitz was so much the central figure in the history of American modernism and his aesthetic of the "American moment" (unmentioned) a determinant of Williams' idea of contact. I would suggest also that Williams' remarks on a Hartley painting ("a split boulder the two halves eternally separated") probably refers to "Whale's Jaw, Dogtown" and not to "The Old Bars, Dogtown." Finally, I would question the conclusive remark that, after 1940, "No one would talk about an American scene again."

A Revisionist Study

The Visual Text of William Carlos Williams, by Henry Sayre, is exceptional, revisionist and challenging as no other recent study of William Carlos Williams has been. Do not be misled by the title: it names a small book—admirably so, well written and well argued—but not one of narrow scope. "Formal necessity," as Williams himself spoke of his rage for order, one of the deepest urgings of his work, touches on everything. It involves, as any genuine poetics does, matters not only aesthetical but philosophical, cultural, political, psychological, and ethical. Henry Sayre, whose competence in art history and literature is notable, touches on some, if not all, of these matters in setting out Williams' relation to modern poetry and art and to modern (urban) America. In the context he provides, what Williams says about his formal necessities is cogent and not easily dismissed as naïve, and his actual formal achievement now appears to be even greater, and of more importance, than has been believed. "It is at least the latent thesis of this book," Sayre says, "that the realization of a visual text in Williams' late poetry is to American poetry what Jackson Pollock's monumental drip canvases are to American painting." Both, according to him, "define the triumph of American art."

This general revision upward is perhaps less surprising than some of the claims made in its behalf. These include, among others, the repudiation of the following: the epistemological view, represented here by J. Hillis Miller and William Spanos, according to which Williams is said to have yielded the ego by leaping into things, thereby eliminating many of the problems involved in accommodating the dualism of subject and object, self and world; the belief in respect to prosody and form, widely held by many contemporary poets and by Williams himself, that speech, as in "Projective Verse," determines the line, that the "variable foot" depends on sound, and that the poem, accordingly, is "an auditory arrangement, a musical form"; the organicist notion of form (Williams, Sayre says, "avoided the synthetic vision of form and content which an organic theory implies until, in his late work, he shunned it almost altogether"). Instead, Sayre argues that, far from giving over dualism, Williams "embraced it": "His aesthetic was based on an unresolvable dialectical opposition: on the one hand was the mind, the imagination, and its potential to create order and form; on the other was the world, fragmented and chaotic." In this scheme, the visual belongs to the mind, the aural (speech) to the world, and Williams' "variable foot" becomes a visual measure, the basis of a form or design arbitrarily imposed by the mind on the disorderly materials of the world, neither mimetic of it nor, in the projectivist version of organic form, an extension of its content. To put it categorically, as Sayre does, Williams is not an "aural innovator." On the contrary, his achievement is the "discovery of a form based on the eye," that is, a *visual text,* the realization of a verbal space in the visual mode, where speech is only the pigment of the poem and order resides in the abstract visual design provided, in Williams' late work for example, by the triadic stanza or grid.

What is to be noted here is that this abstract design is the work of the mind, of the imagination, and that it is the subjective element in Williams' art. Sayre cites Werner Haftmann (*Painting in the Twentieth Century*) on this salient point: "The modern experience of form was defined [in this instance by Malevich] as the experience of a concrete reality, which belongs to the human mind alone, and in which the mind represents itself." Williams, of course, knew this—knew, as early as *Kora in Hell,* that formal means enabled the mind to "turn itself inside out" and to liberate itself (and the self). Moreover, this is not a new understanding of Williams, for whom *poesis* itself was mimetic of nature, an organic creative act, not copying, either representatively or formally, which we usually think of as mimetic. (Given the gender terms in which Williams viewed this dualism, the "made poem," as he calls it in "The Desert Music," is a *male poem.* Art engenders. The synthesis he early sought figures as a dream of love: the journey to form is a journey to love, and in the end, in "Asphodel," he relies as much on love—and speech—as he does on imagination. How could it be otherwise, when everything in his work acknowledges the eros of imagination?)

Even so, this understanding is worth insisting on and following through in tracing Williams' formal concerns from the early to the late works. In doing this, Sayre builds on, and sometimes corrects, the previous studies of Williams' indebtedness to modern art, chiefly Bram Dijkstra's *The Hieroglyphics of a New Speech: Cubism, Stieglitz and the Early Poetry of William Carlos Williams* and Dickran Tashjian's *Skyscraper Primitives: Dada and the American Avant-Garde.* He finds many of Dijkstra's readings "suspect" and moderates Tashjian's view of the deliberate incoherence of Dada; and he goes beyond their studies by attending most to the late work—*Paterson I–V* and *Pictures from Brueghel*—and in all of this developing not only parallels to visual art but a visual poetics. In discussing the early work he attends most to Juan Gris and Alfred Stieglitz, to the appreciation of abstract form in the one ("abstract form does not . . . describe or define the world . . . [but] elevates the world to the point where we can appreciate it aesthetically") and to the aesthetics of the "American moment," so much involved with the new urban environment, of the other. His readings here are choice and convincing. In going on, however, he does not explicate *Paterson* but, as he says, outlines "the drift of a developing aesthetic." This aesthetic—he borrows the notion from Lawrence Alloway—is one of *heterogeneity,* and considered in its light *Paterson I–IV* is important, the focal text, because in it Williams confronted and overcame his residual Idealism: the desire for unity, the sacred or spiritual valorization of art, and the belief in the privileged creative authority of the writer. In resisting the urge to "unification, totalization, and completion," Williams kept the poem open, and opened the way to *Paterson V,* where again he confronted and conquered an insistent Idealism. In Sayre's view, the "failure" to achieve unity is the measure of the poem's success. As for the last poems he considers, the title poems of *Pictures from Brueghel,* they provide the fullest visual text, the most exemplary artifice, for they are both visual in form and in subject matter, Brueghel's paintings taken up, not verbally transcribed, in new visual designs. This is a triumph of art, of the formal abstracting powers of mind and imagination, because it represents a lifetime struggle to achieve the clarity vouchsafed design and, even more, confirmed Williams' faith in art in the presence of death.

The brilliance of Sayre's argument is not in question, only its extremity and simplification, the design, I might say, by which he achieves so much clarity. It is unfair, for example, to read a consensus concerning Williams' epistemological solution out of Miller and Spanos; indeed, theirs is an extreme view not widely held. Nor is it fair to dismiss the fact that a generation of poets learned from Williams, as Robert Duncan acknowledges, the use of the "operative juncture." The aural text, which Williams stressed so much in the preface to *The Wedge* and which, in turn, has become a touchstone of recent poetics, need not be minimized to the point of exclusion in order to privilege the visual text. Is it, in fact, a true representation of the case, any more so, say, than considering Williams' fundamental creative rhythm of ascent-descent only in respect to ascent? I mention ascent-descent, which Sayre overlooks, because it is the vertical axis and primary polarity (in Bachelard's terms) of Williams' work and reminds us of the dependence of the one on the other and also of the movement of Williams' art. And movement, here, should remind us that dance, again overlooked by Sayre, is the central metaphor of Williams' poetics, the consummate notion, if not the consummate "embrace," of his art. By dancing the poem, Williams was able to be true to both its aural and visual elements as well as to its occasion. Like Pollock, an action painter who danced his paintings, Williams is an action poet who did not, I think, impose his designs. If he did, at the end, it was because he was at the end and could in no other way defy death.

It would not be consistent with Williams' lifetime struggle with Idealism to claim for him a victory of artifice. Ascent, or the formal work of *lifting up* the materials of art to the plane of the imagination, is easily idealized, so that Williams' formal aims had always to resist what might be called the idealistic function of *up-lift*. Idealistic formal solutions such as Stieglitz's, whose "Equivalents" represent an order of mind still correspondentially related to the order of nature, were eventually not possible for him. Form, for him, was composition, not "meaning"; order was not to be imposed but composed because the lifting-up was not hierarchical but aesthetic, or, as he said probably to avoid any notion of aestheticization, structural. To be fully appreciated, it seems to me, Williams' achievement must be seen in such philosophical terms—seen perhaps as a victory of the pragmatistic kind in which ideas are not abandoned (how could the mind do that?) but are regarded only as ideas, not Ideas, and truth becomes a matter not of correspondence but of verification in experience. Once again the desideratum is movement, action of a processual kind; and this reminds me that Williams' work is an eminent example of Frank O'Hara's distinctions between *format,* the visual shape or design of a poem, and its *form,* or inner prosodic movement, which is what we grasp by dancing its words, by reading or saying them. In justice to Williams, both distinctions must be kept in mind.

Romantic Idealist?

The argument of Carl Rapp's *William Carlos Williams and Romantic Idealism* is simple: Williams is a romantic idealist. The argument is strong—Rapp is essentially a theorist who appreciates Williams the theorist—but I am not convinced. Like Henry Sayre's recent revisionist study, *The Visual Text of William Carlos Williams,* Rapp's revisionist work overstates the case. Both oppose J. Hillis Miller's view—"the most stimulating conception yet to appear"—according to which Williams at the outset became a "poet of reality" by yielding the romantic ego and the attendant problems occasioned by the dualism of subject and object, self and world. Sayre insists, rightly, I think, on Williams' lifelong engagement with these problems and believes that Williams' achievement is his victory over the idealist's desire for "unification, totalization, and completion," what Emerson called the mind's tyrannizing desire for unity. His argument concerning the "visual text" is another matter, but it is important to recognize that Williams' designs, for all that they represent the power of the imagination, do not foreclose the openness and inclusivity he also cherished; in *lifting up* materials to an imaginative realm, Williams neither aestheticized nor totalized, the imaginative act itself being his mode of "unbound thinking."

Rapp contests Miller's view in another way, one that discounts Sayre as well, by deconstructively reversing Miller's valorizations. For Rapp, the truth of the case resides in romantic idealism, in the primacy of the self (ego) and its power of using and transcending the world. He argues this unremittingly, with little regard for the merit of opposing views, repudiating Joseph Riddel and James Breslin as well as Miller; and he argues in part by elaborating the assertion that "Williams more nearly resembles Emerson's idea of a poet than any other poet we have had since Emerson, including Whitman, Stevens, and Crane." Many of his theoretical touchstones come from Emerson, more from Hegel. And what he sets out to prove is that Williams' poetic quest was for "absolute authority" (*dominance* and *lordship* are other terms), "first, with respect to the image; then, with respect to the poem as object; and, finally, with respect to the poem as rhythm sample."

Rapp begins where Miller does, with "The Wanderer," Williams' early poem of poetic initiation and vocation. This poem has been read most often, as Williams himself speaks of it, as "the story of growing up," that is, if his recollection of burning his Keatsian *Endymion* imitation is to the point, as a rejection of Keats, his first master, for Whitman and the poetic task of engaging the immediate (modern) world. Both are romantic poets, and the shift, as Williams sees it, was from "elegance" to "raw vigor," Whitman, it should be noted, also impressing him with the opening lines of "Song of Myself." So Rapp's claim that "The Wanderer" is not antiromantic is plausible and his reading of it (the only poem he so closely attends) challenging even though he turns for analogues to Keats rather than Whitman, whom the following summary comment may also evoke: "The narrator of 'The Wanderer' *is* purged of his yearning for transcendence, but only because he achieves it. He *does* give up his private consciousness or ego, but only because that ego or consciousness has suddenly expanded to the point where it now contains everything within it." (Williams, not so insistent on the mind's enclosure of the world, acknowledges this "coextension with the universe.") Then, Rapp continues, concentrating what originally was the mind's expansiveness, "As the 'all' enters his mind, it becomes his idea, while he, on the other hand, becomes the single, transcendent point of unity—the *logos,* the center, the coherence."

Everything Rapp subsequently says is founded on this account of Williams embracing idealism. The evidence he marshalls is carefully selected to support it, in this instance an early essay, "Vortex," which opens with "I affirm my existence." This essay is crucial according to Rapp, who overlooks the projectivist intent of "express[ing] my content," "express[ing] my emotions in the environment in which I . . . happened to be"; crucial because for him it puts the paradox of Williams' work, the need to both affirm and negate the phenomenal world, to admit it to mind yet stand above it. "In the final analysis," Rapp says, "Keatsian empathy and Wordsworthian egoism . . . seem almost indistinguishable." Yes, for Rapp, negative capability becomes ultimate capability.

Is this true? Is the *reference* of Williams' poetic world, its import for the reader, the grandeur of the sovereign ego and not the self-in-the-world, in the field, a self capable of *composing* some of its elements (a poetics of *conjecture,* as Creeley and Olson speak of it) but not of totalizing it as *meaning,* as Idea? Can it be that Williams considered a poem a Sacred Word? Isn't *Paterson* the story of "The Wanderer" writ large, the story of an idealist, enclosed in consciousness and divorced from the world, who must learn to enter the field, "walk in the world," as Williams himself declares? And isn't *walking* the pragmatists' way of using ideas in experience, *ambulation,* not the idealists' overriding of experience by *saltation*?

That experience depends on our perception of things does not necessarily spell idealism. All of us stand at the center of perceptual fields but we are not on that account idealists, that is, if we recognize, as Williams does in his poetics of the dance, that the relationship of self and thing is also important. In Williams' famous dictum, "no ideas but in things," neither term is privileged; this dictum, never addressed by Rapp, acknowledges an act of mind that respects things, and does so, as *idea* (not Idea) tells us, by not using things as symbols, by insisting on particularity. Williams himself remarked toward the end of his life, "I have always had a feeling of identity with nature, but not assertive; I have always believed in keeping myself out of the picture. When I spoke of flowers, I *was* a flower." Determinative here are the words "*not assertive,*" not only the negative capability that enabled him to become the flower but, as Olson would have it, his *will of achievement* rather than *will of power,* the refusal of the egotistical sublime. Rapp misses altogether that Williams, in his practice as a poet, is obedient. To hew to experience, not to dominate it, is his aim: "to get a form," he said, "without deforming the language."

Yet Rapp argues, reading Williams out of Emerson and Hegel and insufficiently out of the poems, that "he was constantly striving *within his art* to express the nature of his own spiritual preeminence, not only with respect to the world of natural phenomena, but also with respect to art itself." We know from Emerson's dream of eating the apple of the world what the project of Idealism is, and this may be the reason Rapp turns to Emerson as the writer more than any other who "provides a key to Williams." He finds the Emersonian direction in the early philosophical essays appended to Williams' *The Embodiment of Knowledge,* notably the essay "Love and Service." These essays are Emersonian (see my review of *The Embodiment of Knowledge*) but they are only initial, the enabling declarations of an outsetting bard, not immutable doctrine, and what they affirm should be weighed with Williams' determination to *embody* knowledge. It may be that the myth of the fall that Rapp believes Williams shares with Emerson involves the fixity, and subsequent idolatry, of symbols—that this set both to keeping them fluxional—but Emerson also knew that *the* fall was the advent of consciousness itself and, accordingly, that it was necessary to recover relationship. Rapp's reading of Emerson's essays on poetry at the expense of his practice as a poet misses the fact, established by David Porter in *Emerson and Literary Change,* that Emerson's legacy is not the poetry whose very symbolic totalizing and transcending distressed him but the essay whose open form fulfilled his poetics of liberation.

Porter's work is a serious omission, but so is the absence in the discussion of Objectivism of any mention of the concerns of those most closely connected with it. In treating Imagism, the first of the three theories of poetry that for Rapp tell the story of Williams' ever-enlarging dominance, he cannot avoid Pound. But in speaking of Objectivism, the second theory, he overlooks Zukofsky, who stressed the sincerity of "thinking with things as they exist," and Oppen, who considered images "the data of experience," that is, of the experience of "the poet's self among things." In discussing the third theory, which involves speech and the "new measure" and correlates with Williams' late poetry of thought, Rapp also overlooks the projectivist poetics that Williams endorsed by including a portion of Olson's anti-idealist "Projective Verse" in his *Autobiography.*

These omissions are compounded by some commissions that test the accuracy of Rapp's assessments. Taking Hegel for his guide, he reads *Paterson* as an example of "romantic humor," valuable chiefly for its ingenuity, not its "epic" intent, and finds its collage composition nothing more than a "crazy mosaic." He does not distinguish among *Paterson, The Cantos, Finnegans Wake,* and *The Waste Land,* considering all of them "monument[s] of romantic egoism." And in reading the late meditative poems as the acme of Williams' sovereignty, he forgets that poems like "To Daphne and Virginia" and "Asphodel, That Greeny Flower" are speech acts addressed to others and that the penetrant odor in both fills the spaces of the world and the self.

Rapp's critical practice, then, enacts his theme: unquestioning and inadmissive, it is idealist in its arrogation and argumentative sovereignty.

PART IV

H.D.

A Modern Master

Susan Friedman's *Psyche Reborn: The Emergence of H.D.* is important because it consolidates and advances the now considerable scholarship devoted to H.D., and exemplifies the intellectual sophistication of Women's Studies. Friedman does for H.D. what H.D. did in her quest for a "woman's mythology" and a "new cultural tradition": she revises, transvalues, restores the hitherto neglected or rejected—in this instance, the reputation and place of a woman writer, a modern master, whose epic task is as valuable and worthy of recognition as those undertaken by her masculine confreres. H.D. is a modern master by virtue of having undertaken an epic task—she is, in my definition, a poet of culture—and that her task was epic, BIG, as Olson would say, no one has shown so well as Friedman.

Friedman's study is best described as intellectual history. Ideas are her primary concern: H.D.'s involvement with the psychoanalytic and religious traditions. She provides source material concerning both, often from unpublished manuscripts and little-known books. This material is essential in reading—decoding—H.D. and makes Friedman's book indispensable, a "companion." For the most part, Friedman treats H.D.'s work thematically, taking up a text at various times as the context of ideas dictates. She is, as she claims women scholars must be, a contextual critic. Only the shortest works are fully treated—or almost so, since even here she too often closes off closer attention to formal matters by referring to "imagist craft." This is unfortunate because, as her readings of "Oread" and "Helen" demonstrate, she is a capable critic, and what is needed finally to support her restoration of a master poet is a better sense of the poetic merit of the work. This is also needed because much of what H.D. achieved—the rebirth of the psyche and the mythology and culture this proposes—was achieved by her work as an artist, achieved *in* the work, poetically realized *there,* validated in the irrefutable way of art.

Intellectually what is notable in H.D. is her study of—researches in—psychoanalytic and syncretist religious thought and her formidable revision and interfusion of both. She recognized their hermeneutical equivalence, and *session* became *seance;* in the phrase *hieroglyph of the unconscious* she joined both. And she *read* both of them to the end of ensouling and of liberating the psyche from patriarchal domination. Her story is a radical transformation of the story of Psyche, who was set her harrowing tasks by the terrible Great Goddess, saved by Eros, and domesticated in the Olympian pantheon. Her story is one *of* transformation: of a woman—worm become butterfly—who herself worked this transformation by transforming the *thought* that constrained her. She is a hero of thought, to be compared with Freud for her intellectual courage, every bit as remarkable as the Mme. Curie her father, the learned astronomer, hoped her to be. The Psyche of *Psyche Reborn* gives birth to herself, and this rebirth "makes it new." Psyche is so conspicuous and appropriate in H.D.'s story that it seems curious on Friedman's part to have forgone the advantage of playing off H.D.'s version against Erich Neumann's, all the more so because Rachel Blau DuPlessis has so sharply questioned its patriarchal pretentions. But, then, Jungians have no place in a study whose central text is *Tribute to Freud.*

Tribute to Freud is a remarkable book, so perfect in its kind that it alone might support a reputation. It is a tribute to Freud not merely because it lovingly portrays him but for the better reason that it renders much of what H.D. learned from him even as she opposed him. She reads Freud himself after the fashion of reading he taught her, and her account of her sessions is in this sense tributary and in many ways provides the key to her subsequent work. This book, as Friedman recognizes, is the key book, and more, I think, than any of the books on Hermetic and religious traditions by Ambelain, De Rougemont, and others, because they were merely books—none of their authors was a personal presence in H.D.'s life, and the only representative of such thought in H.D.'s life, Lord Hugh Dowding, failed (if not, as she felt, betrayed) her. Freud deserves H.D.'s tribute because he was the only man in her life who did not betray her. He is paid tribute again in *Helen in Egypt,* where as Theseus he is the synthesis of male and female, father and mother, the "mid-wife of the soul," who, as Friedman says, "watches over the wavering butterfly of Helen's newly released soul [Psyche]." Freud gave H.D. the unconscious for muse.

Perhaps Freud is also central because, as H.D. saw, he represents both traditions she herself united. Friedman does not make enough of this because her *schema*—her book is divided by these traditions—does not permit her to. Freud figures primarily as the scientist and materialist to be opposed by the artist and idealist. Yet when she turns to the Hermetic tradition she mentions David Bakan's *Sigmund Freud and the Jewish Mystical Tradition,* which corrects this simplistic view and grounds psychoanalysis itself in kabbalistic hermeneutics *and* opposition to rabbinical authority. Like this Freud, H.D. is a rebel, another Moses, as Freud said she was. This is the Freud that H.D. herself put first by turning to the archaic statues on Freud's desk before turning to him. H.D. could become a Priestess of Delphi (the tripod is prominent in her work, in the William Morris table she used for seances, in the triadic structure of her epics) because the Freud who taught her to interpret dreams followed the Delphic command to "Know Thyself."

"I found the thread and followed it through the labyrinth." What H.D. says of her wartime involvement with spiritualism applies to Friedman's work and measures its achievement. She is a good guide, whose always useful work prepares for and culminates in the most brilliant critical foray: the representative anecdote, if you will, of H.D.'s transformation, told stage by stage in detailed accounts of "Helen" (1923), "Callypso Speaks" (1938), *Trilogy* (1946), and *Helen in Egypt* (1961). The progression here is from imagistic poem to epic, from a mute Helen to an angry Callypso to the mythmaking quester, set free by Freud, who, in *Trilogy* and *Helen in Egypt,* restores the good Great Goddess, creates a "woman's mythology" and a "new cultural tradition." "Helen" is nicely played off Poe's "To Helen" and might have been set off to still greater advantage by taking account of Crane's "For the Marriage of Faustus and Helen" and Pound's references to Helen in *The Cantos.* "Callypso Speaks" revises the Homeric epic to which so many modern masters were indebted. (What could Pound do, having a father named Homer, or for that matter, H.D., whose mother's name was Helen?) But isn't it a mistake to think that all men are Odysseus or that all women are betrayed to the extent H.D. felt she had been? But I see that I am already beginning to question—another measure of this book, of its provocation.

The questions I have involve two interconnected matters: Friedman's uncritical endorsement of H.D.'s ideas and the version of modernism that allows her to place H.D. so confidently among—and by the logic of patriarchal displacement, above—the modernist masters. I understand how a critic who fully enters a writer's work may give over critical distance for responsiveness. This is the admirative mode of which I myself am sometimes "guilty" and the reason I find exemplary the critical self-awareness of Michael Bernstein in *The Tale of the Tribe*—a book, incidentally, of use here because it rigorously defines the modern epic and provides a superb context for H.D.'s *dream of the tribe*. H.D.'s epic works are, after all, in kind like those of her fellow modern poets: they are epics of consciousness (that explore the unconscious) in which the heroic feats are intellectual and imaginative; they do not celebrate a culture, they try to "make it new." And her epic task, set as theirs were by war and the collapse of civilization, was not unique, or not as unique as Friedman would have it by casual, touchstone references to their work. Her references to such poems as *The Waste Land, The Cantos, The Bridge,* and *Paterson* are not exact enough nor informed by their complexity. Again, I understand a critic's *parti pris:* how in coming to H.D.'s defense one might even the score, say, with Pound, whose *pounding* H.D. suffered and whose loudness she noted in the character of George Lowndes in *Her*. Yet, *The Cantos* are not entirely a patriarchal poem, not if Leon Surette is right in noting the prominence in them of the Eleusinian mysteries, and not if one recalls that the Pound who wrote them wrote *The Spirit of Romance*. Is it likely that H.D. overlooked this book or failed to appreciate in it what she appreciated in Ambelain's study of Notre Dame and in the heterodox religions, in the Kabbalah, in the religion of courtly love? And was she unique in turning to such sources, in taking stock of the Great Subculture? It seems to me that one of the signal concerns of modernism, from Henry Adams, at least, has been the restoration of matrifocal values, and that H.D. shared this necessary cultural task with others. This is even more the case with postmodern poets, poets like Robert Duncan for whom H.D.'s *Trilogy* was an origin. What needs insisting on, then, is that the concern with the matrifocal is not an exclusively feminine one. And what must be resisted, as in Friedman's study, is the logic of exclusion by which the restoration of matrifocal values is made a female quest, denied the male who, it seems, may adore the Goddess but never understand her.

Another problematical aspect of Friedman's account of modernism is her defense of philosophical idealism. H.D. may have been a philosophical idealist: she believed in correspondences, in the primacy of the spirit, in a hidden order. She is not Oedipa Maas, and none of her epics addresses the perplexities of modern thought in the way *The Crying of Lot 49* does. Temporality and process are not conspicuous elements of her work. If modernism is, as Mina Loy said, a crisis in consciousness, H.D.'s modernism may be suspect. In any case, her philosophical idealism—the mode of thought Friedman champions as necessary now to all subject people—does not accord with the modernist revolt against formalism and, more important, does not accord with matrifocal values. Philosophical idealism is the preeminently patriarchal way of thought; it is the foundation of rationalism, which discredited mythology and mythmaking ways of thought. Plato, who rejected the poets, may be said to be the father of the logocentric, androcentric, hierarchical civilization whose discontents poets in our time have increasingly addressed and sought to ameliorate. This, more than anything else, defines their great common undertaking. They agree with Freud that the present crisis is a matter of life and death, but do not, like Freud, associate civilization and Eros. They know that civilization is not in "the service of Eros."

This reminds me of the fact that in other respects Friedman carries on the feminist deconstruction of Freudian thought. And this necessary work reminds me that intellectual history, the history of ideas, is in large measure a history of discarded ideas—and that, even with, perhaps especially with, current ideas, we should keep this in mind. Exclusionary modes of thought, thought that (needlessly) restores one reputation at the expense of others, are suspect and erode critical authority. So does the kind of neglect that leaves out of account a primary work of such importance to our understanding of the power of H.D.'s work and its central place in modernist and postmodernist traditions as Robert Duncan's *H.D. Book*—a book, moreover, that is exemplary in showing us how to think beyond (patriarchal) *schemas,* to engage in thought, and in its generosity generate being; in a word, to *think,* to be critics, in "the service of Eros."

PART V

Hart Crane

R. W. B. Lewis on Crane

Of all the major poets of our century, Hart Crane has perhaps been less well served by criticism than any other. Critics quickly recognized his remarkable talent in *White Buildings* (1926), but for the most part, did not respond favorably to his major work, *The Bridge* (1930). This personal epic was immediately given representative significance, and Crane was treated as a culture hero whose failure to countervail the course of history and the poetry that presented its meaning for his generation (*The Waste Land* is the chief example) was read as a warning to other poets of optimistic, nationalistic, or misdirected visionary tendency. According to his friend Allen Tate, Crane was "one of the great masters of the Romantic movement," but his "extreme solution of the Romantic problem . . . proved that it cannot be solved." Crane's poem stood at the end of the line; in point of testing the resources of individual consciousness, he was the last Romantic. (And as a cultural nationalist he was also at the end—*was* the end of the utopian Whitman tradition.) Tate noted but did not press the fact that Crane was uneducated; that was left to R. P. Blackmur, who looked to his reading and decided that he had "the wrong masters for his chosen fulfillment"—that he was an extreme case of the "predicament of immaturity." Both critics measured Crane against Eliot, against a sensibility at once "mature" and Christian, and their views, and others like them, settled the matter.

Even now, in devoting *The Poetry of Hart Crane: A Critical Study* to the important work of reassessing Crane's genius and restoring juster critical perspectives, R. W. B. Lewis does not directly challenge these critics. For they are, after all, worthy critics and to them we owe much for the critical endeavor that has now arrived at the point where Crane is better appreciated (as a religious poet) and not so much better as more happily placed (in the Romantic tradition). This book, however, is not a monument to Crane—I do not think that Crane is entirely well served by it. It is a monument, rather, to contemporary criticism: to its rich explorations of the Romantic tradition, its many useful analytical instruments, and its prepotent, often heavily religious, vocabulary (here, especially *visionary, apocalyptic, archetypal*). Mr. Lewis is a good critic, sensitive, intelligent, willing to give himself to the work. His reading of *The Bridge* as an ebb and flow of consciousness is the most helpful I know, and his view of Crane's life (not "tragic, wasted, and bedeviled") and respect for his fine intelligence are sane and salutary. Still, in his book, I am disturbed—because it impedes the work to be done—by the conspicuous methodology, the pedagogical insistence ("this moment is what classical poetic theory called *peri-pateia,* or turning about"), and the style, which, like the book, is too capacious and accommodating.

Mr. Lewis has written an interpretative, not a critical, study. He does not attempt to judge Crane's stature; he assumes it, and declares it. Crane, he claims, is "the religious poet par excellence in his generation." (Is Eliot of his generation?) He reads the poetry to support this claim, but the reader is left to make whatever critical measurements he can, against whatever visionary or religious poets he may know. It is good to have Crane placed in the English Romantic tradition, the "visionary company" led by Blake (the phrase is the title of Harold Bloom's book on the English Romantics, and was taken from Crane's "The Broken Tower," and now, by way of Bloom, provides the fundamental interpretative thread); and it is good to see Crane placed in the tradition of Emerson, Whitman, and Melville. But these placings, by adding the weight of association, more often serve the interpretative cause than the critical judgment.

The essential limitations of this book are to be found, I think, in Mr. Lewis' failure to read the poems as hard as he might have and in his unwillingness to follow his *methods* through. He speaks, at the start, of the "dialectical geography" of Crane's background but does not follow this phenomenological signal with a genuine study of the poet's imagination. His basic tool, very skillfully handled, is the staple (now old-fashioned) one of close reading; but he reads only so closely and just as selectively as he finds necessary for his argument. In the course of the book, he says, perhaps apprehensively, that "analysis of Crane's poetry ought to be exemplary rather than exhaustive"—a supposition to which one cannot assent, especially when the exemplary poems are themselves not exhaustively treated and some of the poems not treated are exemplary, and when what we need most is an exhaustive, thorough reading of Crane's work such as the size of this book afforded.

The close reading sometimes slides into biography, especially at key moments in the poet's creative life, and sometimes yields to cultural history. But Mr. Lewis is not speculative enough in these biographical excursions—does not, for example, consider the possible connection between Crane's homosexuality and his visionary art. Nor does he solidly place Crane in his milieu. Having said that Crane was "blessed with an archetypal imagination" (is it not the point of Northrop Frye's *Anatomy of Criticism* that all poets are?), Mr. Lewis, in a chapter on "Chaplinesque," supports this by relating a tradition of the clown that Crane himself only slightly knew. This is interesting but extraneous, and might better have been replaced by other matter, such as considerations of Crane's relations to the circle of writers connected with *The Seven Arts* (there is a recent study by Robert L. Perry of Crane's relation to Waldo Frank) and to writers like William Carlos Williams, some of whose essays on American history, later published in *In the American Grain,* appeared earlier in *Broom,* a periodical Crane knew (on this, there is a long essay by Joseph Slate).[1] Far more important, I think, than Crane's archetypal imagination is the fact that, like the fascination with Chaplin, the materials of his vision and the compulsion to vision were shared. Crane received the attention and criticism he did because his poetry represented the hope of an articulate group in his time. The announcement of Crane's "failure" was meant to be their defeat.

Mr. Lewis' argument depends upon his reading of a few poems, admittedly some of the best, such as "Chaplinesque," "For the Marriage of Faustus and Helen," "Voyages," *The Bridge,* and "The Broken Tower." In "Chaplinesque," for example, Crane shows us the sorry predicament of the poet in the modern world and also the transforming power of imagination and art with which he meets and overcomes it. In the final lines of the poem—

> but we have seen
> The moon in lonely alleys make
> A grail of laughter of an empty ash can,
> And through all sound of gaiety and quest
> Have heard a kitten in the wilderness

—Mr. Lewis first identifies the theme of the visionary poet, the poet of religious consciousness, who sees in the moonlight an example of his power to transfigure and redeem the fallen world. Yet one wonders—because of the intentional sentimentality and the way in which the kitten's cry in the actual wilderness questions the "laughter," "gaiety and quest," and also because Crane brilliantly appropriated poets to his own purposes and in these lines has E. A. Robinson in mind—whether he did not really understand and see *through* the moonlight radiance. (Mr. Lewis says that in *The Bridge*, "*la lune* really was, once more, *Notre Dame*, an object to be imitated, revered, and trusted.") The sunlit poems of *Key West* are often carefully seen and stark; one might say that they transfigure downwards and are more in keeping with Emerson's than with Mr. Lewis' understanding of the miracle to be seen in the common and low.

According to Mr. Lewis, Crane did not wish to transcend but to transfigure the actual world, and the tension in his life was not occasioned by a suspicion of visionary power but by the difficulty of summoning it. Yet in every poem in which the pitch of vision, the evocation of a sense of transcendent reality, is demanded by all that precedes it, Crane is forced and strained—at the close, for example, of both long poems, "Faustus and Helen" and *The Bridge*. He was, I agree, seeking to celebrate this world, but his difficulty (compounded by his guilt over homosexuality and his need for a saving purity and cool repose) lay in satisfying this personal need for transcendence and the equally strong claims of love and life. One sees this in "Voyages," especially when one places them, as I think they should be placed, between "At Melville's Tomb" and "Repose of Rivers." And one sees Crane shifting the balance of these claims in his last great poem, "The Broken Tower."

If Crane's visionary genius was released, as Mr. Lewis says, by an "anaesthetic revelation" in a dentist's chair (Crane describes this, but the phrase is Paul Benjamin Blood's, and Crane may have come on his account in William James' *The Varieties of Religious Experience*), then it is not unlikely, especially in light of the evidence of "The Broken Tower," that Crane's rewarding love affair with Peggy Baird, along with other restorations like that of relations with his father, might have lessened his need for visionary poetry and turned him to other kinds. "The Broken Tower" is perhaps the finest *Crane* poem, a supreme but valedictory specimen. In it the poet "lift[s] down the eye" in the act of love by which he repossesses the earth. Crane, one suspects, knew the direction in which his poetry should go, but the very mastery exhibited in this poem shows how difficult an apprenticeship to new poetic means would be, and his way back, from Mexico, led to New York, to the "smoked forking spires" on which, unhappily, he knew he might again be forced to turn.

Note

1. On scholarly grounds, I find objectionable Mr. Lewis' admission that he "gave up reading criticism about Crane several years ago."

Crane's Prosody

The modesty and good sense of this book, the just characterization, and the careful examination of Crane's versification, are gratifying. "A poet of almost major proportions" is all that Herbert Leibowitz claims for Crane—a poet who "measured the crisis of modernism with real distinction. . . ." His characterizations often probe deeply (deeper than the subsequent analysis), as in these remarks on "Voyages":

> There is little humor or relaxed play in his love poems: everything is intense because menaced by time, loss, and fear or knowledge of betrayal. The poems are sensual without being physical; sex is usually spiritualized, though Crane does not omit bodily or erotic descriptions. His gallantry in love is as great as Cummings', but he lacks Cummings' childlike celebration of sex. . . . His consciousness is almost always embattled; the stress is on the psychology of love, on the lovers' mixture of volition and coercion. He is ever warding off defeat even in the midst of pleasure. . . . The demand for some kind of absolute fulfillment is movingly presented, and when the anguished joy ebbs, he seeks comfort and permanence in the poem which is created along with the love and survives it.

In the most valuable chapters of *Hart Crane: An Introduction to the Poetry,* he describes and accounts for Crane's poetry with greater attention than ever before. Accompanied by readings of selected poems, he treats Crane's diction, imagery, syntax, verse forms, and metrics. These chapters are both introductory in the sense of leading the reader beyond the difficult surface of Crane's poetry—they are the necessary searchings of a critic—and sometimes conclusive, confirming, for example, Crane's poetic conservatism and the accomplished but not quite virtuoso achievement of his prosody.

In other ways, chiefly because of the design of the book, it is neither introductory nor conclusive. The book fails the usual purposes of introduction by being ill-proportioned; it is lacking in coverage and range. Too few poems are treated and some are treated too briefly: the early apprentice poems, for example, which on this account are considerably more important thematically than Mr. Leibowitz makes out; some, not all, of "Voyages," which he considers Crane's "highest achievement"; only the beginning and end of *The Bridge,* a poem he finds weak but the omission of which limits one's appreciation of Crane's larger forms and contributes to an interesting but perhaps unfair view of the influences that served him; and only a few of the poems in *Key West,* which he values highly. The biographical and cultural bearings of Crane's poetry—which, from brief comments, it is clear that Mr. Leibowitz knows—are also neglected. The book does not give a trajectory of Crane's life and career; it does not place him well enough. It begins by summarizing and taking issue with the criticism of Crane before presenting at firsthand the material for judgment, and it ends with a short excursion in prosody and an unsupported statement that here is a new beginning. Like the appendix (on Crane's views on poetry and the machine) this suggests that Mr. Leibowitz did not have the shape of his book clearly in mind.

The primary reason for this may be found, I think, in the curious fact that Mr. Leibowitz knows more about Crane than he tells us and limits his view of Crane's development to matters of style. He considers three periods: the apprentice period up to 1920, when Crane followed Swinburne, Wilde, Dowson, and Yeats, and wrote such *fin de siècle* poems as "In Shadow" and "Modern Craft"; the period from 1920 to early 1923, when he turned to Eliot, the Elizabethans and Jacobeans, and wrote "For the Marriage of Faustus and Helen," the poem in which he both assimilated Eliot's influence and broke from him, the "turning point" in Crane's career in respect to subject matter and style; and the period from 1923 to 1926, his most prolific years, a time of poetic flowering, when he wrote "Voyages" and "O Carib Isle!" This account is accurate enough but incomplete, and it is incomplete because, for all of his attentiveness to the poetry, Mr. Leibowitz did not attend to the larger situation of the poems, their symbolic action, and their thematic development. By what path, we wonder, did Crane get from *White Buildings* to "The Broken Tower"—especially when we are not provided the "span of consciousness" of *The Bridge*? Why is it that the poet, who in "Faustus and Helen" wishes to "Delve upward," wishes in "The Broken Tower" to "lift down"? What is the connection between the strained rhetoric of exaltation and transfiguration (Crane's best poems are about the failure of vision) and the stunning naturalism, the bleak satanic tropics, of *Key West*?

The most obvious and important conclusion one draws from Mr. Leibowitz's book is that the influence of Whitman on Crane is really negligible. Whitman did not influence the poetry, merely the poetic mission Crane attempted to fulfill in *The Bridge*. By omitting *The Bridge,* Mr. Leibowitz in effect denies what critics of Crane have always assumed—the Whitmanian allegiance and propensity, and their importance (see especially *Start with the Sun: Studies in the Whitman Tradition*). But he does this, I think, not so much to discount Whitman as to force us to consider Crane's merits as a poet on technical grounds. On the other hand, by stressing "Voyages" he raises to prominence the influence of Melville, an influence of such pervasiveness that one might call it kinship: Melville, orphan-voyager-symbolist, as cosmic a writer as Whitman but inhabiting a different cosmos—Melville is Crane's older brother.[1]

Some of the implications of this mute interpretation by stress and omission are of great importance. In stressing "Voyages," Mr. Leibowitz stresses the love poet, the poet of unity and praise, and brings us close to the heart of his suffering and creativity. By omitting *The Bridge,* he avoids Crane's attempt to enact in cultural terms a symbolic reconciliation of his private problems. For this poet of love, who found it so hard to love, who, like Melville, lacked basic trust, is an example of someone whose personal crisis is significant because it bears the weight of historical crisis. (Maybe this is an unstated reason for much of the praise and overpraise of *The Bridge.*) When Crane speaks in "Faustus and Helen" of "things / irreconcilable" and a "world dimensional" he is speaking for all the dualities that cultural critics like Santayana and Van Wyck Brooks had mentioned and for the reconciliation—for him, the transcendence—they demanded. Santayana called the dualities the "two mentalities," thereby indicating that the cultural problem was essentially psychological; Brooks exhibited its consequences in the case histories of writers—Crane's friend, Sherwood Anderson, even played them out. Lyrical-cultural poems like "Faustus and Helen" and *The Bridge* recognize the representative importance of the poet who, like Crane, personally tries to carry the cultural burden of reconciliation (*synthesis* is Crane's term). In these poems Crane addressed some crucial issues of his time and tried, as a poet, to be worthy of the kind of praise Brooks accorded Whitman.

But Crane lacked the very things that, in Whitman's case, homosexuality seems to have strengthened—projective sympathy, the gift of touch, and the ability to become genuinely coextensive with the universe. Whitman was able to celebrate the world because he was able to love and to touch it. Touchless for the most part, Crane reached for heaven and, unsuccessful, found a hellish earth; between such extremes there was little world for him to celebrate, only a world to transfigure. The energy of his poems—a terrible energy: can words do this work?—is directed toward purification, wholeness, transcendence; and it seems to me to have its ostensible source in Crane's homosexuality, or rather in his attitude toward it, his never wholly conquered puritan response to love.

Mr. Leibowitz mentions Crane's homosexuality and sees its relation to his visionary art: "In a peculiar way Crane was an idealist of the senses, and the fact of his homosexuality may have caused him to return so often to the word *white,* since it probably connoted a holy desire unvitiated by guilt or mortification." But he does not pursue this valuable insight. He is as reticent as other critics of Crane, even so reticent as to exclude from his treatment of imagery the obvious phallic meaning of towers. Towers are also, in Crane, symbols of what the imagination achieves: White Buildings, or the Royal Palm (uniting both meanings) that "Climb[s] up as by communings. . . ." "The Broken Tower" is about the failure of imagination, its visionary striving, but it also celebrates heterosexual love, a tower less aspiring, only a "slip / of pebbles," and the unsealed earth. It is a valedictory poem, preparing for a new beginning; and if Crane was unable to begin again it may have been because he could not dissociate poetry from spirituality and suffering. For him poetry was not in fact the mediating agency he thought it was so much as one of the terms to be mediated. An idealist of the senses might succumb to the "malady of the ideal."

Note

1. Why is it that so many critics of Crane, including Mr. Leibowitz, fail to cite the pioneer essay on Melville and Crane by Joseph Warren Beach?

An Inside Biography

We owe John Unterecker a substantial debt for the ten years he has spent in search of Hart Crane. He, too, has voyaged in *Voyager: A Life of Hart Crane*—voyaged back, into, and over a life. This has been arduous and selfless work, carried on with modesty and tact. One measure of this is the fact that we place him not among Crane's critics but among his friends. In gathering the materials of this book—the people, letters, places—he has himself become an insider. His book is an inside biography distinguished more by sympathy than by criticism. This accounts, I think, for the fullness of the record and for Mr. Unterecker's willingness to let so much of the record speak for itself as well as for the indeterminate sense of Crane his work produces. His book permits us to live awhile in the details of Crane's life and invites us to do what he himself seems reluctant to do—shape them into a definite portrait.

Whether this is a proper function of biography is a question biographers (or, perhaps, researchers in biography) ought to ponder. We shall consider it later, after we have answered another question: what difference does this book make in our understanding of Crane?

It makes a considerable difference, I think, the most appreciable being its rectification of the hitherto accepted view of Crane's relationships to his mother and father. Philip Horton, who in writing the first biography of Crane was helped by Mrs. Crane and in turn helped her to play out a devoted mother's part, favored Grace Hart Crane at the expense of Clarence A. Crane. We now learn that the balance is otherwise and from the unimpeachable evidence of their letters.

Mrs. Crane's relationship to her son reminds one of that of Pierre and Mrs. Glendinning at the beginning of Melville's *Pierre*. Hart, who sided with his mother against his father, was her companion and escort and, after her divorce, was necessary not only to her stability but to the life of travel and grand hotels, the glamorous, sexless gentility of which she, a handsome, always-indulged, neurotic woman, was a victim (in middle-age she still aspired to Hollywood). The fierce maternal possessiveness that drove Hart finally to desperate secretive flight is indicated by many things: by their correspondence (to a boy of eighteen, she wrote: "You and I will have to have some serious talks about our plans for the future. . . . I don't want you to be entirely unmindful that you have a duty to me. . . . I am optimistic about my future because it lies with you I *hope*. . . . My most devoted love is yours and you are always my dearest sweetheart"[1]); by their rituals of devotion ("Sunday specials," his letters to her, and her special delivery letters to him); by her illnesses and breakdowns, feigned and real, which summoned him to her; and, after Hart's escape, by her attempt to bring him back by withholding her signature from his inheritance. Hart Crane knew, as he says of the maternal sea in "Voyages I," that "the bottom of the sea is cruel," and he tried to flee his mother as early as 1918, having understood the necessity for doing so from attentive reading of Anderson's *Winesburg, Ohio* and Joyce's *A Portrait of the Artist as a Young Man*. By 1920, he had not only refused to follow his father into business, he had repudiated his mother ("satisfied, shallow, unemotional") and her religion (Christian Science).

If his father was less possessive, he was just as insistent as Grace Crane that Hart be a "success." Nothing is so dismaying in the upper-middle-class business culture of Hart's fairly stereotypical parents as the constant harping on success—it dogged Hart to the end. C. A., who in his letters to Grace before their divorce sounds like Sinclair Lewis' Lowell Schmaltz, was, as he later recognized, a man whose expression was limited to business. He was not unkind nor ungenerous so much as abrupt and business-like in his personal relationships. He had the kind of masculinity that Hart recalled with fearful admiration in "Van Winkle" when he characterized Captain John Smith in the phrase "all beard and certainty," and he offended Hart, who was easily offended, by dictating his letters and sending them on company stationery. He also had a sense of practical affairs and a breadwinner's sense of priorities; he was hostile not to poetry (the early families of the Western Reserve respected it) but to Hart's trying to pursue it before having secured a material base—and Hart foundered in trying to do both. Much that seems harsh and despicable in him is the result of relationships that were never untangled and clarified by divorce (Mrs. Crane and Hart lived with Mrs. Hart across the street from his paternal grandparents), relationships that were mediated mostly by Mrs. Crane and prejudiced by old hurts (Hart was once angry over his father's silence, only to learn later that he had just lost his second wife). C. A. was capable of considerable growth where Grace was not, and he became affectionate and understanding, while Grace, a righteous, injured, all-suffering mother, became more demanding and unyielding (and even after Hart's death: she gathered the evidence of his life but destroyed whatever compromised her). The reconciliation of father and son, shortly before C. A.'s death, and the inn C. A. built in Chagrin Falls as if in answer to Hart's pastoral dream of home, is one of the splendid moments in an often depressing story.[2]

Hart's mother and father are present in this book as in no other. Mr. Unterecker evokes them by means of countless details and, especially, by means of their own words. The correspondence to Hart that he provides is one of the most valuable things in the book; because of it we not only overhear a life but thickly people it. Among Mr. Unterecker's achievements are the portraits of Hart's grandmother, Elizabeth Beldon Hart, Mrs. Sally Simpson, Mrs. Addie Turner, Mrs. Bessie Meacham Crane—all surrogate mothers—and William Sommer—a surrogate father. Almost as good are those of Carl Schmitt and William Wright. Curiously, figures with whom we are familiar from other sources—I mention some of those prominent and important in Hart Crane's life: Waldo Frank, Gorham Munson, Allen Tate, Matthew Josephson, Malcolm and Peggy Cowley, Susan Jenkins, and William Slater Brown—have less presence; and some, like Sam Loveman and Emil Opffer (the lover of "Voyages"), have hardly any presence at all. Of the new people in the book the most vivid are Margaret Robson (one of Hart's protective spirits), Solomon Grunberg (a lay psychoanalyst), and Wilbur Underwood (whom we can now imagine from Hart's letters: the confidant, in particular of Hart's homosexual exploits, who at one time sent him D. H. Lawrence's *The Man Who Died*).

In many ways, Mr. Unterecker adds to the record or sets it straight. Such things as the Crane divorce, the contretemps with the Tates, and Hart's disordered life in Mexico are set down clearly, and the chronicle of events is filled out so that a closer correlation of the life and the poetry becomes possible. The account of Hart's reading is fuller, as is that of each stage of his development, and we now realize better the place that people like Mrs. William Vaughn Moody, Padraic and Mary Colum, Sherwood Anderson, even Elbert Hubbard had in his life. Without arguing the matter, the book, I think, confirms the sense we have of Crane's preference for the country rather than the city and makes us reconsider the extent to which he can be claimed as an urban poet. And of even greater importance, in view of the still common notion that Crane, lacking much formal education, was ill-prepared for the high tasks of poetry he set himself (his letters are enough to repudiate this), is the picture Mr. Unterecker gives us of Cleveland, Ohio, where Hart Crane had his most thorough and significant education—and where "Faustus and Helen" was written and *The Bridge* conceived.

Not only could "genius . . . walk in Cleveland," as Crane said in reference to Ernest Bloch, it could be nurtured there: at Richard Laukhuff's bookstore, where Hart discovered *The Pagan* and *Bruno's Weekly* and kept up with the little magazines; at the great city library, art museum, conservatory, and playhouse (with which his friend Richard Rychtarik was connected); and in a circle of artists that included William Lescaze, a Swiss-French architect who more than anyone introduced him to modernism ("I never found a more stimulating individual in N.Y."), Ernest Nelson, and William Sommer. Sommer, whom Hart celebrated in "Sunday Morning Apples," contributed, as did the painter Carl Schmitt, to his aesthetic education. (Mr. Unterecker relates Sommer's theory, but in a fragmentary way, as the chronology offers, and so never carries the discussion far enough. He also leaves the impression that Sommer's theory was determinative. He does not test this by a reading of the poems, nor does he, anywhere, present Crane's aesthetic as it may be derived from the poems.)

According to Paul Goodman, sixty-six people are required to form the minimal community of human relations in which a child may be healthily reared. Mr. Unterecker's book shows how many more people are needed to nurture and sustain a poet, and by showing this, it seems to me, it becomes a tribute to Hart's friends, to a literary generation, and a period. Though Mr. Unterecker does not point it up, his work helps us see the extent to which *The Bridge* is *the* poem of a generation—a summary expression of its anguish, despair, and hope, its discovery of history, of American "tradition," and of art. That it takes a large canvas to present Crane, and that he actually focuses it is a gauge of his centrality and importance.

The canvas, however, needn't be quite so large as Mr. Unterecker's nor executed in his way. It is needlessly large for several reasons. The prose is loose—the kind of narrative prose that books of such length now seem to require of their authors; colloquial prose, moreover, that eases us into a long story and, by its tone, establishes the narrator as an unassuming, trustworthy inside witness. Though adequate, such prose is often soft or fuzzy, and it may even lull the writer into the carelessness that employs such clichés as "hitting his stride," "difficulties brewing under the surface," "hard put," "pulling down" (for earning money), "in no time flat," and sentences such as this one: "In these early summer days, New York still held wonderful unexplored areas." It may also let him slip away from full explanation: "From Lawrence's *The Plumed Serpent,* which Crane was reading in March, he took more than eagle and serpent. . . ." And besides the superfluity of words, the length is increased by double-telling—Mr. Unterecker often tells us what the passages he quotes tell us.

The art of the book, like the explanation it gives of the most difficult aspects of Crane's life, is simple. The complex device of points of view that Mr. Unterecker tries out in the beginning is soon abandoned. Having no theme—Mr. Horton called his biography "The Life of an American Poet"—but only chronology to follow, Mr. Unterecker finds it hard to maintain momentum and begins again and again. He reminds us at the start and throughout the book of Hart's death, but this element of foreshadowing (and pathos) is not strong enough to shape the book. Neither is the motif, taken from Crane's "My Grandmother's Love Letters," of the poet's difficulty in entering and recapturing another's life that he uses to cover his own efforts.

Perhaps the theme of this biography is biography, its own making. One of the notable things about it is the presence of the researcher in it ("I asked Fredrica Crane, who lived with C. A. and Frances . . . , to tell me what she could of their marriage") and the concern he expresses for the work of research. The researcher, however, is only one aspect or voice of the author and for the most part merges with the narrator, the insider, who stands aside to let others speak. The author seldom intrudes; when he does it is to question evidence: "Maybe it did happen that way—though if Crane tossed out of windows everything that his acquaintances [and friends?] have him tossing, most of America, half of Europe, and all of Mexico would still be littered with far-flung typewriters, perfume bottles, dogs, radios, manuscripts, books, and former friends." Unfortunately, Mr. Unterecker's skepticism is wasted on small matters and, even here, functions to the same end as his inside witness and concern for research—it tends to "normalize" Crane, it tends to minimize such things as his alcoholism and homosexuality.

These are not adequately explained. (One wonders what Erik Erikson would do with the rich materials assembled in this book.) They are not explained by letting Mony Grunberg speak about them at the end, and, insofar as they can be, they are explained away. When I say that Mr. Unterecker's account is simple I also mean safe and genteel. Like Susan Jenkins Brown, in a recent collection of Crane's letters,[3] Mr. Unterecker tries to assure us that these profound problems, which often occur together as Mony Grunberg observed, are not to be taken as seriously as they have been. In recounting Crane's endless sprees, he remarks that he is not going "to perpetuate the false picture of Crane as a thoroughgoing alcoholic, a lush desperately fighting for the next bottle," and he tells us, with the certainty of an insider, that "he was never—even after his trip to Europe, when he was drinking heavily—what anyone would think of as a 'classic' alcoholic." Mrs. Brown speaks of "alcohol [not alcoholism] and homosexuality" as Crane's "two weaknesses" and seems to think that because, as she says, "he never completely gave up the struggle against [them]," they are not of great importance. As for his homosexuality, he was, she claims, an "unwilling" homosexual, merely "a man without a woman." Mr. Unterecker explains it in another way: he speaks of homosexuality as "sexual adventure" and accommodates it by telling us that Crane's friends accepted it as "normal for him." Then, alluding to the range of sexual activities of "normal" people recorded by Kinsey, he says that "Crane's record is unusual only because so much of it has become public property," and that, compared with the case histories in Kinsey, "Crane's affairs seem bland." If only, he adds, Crane had been "just a little more discreet" (but why wasn't he?); if only we would realize that "sex was not the only business of Crane's life. . . ."

In keeping with the drift of this explanation, Mr. Unterecker is discreet in his account of Crane's affair with Emil Opffer and anything but reticent in letting Peggy Cowley and Crane declare Crane's discovery of heterosexual love. He introduces the affair with Opffer by expatiating on Platonic love, by reporting Opffer's comment, "There was nothing dirty in it" (his only testimony in the book), and by stressing Crane's own spiritualization of it. We are left in doubt about the actual nature of the affair, its course, duration, and absolute importance to "Voyages" (among the highest of Crane's achievements, clearly springing from intense experience of love—homosexual love). Mrs. Brown is more informative about Opffer than Mr. Unterecker but also obfuscates this episode: "Many suppose that Emil was an 'inspiration' for Hart's 'voyages.' Hart did, indeed, 'romanticize' Emil, whose warmth and kindness moved Hart deeply since he needed them so much. Later on, finding that this warmth was a general, rather than a particular response, he went through a period of intense disappointment. . . ." So the occasion of "Voyages" goes unexplained. (What does Mr. Unterecker mean by the title of his book?) But the occasion of "The Broken Tower," another poem springing from intense experience of love, is explained, mostly by Peggy Cowley, whose account of this affair, never questioned by Mr. Unterecker, reduces the poem to an epithalamium.

I do not understand the need for such evasiveness, for the reluctance to bear down at just those points, such as Crane's suicide, where we seek and need forthright explanation. I see no benefit in enlarging the record by letting everybody speak, especially those like Katherine Anne Porter who speak nonsense ("His parasites let him commit suicide"). A bigger book is not necessarily a better book—Philip Horton's biography is a better *book*. Gathering materials is valuable when it gives us the subject, helps us collect our ideas about him, an end that might have been achieved equally well, or even better, by an old-fashioned life and letters, with minimal authorial but full editorial comment (Mr. Unterecker supplies new letters and corrected copies of old letters, but he does not give them in their entirety nor date them). But this is not the most serious fault.

This biography would have been better had Mr. Unterecker heeded Thoreau's observation that "poetry is a piece of very private history, which unostentatiously lets us into the secret of a man's life." For the life Thoreau has in mind is not necessarily the life in Mr. Unterecker's subtitle—that life might better be thought of as story. As always, Thoreau prompts one to attend to primary matters. Mr. Unterecker neglects Crane's poetry, his *life*. He presents very few of the poems and reads them unexceptionally or superficially. His work is of little help in understanding them, in appreciating their importance, or in determining their order of achievement. It may be argued that this is not the biographer's work, though understanding Crane's poetic world and Crane's way, as a poet, of being in the world seem to me to be the essential preparation for it. And I would even argue that in the case of a poet it is not enough to show how an individual's story intersects history. Pasternak says that "the poet gives his whole life such a voluntarily steep incline that it is impossible for it to exist in the vertical line of biography where we expect to meet it." But we may find it there, I think, if the biographer considers the poetry and adapts to his own work the methodological hint of Pasternak's *Doctor Zhivago,* where the novel gives us the story of a poet *and* concludes with the poetry in which his life was taken up, the very thing that for him made it worthwhile. The biographical fallacy is not in question here. We are seeking the clues that may lead us through the labyrinth of the poet's story. And something more: only by remembering the triumph of the poetry can we accept—I borrow from Edmund Wilson's comments on Byron and Shelly—the price the poet paid—"and that other people paid—not only in pain and grief, but in sordidness and raw distress."

Notes

1. Crane's awareness of the anomalousness of this relation seems to me to be expressed in the concluding lines of "Indiana" (*The Bridge*), where a mother addresses her departing son: "You, Larry, traveller— / stranger, / son, / —my friend—."

2. The photograph of father and son standing before the Canary Cottage is one of the many excellent illustrations in this book.

3. Susan Jenkins Brown, "Hart Crane; The End of Harvest," *Southern Review,* new ser., IV (1968), 945–1014.

A Personal Biography

A large part of *Robber Rocks,* the letters of Hart Crane to William Slater Brown and Susan Jenkins Brown, was published in the *Southern Review* ("The End of Harvest," October 1968), and "The Last Days of Hart Crane," the concluding memoir by Peggy Baird Cowley, appeared in *Venture* in 1961. To these have been added Crane's letters to Malcolm Cowley and a note by Cowley on the encouragement and help Crane provided in bringing his book of poems, *Blue Juniata,* to publication. Mrs. Brown has revised, amplified, and rearranged the commentary that accompanies the letters, some of which, familiar from Brom Weber's collection, are now given in full along with others hitherto unpublished. The result of her work is a personal biography of considerable value, an account by intimate friends of the poet's life, from the time of his arrival in New York City in 1923 until his death in 1932, that fills in our picture not only of Crane but of the literary milieu of the 1920s.

Robber Rocks, the old colonial farmhouse in Dutchess County, New York, that the Browns bought in 1925, rightly names the book because it establishes the primary geographical center of this period of Crane's life. Even earlier, Crane had lived with Brown and Edward Nagle (a painter) at Woodstock. Later, making what might be considered his only permanent home at Addie Turner's place near Patterson, New York, he shared fully the country life of a fairly extensive group of friends. This is the rural landscape and life Crane commemorated in the "Quaker Hill" section of *The Bridge.* But it is more than his personal landscape, one sustaining his profound pastoral sentiment. It belongs to the era, as the setting of what Cowley, who settled at Sherman, Connecticut, called (in *Exile's Return*) the "Connecticut Migration," an exodus of artists from the city, noted also by Edmund Wilson in *I Thought of Daisy,* to the promised land of a countryside long abandoned. For Crane, as for others, it was a refuge from the city upon which he depended for his meager livelihood and the more intense excitements of the "literary life." In the city he lived in the neighborhoods of Greenwich Village and Columbia Heights (in Brooklyn)—neighborhoods Mrs. Brown knows and remembers well, the first as a result of her work with the Provincetown Players and as an editor of pulp magazines, the second as a result of her intimacy with the Opffers (it was through her that Crane met Emil Opffer, the lover of "Voyages"). The personal center(s) of the book, accordingly, circumscribe a larger public world. Had Mrs. Brown provided an index, the number of familiar names that people it would be readily seen.

But Mrs. Brown, like many of her confreres of the 1920s, is not concerned with scholarly matters—except to belittle them. She spends a page correcting Hyatt Waggoner's belief that Crane misused the word *psychosis,* and makes her point (by being scholarly: checking the dictionary Crane used) at the expense of "the respected critic." This perhaps was added to replace the bias of a remark in the *Southern Review* version that was later amended: "He [Cowley] was misquoted [about Crane's use of "findrinny"] in a subsequent (1963) academic study of Hart Crane's life and works, in a manner that made the incident meaningless." We also note at the outset, where she explains her correction of the texts of the letters, the warning that "for those readers whose aims are other than readability, almost all of the original letters are available in major university libraries." For whom, one wonders, is the book, published by a university press, intended? I'd say scholars, or the likes of them, all those who will be pleased by the inclusion of things Mrs. Brown may have thought antiquarian: a parody of Cummings by Crane, a sample page of Crane's financial records, the details of the Quaker Hill region and of the popular songs of the time, the illustrations.

This essentially harmless bias is an inevitable part of the personal and vintage character of the book. So, I suppose, is the name-dropping and sometimes annoying self-reference ("Hart would be glad to know that the Brown grandson, Jason Slater Brown, exists"), and the long account of Mrs. Brown's divorce from Jimmie Light. For me, nothing characterizes Mrs. Brown so well as her remark that "Bill [Brown] and I came from the American educated middle class"; and as I read her commentary—and Peggy Baird's dramatic account of her experience with Hart Crane in Mexico—I am reminded of Maggie Motive, Richard Chase's representative of the 1920s in *The Democratic Vista.*

The book is personal: a tribute, certainly, to Crane's presence (the presence of absence, as Paul Goodman says) in the life of his friends—survivors who also have a stake in the record and who wish by their testimony to keep it straight. Of most concern to them, it seems, are Crane's homosexuality and alcoholism and an acceptable explanation of his suicide. The first, Mrs. Brown tries immediately to discount: Hart Crane (as Tate is reported saying) was "an extreme example of the unwilling homosexual" (the sentence that follows this in the *Southern Review* is omitted: "He was a man without a woman"); his affair with Emil Opffer is obfuscated, and another affair, with a sailor, is covered by reference to him as Crane's "unlettered occasional drinking companion." Yet Crane referred to Opffer as "Goldylocks"—a name more than "teasing" when one recalls Crane's maternal association with golden hair—and referred to himself in a drunken letter as "the fairy God Mother." And what is Mrs. Brown trying to suggest when she draws attention to what she thinks the "marked facial resemblance between Peggy Baird [with whom Crane had an affair in Mexico] and Grace Hart Crane [his mother]"? As for his alcoholism, it never, she claims, reached the advanced stage, what A.A. calls "low bottom," but nevertheless it seems to have accompanied severe deterioration. It is begging the issue, I think, to say that Crane's violent acts "were few; they occupied a short span of time; they did not add up to a way of life."

What she says about his suicide is sounder: that he couldn't cope with the chaos of the early Depression years, that he was in some sense a victim of this public crisis, which had closed out the financial security on which he heavily counted. Mrs. Brown understands how serious Crane's break with his mother was ("the California period was a catastrophe from which Hart never fully recovered") and by not emphasizing Philip Horton's view of Crane's mother stands with those, like John Unterecker, who acknowledge her faults. But many things are minimized: the immediate causes, the shame Crane felt for his bad behavior in Mexico and especially aboard the *Orizaba,* and the overwhelming anxiety he felt for his poetic future—that is, with what seemed to him to be failing creative power, his ability to continue to exist as a poet, or to exist at all, since poetry was his only way of being in the world. He was not, as Mrs. Brown suggests ("I saw no evidence that he was unduly disturbed"), able to take in stride the critical response to *The Bridge,* and perhaps for the reason, not mentioned, that many of his closest friends did not have faith in his "vision." One need only read Allen Tate's foreword to *White Buildings,* which anticipates all his later criticism of Crane's romanticism, to see an early source of doubt—and a better reason than petty quarrels over household matters for his leaving the Tates in Patterson and going to the Isle of Pines, where so much of *The Bridge* was so suddenly written.

Though this kind of biography is attractive it is also curious. Crane is more immediately alive in the past that is the present of the book than the living who comment on him; his letters belong to the always-present, while their commentary, pointing back, remembering, belongs to the past. As a model for scholarship the format of letter-and-comments is excellent—excellent only to the extent that it is disinterested. The temptations involved in reviewing one's past, even with the intent of serving a friend, are too great. One not only plays his part in an old relationship but inevitably plays his part now (a different part) as a living character who preempts what we have imagined. So this is Sue Jenkins! So this is Malcolm Cowley! Not quite the people Crane depicts or we imagine from his letters. Perhaps the other half of the correspondence, if it exists, should have been permitted to speak. As it is, the book must be discounted—read carefully as a document about Hart Crane's friends who, in devoting themselves to him, are doing what the living always do, mediating the past. Mrs. Brown is absolutely right when she says that "Hart's letters are far better witnesses to his life than the best-intentioned of his friends," a statement to which in the earlier version she graciously added, "including this one."

Family Letters

Readers of this collection (*Letters of Hart Crane and His Family,* edited by Thomas S. W. Lewis) will probably have read the Crane letters in both Brom Weber's collection and in Susan Jenkins Brown's *Robber Rocks;* some may have become familiar with some of them in John Unterecker's *Voyager: A Life of Hart Crane.* Yet having them in this form, with the minimal, careful editing Mr. Lewis provides, has its value.

First of all, the letters in this collection are fuller and provide a center or focus in Crane's life that is absent in other collections. These are family letters, understandably not often at those peaks one finds in Crane's letters to writers and friends, and told in them is how much Crane was concerned with his family. Even more, these letters have what other collections of letters do not, the dramatic power of dialogue. Here are his mother's, grandmother's, and father's letters, which make them living presences. One may complain that many of the letters, and the recurrence of matters of domestic life and economy (always economy: money), are tedious; but life is tedious, too, and the letters clearly offer us a life, yes, a whole upper-middle-class way of life that is fascinating. Such tedious places may be the price the reader has to pay for the dramatic moments: how powerful the last letter of Hart's mother signed "Mother"! One of the valuable things given us by these letters is the warm and intimate relation of Hart and his grandmother. The way in which his mother tried to keep up with and understand his poetry is also significant. And all portraiture is fine, all the little details of social and personal history, such things as the fact that Mrs. Crane called her car "Diana" and consulted a psychoanalyst about her "vocation."

The letters do not explain Crane's genius, but they help us understand the background of his work by evoking the pressures that he felt—and with the intensity with which he felt everything—in the persistent demands of his not-too-unusual family situation. Unterecker's book evokes this, too, but here, in Lewis' collection of the letters, we face it directly, without the biographer's intervention. We live for awhile in Crane's life, not in the life of his poetry, but in the life that in some way, certainly, relates to it.

Crane and Winters

The heart of the matter? Hart's letters to Yvor Winters, forty-four of them, forty-three hitherto unpublished; letters of 1926–1930, the crucial years of seeing *White Buildings* published and of completing *The Bridge;* letters kept by Winters, contrary to his disposition to destroy correspondence. No letters of Winters to Crane, and should any turn up not to be published, according to Winters' will, until 1993. What then of "Their Literary Correspondence?" The subtitle of Thomas Parkinson's *Hart Crane and Yvor Winters* speaks for his own contribution: he has had to learn, with the help of Janet Lewis Winters and Allen Tate, to speak for Winters, to fill out what his letters would probably tell us of a correspondence that was almost exclusively literary, devoted to trying out each other's poems, arguing poetic theory and practice, noting reading, and telling the weather of the literary situation. Tate, one of the most important presences in Crane's life and, like Crane, known to Winters through literary correspondence, is a presence in this book, unnamed in the title but very much there, an increasingly important literary figure whose allegiance to Eliot enabled Winters and Crane to define their initial accord over Whitman and their subsequent divergence. Three young poets then (two of them also on the way to becoming formidable critics): a chapter of what Van Wyck Brooks called "the literary life," which then, as now, depended so much on letters! And how salutary to be reminded in reading this book of how much the generosity of poets nourishes their work—their generativity—and how vulnerable the creative spirit is when generosity fails.

I am very grateful for these letters. They confirm the "poetic spirit . . . and critical intelligence" that we come to expect from reading the three volumes of letters already in print—spirit and intelligence that Parkinson believes has been too little noted. They do not significantly alter our understanding of Crane's life and work; they fill in. They are especially valuable for Crane's comments on *The Bridge,* so much of which, installment by installment, he sent to Winters for scrutiny; for Crane's plan for a "Carib suite," under the title *The Hurricane* (a small volume that even now might be done by hand press); for a better sense of his response to William Carlos Williams (a favorite of Winters); and for his sharp assessment of contemporaries ("Cowley has a rather slow, laborious mind that simply cannot turn out a shoddy sentence"; MacLeish "is really illusive [elusive?]—perhaps not genuinely anything—as he has displayed himself in several successive postures . . .").

And I am grateful for Parkinson's biographical study of Winters, whose early life, education, literary and philosophical concerns we must know in order to appreciate fully his part in the correspondence—his part, as Parkinson stages it, in a trial of poets. The early Winters who wrote free verse and endorsed Whitman is not the Winters we have come to know, the Winters whose critical views took shape in 1928 and account for his altered opinion—his disparagement—of *The Bridge.* To explain this trajectory of opinion has been Parkinson's heaviest task, and he has done it with so much sympathy that "In Defense of Winters" would serve well for a subtitle.

I have no objection to what is clearly his preference for Winters, only to judgments that I find as gratuitous as they are unfounded in a close reading of the poems. It may be that Winters' "main concern was with fully realized experience rather than any system." But how is it then that he failed to appreciate *The Bridge,* which Crane defended on just such grounds? Parkinson's general impression of Crane's poems, moreover, is much too wide of the mark. He says that "the poems communicate the sense of an ongoing poetic life rather than an enterprise, and the appeal is to an antecedent experience rather than one contained and finished." Is this in fact the case? And does he think that Winters' strictures about *The Bridge* are justified by what he himself says about critics (unnamed) who find the poem coherent—that the work "gets assimilated into and transmuted by the sensibility of the critic, which is taken to be the sensibility of Crane himself"?

I find the evidence of peevishness curious. I wonder over the sense of extremity that prompts Parkinson to explain the legal matters involved in publishing letters and, with our common ignorance of this in mind, say that "unfortunately, graduate school training in English is not all it could be." And more seriously, I wonder at his need to defend the New Criticism by reminding us of what is certainly known—that before it became an "Old Orthodoxy" (this deeply troubles him), the New Criticism *was* new, a powerful critical encounter with an eroding civilization. Who denies this? What may be denied is what I feel he would have us believe: that because such criticism was once "new and exciting" its views are acceptable. He says disparagingly, that "it is one thing to take Crane seriously in the 1970s, and quite another to have had the wit and perception [as Winters, Tate, Cowley, and others had] to have taken him seriously in 1927." Yes. But in the 1970s, where we unavoidably are, one takes Crane seriously by assessing what criticism in the intervening years has done to and for his work.

PART VI

Charles Olson

Maximus: *Volume 3* *or Books VII and After*

VII. I'd rather designate the recently published and last installment of *The Maximus Poems* (New York: Grossman, 1975) in this way. There are three volumes of poems, and George Butterick, one of the editors of this volume and editor of *Olson: The Journal of the Charles Olson Archives*, has already, here and in the journal, fixed on Volume 3. But readers of Olson's work know there are seven installments, that *The Maximus Poems* appeared first, in an installment of ten poems, in 1953, that twelve more poems appeared in 1956—that the poems appeared in stages, were consolidated in 1960, and then continued, as *Maximus Poems IV, V, VI* (1968) indicates, by increments that probably have for Olson as much formal occasion as the various sections of *The Cantos*. To those who have made the journey to (of-and-in) place of I–III and IV, V, VI—who have lived long in these poems and awaited the next installment—3 is VII, and that's what I'll call it.

The immediate critical task that this concluding if not conclusive book presents is twofold: to distinguish it from the antecedent poems, to note similarity and difference, continuity and development; and to place it in terms of Charles Olson's lifelong project. So I'll begin with I–III.

I–III. Olson wrote the first Maximus poem ("I, Maximus of Gloucester, to You") to Vincent Ferrini in 1950, and the last poems of III in the spring and early summer of 1959. The poems belong to the most remarkable decade of Olson's life—when he emerged as a poet, took his trip to the Yucatan, and assumed the rectorship of Black Mountain College—and their publication in one volume in 1960, during which *The Distances* also appeared, established his credentials. The poems, in fact, concern and resolve the problem Olson faced in the 1940s, when, disgusted with Truman's politics and dismayed by the atom bomb, he turned to poetry as a vocation. Such early position poems as "The K," "La Préface," and "The Kingfishers" declare the need for radical change, for getting underway and finding a purchase in the world. The poems also conspicuously respect place, and one may say of Olson what he said of Apollonius—that now he was moved by "the stubborn sense, with no false arrogation, that he and Tyana [Gloucester] were bound together and that the binding was an image of health in the world." Increasingly, in each installment of these poems, Olson digs in, inhabits Gloucester by giving it a historical context, and the history that most involves him is the history of discovery and founding, of *origins*. The imaginative task to recover "nakedness," to see both past and present freshly, to stand, as Emerson said, in an original relation to the universe, is a matter of cultural and personal health. For Gloucester is both historical and personal ground, a place first explored by Olson's father, not natal ground yet, because of childhood summer residence there, Olson's ground. Accordingly, the poems recover his story (history) and, as Robert Creeley noted, are a record of his attentions.

Nakedness, attention, self-action. These suggest the new kind of heroism Olson wishes to achieve and exemplify. In the Keatsian terms he employs, he would be a man of achievement, not a man of power; he would live at risk in the open, in the "field," and follow the way of "negative capability"; thus he would overcome the estrangement from the familiar world for which Heraclitus is his spokesman ("man is estranged from that with which he is most familiar"). He would be exemplary, like his model, Maximus, a teacher, like Apollonius, too (he said that the poet was the only true pedagogue left). And he would *use* history—not be used, confined by its linearity, its determinism—to open possibility, to descry the nation ("having descried the nation," he says in VII), or at least make a polis, recover a center, enact the first will, demonstrate in the making of the poem what can be done, what he could do to that end.

These poems build toward a representative event in human history, in the history of westward migration: the successful planting of a place. They treat the discovery of America and Cape Ann, the difficulties and heroism of founding (the center is Stage Fort, the time, 1623–27), and the refounding, in 1642, when Gloucester was made to stick. Olson's activity is also a discovery and founding, involving periplus and mapping and the planting of the oar. Here he both enters and creates his "field." By the end of these poems he is considerably at home in Gloucester.

Finally, these poems, in part and whole, are formally tidy. Many, for example, are carefully made ideograms, and some, like those of the last installment, are composed of couplets, tercets, quatrains, and "fivers." The closure is satisfactory, even as it keeps open the further development of the poem. More than the installments to come, it is a *long poem,* if by this one means a poem whose parts sustain high poetic energy and whose organization is sufficiently tight. Certainly some of the pleasure of these poems resides in this—in the fact that for all of its openness and lack of track it is "woven," as Olson said, the threads all visible enough.

IV, V, VI. Much continues in these installments of 1959–64: place, historical concerns (factual, genealogical, proprietary, economical, etc.). But the form—kinds of entries and their articulation—loosens. Letters, Olson's notable form, give way to daybook or journal, perhaps because Olson is now well underway, better placed, fully caught up in his activity, both poetical and historiographical. The format of the book is larger, the poems framed by wide margins of empty space, and the installments are unpaginated and include working notes and blank pages. The long poem, clearly, has become a *serial* poem, perhaps because Olson has entered a new decade in our culture and is no longer moved by the necessity to be adversary or to compete with Pound and Williams. Certain themes of the previous volume drop away—*pejorocracy, mu-sick*—and with them the Poundian mode of revulsion, the didacticism, the heavily melodramatic moralism.

Even though history remains a term of articulation, the poems now find their expression in other terms hitherto submerged—terms from myth, geology, and geography. Having begun by giving Gloucester a historical context, Olson now gives it a context of myth. This development may be noted as a shift from Herodotus ("I would be an historian as Herodotus was, looking / for oneself," Olson says in III) to Hesiod ("the gospel acc. to Hesiod," he told Joyce Benson, in reference to new work in VII and also to the "big crash-pole of a poem all Hesiod" in VI). Or it may be said to involve a union of Olson's interests in Whitehead and Jung, in cosmology and individuation, in myth and dream. In the first of the poems on Dogtown with which he opens these installments, he enters "this / park of eternal / events"; as Richard Wilhelm says in *The Secret of the Golden Flower,* a text for which Jung provided a commentary, "man participates by nature in all cosmic events," psyche and cosmos are one.

These new terms indicate new depths in Olson's knowing-and-inhabiting place. The events told in myth are "eternal," ever-present. As Olson explains in *Causal Mythology,* myth holds for him "more of a poet's experience than any meaning the word 'mysticism' holds." And what some of these poems enact for us is what myth offered Olson—"the activeness, the possible activeness and personalness of experiencing it [earth] as such." He told Charles Doria that "one wants phenomenology in place, in order that event may rearise," and by recognizing the ever-present myths in Gloucester, this is what, in the most brilliant poems, he provides. Also in behalf of the applicability of myth to his place, Olson traces its westward migration. The concluding notation of V—"Old Norse/Algonquin"—is the briefest indication of this. *Theogony* and *Edda* interfuse in his work and, in VII, Norse myth becomes prominent.

The myths with which Olson identifies express the deepest psychological necessities of his work. Two are especially important here. The first is the myth of Ullikummi, a Hittite-Hurrian myth of the diorite stone, which anticipates Hesiod's account of Typhon's battle with Zeus. These myths speak for the rebellious son, for the resistance to authority that enables Olson to identify with his father even while expressing his resistance to him and taking a generally resistant stance (resi*stance*) to what he considers a pressing, suffocating environment. (Olson assimilates the cosmogonal elements of the *Theogony* but subverts Hesiod's celebration of Zeus.) The second myth, again cosmogonal, is that of the Memphite Theology, which he employs in the Dogtown poems, especially in "The Cow of Dogtown" and the superb poem "Gravelly Hill" ("sitting there," he says, "like / the Memphite lord of / all Creation"). The Memphite Theology not only accords with Olson's geological account of the emergence of Dogtown ("this / terminal moraine: // the rocks the glacier tossed"), but recalls the references to Geb and Nut in "In Cold Hell, in Thicket." In this important early poem—it supplied the title of Olson's first collection of poems—he explores his profound anxiety and, to assuage it, proposes to "trace and arch again / the necessary goddess." Now, notably in the poems on Dogtown, he realizes this part of his project—achieves cosmicity (an indispensable Bachelardian term), and knows a sustaining, mothering earth. Resistance has opened a space, and now, as he so desperately feared there might not be in the "smother" he speaks of in "The Story of an Olson, and Bad Thing," there is air to breathe. He says in "The Cow of Dogtown":

> Nut is over you
>
> . . . .
>
> she leans

from toe to tip of hands
over the earth,
making the Cow-sign
with the earth

(she is the goddess
of earth and heaven and sea)

one could live in the night
because she has to do with it,
encompasses it
in the day on Dogtown the day
is as close as the sky

her air
is as her light
as close
one is not removed even in passing through

the air, moving around, moving from one place
to another, going even across the same field

Nut is in the world

And more: the central symbolic action of these poems is making love to earth, a living earth, 125,000,000 years alive; and when "Okeanos rages . . . to get love loose" (in "Maximus, at the Harbor"), we are in a process world where creation is ceaseless, where we recognize, as Whitman did, the "Urge and urge and urge, / Always the procreant urge of the world."

The geographical center of these installments is Dogtown and, to a lesser degree, the coast, both complementing the treatment of history in the flourishing years of the mid-seventeenth to mid-eighteenth centuries. There are three distinct books, V, for example, having the integrity of its concern with Phoenicia; the overall form, like that of I–III, is complete, though circular. In VI, Olson returns to the harbor, the original center of all these poems, and seems to close the poem in the very act of departing from his cherished place: "I set out now / in a box upon the sea."

VII. The poems of this volume, which is undivided and longer than either of the preceding volumes, were composed during the period from the spring of 1963 to November 1969. (Olson's wife, Betty, was killed in 1964; Olson died in January 1970.) In form and themes this volume is closer to IV, V, VI than to I–III, though the earliest installments may be said to be present in the resumption of the original cultural intent to refound or renew America. Were it not for the last entry (the poems were arranged by Charles Boer and George Butterick), VII would be framed by Olson's wish to "write a Republic"—no longer to immediately change Gloucester, the "root city," but at least envisage it in a poem—and thereby begin "the initiation / of another kind of nation." And with this further difference from I–III: now his awareness of origins is not only historical but mythical.

Olson continues because *The Maximus Poems* are, as Zukofsky would say, the one poem a man writes all of his life, that he both lives for and with. The poems, as Olson said of *The Cantos*, are "a walker" ("something"—I quote Creeley—"you could take a walk with daily, and have as experience of daily possibility"). Olson is very much a walker who comes, as he says, "from the last walking period of man." And a talker. As he said of Apollonius (and proved in *Reading at Berkeley*), he "talked to live." Olson's poems follow the directives of "Projective Verse," are in the oral mode. Breath-phrasing determines the line, and although some of the poems do not seem to scan in this way, Olson successfully follows their scoring when he reads them on Folkways Records (FL 9738). Movement of thought creates their shape. Sometimes the movement is simple, direct, lyrical—some poems are "songs." More often, since their work is meditation, the poems are complex and have the many-dimensionality of, say, a Kerouac sentence. Where Creeley's poems, following these directives, are small, Olson's, in keeping with his energy and expansiveness, have "size." In this the poems are similar to the remarkable letters in *Letters for Origin* and *Mayan Letters*. These characteristics of his work may be sampled in the poems and fragments of poems cited below.

Olson also continues because what he thought he had finished in VI ("*The River Map* and we're done") had not been finished; he had not completely charted his place, the "mappemunde" of self-and-world. In fact, the next-to-last poem on the river prefigures and projects VII, where Olson now explores the river and parts of Gloucester hitherto unnoticed, chiefly West Gloucester—west having its immemorial association with death. (Ferrini, commenting on the last lonely years of Olson's life, said that "he had that hunch about time he knew so well.")

Restatement of the poem's cultural project provides a way of beginning again, only further on, "in gloom on Watch-House Point." This restatement also recalls Pound, the master to whom Olson is again responding, for Olson's desire "to build out of sound the wall / of a city" echoes Pound's "To build the city of Dioce" in *The Cantos* (LXXIV); Pound is also involved here in that his poetics of action, enunciated by Olson in "ABCs," is present. Where Olson goes beyond Pound is in the cosmic reach of his attention, for he would attend "the world (over the / *marshes* to the outer limits where minutiae / hold & swim in the electro-magnetic / strain"—reach which also takes him beyond Williams and links him with Whitman.

Olson's immediate self-characterization, his nosiness, is conspicuously Williamsian:

> Said Mrs. Tarantino,
> occupying the yellow house
> on fort constructed like
> a blockhouse house said
> You have a long nose, meaning
> you stick it into every other person's
> business, do you not? And I couldn't
> say anything
> but that I
> do

It is also associated with maritime discovery ("like Gomez / pushing / his nose into everything westward") and brings the reward of intimate knowledge of place, but with a deeper awareness than in Williams of all that is still present:

> I told the woman
> about the spring
> on the other side of Freshwater
> Cove which lies
> right on the edge of the
> marsh and is flooded
> each high tide by
> the Ocean which it then
> expells it runs so fast itself
> from its sources and to drink it
> the moment the tide has pulled off even one little bit
> is a water untasteable elsewhere.

I showed her the trees
under which it sits
from where we were standing
on the Dolliver Neck side
with the tide all out

Olson is indeed a "tireless Intichiuma" going over the ground. And over historical ground, old and new. We hear again of Dogtown and Stage Fort, of John Watts, Osmund Dutch, and Homer Barrett, of fishing, of Winthrop and, especially, of William Stevens, the first Maximus, who is now extolled and, in his rebelliousness, joined with Olson's father. Local history is extended: to the French attacks on the "frontier" at Cape Ann, to the Norse migrations, to the "new coast types" like Osmund Dutch, John Gallop, and Abraham Robinson, with whom, in his loneliness, Olson now feels close and, in "Maximus, in Gloucester Sunday, LXV," inscribes his name. With deepening wonder and sense of environing place, he explores new areas, chiefly, as noted, the tidal river and West Gloucester. At the Polls (or Poles), another height, near the river, comparable geologically and mythically to Dogtown, he idles "overlooking / creation," finding out "there is no doorstep / equal to the heart / of God," that he is "on the throne [of creation] // of the diorite, and the air alone / is what I set in // among the edges / of the plagioclase." And in one of the outstanding poems, and one of the longest (pp. 155–61), he enacts a nighttime ramble-meditation-writing-of-the-poem which tells of his solitary nocturnal way of life and what sustains it:

Excuse please   no boast
    only the glory of
            celebrating

the processes
    of Earth
            and man.

    And no one
to tell it to
    but you

for
Robert Hogg, Dan Rice, and
Jeremy Prynne

And the smell
of summer night
and new moan
hay

And the moon
now gone a quarter toward
last quarter comes
out

West Gloucester, where he also takes excursions, not only reminds him that the wealthiest persons in Gloucester at the end of the seventeenth century were farmers who raised grain but, in the poem "Cole's Island," becomes the place where he meets "Death" ("We did exchange some glance. That is the fullest possible / account I can give, of the encounter"). This encounter, narrated, quiet, of unusual equanimity, compares with "The Story of an Olson, and Bad Thing," an early poem in which Death is no sportsman but the "Enemie" who apprised him of "shortness of life" and forced him to turn time into space.

Other places, mentioned in earlier poems but now important enough to be minor motifs, are Shag Rock and Settlement Cove, with its "cromlechs" and "menhirs."

More than before, myth is present in Olson's world, his language, his way of seeing and experiencing:

To have the bright body of sex and love
back in the world—the moon
has her legs up,
in the sky of Egypt

* * *

I am the
Child, Jupiter
furens—Ocean's
Child; I am
Round Rock Shoal

I am the one from whom the Kouretes
bang their platters

* * *

I looked up
and saw
I was faced
to the left

Okeanos,
the wobbling
ring

* * *

Hector-body,
my Cow to the left my Cow to the right:
Goddess-

shield Ajax
or the Knossian
who is compared to Enyalios

crossed in Helladic to
Troy
now moves on east from
west of Albany

[Olson taught at the State University of New York, at Buffalo.]

got home again,
Wednesday
January 20th
1965

And there is more myth: the motif of the lotus growing upside down, an image, for Olson, of paradise, the tree of life, a finite world:

Imbued
with the light

the flower
grows down

the air
of heaven

* * *

There is solely
the Lotus
upside down. When the World is one again

with the Universal the Flower
will grow down, the Sun
will be stamped
on the leather
like a growing
Coin, the earth
will be the light, the air and the dust
of the air will be the perfume

Another motif, whose source eludes me—that of Bulgar and his four sons—seems to be related to NNW migration, perhaps to Stefansson's theory of movement toward the polar region. The Hindu myth of Ganesh and the Hindu vision of destruction-creation are new here, as is the Norse myth of Fenris and Tyr, Tyr being a god with whom Olson identifies as well as with whom he associates Enyalion (a new hero of these poems), Stevens, and his father.

Olson's myths are essentially cosmogonal. They concern creation, a living world whose life he also recognizes in the migration of continents. The cover of IV, V, VI depicts Gondwanaland, "Earth (and Ocean)," Olson notes, "before Earth started to come apart at the seams, some 125 million years awhile back. . . ." Now, in VII, he recalls that time, when Newfoundland was almost joined to Biscay and the North Atlantic was merely "ponds." And in a poem on his Portuguese neighbors, to which he brings both Greek and Norse accounts of creation, he tells his awareness of the mid-Mesozoic time, when Gloucester was Terceira and began its still-continuing drift westward. Yes, recognizing the eyes of the Guanches in those of his neighbors, he knows that "my City she too came from the / Islands." He sees evidence of a similar kind in a canoe which he identifies as a "Pleistocene / 'boat.'" And more than he had in the earlier books, he treats migration: in respect to the work of Eratosthenes ("Phoenician is a chorography carrying / Gloucester as / I go"), as a constant in history (for plants, animals, men, and gods seek suitable environments and new centers), and as a westward push of myths.

These considerations matter because, as Olson says in one of the last poems, "there has been / no break—there is now no break in the / future. . . ." The world is "continuous," which is why, he remarks, "I raise monuments / by this River and have sd it does take a mole to join Gloucester to / the Nation." Even as he looks out in the gloom of Watch-

House Point or notes the ecological destruction of our time—he is aware that his daughter may not "live in a world on an Earth like this one we / few American poets have / carved out of Nature and of God"—he places his faith in the actual, physical world. He concluded the NET film featuring him by saying that we need only love the earth, and that is his conclusion here: "Love the World—and stay inside it." A last poem says all he means by *typos, tropos, topos:*

   the blow is Creation
& the Twist   the Nasturtium
is any one of Ourselves
And the Place of it All?
   Mother   Earth   Alone

We do not doubt him when he says, "I'm going to hate to leave this Earthly Paradise." Desperately lonely, living a monkish life, the poems confirm his hunger for "every thing."

For all of Olson's celebration of Earth, this book is the book of the Father, where IV, V, VI was the book of the Mother. Its motif, expressed at the outset, refers to the cover-picture of *The Post Office,* Olson's reconciliatory memoir of his father[1]—a picture of Olson as an infant standing, protectively held by his father, in his father's mailbag:

The Return to the Mail-Bag, or,

         The Postal Union

   of the Son with the Father

What he asks in a prayer to Great Washing Rock—"renew one's faith in the fathers"—he achieves here. He early admits that he has been Fenris to his father's Tyr; and in the central portion of the book (pp. 101–34), where he works through a spiritual crisis of vocation and individuation in relation to the winter solstice and the renewal of spring (1965–66), he acknowledges:

   I have been an ability—a machine—up to
now, An act of "history", my own, and my father's,
together, a *queer* [Gloucester-sense] combination
of completing something both visionary—or illusions (projection?
                                                            literally

lantern-slides, on the sheet, in the front-room Worcester,
on the wall, and the lantern always getting too hot
and I burning my fingers—& burning my
nerves   as in fact John says or Vincent Ferrini they too
had to deal with their father's existence.   My own
was so loaded in his favor as in fact so patently
against my mother that I have been like his stained shingle
ever since   Or once   or forever   It doesn't matter   The Love I
learned

from my father has stood me in good stead
—home stead—I maintained this "strand" to
this very day. My father's   And now my own

In "*Golden Venetian Light From / Back of Agamenticus Height Falling / Like Zeus' dust All Over the River & Marsh . . .* ," he tells of his worship of the sun "at least once a day," at sunset. The golden Venetian light reminds us again that the book of the father is a book of light (and air).

Which brings us to Fitz Hugh Lane and Luminism, distinctive elements of VII.

Olson identifies with Lane (1804–65), a native Gloucester painter of its sea- and landscapes, the exemplar, in Barbara Novak's account of nineteenth-century American painting, of Luminism, an indigenous tradition related to Emersonian transcendentalism in its fidelity to things and recognition of their animating spirit. Olson turns to Lane because no artist, besides himself, was so devoted to Gloucester, so responsive to place, to geography, topography, climate, and saw so well what he saw (and what we may still see: "the sky, / of Gloucester / perfect bowl / of land and sea"). That his father, as he remarks, had painted these scenes is important, but Olson turns to Lane because in his own work he is now composing a "poetry of light":

low tide night is
just the same the bright white moon
light slashing harbor water as
differently in look & sound as
water noises coming up beside

this Ragged Arse Rock Earth
divine

upon such August low tide night
I celebrate what Fitz Hugh Lane
                                        too
                                        saw

What Lane saw was the "still handsome & efficacious / environment"—

The Island, the River, the shore,
the Stage Heads, the land, itself,
isolated, encased on three sides by
the sea and water
on the 4th side, Eastern Point an arm
such as Enyalion's to protect
the body from the onslaught of
too much and give Gloucester
occasion, give her Champlain's channel
in & out (as her river
refluxes), a body of land, hard on granite yet
arched by such skies favored by such sea and
sweetened in the air so briar-roses grow
right on her rock and at Brace's Cove kelp
redolents the air. . . .

Lane speaks for Olson's achievement in *The Maximus Poems*—that of having fully possessed place:

                Heaven is
                Mind (drawn to
Gloucester. . . .
. . . .
                In one place
—in the place where God rests—
the Earth glows, in the light
of Heaven

This wonderful poem is wonder-filled:

                I bend my ear, as,
if I were Amoghasiddi and
here on this plain where
like my mole [a star-nosed mole] I have
been knocked flat, attend,

to turn & turn within
the steady stream & collect which
within me ends as in her hall and I

hear all, the new moon new in all
the ancient sky

The confidence and ease with which Olson uses his terms is notable. Not since "Letter 12" of I–III has he been so open with himself, and, unlike the admissions of that early letter, able to live in difficulty without yielding to despair. Never before has he bestowed so much love. Besides, he has achieved "nakedness" ("And one, desire, / that the soul / be naked / at the end // of time"), not merely the freshness of perception of the discovery of the New World but the perception of earth as it was perceived at the beginning of time in the great cosmogonal myths. As he said of Apollonius of Tyana, whose life he made the fable of his own, he has "made his birthplace capable of verticality," has learned to dance in place, to avoid dispersion, so that, as he found in the last walk recorded in VII, a walk in "Man's field" (near Mansfield, Connecticut), he walks in "Tartarian-Erojan, Geaan-Ouranian / time. . . ." He has recovered origin, and doubly so since the myths he recognizes as his own treat the universe in terms of parents. Like Thoreau he has learned that "there is a truer account of [America: nature: place] in mythology than in any history of America," and the great reward of this lifetime endeavor is the realization he has in VII that "Physically, I am home."

This speaks for individuation; VII is markedly "spiritual," and Maximus has pretty much disappeared, taken up by Olson. But it also speaks for Olson's primary work as scholar-poet-archaeologist of morning: his repudiation of Humanism, the Western tradition served by Eliot and Pound. Humanism, he said, "is (homer) coming in, and (melville) going out," and his project, announced in *Call Me Ishmael,* is the radical and daring one of going "backward and outside" the inherited tradition, the "culture trap" of Western history, in order to repossess the familiar world. Even as scholarship, Olson's work to this end is significant, representative of major intellectual explorations in our time. (Knowledge of the going reality, he told Cid Corman, is what art and culture build on; and culture, he knew, was confidence.) But of greater importance is the poetic result of this work, the considerable extent to which Olson has realized this in his poems.

What the entire work enacts and Olson exemplifies is a new way of being, of standing in an actual world, in process: of entering a "field," accepting risk, attending (to self-and-world), locating, mapping, inhabiting space and thereby making it place. No other work of our time—not even *Paterson*—is so much of and in place. In seeking comparisons and measures of his achievement, I most readily turn back to *Walden* and, in spite of Olson's revulsion from romantic egoism, to Emerson and Whitman. His poetics advances theirs, and he is the "actual willful man" of his most Emersonian book, *The Special View of History,* where history is again prospective, an open possibility. Like Emerson he gives us a new man in a new universe: self-active man, a thing among things, in a universe in process. Like Whitman—whom he never praised as he did Melville but whom he called "our greatest voice because he gave us hope"—he gives us hope, thus fulfilling one of the great offices of literature.

Note

1. Published in 1975, it was written in 1948, one of the necessary acts of Olson's emergence. In an early autobiographical statement, Olson confessed himself "still, at 40, hugely engaged with my parents." He was hugely engaged with them all of his life.

Olson and Pound

The subtitle of *Charles Olson and Ezra Pound: An Encounter at St. Elizabeths*, edited by Catherine Seelye, is accurate. Olson's visits to Pound at St. Elizabeths, 4 January 1946 to 6 February 1948, were an encounter: they involved not only conflict but the profound response to another, moved by love, that necessitates change. Olson addresses encounter in "This" ("you / have been / asked"—which calls up Rilke's "You must change your life"). His visits to Pound changed his life, and fixed his allegiance to change.

When he went to St. Elizabeths to serve Pound, a poet he revered and always acknowledged as master, Olson was at a watershed of his life. He was thirty-five years old, between vocations. No longer a governmental official and not yet confirmed as a poet, he was casting about for direction, for a project with which to take hold. Those he mentions, such as the books on the West and on the human body, were not undertaken because, as much as anything, the work of his emergence was of another kind, the kind recorded here.

The work of emergence was begun in *Call Me Ishmael*, finished six months before he met Pound, and it was carried on in *The Post Office*, written early in 1948, about the time of his last visit to Pound. *The Post Office* (published in 1975) is a memoir of Olson's father, a postman, and its therapeutic work is accomplished only at the end when Olson tells of the cause of their estrangement. His emergence is an affair of fathers, of making peace with his own father (he implores his recognition in *Call Me Ishmael:* "O fahter, fahter / gone amoong // O eeys that loke // Loke, fahter: / your sone!"—and in the last volume of *Maximus*, just published, he is still seeking "The Return to the Mail-Bag, or, / The Postal Union / of the Son with the Father"); of rejecting others, Edward Dahlberg, his first mentor, and Pound; of finding others like Carl Sauer, the geographer, whom, significantly, he met in the interval between his visits to Pound and who gave direction to his subsequent work. Serving, then rejecting Pound—he entitled his farewell "GrandPa, GoodBye," and sent it to William Carlos Williams for approval!—is representative of a persistent emotional pattern, and perhaps the depth of Olson's relation to Pound is measured, like that of his relation to his own father, by his almost lifelong concern with it.

The materials that Catherine Seelye has collected and so helpfully edited and introduced in *Charles Olson and Ezra Pound* are part of the necessary therapeutic work of this period of Olson's life. Pound-the-Fascist may be said to have precipitated Olson-the-poet, though Olson, in any case, could not have gone the way he went without breaking with Pound—a way, we realize here as elsewhere in his work, that required the presence of Williams, whom, wisely, for some reason, he spared the inevitable trials of fatherhood (not that in less violent ways he did not reject him, as in his unfounded view that Williams "didn't know fr nothing abt what a city *is*"). Olson's earliest poem, "Lower Field—Enniscorthy," borrows images from Pound—from the first *Pisan Canto,* which Olson read in manuscript. Of more importance, the great position poems, "The Kingfishers" and "To Gerhardt . . . ," work through for progammatic ends Olson's repudiation of Pound. Other poems, less good, like "Issue, Mood" and "I, Mencius, Pupil of the Master . . . ," simply, sometimes unkindly, make fun of him. But even "The Song of Ullikummi," read by Olson before Pound at Spoleto in 1965 to honor him, perhaps unwittingly (and perhaps not) puts him down by parodying his method of translation, by choosing a myth beyond his scope, one, moreover, whose import of father-son is only alluded to in the title and whose burden, in the passage rendered, recalls Pound's suspect notion of the relation of clear thought and coition.

The biographical value of this book is indisputable not only for what it adds to our knowledge of Olson's obsessive concern with fathers and sons (see also *Reading at Berkeley,* and the recently published *Charles Olson in Connecticut,* by Charles Boer) but for the portrait it gives us of the young man, so much the same yet so different from the often self-indulgent older man recalled by Boer, and for that matter not quite the full-fledged Olson who comes at us in *Letters for Origin* and *Mayan Letters.* One misses his familiar, characteristic *push,* but one finds a man of great attentiveness, of sensitivity, care, and compassion, who believes in his ideas and worries over them. The reports of his visits to Pound—he calls them "Cantos"—inspire confidence because of his evident fidelity to their complex, difficult occasions, and his judgments of Pound win our respect (and often assent) because he earned them by doing what he thought should be done in a trial of Pound—consider, on the basis of Pound's work, how the poet became a spokesman of Fascism. For Olson, who believed that Pound's treason to the state was a crime of less importance than his treason to art—that "no man can attack a race and remain useful to anyone as an artist"—what needed to be fathomed was the fact he found incomprehensible: "That a poet should choose hate!" Olson's encounter with Pound is of value, then, and not merely for literary history, because it is so deeply engaged and of such ultimate importance to him (and to us, who since the 1940s, may have found less outrageous the association of art and hate). The encounter is also a trial of Olson, who wanted in his dealings with this "tragic Double of our day" to keep the "open man, the poet" in spite of his revulsion at the man who "throws his bowels in my face." He had already judged Pound's action before he met him and believed he should be confined, and the difficulty he had (almost immediately) in resolving to help him is obvious in his remarks: "Shall we talk a 100 Cantos and not answer the anti-semite who wrote them? Shall we learn from his line and not answer his lie?"

Olson was a New Deal democrat. His political work had been with minority and immigrant groups. He himself was the son of immigrants and identified with immigrants, with the Portuguese of Gloucester, for example. Pound's snobbism and elitism as much as his anti-Semitism offended him, were morally repugnant. He could not stomach (the right word in view of Pound's "vomit") Pound's WASP assurance of birth, class, and privilege; and he traced Pound's hunger for power and name and his concern for "civic responsibility" to the status revolution that had eroded WASP leadership. The touchstone of Pound's attitudes is a conversation Olson had with Miss Maple, an old Philadelphia lady who had known Pound all his life and had asked Olson if he were English: "I went on [he replied], my father was Swedish and my mother Irish, which makes me very American. She looks up at me, and says, 'Then you must have a sense of humor!'" This exchange prompted the following statement of Olson's grounds of disapproval:

> What's shallow about it [Pound's feeling for civic responsibility] is the deadness of it, the 18th century *lag* in it, the moan for the lost republican purity, the wish to return America to its condition of a

> small nation of farmers and city-state patricians, all Boston brahmin, and Philadelphia brick. Nothing wrong in that either, except what happens to political action now if it is so motivated. It turns out to be reactionary and fascist. For what are the positions it leads to? (1) an antagonism to immigration; (2) a hate for "foreign" elements; (3) a feeling of a Jewish conspiracy; (4) the old ways of "free enterprise"; (5) a Civil Liberties Union concept of the bill of rights; etc. In other words, a pitiful, sick and dangerous defense of all that *was*, which forever and anywhere and in all things, fears anything forward.

Olson was willing to forfeit neither present nor future to the past ("I'll live on into what's coming up"), and for him Pound was the exception to the proposition with which he began "The Kingfishers": "What does not change / is the will to change." Pound, he realized in the summing-up of "GrandPa GoodBye," had built his career on "remembering," and the best of his work captured a "mood of loss"; it was, he felt, "a structure of memories raised on a reed, nostalgia." Moreover, its roots were dry, as if he were lacking in "the amorous" and had failed to inhabit his experience. The result of all of this was the aestheticism of which Olson complained:

> You feel him imagining himself as the last rock of culture and civilization being swept over by a wave of barbarism and Jews (communism and commercialism), the saviour of more than the Constitution, the saviour of all that has been culture, the snob of the West. For he is the AESTHETE, as I had Yeats speak of him [in "This Is Yeats Speaking," reprinted here]. All—his pride in his memory, his sense of the internationale of writers, painters, musicians, and the aristocrats, his study of form as technique (no contours, no edges, intellectual concepts, but rounding, thrusting, as a splash of color, as Yeats described his aim in the Cantos, after Porteous disastrous painting) it is all a huge AESTHETICISM, ending in hate for Jews, Reds, change, the content and matter often of disaster, a loss of future, and in that a fatality as death-full as those for whom the atom bomb is Armageddon, not Apocalypse.

It remained only to say what Olson had had Yeats say for him: not that "behind his [Pound's] art lies a respect for authority and behind that respect lies a disrespect for democracy" (which was bad enough, a fact for Olson that also put in question the achievement of other great modernists) but that he was false, in the way most damning to an artist, "when he subordinated his critical intelligence to the objects of authority in others." For in doing this Pound betrayed art, yielded his responsibility as a writer to "his own sense of life, without regard to state, to system, to idea or to justice."

Dancing the Man

Robert Duncan says that "Maximus calld us to dance the Man," an exact statement by which I think he means that Olson, in Maximus and the unfolding movement of *The Maximus Poems,* proposes a new ontological possibility, or rather an old one that is new to us. The conjunction of Olson and Whitman in Duncan's poem "The Dance" confirms this; and the fact that this poem is a companion to "Often I Am Permitted to Return to a Meadow" indicates the centrality of dance in *The Opening of the Field,* a title to be read as the declaration of the work of a generation of poets. The open or field poetics of "Projective Verse"—so much a matter of physiology, stance, and self-originating movement—is also a poetics of dance. Olson spelled it out in "A Syllabary for a Dancer." And it may be that dance, with which Olson was familiar from youth, had for him the priority it had in human history—and was necessary now because the requisite of the will to change was the will to move, an idea he pushed at Black Mountain College, where dance was more than an attendant art.

Like his theatrical experience, Olson's critical and literary work in the drama was considerable. There is the fine essay on Shakespeare's late plays, which warrants the publication of the chapters on Shakespeare Olson wrote in 1954—following Melville in his appreciation and hoping perhaps for a similar Corinth. And there is evidence in the eleven plays collected in *The Fiery Hunt and Other Plays*—play, dance, dance-and-verse, opera—that Olson knew the various theaters of the classic Greeks, of Noh, of the masque, and of such exemplary contemporary companies as the Yiddish Art Theatre. None of this work—and not necessarily for lack of merit—has been performed. Yet all of it, as George Butterick says in an admirable introduction, is "notable for [Olson's] willingness to explore the formal possibilities of theater."

Olson was impatient with "straight theatre," which he felt was too much concerned with "contemporary realism." He wanted "enlargements and poets' treatment," a drama, Butterick explains, antedating Greek comedy and tragedy, emphatically given over to language and movement and to the single actor. This possibility, which Olson later recognized in Mayan glyphs, inspired Katherine Litz's *Glyph* and his own *Apollonius of Tyana*. From the start his predilection was for a minimal company: for the single actor who exemplified heroism, danced the Man ("the Figure of a most normal man is there," he notes at the close of *Wild Man Fragment*) and for the very few who were necessary to dance out his moral equations. Butterick says that Olson turned to drama because of impatience with narrative, but this impatience might well derive from his conspicuous didacticism and his inclination to see issues graphically and dynamically in a binary way. What interests him especially in Shakespeare's late plays is the opposition of innocence and sensuality.

Butterick's introduction is expert, and I will not rehearse its wealth of information, tempting as that is, but only remark how much he knows of what there is still to be learned of Olson—how much the kind of detail he presents here promises for the biography he will someday write. Since the reader will certainly turn to his introduction, it is only necessary to add to it my own response to these primary plays. I call them primary because what also makes them notable is their singular emphasis on dancing the Man and, in doing so, dancing out Olson's own developing fable. Anyone familiar with *Apollonius of Tyana* will have remarked Olson's didacticism and the extent to which the dance patently fables him. Now, reading these plays, he will find that this is not unusual but characteristic. Olson defined man, in Vedic fashion, as a "dancing thinker," but in respect to him we might modify this to "dancing pedagogue," bringing over the insistence on single intelligence and adding the insistence on the *work* to be done.

Except for *The Nineteenth of April*, the last unfinished play on Paul Revere written some time between 1960 and 1963, all of Olson's plays are occasional. Unless *Cabeza de Vaca* was written in 1947, the earliest is *The Fiery Hunt*, a dance-drama based on *Moby Dick*, commissioned by Erick Hawkins in 1948. Of the first group of six plays, all written between 1947(?) and 1953 and all concerned with Olson's emergence, three were written at Black Mountain College, prompted by the revival there of modern dance and the presence of Merce Cunningham and Katherine Litz. The remaining plays belong to the early 1960s, chiefly

1961, when Olson did three, perhaps four, for Leon Katz at Manhattanville College.

All of these plays are occasional also in being clearly the result of Olson's occasions. For example, *The Fiery Hunt,* a remarkable finished work, enacts the problem of father(s) and son which was such a critical matter in Olson's career. Apart from the ways in which Olson transforms Melville's novel—uses it for scenario—the interest resides in his conception of Ahab as wholly evil, comparable to Huitzilopochtli, and as father ("It is not Ishmael's young, still questioning plunge into the waters of event, the son entering his majority, but the resignation of a father . . ."), and his conception of Ishmael as wiser than Melville's Ishmael, worthy of being his own spokesman ("Call Me Ishmael," indeed!). *Troilus* treats Olson's acute sense of the desolation of cities—of civilization—in World War II and the desolation of love ("Love is a fallen thing"—the male conviction, he says, even admitted by women, yet even so *the* value to be restored). And *Cabeza de Vaca,* an idea for an opera, merges several elements of Olson's early thought: the concern—anticipating our present concern by a generation—with the Red, the Black, and the White in the settlement of the West, of America (the materials of this abandoned or otherwise assimilated project may be found in *Olson: The Journal of the Charles Olson Archives,* V [Spring 1976]); the interest in the hero as man of achievement rather than man of power, in this instance as healer teaching "the only *proper* individualism" and that "the only endurances are structures of activity," a man such as he himself wished to be, "singing of the beauty of things and of man alive in the phenomenal world"; and the anxiety prompted by his sense that man is inevitably overcome by evil, here by the Grandfather, representing material greed ("this greed is what plays on men, anywhere, what eats us"; he called it Bad Thing, his enemy death, in "The Story of an Olson, and Bad Thing").

Of the plays written at Black Mountain College, two, companion pieces, the work of the summer of 1951, are especially fine: *Apollonius of Tyana* and *The Born Dancer.* The first, "A Dance, with Some [Many] Words," dramatizes Olson's second birth and self-shaping, the vocational choice that he had made in undertaking *The Maximus Poems,* that great poem of place. Thematically it is the richest of Olson's dance-dramas, the only one hitherto published and well known. The second, treating Nijinsky, is appropriately pure dance, and dance here, with a brilliance not to be found in any of the others, itself becomes Olson's projective speech. It tells of Olson's respect for the human body, of his awareness of sexuality in the growth of consciousness, and of his hatred of all that impedes its proper (*tropic*) development. Nijinsky's first dance, celebrating the body, is "the dance of man as born god because he is child of nature in the full sense of planets as well as plants. . . ." But this innocent Nijinsky, so much like Billy Budd, is confronted by evil, by Diaghilev, "power as the world is power . . . [the] male-raper—sensual in the sexual sense, due to no center, no intimate center innate as Nijinsky has. . . ." Diaghilev is a Claggart, but there is no mystery in his iniquity. What Olson abominates is his homosexuality. Here, the inordinate sense of evil is truly projective, for Olson feared that his own dependence on fathers (Dahlberg, Pound, Cagli, etc.) might be evidence of homosexuality. Nevertheless, he also sees it, as he so often sees things, dialectically, as part of the necessary development from hermaphroditic (uroboric) to "normal" sexuality, the last achieved by Nijinsky in his relation with Romola, who stands to his right as Diaghilev to his left. Later, when Nijinsky is confined in an insane asylum, Olson considers him a second Rimbaud and stresses, as before, his resistance—and victory ("the story should be the Victory of, Metempsychotic [not Psychotic] Man over Humanism"). The vertical arrowlike (diorite stonelike) Nijinsky at the end of the second act prefigures this victory, and it is achieved on his escape, when, meeting the Russian soldiers, he dances, according to Olson's instructions, "as Shiva might . . . until, at the end, how I don't know, it is as though he shot straight *up* into the air." This, for me, is one of the supreme imaginations in Olson's work, and supremely Olsonian.

None of Olson's later work is moved by the intensity that informs the early work. In these plays of the 1960s, Olson is a parodist-social critic, somewhat removed from the artwork, often moved by disgust. In *Telepinus* ("a Christmas Entertainment for Manhattanville"!) Telepinus, the Hittite god of fertility whose name heavily puns, still seems to be angry and withdrawn, reluctant to do the work of the solstice. In his speeches he refers to the "futile masses"—"The masses / are all over the place"; "Too many people / all over the place // No hope when more / are made every day." He also hates the "decisions of / the middle class" and believes that the socialists will never "catch up with agriculture." "I am merry now," he says. "Are you?" Mary, the Mother of Jesus, identifies herself: "I am the cherry / rosy & red." And the following comment of hers seems (even so early and in all likelihood addressed to Americans and Russians) to foreclose the counterculture: "You are all relaxed / in your midget cars / or messed up good / in communes." In *Fluff* ("a 'Temperament' of Four Natures"), a characteristic speech is the following of Lady 1: "I am / wiggle / ass / Doris / Day / I am pastry / in your stomach / I am / bullshit / all over." Hyacinthus says, "I use / democracy // . . . I don't believe / in anything. . . ." This brief play collapses into "rottenness"; the grossness of the characters overwhelms the author who ends it all in brawl, "literally, a vulgar dirty mess." Olson, the black humorist, writer of satyr plays?

Even the *Wild Man Fragment,* resuming Olson's most serious theme, breaks off in hopeless hopefulness. The wild man, who is "nature" and has "native (neolithic) powers," lives in fear of "much today which / is [hostile]." His antagonist is "Pointed Beard" ["scientist modernism commercial-success present intellectual best (exponential IBM computer future), the full miserable self-autonomy of the intellectual as it now is"]. These stock characters—catchwords, Van Wyck Brooks would have said—define for us, as our critical situation, the endless opposition of Nature and Culture. They identify Olson's allegiance and the large theme—the great theme of myth—his work addresses. Curiously, they provoke little action; the enterprise is almost static. Threatened by Pointed Beard, Wild Man lifts his stick and Pointed Beard retreats. Olson seems satisfied, saying of Pointed Beard, "that he ain't got it all made the way he thinks he has," but noting also that "so far he is tops." At which point, according to stage directions, there is a stirring out of "a previous nonevidentness" and the wished-for middle term miraculously appears in the "Figure of a most normal man. . . ." But here the Brooksian legerdemain of terms—extremes begetting a satisfactory middle term—fails and the nonevidentness is apparent.

Olson's success in realizing the most normal man was greater in *The Maximus Poems.* There the miracles are genuine—miracles of experience, Emerson called them. There is evidence and the way is evident, and in every sense he dances the Man.

Birds, Landscape, Place, Cosmicity

I want to talk about several related things: birds, landscape, place, cosmicity.

Birds. To live in Gloucester, at the harbor as Olson did at Fort Square, is to be aware, always, of gulls. They animate the air, and contribute to the motion of that "perfect bowl / of land and sea." They are immemorial presences, as Olson, looking out of the six tenement windows of his aerie, tells us in the *Maximus* poem of his first winter's occupancy, when he realized the newness experienced by the fishermen of the Dorchester Company—

> and the snow flew
> where gulls now paper
> the skies
>
> where the fishing continues
> and my heart lies

Gulls figure in one of Olson's earliest poems—in the river landscape, which, with the harbor, is of greatest psychic significance to him. They figure as tutelary birds; doves of ascent, teaching us that flight is attained only by love. Or, as we have it in the first *Maximus* poem, teaching us that to take possession of place by planting the mast, the vertical of the self, we must do the work enjoined by the declaration "Love is form." Olson's gulls are notable, among other things, because they are never depicted as scavengers. They do not seem to be kin to the gulls of *Paterson IV* but to those of *The Bridge:* they release the creative spirit—the flight of imagination—to the end, in Olson's case, not of transcending but of inhabiting space. The flight of the gull, with the love it summons, gives one a privileged landscape, the total or circumambient landscape—and the correlative psychic wholeness—that Olson sought in his lifetime's devotion to place.

I begin with birds because Olson's deepest imagination of being involves them. Let me cite two instances whose intensity makes them indelible. The first is the account of the chii-mi at the beginning of the *Mayan Letters*.

> Birds, lad: my god what birds. Last evening a thing like our hawk. And that woman of mine (again) most alert to their nature. It happened this way. I was down the beach bargaining to buy a piece of their best fish here, what sounds like madrigal, only it comes out smedreegal. I had my back turned no more than three minutes, when, turning, to come back to the house (Con was on the terraza out over the sea, surrounded by a dozen of these gabbling kids), below her, on the water line, I noticed these huge wings fluttering wrong. My guess was, one of the kids, all of whom carry sling-shots, had brought down a zopalote (our vulture, "brother v," as Con named them). But when I came near, I noticed, just as Con cried down, that it was no vulture but another bird which is quite beautiful here, in Maya a chii-mi (chee-me): flies in flock over the waterline, soaring like hawks, high, and is marked by a long splittail ((by god, I was right: just checked dictionary and is, as I thought, our frigate bird))
>
> there it was, poor chii-mi, stoned by one of these little bastards, and the others, throwing more stones at it, and a couple, kicking it. And it working those three foot wings, hard, but not wild: very sure of itself, tho downed. By the time I came up, it had managed to get itself over, and was already out into the water, to get away from the kids. But each wave was wetting it down, and the misery was, that it drown.
>
> My assumption was, the stone had broken its wing. But Con had seen it happen, and seems to have known it was only its head that had been struck (it was out cold, she told me later, for a minute or so, and then, on its back, had disgorged its last fish). Anyhow, she had the brains to send down one of the older boys to bring it out of the water, and up on the terraza. And when I came up, there it was, quiet, looking hard at everyone, with its gular pouch

swollen like my Aunt Vandla's goiter, and its eye, not at all as a bird's is, when it is scared, or as, so quickly, they weaken, and that film drops over the eye. Not at all: this chii-mi was more like an animal, in its strength. Yet I still thought it was done for, something in the wings gone.

Just about then it started to work its way forward, pulling its wings in to its body, and making it look so much more like, say, a duck. What it had in mind, was to try to lift itself the two feet up to the wall that goes round the terraza. But it could not. It had worked itself into the inner angle of a corner. So I reached down and raised the right wing up to the top of the wall. Then the left. And, itself, it pulled its body up, perched for an instant, and swung off, off and up, into the sky, god help us, up and out over the sea, higher and higher, and, not like the others but working its wings in shorter, quicker strokes, it pulled off and off, out over the shrimp ship moored out in the deeper water, inside the bar, from which it swung inland again, and, as I watched it a good five minutes, kept turning more and more to the west, into the sun, until that peculiar movement of the wings began to give way to the more usual flight of a chii-mi. And I figure, as it disappeared, it was all right, all right.

God, it was wonderful, black, wonderful long feathers, and the wing spread, overall, what, five to six feet. Never got such a sense of a bird's strength, inside strength, as this one gave, like I say, more animal, seemingly, and sure, none of that small beating heart. That's why its victory, over these mean little pricks, was so fine.

Here victory is enhanced by victimization, by Olson's sensitivity to exigencies of resistance. The triumph of beautiful being over death is moral: of indomitable heart, spirit, will. In depicting the chii-mi with "maximal attention," Olson makes its spirit his own; his projective act gives him "secrets objects share."

In "A Round & A Canon," he speaks of "a lovely bird of a wild human motion," assimilating the bird to the movement of a child swinging—and, more important, to his own precarious equipoise.

A bird
knows too much, or it strikes me he knows enough
to awake to a day to sing a day down

And when he falls—o
all saints & recitals, consider
what a very high heart, what a high heat

such nerves
I cannot keep him alive, holding
him in my hand, winged or pawed, he fell
from his own world, his own careful context, those
balances

Even a spoon
of the finest honey, or a splint, or,
tried down his throat like his father,
the finest worm.

Won't do. He dies, his eyes
close upward, the film first, the milky way
of his dying
(as the Two who shyly rule
off the north in the night settle, distractedly,
in the sea

He ceases to fly or to sing. And no reference
to the twisting of the neck of
the spitting black goose

he dies
as the instant dies, as I die
for an instant listening
to the slightest
error

I underscore *his own world, his own careful context, those / balances.* For the bird is an exemplary inhabitant of space. Its dynamic will maintains a dynamic state; it is always at home in a forever-changing world, the careful context, the cosmos of its fluid circumscriptions.

The bird is remarkable for both its resistance and its stance. It lives in the fields of air as Olson wished to live in the fields of life and poetry. (We may speak of *air* in the Bachelardian way, as one of Olson's characterizing elements. The free-soaring bird, of course, contributes to its valorization. But there is also the air we breathe, the inspiriting element of life and poetry. For Olson field composition involves breath because space is air and we are lungs: "space . . . the air that it is and the lungs we are to live in it as our element." Although the meditation on metacenter in "Tyrian Businesses" provides an aqueous example of "those / balances," Olson is not, I think, primarily a poet of water. It is too much the element of smother—an interesting association with mother and with the choking of the flesh—a fearful, denying, death-dealing element. Air, then, and for the great reason Bachelard gives: "anguish is factitious: we are made to breathe easy.")

But what of stance? Olson saw the chii-mi in Yucatan, where he was also overwhelmed by the Mayan glyphs. These were built around "ONE central HUMAN figure," and in them, as he said, the human figure is part of the universe of things, individuated only by acts of attention, by its "own special selection from the phenomenal field." Like the bird, the human figure is within its world. It is not estranged from the familiar world; it inhabits this "human universe." What Olson saw in the Mayan glyphs he also recognized in the Hopi and Whiteheadian cosmologies: a space-time centered on the individual, bending around him, creating an intimate space of here/now peopled by particular things that, impinging on him, solicit his attention. *Familiar. Intimate.* It must be emphasized that Olson wished to bring us out of hostile or indifferent into intimate space. He did not wish to conquer space but to live in place, and he valued cosmologies that "reset man in his field"—cosmologies that gave him a veritable cosmos with its virtue of cosmicity, of well-being.

Olson's achievement is of the highest order because, in his concern with cosmology and psychology (his studies in myth join both), he transvalues our primary conceptions of nature and self and gives us a new ontological possibility. Resetting man in his field is the cosmological work; restoring his dynamic is the psychological work. And the bird in its own careful context—perhaps we should note here a relevant Creeley title: *Contexts of Poetry*—the bird tells us that care, as requisite as attention, is a condition of being and of being in the field, of having such a cosmos. Olson's field is not for spectators but vigilant participants. Creeley provides a corollary when he says that poets are only poets when they are writing poems. And Paul Goodman, commenting on the sadness of writing about rather than doing something, adds another: "Poetry is not sad, it is an action."

Olson notes in *The Special View of History* that these lectures on "actual willful man" most fully develop the dynamic view first presented in the essay "Projective Verse." One of the most remarkable things in this essay is the use Olson makes of the following passage from Fenollosa:

> There is in reality no such verb as a pure copula, no such original conception: our very word *exist* means "to stand forth," to show oneself by a definite act. "Is" comes from the Aryan root *as,* to breath. "Be" is from *bhu,* to grow.

A summary declaration of *The Special View* puts this succinctly: "Man is, He acts." Olson's poetics of breath, accordingly, is a poetics of self-action. All act springs from the breath; to breathe is to act, to stand forth, to grow. Every thing—and we are things among things—every thing in Olson's universe manifests energy, is efficacious. And so he speaks to us of a morality of motion and challenges us to move, to put ourselves in motion. What is the will to change without the power to move oneself?

The bird, always in motion, moves itself, and this is why Olson dedicated "A Round & A Canon" to a dancer. In dance, the kinetic art closest to Olson's physiological conception of poetry, one moves oneself, and gloriously in defiance of gravity. His meditation on the relation of *M* to *G,* metacenter to gravity, Maximus to Gloucester, addresses this. But the supreme imagination of this relationship is in the dance scenario Olson composed depicting episodes of Nijinsky's life and patently fabling his own deepest desire. I cite the second indelible instance of imagination of being, this one the concluding instructions of "The Born Dancer." Olson describes the occasion: having fled the insane asylum, Nijinsky wanders in the forest where he meets the soldiers who recognize him and plague him to dance. Then he says,

> So he does it. He starts, and, from pain, it comes, all the way, until, you shall dance beyond what Act II is, you shall dance as Shiva might, say. Until, at the end, how I don't know, it is as though he shot straight *up* into the air.

Nijinsky's leap is vertical flight, an image of mobility akin to the most mobile of powers, that of imagination; and it is a more felicitous image of vital imperatives than the diorite stone. In the context of a troubled sexual and personal life—again Olson stresses victimization—this wonderful leap enacts the ultimate tropic liberation of self and fulfillment of being. Clearly the leap is transcendent, an apotheosis. But it is also a figure of the wholeness whose attainment includes the other stations of the vertical of the self: hell and earth (Diaghilev and Romola). Duncan says that "Maximus calld us to dance the Man." Maximus does, and fortunately in a way more commensurate with our powers than Nijinksy's. He calls us to walk in the world, or, in the lovely admission of the last volume of *The Maximus Poems,* to find our satisfaction in the laborious and limited—yes, earthbound—flight of the cormorant.

In calling us to dance the Man, Maximus also calls us to the dance of imagination and the creation of form. *Love is form.* What form? Considering the exemplary bird, could it be anything but a nest? "O Gloucesterman / weave"; "The nest, I say, to you, I Maximus, say"—these imperatives initiate the work, which has for its goal the initiation of another kind of nation. Love is form because cosmos is the work of Eros. (A distinguishing feature of Olson's studies in mythology, as in Duncan's too, is the primacy accorded Eros.) We are, Olson says, *amorvores;* and the forms we love are born and torn from ourselves in our necessary engagement with the environment. Love is not easy because our environments revulse us; they are strewn with the "rubbish of creation," the detritus of civilization. Yet, as Olson demonstrates, we must make our forms—our nests—from the available pickings.

The bird is exemplary because it makes a shelter of such inhospitable materials—because it does what all of us would literally like to do, make our own houses. Isn't a nest, as Bachelard reminds us, isn't this place of primitive warmth, a bird's *house*? And doesn't it stir in us the deepest reverberations? When Kerouac (about whom I have been reading in Victor-Lévy Beaulieu's chicken essay) remembers the kitchen of his childhood he recovers a "feeling of indescribable peace" in the "warm home time." In their literal activity, poets, of course, make houses. (Creeley's "The House" is an apt example.) *The Maximus Poems* is a house to be remembered along with Capt. Levett's and Roger Conant's, in my mind, at least, situated in Olson's essential unspoiled landscape, the pristine America—

> by fish flakes and stages
> on rocks near water with trees
> against sea . . .

We might linger to enjoy the reverie *nest* awakens, but let me simply touch on some of the relevant associations Bachelard develops in *The Poetics of Space*. Nests, he says, call up our childhood wonder (and the wonder of childhood). They are associated with the ideas of return and lost intimacy, with the desire for cosmicity. To have a house for the self, and one so conformable and comfortable! "To make a world"—the imperative need of childhood, according to Edith Cobb—"to make a world in which to find a place to discover a self"! The nest, in the first *Maximus* poem, is the center of the cosmos; at the end of *The Maximus Poems* the cosmos itself is a nest. Gloucester, the perfect bowl of land and sea, is a place where Olson, at last, is physically at home.

The nest is the model of poem, polis, and cosmos. Olson's great poem is a polis—the polis of Gloucester exists only in the poem—and this polis, this Gloucester, is finally, because of his labors, a cosmos-polis, a true cosmopolis. And to live there, in the place of that poem, is to know again what moved the bird and the poet to make nests. "Would a bird build its nest," Bachelard asks, "if it did not have its instinct for confidence in the world?"

A reading of *Apollonius of Tyana* confirms the equation of nesting place and natal place, and reminds us that both involve return—the "human returning," according to Bachelard, that "takes place in the great rhythm of human life." Worcester, not Gloucester, was Olson's natal place, but Gloucester was a childhood place cherished, as we know from "The Twist," where places often count most, in dreams. I cannot think of that poem, nor of *The Maximus Poems,* without recalling Thoreau. He too made a nest beside the water. And he sufficiently accounts for the labor of inhabiting Walden when he says that he well remembered, when only four years old, being "brought from Boston to this my native town, through these very woods and this field, to the pond." The sentence moves inward, centering in what he says is one of his oldest—earliest, deepest—memories, evoking for him "that fabulous landscape of my infant dreams." It may well be a landscape dreamed then, but it is clearly a landscape dreamed now again, advising us to remember in reading *Walden* and *The Maximus Poems* that "childhood"—how well Bachelard says it—"is at the origin of the greatest landscapes."

How is it then that Olson, one of our greatest poets of landscape (because he gives us the greatest landscape)—how is it that such a close student of the landscapes of Fitz Hugh Lane is silent about Thoreau, Lane's contemporary? One reason—I will offer another later on—is Olson's repudiation of the Romantic-Transcendentalist legacy. Everything in his thought refuses the dualism of subject/object, consciousness/nature, and its resolution on the side of the Ego in the aggrandizement of the symbol-making imagination. Matters of this kind, as we now say, were Thoreau's constant *problematic,* but they were not Olson's, once he had overcome them.

This can be seen in terms of Olson's transformation of the conventional view of landscape. I take the briefest formula for this from the title of John Barrell's brilliant book on John Clare: *The Idea of Landscape and the Sense of Place.* The idea of landscape is the correlative of the Cartesian way of seeing and, with the old discourse, contributes to our estrangement from the familiar world. In *Proprioception,* where Olson sets forth the fundamentals of a new discourse, he defines landscape by citing the entry in the dictionary: "a portion of land which the eye / can comprehend in a single view. . . ." This is the familiar spectatorial, pictorial definition. Landscape is *scene.* In the nineteenth century, that great age of landscape, it is always *scenery:* one not only took the waters but took in the views, and for similar tonic reasons. The definition tells us that to see is only to *comprehend,* to grasp the meaning mentally, to understand. Romantic landscape is predicated on a geometry of inside/outside and on an epistemology of subject/object. The land becomes a "landscape," a picture, because we are predisposed and disposed to see it that way. We come to it with an "idea" in mind: we look for "views."

Now for Olson in search of intimate being (he will endorse the notion of contact, of the skin as sensitive interface), such landscape required that he open the field, enter "outside" space, become active within it and so inhabit it. The emendation in *Proprioception* suggests this:

to bring the land into the eye's view

This evokes for me the act of discovery Olson associated with *periplus,* with the fresh experience of sailors at sea and the wonderfilled moment when the eye, straining to grasp the unseen, finds the land emerging in its sight. The occasion is such—is so Whiteheadean—that I hear *prehend* instead of *comprehend.* And *view* becomes *viewing,* an activity that gathers the land into and about oneself, as a further notation suggests:

Cosmos
creation
a verb

Cosmos is creation resulting from activity: we attack chaos by work. But "*a verb,*" charged inevitably by Olson's reading of Fenollosa, also tells us that the cosmos itself is a verb: the universe is a process. We live in the world of fishermen and gulls, not a world of fixities (subjects and objects) but of energies (verbs). "*The verb,*" Fenollosa says, "must be the primary fact of nature, since motion and change are all that we can recognise in her." So we see again the intellectual magnitude of the task of making space place and appreciate the justice of Ed Dorn's comment on *The Maximus Poems:* "You don't have a place just because you barge in on it as a literal physical reality, or want it to prosper because you live there. . . . Place, you have to have a man bring it to you." A man, I might add, doing what Dorn depicts Olson doing in "From Gloucester Out."

Olson gives us Gloucester because he learned how to stand in the landscape. The problem, he knew, was one of "landscape," and in "Lower Field—Enniscorthy," an early poem originally called "Field notes," we see him trying to solve it.

The sheep like soldiers
black leggings black face
lie boulders
in the pines' shade
at the field's sharp edge:
ambush and bivouac

A convocation of crows overhead
mucks
in their own mud and squawk

makes of the sky
a sty

A bee is deceived
takes the rot of a stump
for honeycomb

Two black snakes cross
in a flat spiral
the undisciplined path

Report: over all
the sun.

The fundamental difficulty presented in this poem involves the "stance toward reality" that Olson said in "Projective Verse" "brings such verse into being. . . ." This is a matter not only of acts of attention (as with Lawrence and Williams) which Olson is obviously practicing; it is a matter of composing things in a way that avoids the conventions and expectations of landscape poetry and painting. "Field notes" is an accurate title. This poem is not a "landscape" even though a place is named and an observer assumed, and it begins with a distant view taking in the field. The arrangement of verses does not compose a landscape, though, interestingly, the movement of the eye is not unlike that in a poem by Thomson or a painting by Claude. But Olson, who avoids syntax in the juxtaposition of verses, cannot organize it as Thomson did his Claudean views. He cannot organize it at all, unless we consider it collage, a composition, in this instance, following only the serial order of the poet's random acts of attention, desperately closed by a terminal period and the hopefully conclusive enclosing awareness of the "over all" sun.

Olson sees things, not landscape, because he has relinquished the "idea of landscape," the *a priori* conception of how to compose one, the desire to manipulate the world. This is notable. The sheep he sees might have evoked a familiar romantic landscape but now call up a legacy to be refused. The simile of "sheep like soldiers" and the impression of "ambush and bivouac" are owing to his recollection of the "dark sheep in the drill field" in the first *Pisan Canto*. Pound, much in his mind at this time, mediates his seeing. And with the simile, such things as the supposition that the bee is "deceived" and the path "undisciplined" call attention to

Olson's act of seeing and not, as the suppression of the "I" throughout the poem intends, to the primacy of things seen. Olson is troubled because in putting aside the idea of landscape he has not yet put aside the "I." He remains as much outside the field as a romantic painter and is perhaps more aware of estrangement because he refuses to employ the romantic resources of consciousness to overcome it.

His problem is not to compose but enter the field, to do this by merging the "I" in the "eye," where the eye, as Creeley says of Zukofsky, is "a locus of experience, not a presupposition of expected value." His problem is not to dominate nature but to participate in it, to become, as Francis Ponge says so well, "not just the site where ideas and feelings are produced, but also the crossroads where they divide and mingle. . . ." Perhaps the closing verse ("Report: over all / the sun") accomplishes this. With sudden release the attention leaps from sheep, crows, bee, snakes to totality, as if Olson recognized that these things are all *in* a field. The sudden "Report" destroys the several perspectives of the previous acts of attention. The sun, over all, establishes the poet at the center of a hemisphere, in a field, arched by the sky.

Even so, "landscape" has not yielded to place. The field at Enniscorthy is too empty. It lacks the fullness of place. It is space. Olson has not inhabited it. He gives us very little sense of what it is like to be there. He has yet to introduce us, in John Clare's words for a place lived in, to "a landscape heard and felt and seen."

Olson continues to use the word *landscape* because, as he goes on, he associates it less with the tradition of landscape painting and more with the areal tradition of chorography and geography. One of his early teachers was Carl Sauer, the eminent geographer—in "The Area, and the Discipline of, Totality," a valuable unpublished essay on his essential themes, he speaks of Sauer as his master. It is true that Olson pays tribute to Fitz Hugh Lane. He does this in the last volumes of *The Maximus Poems,* where Lane's practice supports his own. Olson appreciates most "Lane's eye-view of Gloucester"; this is equivalent to a "Phoenician eye-view," that is, to the active seeing associated with *periplus*. Lane is remarkable among American landscapists because he does not devote himself to wilderness views. He devotes himself to Gloucester and with exact detail renders the life of the place, gives us its geography and weather and, especially, its remarkable light. Olson puts Lane in the *areal* tradition that he connects with discovery, with the first/fresh viewing of such American contemporaries of Lane as John Stephens, William Prescott, Francis Parkman, and Noah Webster; a tradition he also associates with the conspicuous practice—the practice of close attention—of the pragmatists. This is to say that he places Lane in a tradition where act precedes idea, where experience is primary and one considers organism-in-environment.

From Sauer, Olson learned that landscape is an area, a physical, geographical region, to be understood only when one "'has learned to see it as an organic unit, to comprehend land and life in terms of each other.'" The concluding phrase contains the title of Sauer's collected writings, *Land and Life,* and gives us the gist of cultural geography: land, itself a living thing, is a place of—and for—life; life is an activity of—and in—place. Now Sauer, with Olson, means human life, the life, as we are fearfully learning, that so radically modifies the natural landscape. With Sauer, as with Olson, we do not find ourselves in pristine wilderness but in a cultural landscape. Geography gives us the facts of place, history gives us the facts of time; bringing these facts together, cultural geography gives us time in space, an account of what happened there and transformed it, human history of the most significant kind. The immediate point of these considerations is that "in this view," as Sauer says, "there is no place for a dualism of landscape. . . . In the sense used here, landscape is not simply an actual scene viewed by an observer."

The areal definition of landscape resets man in the field and gives him practical field work to do. By means of the human sciences—Olson called them the sciences of man, among them those particularly his, historiography, archeology, mythology—he recovers the life, the sense of place. Olson's initial "dramatic reconnaissances" in Gloucester follow Sauer's practice. He looks for evidence of time in space, and this is first of all a matter of walking. Walking, as in Thoreau's excursions and Williams' *Paterson,* is the mode of *The Maximus Poems,* a mode of attention and meditation. And Olson is a walker, coming, as he says, from "the last walking period of man"—a phrase in one of the last poems that tells the pleasure he now finds in the "still handsome & efficacious environment":

> And so I walked
> thinking as I did so, I come

from the last walking period
of man, homeward,
happy and renewed, in that sense, by the
sight of the
original cave of the City populated
megalithically, & pure Brythonic

This sense of place comes, of course, from all the previous walking, those daily walks that make his poem a "walker," all those excursions in which Olson practices "genetic human geography." In his field work Olson also follows Herodotus—he personally looks for evidence of what was said—Herodotus, endorsed by Sauer in a footnote citing Alexander von Humboldt's appreciation of the ancient historians who attractively intermingled physical geography and history. Now in doing this work, Olson finds, as Sauer promised, that "it is real discovery . . . to take old documents into the field and relocate forgotten places"; he even realizes the "high moment," when, as Sauer says, "the picture begins to fit together" and "the past is clear, and the contrasts with the present are understood."

We know, in Volume One of *The Maximus Poems*, how dismaying Olson's realization is. Not only was the newness of America dirtied from the start but the spirit of enterprise was such that "Venus / does not arise from / these waters. . . ." As Olson's researches people America, give it a history, the landscape that matters to him empties. The present is "dreamless"; it is "worse," he says in the most disconsolate verses, where, lamenting the lack of mythic understanding, he projects his future work. Finding "America" in history, Olson finds only "the lost America of love," as we might say with Ginsberg, who identifies this theme with Whitman and so with much of American literature. And Olson feels this loss because he knows it in his own lack of psychic wholeness—and knows it in Gloucester, where the very landscape declares it.

A footnote in Volume One explains this and the departure of his subsequent work. He speaks in the footnote of the Hopi language as "adjusted to the topological as a prime and libidinal character of a man, and therefore of all of his proximities, metric is then mapping. . . ." Space and self, landscape and psyche correspond, as do mapping and metric, field work and poetry. Olson wants us to appreciate the fact that in *The Maximus Poems* he locates himself in the Hopi fashion—he is concerned with

"Gloucester, and myself as here-a-bouts." But the word that strikes us is *libidinal.* The topological, he says, is a libidinal character of a man: the topological is not separate from us; it is intimately ours, and so we cannot fail to respond to it, and, in the instance of the first *Maximus Poems,* as loveless. Our task is to fill the loveless space with love, not only by loving attention but by realizing in mythic awareness—and this means an awareness of the presence of myth—the still-active, living processes of earth; by realizing that these processes are themselves erotic, that Eros, Love, as Olson argues in his Hesiod poem, was there at the beginning, in the first acts of cosmological creation. When, at the end of *The Maximus Poems,* Olson gives us the gift of "an actual earth of value," the actual earth has value not only because his love has valorized it but because it is love.

The fact that the topological is a libidinal character of a man allows Olson to complement Sauer with Jung. Myth, which he reads as earth history and archetypal experience, enables him to follow both masters, though there is the displacement he notes when he speaks of turning from Herodotus to Hesiod. He is looking now, in the later installments of his poem, for primordial beginnings, for the ground of *begründen,* the rich word, glossed by Kerényi in *Essays on a Science of Mythology,* that proposes Olson's work: the grounding of the self that is the founding of a city, the achievement of "cosmos of being" (as Olson said of Whitman) and cosmopolis. Kerényi's book, written in collaboration with Jung, was published in 1949, and we need read only these lines to assess its importance to Olson and to learn why Maximus, not Gloucester, identifies the poems: "To rebuild the world from that point *about* which and *from* which the 'fundamentalist' [*Begründer*] himself is organized. . . ."

Though there are particular landscapes or views in *The Maximus Poems,* it is the circumambient landscape of the complete work that accords with Olson's notion of self-and-cosmos and provides the sense of place. Space is merely the extensive plane of history, the dimension of dispersion, where place, including this horizontal dimension, is round and coherent. It is a sphere that turns on the vertical self and includes all the topologies, all the landscapes of being—underworld, earth, and heaven. And so to inhabit it, to map it, as Olson does in making his *mappemunde,* is, in Jung's terms, to experience wholeness and know the healing of individuation. We may read Olson's map as the record of a remarkable journey to individuation. And one of the notable things about it, as he said of the writing of John Smith, is that "the *geographic,* the sudden *land* of the place, is . . . there. . . ." Just as it is no longer a view, so Olson's landscape is not a psychic landscape, a symbolic projection of the Ego. He knows that the world is not completed when one takes it into oneself; to eat the apple of the entire world, as Emerson in a dream of consciousness dreamed of doing, is no longer the way. Olson's landscape is a real landscape—an areal landscape—in which the self has a place and finds itself at home. *The Maximus Poems* are the consummate landscape of this consummation.

To transcendentalize is to transubstantiate, as Olson said of the painting of Marsden Hartley. This is one of the reasons he didn't countenance Thoreau, the writer whose concern with place equals his and whose work in so many ways is comparable with his own. Walden and Gloucester are places, given to us in the way Dorn mentions, and so they are sacred to us—and sacred in Eliade's use of the word, places to be differentiated from profane space. Olson was not, I think, a sympathetic reader of Eliade chiefly because he wished to remain in history, and to use history, rather than look back to and repeat archaic ways. Though he recognizes the qualitative difference between the profane and the sacred, he doesn't see them in Eliade's antithetical fashion. This suggests another reason for his dismissing Thoreau.

In American thought the profane and the sacred have been variously translated into such oppositions as Europe vs. America, Civilization vs. Nature, City vs. Wilderness. We know where Thoreau stands in respect to all of them, and some of us, following Thoreau, subscribe to an ethic that holds the wilderness—unsullied Nature—sacred. But not Olson, whose place is a city, who wished to ground the city in nature, who would not divorce but join the elements of Nature and Culture he first appreciated in *Gilgamesh.* Olson, so much more social than Thoreau, is a man of the polis, that "nest of solidarity," in Richard Schechner's fitting phrase. Maximus of Tyre not Thoreau of Walden (or even Concord) is Olson's model. Of his public task—the initiation of another kind of nation—we may say that he has the distinction of giving us another kind of place, an urban place hitherto denied in our thought. And with this, he has the distinction of teaching us, in his poetics and his practice, how to relocate where we are, how to renew the spaces of our lives, to make them, as Apollonius made Tyana and he made Gloucester, "capable of verticality," places, therefore, where we willingly stay put and dance sitting down.

For there we will celebrate "the joys of the rounded cosmos in which we live happily." Being, Bachelard insists in the wonderful rounding off of his phenomenology of roundness—"being is round." We know already the image that confirms this for him. It is the bird, whose being in its cosmic condition, he says, had been thought of by Michelet as "a centralization of life guarded on every side, enclosed in a live ball. . . ."

Olson's chii-mi, the gulls of Gloucester harbor departing the ridgepoles, the cormorant and the spindle of Shag Rock invite us to centralize in this way and so recover "the being of round life." These tutelary birds—birds are muses in Olson's meditation on the vocational choice he had made—these birds led him to the dominion of song:

we speak with water
on our tongues when
Earth
has made us parts of the World again,
Poets, & the Airs which
belong to Birds have
led our lives to be these things instead of
Kings

A Letter on Olson and Burke

Cass Lake, Minn. 56633
2 June 1981

Dear Roy:[1]

I had been forewarned by George Butterick and had already begun to ponder Burke and Olson when your letter arrived yesterday morning. We no longer get our mail delivered by boat—this is one of the new economies—and go to town maybe twice a week to get it. So now, since it is raining and I can excusably stay indoors, I'll answer you in this form, a meditative form after all, and write out what comes to mind as it comes, unaided by all the scholarly props I left behind in Iowa City. Had your deadline been less demanding, I would have waited until I returned, if only to be able to intersperse what I say with such wonderful, truly Burkean remarks as "Where there's life, it's hopeless," which reminds me that when I talked with Burke several years ago I remarked, in his spirit and very much in the spirit of his work, that his *ars poetica* was an *arse poetica*. Which recalls the salient remark of Olson about the *firmament* and the *fundament,* and reminds me how much Burke and Olson are fundamentalists.

You say that you come to Burke after Olson. It's the other way round with me. So when I wrote about Olson, that is, when I thought about him, I thought in ways, among others, that Burke had taught me, which is why it pleases me to write about him and add my testimony to the long-deserved celebration of his genius, though I acknowledged my debt to Burke in the preface to *Hart's Bridge.*

What Burke and Olson have in common (and in common with an increasing fellowship) is their sense of the crisis of the crisis of civilization: Burke, in *Counter-Statement,* seeing in the technological breakdown of the Depression something as ominous as the war he would purify by symbolic action; Olson, on the explosion of the atom bomb, taking up the vocation of poet and the undertaking—veritable symbolic action: "Man is; He acts"—of initiating another kind of nation, a *polis,* which is to say, a city worthy of belonging to Burke's *commune* cluster. (And I think now of the commune in Duncan and McGrath.) And both, of course, men of the word, answering back, countering with statement (Olson's push a counter-punch), speech itself, which we had in the beginning, our last resort; *song,* as Olson's daughter exemplifies it in *The Maximus Poems,* a form of resistance. The physiology of speech; the activity of language.

My friend Bill Rueckert, whose work on Burke is indispensable, considers Burke and Frye the preeminent literary critics of the 20th century because of the originality and thoroughness of their theoretical contributions. I appreciate the grandeur of such entelechially-achieved projects but am less concerned with systems than with the incidental practical tools they offer me, for example, Burke's "clustering." I am sure that Burke's ratios, as you suggest, apply—or can be applied—to *The Maximus Poems;* that, for all that it might lead to a spatial or static reading, one could read these poems, with considerable gain, in Burkean terms. I am sure that Maximus-Olson's journey of individuation answers to Burke's purgative-redemptive journey. I am especially tantalized (to take up your verb) by your suggestion that "O's poetics [is] a rhetoric of landscape." I wouldn't hesitate to say that it is, he himself having said in *Maximus 1* that metric is mapping and having, in his use of *projective,* a mapping term also in mind. Could it be otherwise in a poet so much concerned with our relation to space, with how to locate there, *be* there (*dwell:* Heidegger)? I have myself meditated on the following terms in respect to Olson's work: *birds, space/place, landscape, cosmicity.* My approach is neither Burkean nor systematic (coming up with a "rhetoric") but Bachelardian. Still I think you might find it useful in discovering such a rhetoric.

Though I failed to say so in adopting Burke's notion of "offices" in my account of Olson, I recognize their importance in establishing the centrality and usefulness of the poet. Both Burke and Olson believe in the centrality of the poet (isn't it significant that Burke treats the offices in a discussion of Emerson?), though they themselves, and other poets and writers, are marginal. It has always pleased me (is it because I gravitate that way?) that Burke lives on a farm and that Olson lived in a decaying fishing port. Of course I think of Thoreau when I think of margins—he said we need a large margin to our lives, which is what we go to the margins to get, as here. But I also think of Wendell Berry who speaks of margins as a counter-theme to the dominant theme of exploitation. And I think (to praise Burke and Olson) of the counter-move of their lives in taking up voluntary poverty, and of the marginal colleges, Bennington and Black Mountain, that helped them endure it. This spring Bill Rueckert and I had a long set-to over my according Olson only three of the offices, not all of the seven. I don't have our correspondence here and can't rehearse it with the fullness Bill's argument deserves. I assured him that I did not deny Olson the full complement of offices—certainly not the political, which Bill so much insisted on—but that the ones I chose particularly characterized Olson for me. What were they? The pedagogical, the pleasure-giving, the pontificating?

What I appreciate most in Burke, to whom these offices also apply, is his comic perspective. He has the ameliorative, social attitude and the pragmatic attitude I also find in Paul Goodman—the willingness to "tinker" so that we may all "live on a little." Olson, for all of his concern with *polis,* is a poet of the cosmos, like Whitman, as Dorn shows so well in "From Gloucester Out"; but in his way, too, he is indebted to pragmatism. (Wouldn't Burke note here that *comic* is *cosmic* without the *s*?) I also appreciate Burke's humor, his playfulness, the dialectical both/and way he thinks, all of these things suggesting to me the inclusivity and openness of an open poetics, the abdication of the absolute, categorical, restrictive. Might we not read his work as a long, serial poem, the one poem a man writes all of his life? A life's work? Hasn't he taught us to look at the life and the work in this way?

I don't know if Burke influenced Olson in the way, say, that he did Ellison. I don't think Burke was one of Olson's *teachers,* like Merk and Sauer, Jung and Whitehead. Burke is not mentioned in the bibliographical remarks that punctuate Olson's letters, that remind his correspondents of the originality and groundwork of American scholarship (of "American builders," to use your good phrase). Isn't this strange considering how widely influential Burke has been and how attentive Olson was? Can we account for it? It may be that he was too readily associated with the New Critics, as he still is, mistakenly I think, in Grant Webster's *The Republic of Letters,* though considering Burke's emphasis on the *Word* there is perhaps reason for it. Then, Burke is a systematic thinker, or should I say a theoretician concerned with system, and the model of his system, the one, as we say now, that he finds paradigmatic, is logo-theological (patriarchal, the feminists would say) with emphasis on the negative (thou shalt not), the hierarchical, and victimage. I think we may gather something of the weather of our time from the fact that during a thesis examination on, among others, Burke and Hugh Duncan that I sat in on recently, the most debated issue was Burke's view of hierarchy (there are no hierarchies, Olson declares in *Maximus*) and his view of victimage, of the fact that in his system there must always be some victims, however much someone like Hugh Duncan would improve their condition or adjust them to it. Perhaps Olson would say of Burke what he said of Pound, that he was limited because he was caught in the Western box, never got outside that tradition, *back* and *outside,* as he himself did, looking for alternatives rather than an explanation (salutary as that is) of the system. Maybe their point of difference has something to do with Burke's desire to use language to purify war (any contention) and Olson's to transfer energy. I have not, as Rueckert properly instructs me to, systematically laid out Olson's thought, but I suspect that it derives from a different model than Burke's. Maybe cybernetics.

Curiously, I have been profoundly influenced by both Burke and Olson; they live compatibly in my mind. Thinking of them now, in thinking what joins them, I remember that what Olson said of Apollonius applies to them: great talkers both, who talked to live. Who thereby live.

Ever,
Sherman Paul

Note

1. *Olson's Push,* by Sherman Paul, is among the first studies of Olson and is an especially sympathetic and culturally rich placement of Olson in the American tradition. Paul, like Olson, was trained in the American Studies program at Harvard, and he performs an important act of recognition, for Olson speaks from the deepest sources in American writing. Throughout his book, Paul uses the work of Kenneth Burke and concludes by referring to Burke's adaptation of the seven offices to summarize Olson's accomplishment:

> Of the seven official human offices, Olson performed especially those of teaching, giving pleasure, and consoling. For him, as has been remarked of Jane Austen, the true relation between people was pedagogic—it was chiefly in the generous way of his teaching that he gave pleasure and consolation.

> Such pedagogy—an antonym for demagogy?—is one of his conspicuous New England traits. Kenneth Burke . . . replaces "console," his initial choice for the last office, with a word that better explains its function: "pontificate; that is 'to make a bridge.'" This reminds us that Maximus, in the first instance and always a teacher, is also a Pontifex Maximus. . . .
>
> But Olson's pontification is not of the transcending kind Burke has in mind in treating Emerson. The symbolic action of Olson's work follows the path of descendence rather than transcendence. It does not provide a bridge from here to elsewhere—to a realm beyond, higher, heavenly: transcendent. . . . Instead it bridges down and back from here to beneath . . . to the ever present archaic fundament. . . . [*Olson's Push* (Louisiana State University Press, 1978), pp. 247–248.]

I wrote to Sherman Paul, telling him how I had gone to Burke after reading Olson, looking for a philosophy of rhetoric and thinking Burke's scene/act ratios applied to Maximus. I wrote that Burke and Olson were especially American builders and asked him to build a bridge between them.

Roy Skodnick

An Olson Primer

Primer: (1) a small book for teaching children to read; (2) a small introductory book on a subject (Webster's). I begin my morning work in Olson's fashion, and I note that in this instance meanings 1 and 2 overlap and that *primer* ("used to ignite an explosive charge") also applies, as meaning 3. Thomas Merrill's *The Poetry of Charles Olson: A Primer* is a small book, curiously so, since it is kept small by treating in a minimal way what merits extensive treatment, the last two volumes of Olson's major work, *The Maximus Poems.* Was it foreshortened out of weariness or, to take the concluding pages at face value (*primer,* meaning 3), out of lack of interest in the subject? The *subject*? Not the poetry of Charles Olson, as announced, but the "system" that may be said to inform it and that enables Thomas Merrill to reduce it to its intellectual content, to hand over its meaning and thereby achieve, as we were once taught by the very poets and critics whom Olson resists, the "understanding" of poetry.

The daring of the book is Merrill's acknowledged use of "traditional methods of explication," the "hermeneutical midwifery" with which he tries to deliver the poetry of a poet whose assumptions he understands very well—so well I assume that he endorses them—yet refuses to assimilate to his own critical practice. Does this mean that he rejects Olson's ideas, denies their validity, or only that he thinks them eccentric, comparable, say, to Yeats's, and of limited use? But what then of other poets who have found them useful—Allen Ginsberg, for example, about whom Merrill has written a book? In any case, I would not like children to be taught to read in this way. I am skeptical of an enterprise that tries to explain a poet to those who are ignorant of his work—that is, who think, as Merrill seems to, that one turns to the primer before turning to the poem. To do so, of course, is to be defrauded of the wonderful risk and reward of *participating* in the poetry (the verbal action), of discovering its "meanings" *in the poetry.* Merrill knows this, and works against it: "It must try to explain . . . when it ought simply [oh not so simply!] to experience [participate]." The vocabulary of his introductory remarks—*counterfeit, fraud, lure, engineer, apologetics*—does not disarm me; it disturbs me. Does a poet need "exegetical seasoning"; is poetry an "acquired taste"? And the cover photograph, Leonard Craske's "Man at the Wheel," which Olson deplored, is enough to suggest the fundamental cross-purpose of the book. It may even forewarn the reader that the good this book does will be canceled by the peremptory conclusion that Olson is a cult figure whose work demands that we "convert," buy "the whole package" of "rigid doctrines." This, of course, is not true, though, in Merrill's case, one can see how it follows from his belief that "the engines that drive it [the poetry] hum in the pages of Olson's theoretical prose."

Merrill does not participate in the poetry to the extent that he participates in Olson's theoretical prose, though this is neither fully treated nor ever considered, work by work, as having the same integrity as a poem. Yet his contribution to Olson scholarship is here, in his grasp of Olson's governing ideas and his systematization of them. This is not to say that his work supersedes the profound understanding of Olson's ideas in Don Byrd's *Charles Olson's Maximus* or the thorough and close understanding of Olson's reading and use of Jung in Charles Stein's thesis, on deposit in the Olson Archives. Merrill makes very little overt use of previous critical work and may have called his book a primer to distinguish it from these introductory studies. I say this with his fullest reading in mind, a chapter devoted to "The Kingfishers" as an exemplary text; exemplary, that is, of the ideas treated in the preceding chapters, not of the verse, since no attention is paid to the current poetic situation in which the poem figures and to which it answers, nor to the formal nature of the poem as collage and the action it performs. Merrill denies the allusions to Christianity in the poem by categorical dismissal, and instead of bringing to focus what has already been done—an obligation of an explicator following, indeed building on, other explicators—reduces the reading of the poem.

What pleases Merrill in *The Distances* is that it is "overtly 'composed'," a book of variations on a theme (nominalization, chiefly) that he can set out. He treats *Archaeologist of Morning,* the most inclusive collection of Olson's verse, in a similar way, for the procedure is to establish the system and then read it back into the poems. This is why he considers Olson a poet who, in his verse, delivers his ideas, his "ethical dogmas," and not as a poet struggling, contesting with reality in his verse, in order to attain to and enact his ideas. Merrill makes programmatic (thematic) what arose in an occasion as an insistence. So the earliest poems, which happen to be in *Archaeologist of Morning,* are treated in the fifth chapter, in what presumably is the chronology of works and not in the chronology of the poet's life. Accordingly, we lose the sense of poetry that Olson wanted to restore—that it is act, not intellection alone, the way one, for life's sake, hews to experience.

Merrill appreciates this, theoretically. The phrase *hews to experience* (from Olson's essential essay, "Human Universe") reminds me of Emerson, whom Olson dogmatically proscribed but who nevertheless in respect to experience and much besides is to be associated with him. In this instance, it is Merrill's concern with *obedience* that supports the association. Now, for me, this is the most rewarding aspect of his study and what, if I may say so, should have been its subject. He names it early in his treatment of the stance toward reality in "Projective Verse": "the larger philosophy of obedience that so significantly informs Olson's work as a whole." Still earlier, he explains Olson's "patient willful obstinacy" by saying that

> it comes from obedience. Olson was an obedient man and an obedient writer. "The mark of life," he was fond of saying, "is that what we obey to is who and what we are."

Like Emerson, Olson knew that "the true self is not the asserting function but the obeying one" (I cite *The Special View of History*) and that the secret of the power to be recovered in the will to achievement and the will to cohere is here. And like Emerson, he knew that another name for obedience is love; as he says at the outset in "Troilus," "The way, love is / the way!" All of which might be read in terms of critical stance, as Merrill does in speaking of Sam Charters' "willingness to obey its [Olson's poetry's] energies and acts rather than its meanings."

Energies and acts vs. meanings. This brings me back to *understanding poetry,* which is a contradiction in terms that derives from Plato, who put the way of rational understanding against the experiential way of poetry and knew that to understand it was to destroy it. I mention this because Olson's project (and not his alone) is nothing less than the restoration of the poetic way of hewing to experience that antedated Plato's discourse and was the very thing that gave birth to Platonism. Eric Havelock, in *Preface to Plato,* is as informative in respect to Olson as he is to Greek culture because the preliterate culture of the Homeric *paideia* had a stance toward reality and a language and syntax that have much in common with Olson's. Again, Merrill understands this, and treats it well in a chapter entitled "The Grammar of Illiteracy." He knows that "the grammar of illiteracy is the grammar of talk," that *illiteracy* should be *preliteracy* or *nonliteracy* and that what should be emphasized is an oral culture and what follows from its dependence on speech. Yet he chooses a pejorative term and, in explaining "La Torre," identifies his own point of view when he says that the "perspective from the old tower [Platonic literacy] sees this as illiteracy." As a result, he overlooks much that, followed up, would have increased the value of his work: that Olson's pedagogic concerns as a teacher and poet, for example, accord with the function of poetry in a preliterate culture and that his *Maximus,* in many ways, is an epic of the Homeric kind, encyclopedic and didactic, intent on handing over the *nomoi* and *ethe,* except that for Olson the nation for which they are intended is still to be initiated.

Knowing the labor and obedience required in undertaking the study of Olson, I am dismayed in Merrill's primer by what I think may be justly called critical futility. What, I wonder, inspired Merrill to read Olson? What, to borrow from Merleau-Ponty, was the "motive" of the event, the "attention-lure" that started the whole process?

PART VII

Robert Creeley

A Letter on Rosenthal's "Problems of Robert Creeley"

Dear Editor:
I have never written a letter of this kind before, having preferred to let criticism, as a general activity, do its remedial work. But M. L. Rosenthal's review of Creeley, in *Parnassus* (Fall/Winter 1973), addresses me as an occasion and asks me, in Creeley's and Olson's sense, to keep faith with a criticism of "use." And Olson provides my precedent: "This man, Grover Smith, 'On Poets and Poetry,' in your 1953 Autumn issue. He's a glib one."

Anyone whose work has been criticized knows the deplorable inattentiveness and inexactness of most criticism. Of what use is criticism when as Creeley observes in a recent interview collected in *Contexts of Poetry* (reviewed by Rosenthal), "there is *no* correspondence of any interest to me between the activities of contemporary criticism and that poetry I am myself engaged with". . . ? The example he cites in this interview of December 1969 is Richard Howard's *Alone with America,* which he comments on with characteristic incisiveness: "there are gaps I so deeply question that the book itself becomes a fine instance of *mandarin* writing—i.e., an 'entertainment' of 'sensibility.'" What, I wonder, would he say to Rosenthal's *The New Poets* (1967) or his "Problems of Robert Creeley," the latter establishing in its initial sentence this critic's attitude and imprecision: "Despite a tendency to regard as quintessential poetry any twist of phrase that happens into his mind, Robert Creeley has written some real poems. . ."? Whether poetry of the projectivist kind is "real" poetry seems doubtful. But then "real," for Rosenthal, is a multipurpose, approbative adjective—in the comparison with Williams' work by which he measures Creeley's he says of a scene in *A Dream of Love* that the poem, "Love Song," is "directed by a real, grown-up man in a real, everyday world to a real woman." Not all of the problems, clearly, are Creeley's.

To be "a major domo of modern poetry criticism" (I cite the designation in "Contributors") is not an enviable position. The household of contemporary poetry is too large; there is too much to keep in order, to keep up with. Ignorance is inevitable, allowable, though not in the case of an important poet one chooses to review and has written on before and whose career one has presumably followed. To say of *Contexts of Poetry,* as Rosenthal does, that it contains considerable material on "Mr. Creeley's vague but assertive poetics" makes one question not only the care with which he read the interviews but whether, in fact, he has read *A Quick Graph* (1970), the best critical book on (of) what Rosenthal calls "The 'Projectivist' Movement," and one of the finest, most useful and necessary works of critical intelligence in our time, a work in which Creeley amply pays his debt to Pound's critical practice. The evidence of the review suggests that Rosenthal has come no further in understanding Creeley's "terms" and "insistences" and in entering his work than he had in *The New Poets.*

"Problems of Robert Creeley" is focussed chiefly on *A Day Book,* Creeley's most recent large work, but it cannot be understood or fairly considered, as Rosenthal seems to think it can be, without understanding the importance of "context," a term of Creeley's carefully employed in the title of his collection of interviews. Context, to borrow Olson's words, refers to the limits any one of us are inside of ("Limits / are what any of us / are inside of"); one's context is one's "field," all the particular things to which one actually refers, in which one's poetry has its occasion and beyond which it may seek to move. A book devoted to contexts—what, for understanding a poet who wants to bring the poem as close to the fact of his life as he can, is more useful to the critic? Yet Rosenthal dismisses *Contexts of Poetry* in a paragraph, or in two, if one counts his animadversions on Creeley's comments on the academic reputations of Whitman and Williams—comments in spirit not without some truth and again to be considered in the contexts of Creeley's correspondence with Williams from 1950 to 1962 (it is available in the Beinecke Rare Book and Manuscript Library of Yale University) and of his own *Whitman* (1973), a volume of selections, edited with an introduction, in the Penguin Poet to Poet series.

Not only does Rosenthal appear to be uninformed, he is still admonishing Creeley in the way he had in *The New Poets* by attending pretty much to one poem—a real but unexceptional one—and holding up to him what he considers the superior practice of Williams. In *The New*

Poets, "The Riddle" is placed against the Corydon passages of *Paterson IV,* in the present review, "The Edge" against "Love Song." But in neither instance is the comparison just nor the Creeley poem opened, in the useful, admirative fashion, say, of Samuel Charters in *Some Poets/Poems: Studies in American Underground Poetry since 1945* (1971), to permit one to enter his world. The attention is not so much on the Creeley poem as on the poem with which it is compared, and in the instance of "The Edge," the poem may have been chosen not because *edge* is a term of increasing significance to Creeley ("at the edge of the world, / the edge beyond that edge") but because here Creeley has meditated on "Love Song," a poem properly valued by Rosenthal, who expatiates on it as he had, in another context, at the recent MLA meetings. Rosenthal, incidentally, chides Creeley for not acknowledging his borrowing from Williams, when the borrowing, if it is that, is acknowledgment enough. For Creeley, too, values this poem: it entered his thought—he thought with it—as early as "Love" (1951), and he is aware—he treats it in *Contexts of Poetry*—of what is involved in acknowledging another writer. But putting such matters aside, my objection is that one no more discovers the Creeley of *For Love* in *The New Poets* than the Creeley of *A Day Book* in "Problems of Robert Creeley."

The resistance in Rosenthal's treatment of Creeley—the refusal to engage him directly—derives, I think, from his unwillingness to acknowledge the magnitude of change introduced by the "projectivists." His treatment of "Projective Verse" in *The New Poets* is scant, omitting altogether Olson's considerations in Part 2 of stance, of the new universe and how one stands *in* it, and, accordingly, as Olson explains in Part 1, now engages in writing. Creeley has written extensively about this in *A Quick Graph*—it was a central fact of his defense of Hart Crane in 1953—and he comments on it in *Contexts of Poetry* ("Writing, and all of the arts as well, have entered the altered consciousness of men's situation in the world"). In fact, the possibility introduced by a process world of which he himself is a part (the universe is Whiteheadean and the poem is an "event" in it) is what he has found most liberating. And it is possibility, another term of Creeley's, that compels him, in *Pieces* and *A Day Book,* to move in ways that many critics have not approved. That he has taken this risk and recovered possibility is the chief excitement of these works ("writing," he said in 1967, in "I'm given to write poems," the great testamentary essay in which he told his faith in poetry as a way of being in the world and so prepared himself for the departure of these sequences—

"writing is for me the most viable and open condition of possibility in the world. . . . In poems I have both discovered and born testament to my life in ways no other possibility has given me"). "Poetry," according to Thoreau, another New Englander, to whom Creeley pays tribute,[1] "is a piece of very private history, which unostentatiously lets us into the secret of a man's life." And so it is for Creeley, who, in "Inside Out" (*Sparrow* No. 14, 1973), speaks of autobiography as "a life tracking itself," which, of course, is the essential activity of his writing, as Olson noted when he said of Creeley's stories that the narrator makes clear "by way of his own person that life is preoccupation with itself. . . ."

Though Creeley's poems are often spare and small and his insistences always personal, there is, in view of his standing in the "primary situations" of his experience, nothing that merits the usual limiting characterizations of his work: minimal, domestic. He understood early what Olson told Cid Corman, that the poet starts with nothing, with only his personal details, with what he actually knows, and he was ready to accept "nakedness," the shedding of preconceptions by which one finds himself, in Emerson's words, in an original relation to the universe. Nakedness has antecedents in American literature just as projectivist verse has: it simply states the condition of the intrinsic form proposed by Emerson and the free verse practiced by Whitman—and reminds us of the body, and the physical aspect of this poetry. Creeley takes the term from Olson, who, in *Maximus,* provides, among others, the following instance:

He left him naked,
the man said, and
nakedness
is what one means

that all start up
to the eye and soul
as though it had never
happened before

And Creeley says, in explanation, that "'Nakedness' is to stand manifestly in one's own condition, in that necessary *freshness,* however exposed, because all things are particular and reality itself is the specific content of an instant's possibility."

What needs emphasis here is exposure, risk, and the heroic stance conveyed in Creeley's account of his "saints of this exposure" and in Olson's dedication of *Maximus* to Creeley, "the Figure of Outward," because literary history, for example Rosenthal's and Walter Sutton's *American Free Verse,* minimizes them. We tend, I think, to forget how much the change from extrinsic to intrinsic form and from subject to the activity of writing itself demands of the poet: that he change his life, his way of being in the world, his attentions. The "unbound thinking" of which Williams spoke—and he reminds us that the poet thinks with his poem—is neither easy nor safe. The poet is moved to it, as Williams was in "The Desert Music," a superb example of the new poetics and the Williams poem most esteemed by Creeley and Olson, because only in the poem, in the dancing of its words, can he find the possibility and being that insure his survival. Poetry, for Creeley, is the cry of its occasion, a necessary way of having life, "an agony of self-realization [Williams wrote in "The Desert Music"] / bound into a whole / by that which surrounds us." And it saves the poet: "Again and again, I find myself saved, in words," Creeley says, "—helped, allowed, returned to possibility and hope. In the dilemma of some literal context a way is found in words which may speak of it." This view of the extreme condition and function of poetry accounts for his belief that "in America, we are certainly not poets simply, nor much of the time." As he said recently, we are poets only when we are writing poems, and perhaps most often when, as he noted of Williams, we find "location in difficulty"—and "find and build happiness."

This brings us to *Pieces* and *A Day Book,* companion book-length poems concerned with survival.

Pieces ends on August 16, 1968, and *A Day Book* resumes the entries which comprise this journal-keeping on November 19, 1968.[2] Both books insist on continuity—"one continuity instead of a single poem"—which is to say that Creeley wants, as in the writing of *The Island,* a novel that he considers his first long poem, a form of writing that admits more than and carries him beyond the "single instance" of his usual poem. (The lack of pagination in *A Day Book,* lamented by Rosenthal, is deliberate.) Both books treat a continuing crisis, what might be called the crisis of middle age (Erikson's crisis of generativity?), which involves the recognition of biological age and entropy, time and death, and prompts, increasingly, a reverie toward childhood, a return to and recovery of the past (what Rosenthal calls "Proustian recollection"). The insistences that have always concerned him are present—love, place, and being as they are jeopardized by the locked-in, thinking self—but he is not now, at least in *Pieces,* as overwhelmed by them as he once was, and is accepting ("This life cannot be lived / apart from what it must forgive"), knowing now that even though he cannot wholly overcome the otherness of his situation, he sometimes is permitted to have being, to live in the here and now, in his body and in the world:

> Here now [in his ageing body] I am at best
> or what I think I am
> must follow as the rest
> and live the best it can.

Both books risk what Williams called "descent," a necessary loosening-up process, and one key to them, cited in *Pieces,* is Olson's "we are as we find out we are." Another, describing the undertaking, might be "This is the exercise for this morning," from Olson's "Tyrian Businesses." Because of this as well as the lack of sustained intensity and obvious formal coherence, I think of these long poems in terms of Williams' *Kora in Hell* and Ammons' *Tape for the Turn of the Year* rather than *Paterson* and *Maximus. Pieces,* more than *A Day Book,* which is broken by its prose and poetry sections, offers the reader familiar with Creeley's work the pleasure and excitement of sustained reading. It is a unified book, having of course the single ground of the poet's consciousness, of his poetic activity, and it may be sufficiently energized, as some believe, to warrant consideration as a long poem rather than a sequence. But the title is *Pieces,* and pieces, we learn in *Words,* are fragments, the expression of fractured being, of something less than a state of being. Pieces belong to the condition spoken of in the entry for March 13, 1968: "So tired / it falls / apart." Yet because such entries are included, the splendid poems that appear are wonderful, both arising from and creating the place for which pieces search. The activity of writing in the way he has insures these forms ("No forms / less than activity"—and no forms unless there is activity). In fact, the book begins with its own activity, one that creates possibility, the open form the work moves into, the book becomes, by transforming an end into a beginning:

> As real as thinking
> wonders created
>   by the possibility—
>
> forms. A period
> at the end of a sentence
> which

began *it was*
into a present,
  a presence

saying
something
as it goes.

Creeley discards the sentence, or syntactical prescription (as, for example, in the two fragments that comprise the poem), and by transforming end, associated with the past tense, past time, and remembering in which the self is no longer in its occasion, comes into the present and the very activity of the poem. The initial, necessary, and therapeutic act is to become "a presence"—one fully present and in motion, "saying / something / as it goes." In this way, he avoids stasis, lives in, explores, and works through his situation, a recurrent effort, represented by daily clusters of entries as well as by "Mazatlan: Sea," the longest, concluding, paradigmatic sequence of the book.

A Day Book does not open or move so easily. It begins difficultly, in prose, with Creeley confined to his head, enclosed in a room, shut out of the world. It is not a comfortable place for either reader or writer—it reminds one of the situation of John in *The Island.* But what happens there—the meditation, reverie, fantasy, and the activity of writing and writing about writing—is necessary to the "turning occasion," the eventual resolution this section of the book achieves. The major events of this section are the deaths of John Altoon (a painter, identified in *Contexts of Poetry,* who may be said to represent the first, annunciatory death of a generation of artists: "this will happen more frequently now") and Creeley's Aunt Bernice, and the decision to leave the house in Placitas, New Mexico, for Annisquam, Massachusetts. (The larger movement of the book is from Placitas to Bolinas, California.) Among other contributing events are the telephone call from Creeley's first wife, and various occurrences of domestic life, of teaching and poetry readings. All feed a deepening crisis which now involves the house in Placitas, a context and place his success as a poet has created, that he finds comfortable and might rest in, but which has also become, like the fixed circumference of the self (in Emerson's account of "Circles") a limitation to outward expansion, a shell, a "scab of previous condition," Creeley says, that must be picked off. The issue for him, aggravated by diminished energy and "deadly tiredness," is to bring himself to leave "a place [no longer] made clear in living," to move to "the place of whatever renewal of energies seems to be possible."

Writing is the activity by which this is done. And one feels this in the writing, which moves toward "clarity," away from self-reflection toward the external world, and which *moves,* more directly, liberated. There is also movement from head to body, and from head/house to body/road. As much as the unbound thinking—or, here, the unbinding of his thinking—he practices, Creeley seeks unbound being, like that of Buck Rogers, the floating of highs, or the hippies "in the world unequivocally . . . literally on the road, in the fact of their own bodies." And at the end of this section, he is again the wanderer, welcoming movement, the risk that promises renewal. Death, he realizes, is stasis, and his crisis is one of moving, the resolution of which is emblemized in the account of enplaning at Denver ("Tired of dying. Wanted only a trace. Sense of deer tracks, or rabbit—out there, in the snow. Sentimental—thought full of feeling. Welcome, stranger! Come in the door with bag in hand, smiling. Anyone. Anywhere"). And like the wanderer of his previous poems, the poet for whom "The Finger," in *Pieces,* is the representative fable, a fable recalling Williams' in "The Wanderer"—like the wanderer, he is moved to move because he still seeks the goddess: "I do keep looking, in that sense. . . ."

The complete break and shift to poetry in Part 2 marks another stage of crisis. "In London," as this part is called, is not limited to Creeley's stay in London. That title and the epigraph establish a point of beginning, which is actually one of displacement, disorientation, and vocational crisis. Williams' words from *A Voyage to Pagany* ("But what to do? and / What to do next?") are appropriate—that voyage was a crisis in Williams' career. And by association with a wasteland atmosphere, which "London" evokes, and with his Gerontion-feelings ("You have nor face nor hands / nor eyes nor head either"), the epigraph sets up Creeley's crisis in terms of Eliot and Williams.

The atmosphere at the start is Eliotic. It is autumn, and Creeley is weary, low, homesick, much concerned with the past. He is, to quote Eliot, dying with a little patience:

> We'll die
> soon enough
> and be dead—

whence the whole
system
will fade from my head—

Without energy, spiritless, his activity is mental—and that, minimal, able only to note the issue:

Die. Dead,
come alive

He is enclosed ("all in the head"), suffocating ("No air is / in this / room"). He knows what he should do—what the great poems of the book subsequently vouchsafe—

Love—
let it

Out,
open up

Very,
very *voraciously*—

Everywhere,
everyone.

But he can only state his desire ("Dance. Make happiness . . ."), not release it and be released by it.

This is the context of "The Edge," which, incidentally, is preceded by "Bobbie," a poem erotic enough, I should think, to satisfy Rosenthal. "The Edge," like Williams' "Love Song" ("I lie here thinking of you"; "you far off there . . ."), addresses loneliness.

Place it,
make the space

of it. Yellow
that was a time.

He saw the stain of love
was upon the world,

a selvage, a faint
afteredge of color fading

at the edge of the world,
the edge beyond that edge.

Here Creeley uses Williams in the context of his own dispiritedness, one determined by the past tense and the meanings *fading* and *edge* have for him. ("Neither sadness nor desire / seems the edge: this precipice" and "Love's faint trace . . ."—subsequent entries—turn us back to "The Edge.") The Williams recalled in the poem is exemplary, and Williams throughout *A Day Book* is the model of poetic activity and recovery.

There is, for example, "Kiki," which may refer to Williams' "Young Love," the ninth poem of *Spring and All*, but certainly calls up the deepest similarity between Creeley and Williams—their dependence on woman, their service to love.

World in a
plastic octa-
gon from a
most perspica-
cious daughter.

Kiki, named after Kiki of Montparnasse, is a doll in a plastic container. She is the symbolic representation of his world, one with which he cannot now make contact; and she—woman, muse—is very much the explanation for Creeley of the question Williams asks in his poem ("What about all this writing?").

"An Illness" also alludes, in "all dignity of / entrance," to "By the Road to the Contagious Hospital." But more important than such echoes is the notable fact that in this part of *A Day Book* the meditative tone and movement is very much like that of Williams' last great poems and for the reason that Creeley, too, is confronting death and petitioning his wife for love. In "The Act of Love," Creeley's confession of love overcomes the distance from his wife occasioned by his devotion to writing and by his sensualism. In respect to the issue of writing, one thinks of course, of innumerable instances in Williams' work—*A Dream of Love* is one—but especially of "Asphodel, That Greeny Flower," where the very act of writing declares the love that wins him forgiveness. And again one thinks of

"Asphodel" when reading "An Illness" because of the situation and the meditative logic, tone, and cadence:

Across from me [in the hospital]

a young woman, dark
haired, and in
her eyes much dis-

traction, and fear. The
other one, I
remember was also

young, a man, with
lovely eyes, a greyish
blue. He was

struck by what
we were
hearing, a voice,

on a tape, of an
old friend, recently dead.
Have you noticed

the prevalence
of grey blue eyes?
Is it

silly, somehow,
so to see them?
Your breasts

grow softer now
upon their
curious stem. In

bed I yearn
for softness, turning
always to you. Don't,

one wants to cry,
desert me! Have I
studied

all such isolation
just to
be alone?

. . . . .

Accesses of being occur in the sequence, and even at the end, where the gathering of great poems, beginning with "A Testament," is remarkable, lesser moments are acknowledged, as in "Kid":

The kid left
out back waits
for his mother's

face to
reappear
in

a win-
dow,
waving.

This is the measure of Creeley's honesty and of his world, where he treats each day what is given him, where there are no destinations and nothing remains fixed. Resistance to death distinguishes these poems, and in them more often than ever before he accepts his body and tells his need for friends, wife, children, people, for the world outside the window. One feels in them the presence of Whitman as well as Williams. An obsessive word of this volume is *around* (as in "See / the things around you"; "I felt around myself"; "See / the night / all around"). And in this part there is a significant change from wandering to walking.

"You" establishes the context:

Back and forth across
time, lots of things
one needs one's

hand held for. Don't
stumble, in the dark. Keep
walking. This is life

Walking not only enjoins movement, as in Part 1; it accords with Williams' injunction to Paterson to walk in the world. One is no longer, or not quite, the romantic wanderer so prominent in Creeley's poems, though he may still be present in "I / walk down a road / you make ahead." A more fitting example is "For Betsy and Tom":

> We are again
> walking in a
> straight line—feet
>
> fall, footsteps. We
> walk! I am
> happy, foolish I
>
> stumble on to the next
> person, I think
> to myself, charming in
>
> the peace she so manifestly
> carries with her. All the
> children follow us. The
>
> dogs walk also,
> with a sort of sedateness.
> They think
>
> they think. We
> whistle. I want to
> love everyone alive!

Or in "'Bolinas and Me. . . ,'" which tells also of wandering, and of homecoming: "Walking / and walking, dream of those / voices, people again. . . ."

Among the great poems toward the end of the book are "A Testament," "The Act of Love," "The Birds," "An Illness," "People," "For Benny and Sabina," "For Betsy and Tom," and "'Bolinas and Me. . . .'" (Of these Rosenthal mentions only "People.") Subsidence occurs toward the very end, and "'Bolinas and Me . . .'" works through many difficulties to affirmation. In the small closing verses the world again is open for the poet. It seems, in "Sea," that he has dismissed the "wake" that, in Part 1, had figured, as in Hart Crane's "Southern Cross," the perils of retrospection. Reverie toward childhood now brings him home ("it all comes home").[3] *Place* is what he has in mind when, in the concluding poem, he denies that "you can't / get back / what's gone by." In that poem he tells his daughter that "We live in a circle"; this gainsays an earlier entry: "You think in the circle / round the whole [hole?]." The "we" is salutary, and so are the thinking of others and the act of memory it has now stirred him to undertake.

A few words on *Listen,* and I'm done. The play deals with the usurpation or possession of another person; this is what the women, all of them designated by "You," the other in the protagonist's mind, protest. The most excruciating instance of such relationship is treated in *The Island.* Creeley ponders that situation in *A Day Book* when he says, "No one owns. I think the most useful truth I've been given to acknowledge of others, as a man, is that in one's own experience another's is not necessarily denied nor increased." In *Pieces,* he tells the arrogance of thought that owns and must be humbled:

There was no one there.
Rather I thought I saw her,
and named her beauty.

For that time we lived
all in my mind
with what time gives.

The substance of one
is not two. No thought
can ever come to that.

I could fashion another
were I to lose her.
Such is thought.

The American production, which is the only one I've heard, sometimes achieves a pleasant antiphony and nostalgic tone, but the opening fanfare announcing it is embarrassingly arty—and time-filling—and the enunciation, as often with actors, is too deliberate, perhaps too British.

Notes

1. An appropriate title for an essay on Creeley might be "Where I Lived and What I Lived For."

2. Mary Novik's *Robert Creeley: An Inventory, 1945–1970* (Kent State Uni-

versity Press, 1973), now enables us to date Creeley's poems, which have always been ordered chronologically and constitute, as he appreciates in Zukofsky's work, the one poem a poet writes all his life.

3. The lines summon for me "The Picnic" (in *The Charm*), the finest poem on this theme. It concludes:

> Time we all went home,
> or back,
> to where it all was,
> where it all was.

Understanding Creeley

Cynthia Edelberg's *Robert Creeley's Poetry: A Critical Introduction*—the first book-length treatment of Creeley's work—is limited to his poetry and, even then, treats only *For Love, Words, Pieces,* and "In London," the section of poems in *A Day Book. The Charm,* a volume of early and hitherto uncollected poems, is not considered in this study of poetic development for the following (questionable) reasons: "I do not include this volume . . . because the poems collected here do not indicate the way in which Creeley's poetic voice will develop. Furthermore, the poems themselves have little merit." The substantial body of Creeley's work—novel, stories, play, essays, criticism—which Creeley says, and a critic should assume, are continuous with the poems, of the totality of his *writing,* hardly figures at all, with the result that what Creeley means by the title *Contexts of Poetry* (interviews that help us recover occasions) is absent. Much that might have deepened the reading of the poems and restrained or qualified interpretative zeal is foregone: the context Creeley himself so generously provides and the context of postmodern poetry, the enterprise Creeley so fully shared with others.

An exceptionally fine photograph of Creeley by Elsa Dorfman serves as a frontispiece. The poet's expressive face suggests not only the burdens we encounter in the poems but perhaps his response in the appended transcriptions to Edelberg's insistent interpretations ("Yeah, I suppose . . ."; "Yeah, well, I'm sorry . . ."). For this book, if not a thesis, has a thesis, in the trying sense of thesis-ridden. It involves three themes or continuing preoccupations of the poet—his concern with thought, love, and poetry—and the development of these concerns. (For example: "*Words* is a transitional volume. . . . At the core of it is his rejection of Valéry's perspective and his acceptance of Olson's.") Instead of *theme,* Creeley, who supplies the needed critical terms in *A Quick Graph* and *Contexts of Po-*

etry, would undoubtedly have preferred *insistences;* instead of *development,* with its suggestion of linear, step-by-step "progress," perhaps *course* or *trajectory,* which are more in accord with the way his poems variously issue from the manifold immediate occasions of his life. Furthermore, while appreciating Edelberg's recognition of his debt to Valéry's *Monsieur Teste* and to Zukofsky's *It Was,* he would most likely have questioned the way in which, in the first instance, she presses it too hard, in the second misuses it.

An instructive essay by Cid Corman, "Corman on Warren on Frost" in *At Their Word,* addresses the essential problem raised by Edelberg's book: how a critic can displace a poem and induce specious readings—how, in a book-length work such as *Robert Creeley's Poetry,* she can violate both poems and poet by refusing to take the poet *at his word,* in the literal activity of his work. I cite Corman on R. P. Warren because what is involved are habits of reading and interpretation fostered by *Understanding Poetry.* The predilection here is to impose a scheme, to validate a poem by adducing an extrinsic meaning. Edelberg says that Creeley, in *Pieces,* asks the reader to participate in the poems to the end of fitting what he finds there "into a coherent pattern." She speaks of "the conceptual framework of the sequence"; she says that "the romance convention shapes *Pieces.*" But does a poet who himself rejects extrinsic order expect us, want us, to supply it? Creeley writes, in *Pieces:*

> My plan is
> these little boxes
> make sequences . . .
> Lift me
> from such I
> makes such declaration.

Well, the boxes do make a sequence, are sequential: the poetic notations for each day are divided by a dot (.), and a day's work by three dots (. . .), a matter of form Edelberg overlooks in *Pieces,* preferring to adapt it to "In London," which she values for the very risk Creeley had taken in the earlier book. Why? Because she reads *Pieces* literally in terms of Northrop Frye's version of the romantic quest and gives it the coherence it lacks. Lacks? Was never "intended" to have. Now *The Charm,* among other early work, depicts a romantic (and postromantic) wanderer, and the burdens of the wanderer are among the insistences of the poems in *Pieces,* very much so in one of its finest and longest poems, "The Finger."

Can't this be recognized rather than made into a scheme? Is it necessary to make the poet a "hero" who undertakes a "perilous journey" and confronts a "sea monster"? Isn't the poet simply a person (not a *persona*) in the actual, literal occasions of the poems? Sea monster?

An unexamined hump
at first of no
interest lifting out
of the beach at
last devoured us all.

Devour here takes its meaning from *unexamined* and *of no interest;* it means "consumed us in our interest" and the context of entries on attention supports this rather than some notion of being eaten by a dragon. No dragon, and no Perseus; probably just a sea turtle, as the next entry, omitted by Edelberg, informs us: "Sell the motherfucker for / several hundred dollars." I do not question the centrality of "The Finger" but the way Edelberg construes the mythic material it employs, thereby dismissing the profounder depth at which it works—moves—in the poem.

She does not find Creeley's treatment of women, either in archetypal terms (as Goddess) or in human terms, credible; one, she says, is fantasy, the other stereotype. (An excursion into the stories, say "Mabel," or into the novel, *The Island,* might have put in question such convictions.) In *For Love,* she finds his "addresses to the 'Lady' . . . devoid of humility and reverence"; his response to the "Lady" is "silly, stylized, agonized." So she is not inclined to acknowledge what "The Finger" means to *Creeley*—she does not include his account of the poem in *Contexts of Poetry*—how much the erotic content means to him and how it finds expression in another visionary poem, the penultimate poem of *Pieces,* where he realizes (to use Whitman's words) that the kelson of creation is love. No, for her this vision is a "farce"; it is not the burden that his generation of poets so conspicuously bears (Olson: "Venus / does not arise from / these waters. Fish / do"). Later on, in "In London," a similar inability to accommodate the dimensions of the poem confounds her reading of "People." She says the poem is full of "fantastic notions." But then she doesn't pick up Creeley's account of the fairies he once believed inhabited the woods nor respond to the sense of nature that informs "The Rhythm" and distinguishes *Words*—and in a subsequent poem on the death of his mother is wonderfully expressed.

Underfurnished. Archival material has not been used—none of the letters of Olson and Creeley, very little of the correspondence with Williams, none of the abundant manuscript and other material readily available. Too much is at second-hand, and there are too many inaccuracies (Olson began to teach at Black Mountain in 1948, not 1945: Williams' trip to Europe in 1924 was not "year-long," etc.). This neglect, combined with arbitrary and repetitive exposition and brief, schematic, and for the most part inadequate readings of the poems, undermines the authority with which a critic wins our confidence. Cynthia Edelberg's book puts one on guard, in an adversary position, checking every reading and resisting much that, inadvertently, diminishes the poet. This "introduction" does not serve Creeley well.

PART VIII

The Correspondence of Charles Olson and Robert Creeley

Gripping, Pushing, Moving

I

I suspect that Robert Creeley was always a letter writer and that he began to write voluminously—became a man of letters—simply because sometime toward the end of 1949 or the beginning of 1950 his dismay with the situation in poetry provoked him to publish, with his friend Jacob Leed, a little magazine. I hear myself saying, "Yet another little magazine!" and I say it now because the failure to launch *The Lititz Review,* which was only, finally, a mechanical failure, the result of a faulty press, remains instructive. These letters—the first two volumes of *Charles Olson and Robert Creeley,* a projected multivolume correspondence edited by George Butterick, cover the brief period April 21 to September 21, 1950—are Creeley's show in the absence of many of Charles Olson's letters; and Creeley's concern with the magazine, especially as the correspondence itself clarifies the issues and proposes the work it should push, is very much part of the story. If nothing else, the letters, along with those to Leed, Pound, William Carlos Williams, Cid Corman, and Vincent Ferrini published or available elsewhere, provide an essential (heroic) chapter in the history of little magazines and American literature because, as it turned out, the failure of *The Lititz Review* was made good in *Origin,* begun by Corman in 1951, and *The Black Mountain Review,* begun by Creeley in 1954. The writers whose work Creeley had so arduously solicited became the nucleus of Corman's magazine (the first two issues featured Olson and Creeley), and Corman's achievement, somewhat distorted by the one-sided correspondence of Olson's *Letters for Origin,* is not diminished by recognizing how much in the matter of setting things in motion was Creeley's work. The new movement in American letters was to a large extent encouraged by letters—when, it should be noted, first-class postage was three cents.

The architect Daniel Burnham used to admonish his colleagues to "make no little plans," where Louis Sullivan asked them to "remember the seed-germ." Reading these letters reminds us that little magazines are seed-germs; that two people, one pretty much alone on a farm in Littleton, New Hampshire, the other about as solitary and unnoticed in Washington, D.C., may do greater things than they know by writing letters ("let language be our tie!" Olson exclaims early on), by thus confronting their isolation and transferring, and compounding, their energies. Of most importance then—and now—was the crystallization of ideas fostered by this correspondence; it formed two distinguished careers; and it gave rise to a new poetics, a new charter, to use Grant Webster's term. (" . . . isn't time," Pound wrote Creeley, "for Creel's generation to revolt against the dead hand, dating from Dial or before / backwash of aestheticism. . . ?") The letters themselves are sometimes drafts of what was subsequently published ("Projective Verse" and "The Gate and the Center") and are valuable because they deepen our understanding of projective writing, whether in verse or prose. They exemplify the very theory discussed in them, one of the best forms for projective expression, which Creeley acknowledged by publishing Olson's *Mayan Letters*—and Corman, too, by making letters a distinctive feature of *Origin*. The letters, then, are not merely documents; they bring us immediately into the current of life. Sometimes they are so stunning, of such force of mind and heart, that one feels compelled to say, as Creeley did on first recognizing Olson's work, "Too much! too much!" (a phrase, picked up from jazz musicians by Creeley, that Olson, his senior by sixteen years, asked him to gloss). Or compelled to cite Williams' reply to Creeley: "I am really startled at what you see and how clearly you see it. It's stimulating to me to realize your clarity of purpose . . . your drive."

To adapt Williams: no little magazines (of any worth) without ideas. And no little magazines without generalship. Discussing Creeley's force with my colleague Donald Marshall, he remarked that Plato was wrong about poets, that they, not philosopher-kings, should rule—which may not be wide-of-the-mark of Olson's belief in the sovereign power of the poet as pedagogue, a role he himself filled when he gave up a political career. Creeley's letters—these and the others, all notable for their various styles, each respectively taking the measure of the recipient—belie whatever impression of reticence, hesitancy, or stumbling his poems give, though these, one comes to realize, are hard ("conglomerates" is his word), evidence of the *grip* he so often demands in the letters, of having things directly in, and under, *hand.* The Creeley of the letters is forward, fearless, and commanding, so much so that both Pound and Williams, to whom he turned for help, took the trouble to keep up a correspondence with a young man of 23.

Olson's letters are modelled on Pound's, though they soon become as open, as free formally and visually provocative, as those in *Letters for Origin* and *Mayan Letters.* Creeley's letters to Olson are composed of sentences broken into small breath phrases by heavy, unusual punctuation (colon and slash), marked by abbreviations and syntactical inversion. Their effect is of rapid fire, a brisk shorthand, even though they must be read word by word, as carefully as poems, alertly. And they are often poems, as in the following indebted to Charlie Parker: "Tell yez / wd, to get out, to get clear: to renew / this life. Give much to be anywhere / . . . chewing the fat / slide & slip. Going dead." They fulfill his demand for sound; they go by ear. There is the frequent aside, "like they say" (still a signature), and often a final turn, undercutting his aggressiveness and extremity of feeling with the knife of self-awareness. They are urgent, so it may not be farfetched to recall the example of General Grant, whose prose-dispatch was prompted by the battlefield. (And didn't it require generalship to outflank Pound's campaign to use the magazine to his ends?) It is understandable, then, that in dedicating *The Maximus Poems*—begun at this time in a *letter* to Ferrini—Olson thought of Creeley as "the Figure of Outward," an "opposite to a / personality which so completely does (did) / stay at home." He was the person who enabled him by correspondence ("why *was* the pt. then to write Creeley / daily?") to have the "'World.'"

That Pound and Williams needed Creeley as much as he needed them tells us a great deal about the situation in poetry in 1950. Creeley recalls that at Harvard his teacher, F. O. Matthiessen, didn't include Pound in the course on contemporary poetry, nor Hart Crane—avoidances whose importance he indicates when he remarks, in an unfavorable context, that "in 2000 years, maybe all such: will be grouped under general heading / Ez Pound." (He comments extensively on Crane in the letters.) The guiding poets of the time were Stevens and Auden, the former much respected by him though said to have "fallen to the questionable fact of a device" ("Stevens ain't got the push, any more. It is a method / holds him up. NOT a content"), the latter dismissed for "a socially based use of irony

[that] became the uselessly exact rigor of repetitive verse patterns. . . ." Creeley felt, as Williams insisted, that "the measure itself / had been lost," and that too many young writers of his generation had failed to school themselves in the *art* of poetry in the work of Pound and Williams—failed, as Olson has Yeats say in Pound's defense, to take up and carry on "the advances we made for you." When Creeley wrote to Corman in December 1949, in what must be one of the first salvos of the advance, he complained of *Poetry* on two scores: its kind of lyricism ("I can't see very much that they've published in the last 4 or 5 years, new, that is, that's been worth the effort") and its failure to maintain its initial force ("And we don't need the tradition so much as we do the kind of force & straightness that brought it into being"). Creeley and Olson consider many little magazines in the course of the correspondence—they are busy submitting manuscripts to some of them and know the timidity and dilatoriness of editors, the lack of force and straightness; and they have been rejected, perhaps the most remarkable instance being the refusal by *The Kenyon Review* of a Creeley story, accepted and paid for but then returned when John Crowe Ransom concurred in R. P. Warren's opinion that it lacked "plot." It should not surprise anyone who knows this time that Creeley and Leed planned to devote an early issue of *The Lititz Review* to education, that is, to the University; that they took issue with it, knew that as much as the little magazines, the academy contributed to the tightness and settled state of things. By this time the New Critics dominated the schools and even the New York intellectuals were turning to them, and to magazines like *The Kenyon Review,* for support. Corman wisely refused the institutional backing of Brandeis when he undertook *Origin,* and Creeley and Olson also stood outside the circle of such support. The obsessive words of their correspondence are *push* (noun and verb) and *move.* The mounting anger of these letters is caused by stasis, the impasse and impotence of thwarted hope and energy; the humor is caused by the fact, noted in "Le Fou" and probably recognized only by them, that "they are waving" (the others, standing still) and "we are moving."

The poetics that they work out in the letters—Olson from the vantage of poetry and Creeley from that of prose—is also one of push and movement, eminently projective. Its gist appears in Creeley's early comment that the head should determine form as "an extension of its own center," not do "menial / enclosed / work. . . ." Or phrased another way, "the compression & push of poetry: toward a single 'action' of comprehension. . . ." By restoring the "subjective," he would join art and life, make writing "personal," the work of what he calls the "Single Intelligence," that center from which one pushes his own content. It is "the usable content of a man," his "coherence"; and it is pushed / moved so that "what was of me, in, is it: out." (Turn the inside out, Williams said.) So form is the extension of content: in the very language, the literal activity, of the poem, we have the particular history (his-story, Olson would later pun) of a man who knows directly, and firmly grips, what he is writing about, delivers it straight, exactly. When given this notion by Creeley, Olson adduced Whitman.

Creeley adduces Lawrence, the prose writer whom, with Stendhal and Dostoevsky, he admires most, and, with some reservations, Crane, the poet, who, he believes, "push[es] way out," farther than Pound, Williams, and Stevens. To use one of Creeley's more recent formulations, Crane is an example of life tracking life. In the letters there is a statement addressing the heart of this undertaking: "Too much / those things. I mean: of the heart, that which can be tracked. . . ." Crane, he says, tracks the heart by feel, or as Olson says in another context, "he goeth by / langwitch." Charlie Parker, an exemplar for Creeley of the going by ear—the sound—both prose and poetry now require, is another who "live[s] by feel"; he "pushed out too far." Lawrence, too, goes "by the head & heart." Heart? Yes, taking one's feelings straight, as Creeley wished to advise Ferrini to do; permitting "a direct reaction," which has been blocked in recent poetry ("there are countries where men can cry"). This is why he frequently cites Williams' "Why do I write today" (from "The Apology") and why for him the value of the new poetics is that it doesn't "stifle feel / grip: by preconceptions . . . ONLY as the coming out: makes it."

Of the many implications of this poetics perhaps the most radical at the time and the most necessary for Olson and Creeley were the following: that content is the evidence of originality ("A man, each man, is NEW. If his method, his form IS the logic of his content: he cannot be but: NEW / 'original'"); that "conjecture," an active, searching attention, is requisite; and that memory must become a condition of the present ("You can't go 'back'—you got to pull 'to'"), a problem that Creeley was confronting in his stories and Olson would soon confront in working out the historiographical difficulties of *The Maximus Poems*. Creeley may be said to summarize the case, when, exasperated by reading anthologies of poetry, he says, "I don't want the remembering. I want the straight thing. The straight open breath of it, the freshness, the love, exact & living." Olson says it in a letter to Ferrini: "when I also speak of PV [Projective

Verse] as propellant, I think of the man as his own muzzle—and charge." And as he remarked to Creeley at the outset, when he announced the battle: "a man . . . / has to come up with his own lang., syntax and song both, but also each poem under hand has its own language. . . ."

II

Of course, it is not necessary to join the battle or to use the letters as a textbook of poetics in order to enjoy them and welcome their publication. Their importance is assured: this is unquestionably one of the great correspondences of the twentieth century. So it is assuring to have the letters in the care of a capable editor and courageous publisher. George Butterick respects the text and doesn't tamper with it. His notes, as always, are ample and invariably helpful: resourceful. His Introduction, brief yet summary, is surely modest in the light of the many volumes of correspondence still to come. The illustrations he has selected for each volume are excellent, and the indexes of persons named in the letters and of works by Olson and Creeley referred to there are very convenient. The format of the volumes is the usual handsome one that identifies the Black Sparrow Press. Like many of the volumes John Martin has published, these confirm the value of his enterprise, his push, the way he keeps (good) things moving.

Like all great letters the appeal of these lies in their unguarded expression and revelation of human quality. They have *size,* as Olson said of the Sumerian kings, when, in "The Gate and the Center," he addressed the issue of education; they exhibit extensible energy and offer us the "IMAGE of possibilities implicit in the energy," that is, to cite his own statement of purpose at the end of *The Maximus Poems,* give us "an image / of man, 'The nobleness, and the arete.'" This installment also has the excitement of beginnings, of being on hand to witness what Olson called "Corinth." He said of the happy accident of Melville discovering Shakespeare that "Melville and Shakespeare had made a Corinth and out of the burning came *Moby-Dick,* bronze." This speaks for an intellectual event, where the Corinth of Olson and Creeley is that and also a personal event, the beginning of a lifelong friendship, more enduring than that of Hawthorne and Melville, but of that kind.

I read these letters as much as anything for such tokens of necessary generosity as Olson's almost immediate encouragement ("above all things resist, to be sick at heart: we are forward, and it is such gratification, that you are ready to go with me / / love, / Olson") and his immediate remittance of the money Creeley needed to procure library privileges at Dartmouth College; and on Creeley's part for such admissions as "Because / much talk from the others: but from yrself: the facts of the poems / the prose of P / & the verse. The letters. That wd be enough, any one of them," and "Jesus / O / I ask nothing, absolutely, nothing from you but that you stay within reach: letters—let[s] build this thing." So much is moving inside, within them, and so little is moving outside that they have often to grapple each other close (Olson: "this / correspondence, you and me"; Creeley, echoing Lear?: "Let's you and I, by God, write for each other!"). And inescapable throughout the letters, almost from the start, is the groundtone of Creeley's desire to see Olson, whom, in fact, he didn't meet until March 1954, when he came to Black Mountain College—a disappointment as great as the failure of his magazine.

There is, inevitably, much here of biographical interest and much to satisfy the hunger, whetted by the distance of time, for literary gossip. Olson describes his curious working day from 1 to 9 PM, determined, he explains, by his wife's "crazy" shift, and their apartment near the railroad tracks ("this small two room jewel in brick, with garden"). He notes, in speaking of particularists and generalizers, that T. S. Eliot has misused "my, *my* madonna, buona viaggi"—this before he had begun *The Maximus Poems* and Creeley could pick up the reference. Compared with Creeley, he's reticent, or maybe it's that what personally concerns him most in the letters is his relationship with Pound. He had broken with Pound two years earlier but mentions it only when Pound writes Creeley of Olson's defection: "Believe Olson FUNDAMENTALLY (not superficially) wrong, tendency which will sterilize anything it touches. i.e., AGAINST nature's increase, etc." Creeley found this kind of literary politics disturbing, and petty. It posed a serious question of loyalty for him, as it had for Olson, who said that "the big struggle, after the decision to leave politics . . . , was to leave Ez." Creeley admitted his struggle, and that he had been "holding to you, as against him. . . ." He knew what he owed Pound, recognized his power, his "ways and means," but almost immediately held with Olson, a decision of considerable consequence for his magazine and one that brought forward as its presiding elder the gentler, less officious Williams.

For his part, Creeley writes vividly of his life on the farm at Littleton and of the years preceding it, the time at Cape Cod, at Harvard, in India and Burma during the war. He explains his awkwardness in cities, how he went under in Boston ("cd not hold myself / or work"); his singleness ("I cant see that one writes / or does anything / to be among others: but only to be: himself"); his fierceness ("Christ: get there if you can and see the land you once were proud to own, etc., or: shit. Keep clear & go with & by yrself. Who is there / that can make that difference. I am ready, dammit, I am ready: to leave anywhere, anything: at any time"), and his egoism ("My egoism is very great. I believe in all sincerity that what I say is important"). So constituted what could he do but make his push with a magazine or, later, with the Divers Press? His dilemma: "how to take on what I think are valid / actual: responsibilities, without sacrificing the aloneness." He writes of his love of cars, his good relations with his mother, family history, the need for roots. His several accounts of jazz, especially of the "Bird," are notable (to "Le Fou," he appends, "Thank you—Charles Parker. Et tu—Thelonius Bach"). More than Olson he tells of his intellectual and social life, his reading, for example, of Lawrence ("Lawrence is worth 50,000 Pounds in any market") and Dahlberg ("Sick, sick bk / man"), the visits of Slater Brown, a valuable, generous friend and mentor, and of Mitchell Goodman and Denise Levertov, the latter, it seems, spoiling for him a much-used book, Rilke's *Letters to a Young Poet*.

But enough. There are riches here, and much advice to put with Rilke's. Olson dated postmodern, in these letters anyway, with Hiroshima. I hear postmortem in the word, but also postpartem. And I think of "La Préface," where Olson might just as well be speaking of Creeley as of Cagli when he says, "We are the new born" and this means that there is "no parenthesis." These letters are an opening, and bring us into the open. Creeley wrote in "Hart Crane," the poem that initiates his work, that for Crane letters proved insufficient. The measure of these letters is that they proved sufficient and enabled Olson and Creeley to make "the push / beyond. . . ."

Holding

I

These volumes, numbers three and four of the Charles Olson-Robert Creeley correspondence, take up where the previous volumes end, on 21 September 1950, and carry forward to 11 February 1951, so that we now have about ten months of the story of two poets whose emergence was coextensive with that of a new literary generation. Their story, to pun on Olson's equation of *his story* and *history,* is history, a matter of literary history anyway, of persons, places and things (little magazines, especially). There are many letters, often more than one a day, and this gives the impression of a long time, though the time is short, a few months during which both writers continue their solitary lives, sustained in large part by the correspondence. (Mail service then almost kept pace with thought; even in Lerma, Campeche, Olson expected delivery in two days.) The correspondence is eminently literary, the threshing ground of the new poetics of verse and prose they seek to demonstrate in their work and the intelligence center/command post of their various sorties of literary advance (*push* is their word, accompanied by the usual military expletives; a conspicuous new word, appropriated from jazz musicians by Creeley, is *gig*).

Still unknown to each other except through their work and the letters (recordings and phone calls are special, rare occasions), Olson and Creeley come together here, as George Butterick notes in his brief introduction, in absolute trust, each the confidant of the other. The integrity of their friendship is one with the integrity of their literary concerns—their vocations, *commitment,* a word that finds its way into their poetics. They may be said to be living their lives according to the proposals of field composition, certainly with the risk of openness; and their letters, too, are seldom merely communications but examples of conjectural form. Commenting on Creeley's use of *conjecture,* a central term in his poetics, Olson says: "if a man (the writer) is in there, committed, what he has to say is as open, as, in fact, a man who is same is, then any page, any word, may blow you the hell, yr life, *change.*" These letters are notable—however much their abundance may tire one, or it may be the attention sometimes required to parse Creeley's bop syntax—because the writers are in there, committed, the literary life something other than the usual game.

To cite another idea Creeley takes up in regard to short stories, these writers are not in *opposition* but in *apposition;* they relate to each other, are as critically generous and true as, say, Pound in taking up *The Waste Land,* and as careful of the other's needs as, again, Pound was in the case of the overworked and harassed Eliot. Olson sends Creeley postage stamps—a considerable expense when one remembers that Creeley was writing to others besides Olson, typing up manuscripts, his and others, and sending them off—and immediately provides the requisite travel and household information about Yucatan, should Creeley decide to go there. On his part, Creeley offers to send "loot" to help Olson on his way, to Yucatan. (One of the finest sentences is Creeley's "if we can be of help, re yr getting there, for the love, finally, of some things in this life, please let us know.") Though brought together by their uncommonly common literary concerns, their friendship itself has already become transcendent. As Creeley says, "There was these two men, see. . . ." He signs his letters "Yr lad" (he is 24, Olson 40). And when things get *tight—tightness* and *deadness* are conditions Creeley amply acknowledges—he writes, "WHAT ELSE, BUT yr letters, have held me, DO, over the fucking bumps."

Have held me. Yes, no question about the letters during this troubled time of increasing physical cold and spiritual discontent, when nothing *moves,* at least not as rapidly as Olson and Creeley wish, and all that can be done, it seems, is "hold."

II

To hold (on) when they know that what they are joined in is "the MOVE, the NEXT move"—that's part of starting out in the 1950s, from Rock Pool, a small subsistence farm in Littleton, New Hampshire, where Creeley has been living for nearly three years with Ann and their son

David, and from a two-room apartment in Washington, D.C., where Olson has been living with his wife Con. (Fielding Dawson describes Olson's "beautiful, magic, little house" in "On Olson, with References to Guy Davenport," *Sagetrieb,* I [Spring 1982].) Both are fully engaged by their work, but neither, as we say, is gainfully employed. Both are supported by their wives, Creeley by a small trust fund of Ann's (when it becomes inadequate because of increasing expenses, he does not choose to supplement it but to move to a place where it will suffice), Olson by Con's work as an office manager. Worth mentioning? Only because neither Ann nor Con figures conspicuously in the letters in the way, say, Cid Corman now does, which of course is not unusual, but just the same. . . . Ann, Creeley admits, is part of his "ground," one of the few the soul selects. But she is here, nevertheless, by virtue of "this thing" Creeley has with women, "that there is a force of them, pulls or throws." Ann is such a *force,* all the more so because she is pregnant and the pregnancy, complicated by the Rh factor, is also, it seems, on hold. And just as important, she is a literary force: "Ann has continued to yowl abt: lack of woman's 'point of view,' etc., etc. [in "Mr. Blue"]"; "My wife (DAMN her) just sez: it seems to me, that moon [in Olson's "The Moon is the Number 18," unsuccessfully glossed by Creeley] is from the tarot pack"; "as Ann says (me saying: but NOTHING OUT, MYSELF): o well/it's all right, you just haven't had any ideas." From such casual hints and others concerning sexual importunity—irritation with the ever-tired wife, the sleeping wife, and the postpartum abstinence that he thinks, having searched out this questionable notion in Freud, "dries me out"—much is adumbrated, poems, stories, novel.

Olson himself is hardly present here, represented by only eleven letters, and little is said about his domestic life. Again, as in the previous volumes, these are Creeley's letters, and the story, to that extent, is partial, one-sided. It might be summed up by saying that it involves getting things out—getting into print, establishing a foothold, preparing for such things as a Guggenheim fellowship—and getting out—getting out of the present stasis (deadness), moving on, not so much for financial reasons as for deeper reasons of spiritual economy. To move, it seems, is the desideratum, any move. Creeley prizes life on the farm; it accords with his fierce need for singleness. "Here," he says, "as things go, I have a life, of my & our own, which means, none of the shit." Still the pressure to move, on Ann's part as well as his, is irresistible, abetted by Olson's sudden move to Yucatan in January ("i am moving   moving, lad!") and what this induces, "that taste, & what exact, want again, to be moving" he revives for himself in telling Olson of Lawrence's travels and his own travels during his time in the American Field Service. *To be moving*—this is fundamental, the necessary rhythm whereby Creeley overcomes the deadness (see *A Day Book, Hello*). Coming now—he will soon go to France, a roundabout way to Yucatan!—it signals, as did Olson's move, a significant change. By the time this portion of the correspondence concludes, many things on hold are about to begin or have begun to move. Now it would be more appropriate than it was early on to cite "Le Fou": "we are moving."

III

A number of things makes this a troublesome, crucial time for Creeley, and the number of times he rehearses them tells their importance to him. In a letter of 13 November 1950, with this marginalia ("All too tight—breaks gig—Ann, Kid, Me"), he lists some of them:

> . . . for myself: too much hanging, and/or
>
> the baby
> the place to live
>
> the chap bk
>
> the divers things out, with no word
>
> cid
> (and could here list characters like:
> Emerson, et al)
>
> stop of push, which dated with gug
>
> . . . .

It's the waiting ("too much hanging") that bothers him, especially when the delay in publication jeopardizes the Guggenheim fellowship that he counts on so much. To apply at all seems audacious, but then Olson had received one, with little to go on but good academic credentials. Creeley, as he knows, has nothing to offer: "24 yrs / no degrees / no occupation other than small farm / no honors, no printed works / no appearance of sternness, the good life / no evidence of seriousness other than hysteria /

no no no." And, as he finds out, he has no one he can trust for references except Olson—"who else (FOR ME) but yrself."

The proposal for this fellowship is a central document carefully worked out and revised in consultation with Olson, and it turns on everything Creeley is doing at this time. The chapbook he mentions is a collection of five stories ("In the Summer," "The Seance," "3 Fate Tales," "The Lover," and "Mr. Blue") that he hopes Richard Wirtz Emerson will publish at the Golden Goose Press. In addition, these stories are to be accompanied by his "Notes for a New Prose" and Olson's "Introduction to Robert Creeley," major statements discussed at length in the letters and worked into the fellowship proposal as justification for the significance of Creeley's demonstration.

As in the previous volumes, Creeley is concerned primarily with prose and with narrative theory—a poetics of narrative that belongs with Olson's recently published "Projective Verse" and that with it, and such ponderings here as Olson's on sleep, may be said to constitute a field theory. To call it such is to acknowledge its scope, the necessary connection, as in "Projective Verse," of writing and stance, language and reality. This inclusiveness, or profundity, explains the way in which much that Olson and Creeley discuss (for example, Sumer—Olson's "The Gate & The Center" and the will to cohere) feeds into it.

In one of the first of the letters from Yucatan, Olson distinguishes between the old and the new in a summary way: "the new is of the making of our own lives & references. . . ." The old is humanism: "that itch to conclude," Creeley says; "To find pattern / external / continual." Elsewhere he notes the difference between *understanding* and *realization,* the former, as in *Understanding Poetry,* equating with analysis. Or he speaks of plot or frame ("all such 'frame' is SHIT"), refusing them as limiting, modes of domination (and: "No man has yet figured a way to dominate EXCEPT by crippling"). To these present requisites of narrative—for lack of which his stories are refused—he prefers to "ride," to go with what the writing itself proposes, or what the objects, themselves having force, propose in their relation to him, in their eventfulness. Instead of fixing, he wants fixes. What matter to him are the ongoing relations of objects to a narrator who, though the story necessarily swings on him, is also an object in a field of experience larger than himself, with more alternatives than he can command.

This is why Creeley's covering term is *conjecture.* "My own world," he explains, "is conjectural. . . . What each thing is, is so, because—at last—it couldn't be anything else. I limit it / but not limit: simply find its fix." This conjectural world is both processual and relational: "Man looks for RELATION . . . looks for fix of forces, as he is, & IS, a part. He plots with his only instrument: conjecture." Neither the *a priori* nor the past is determining, but rather the present, the vantage in terms of which what is past becomes relational, acquires significance. In Olson's terms in "Introduction to Robert Creeley," conjecture involves a narrator who is the *total in* (as opposed to document, the *total out,* distinctions Creeley doesn't endorse), and in such terms it is easy to see why conjecture answers to Creeley's need for singleness and his sense of commitment, the preoccupation of life with itself referred to by Olson. Conjecture is both the way in which one can come closest to oneself and precisely deliver that content and the way to stay "open" (matters discussed here in respect to Lawrence, the writer Creeley admires most and whom Olson considers in "Notes on Lawrence & the Real"). Writing, now, is to be judged by enactment rather than by representation—Olson will soon speak of language as the act of the instant, not thought about the instant. The poetics is one of present experience and is valued for "the writer's contesting with reality," the drama of "this open man, staying open in there," committed to that.

Anyone interested in Creeley's stories will appreciate these volumes for these theoretical considerations, accompanied as they are by close attention to the stories then in hand, especially "Mr. Blue," one of Creeley's finest. And after all of the reported misunderstandings of Creeley's work, the response of Katue Kitasono, from Japan, will be appreciated: "My first impressions of these works are such exquisite psychological Variations going to be reeled out in that stuttering but elastic rhythmic style of you." Has anyone more perceptively seized on "the unique of you"? Testimony of this kind—unexpected, immediately generous and true—is one of the heartening signs of movement. Another is the response of Rainer Maria Gerhardt, in Germany. These letters are especially important for filling out our knowledge of Creeley's and Olson's connection with Gerhardt's *Fragmente,* and amusing, besides, because Creeley's German is not always adequate to a correspondence, again, often concerned with theoretical and methodological matters.

Placing work, getting it recognized and printed, is of course the most frequent business of the correspondence. It is a tedious story of complications and frustrations, which is why, I suppose, I mention first the gratifying instances of Kitasono and Gerhardt, whose conduct of literary affairs was, in fact, the measure by which Creeley himself liked to proceed and judged others. Judge he does, not necessarily unjustly (though *in time* things turn out well) but harshly, bitterly, willing, as he says, to do battle "if it's root." And it was: literary survival, dependent now chiefly on Cid Corman's efforts to start *Origin,* which were not, as they seemed, on the point of being compromised by the temptation of backing from Brandeis University, and Richard Emerson's efforts to keep things going at the Golden Goose Press. Corman, whom the index shows to be the most frequently mentioned person in the correspondence, enters the stage of literary history here, in the role of victim, comic butt. Creeley's account of his dealings with Corman is of course true to the occasion, that is, *his occasions;* but after-the-fact it often seems unfair and cruel. He himself speaks of his envy of Corman, whose magazine initially took over material Creeley had gathered for his own never-realized magazine. This reminds us that Pound, who had helped Creeley make connections (Pound makes the connection with Gerhardt), is still on the scene, manipulating from St. Elizabeth's. It also puts in perspective the relations of both Creeley and Olson to *Origin,* which served them well, but which in a way they may be said to have abandoned by starting *The Black Mountain Review.*

IV

This would be a poor correspondence, unworthy of considering great, if it offered only such matters of "gloss" as I have so far mentioned and were not in itself, intrinsically, valuable, a stirring human document. It is true that it deals with the business at hand, but it is always *writing,* and this means that it opens to recollections and revelations, to anecdotes, stories, descriptions, curious details, reading, and so on. There are, for example, splendid accounts of Creeley's pigeon-raising and pigeon-showing; and one on the Rollers who stay up too long and eventually return only to have one of them seized by a hawk seems to me to have prompted the "answer" of Olson's equally fine account of the chi-mii in the first of *Mayan Letters.* Of the several glimpses we are granted of Creeley's sentiment of being, one concerns the Rollers: "Wish I was a bird." Others involve wonder: that of writing ("just sitting here, writing these words, at this time of night—it reaches OUT. Feel, forever, cd be doing this, which IS, or so I take it, the feel. Is the end. Too much. Language—beautiful beautiful thing you are") and that of the birth of his second son ("Is the real thing / such times; none greater. . . . Anyhow: too much / goddam REAL: wonder"). There is a fine story of how he wrecked a car, a tire having been deflated by a man who disliked him, and vivid recollections, made so by yearning, of his travels as a boy and young man. The writing sometimes reveals him to himself ("it hits me now . . . he [Slater Brown] is, I expect, just that, my father") and reveals him to others: his love for the old car he buys and for the telescope he barters from some children. The way he reads, not just what he reads, is exciting, and after following his remarks one is eager to go back to Parkman, to Klee, whom he has just discovered, to *Mornings in Mexico,* here the focal Lawrence text.

And Olson? The most important letter concerns talk and sleep: *talk* ("Talkin to myself. Which is what I'm left with, mostly. . . . Talk, the REAL push. . . . Conjecture. Talk it is") and *sleep* ("THE PLACE. where time and space collapse. . . . a base which never ceases") which he connects with myth and the primordial and uses to amend Creeley's singleness ("keep it open: is, don't isolate"). Then, there is a remarkable long letter of dismay on hearing E. E. Cummings read ("what a dirty little man, dirty old man, death muggin man, this man who was so long poet to me, is . . . I can't believe it, but [it] comes out all death . . ."). This prompts a foolish letter of gossip (biographical phallusy, indeed) in which Creeley transmits Slater Brown's view that it's all because "cummings has a very small prick" and, on his part adds, "no balls."

Well, enough. As Louis Sullivan says, nature neither hastens nor delays. The baby arrives, Kitasono and Gerhardt enter the scene, Corman holds ("Cid's virtue. The tenacity"), Olson is in Yucatan and the first exuberant Mayan letters have come, and spring, the February intimations of which have relieved the tightness, is about to make its move.

Entering

Enter OLSON, center stage, "on this horst / on the Heat Equator," as he said in answer to Gerhardt's "Brief," locating himself in Yucatan, where other discoverers had come before him. The time: 13 February–26 April 1951; that is, of the correspondence presented in the fifth volume, since the Mayan letters had already begun and would continue until Olson's departure for Black Mountain College in July.

I

I had thought to take the title from Olson's remark to Creeley from Lerma, Campeche, "I long ago learned that I range, or I go dead." But *entering,* as in *entering on,* contains the idea of *ranging* as well as the idea of *beginning,* and as a stage direction is appropriate to Olson's dynamic view of man as actor ("Man is; He acts"). Olson's predilection for drama—drama, Hannah Arendt notes at this very time, flourishes where political life, the life of the *polis,* is still vital—accords with his view of history, with his deconstruction of HISTORY, a metaphysical absolute, and recovery of *his story,* the acts any human being initiates—and *tells,* since to tell one's story, which is necessarily after the f(act), is *history* in a genuinely human sense. Olson's subject, as he would take it up in *The Special View of History,* is "actual willful man," where willfulness is not an insistence of the ego but the readiness to willingly attend (obey) the things of one's experience. Maximus, in *The Maximus Poems,* is a center of such attentions, the most fully achieved literary example of what, in the present letters, Olson found to be true of glyphs. But Olson, in these letters, is himself a remarkable example, a representative because represented man.

It is not getting ahead of the story to mention glyphs now, for in ranging far afield Olson had not forgotten the primary interest of the previous letters. He went in search of the Maya because "such a demarche," he explained at the start, had everything to do with his "bases of verse." This interest finds its focus in his realization that a Mayan glyph, like a Sumerian poem (for Sumer is much in his mind), is "more pertinent to our purposes than anything else, because each of these people . . . had forms which unfolded directly from content [recall "Projective Verse": "FORM IS NEVER MORE THAN AN EXTENSION OF CONTENT"] . . . sd content itself a disposition toward reality ["the projective involves a stance toward reality"]." The Mayan glyphs, he told Creeley, are "built around *a single human figure* . . . as part of universe of things."

So are these letters, which are now mostly Olson's because Creeley's, water-damaged, are beyond redemption. In this respect, they are comparable to *Mayan Letters,* which Creeley edited from the correspondence by eliminating his own presence—and almost everything that was not central to and thereby detracted from and diminished the intellectual excitement of Olson's field work and the exhilaration of finding himself, after "22 yrs in the Pen," free to search in his independent, negatively capable, conjectural fashion. As it turns out, this is the supreme and most dramatic of Olson's projects, so much so that George Butterick is reminded by it of the great amateurs, Heinrich Schliemann and Benjamin Lee Whorf; of Herodotus, too, whom Olson esteemed for "finding out for oneself," and, I would add, Frobenius, who is here because of Olson's concern with culture morphology.

As a record of attentions, whether in the briefer *Mayan Letters* or in the full account this installment begins, there are few books that equal it. Creeley knew this when, in 1953, he published *Mayan Letters* in the beautiful large edition with glyphs on the cover (a collector's item now) and again, in *Selected Writings,* where he placed it after the crucial theoretical essays and played it off *Apollonius of Tyana,* a comparable dance-drama of discovery. *Mayan* letters, after all, are glyphs, and the composite glyph he composed spelled *Olson,* as only his attentions spelled him out. In this way he put Olson forward and helped to make their push. But he also knew and asked us to recognize that letters of this kind, as concurrently in the initial *Maximus* poems, were Olson's mode, a conspicuously new literary form. The reissue of *Mayan Letters* in Cape Editions, in 1968, moreover, owed much not only to Nathaniel Tarn's professional interest in its anthropology but to his realization that this unique book marks the beginning of the poetic movement with which he associated himself; unique also, it should be noted, in bringing together anthropology (or archeology, as Olson practiced this human science of beginnings) and poetry, a notable union to be found at this time in Gary Snyder's undergraduate thesis on a Haida myth. *Mayan Letters,* finally, is especially compelling—it is one of my favorite books, read on the Isle Mujeres—because it is an instance of the rarely hazarded abandonment by which Emerson says we pursue the onward way, find that the way is not dead or history foreclosed. Had Olson written nothing else, he would be remembered, I believe, for this book, which, in the present version, includes a sentence of Whitehead's that it corroborates: "The only endurances are structures of activities."

Reading it now, informed by what the added letters tell us, prompts the thought that, had Olson had the money to stay on, this book might have been his *Maximus,* a book, say, to put with J. L. Stephens' several volumes of travel in Yucatan and Carl Sauer's studies of the cultural geography of Mexico, a conquest of another kind, worthy to stand with Prescott's history. Isn't Yucatan a cape on the very coast marked by Cape Ann, a site to delight a culture morphologist for whom migration, sea-people, and myth were especially challenging, and to excite a poet, who had, in Kukulcán, a founder and *writer,* a Maximus? And wouldn't the exploration and charting of the ruins of this *human universe* have explained the declaration with which *Maximus* all but ends—"the initiation of another kind of nation"? If only Olson had been able to do a few of the things he proposed in these letters and those to Cid Corman (in *Letters for Origin*), he would have had a pre-Columbian book to balance *Maximus* and give it perspective. He would have contributed to the understanding of continental America that Jerome Rothenberg and George Quasha call for in *America a Prophecy* and, as Rothenberg's appreciation of Olson's remarks on Mayan myth indicates, have certified his part in the search for the primitive, the signal project of a generation of poets he inspired in other ways. There is no question of Olson's priority in finding this way, the direction in which so many American writers have gone, nor of Creeley's part in making it known.

II

One measure of the importance of Olson's undertaking is the way in which Creeley, his wife Ann, and his friend Slater Brown rallied and contributed to it. Hence, this account, though fuller than that of *Mayan*

Letters, retains its glyphic power. Creeley's letters remind us that the correspondence was necessarily dialogic and that by participating in Olson's "occasion," as he calls it in the preface to *Mayan Letters,* he enabled his friend. What Olson acknowledged in regard to his writing ("i go a good deal on, how you take a thing") covered as well his need of Creeley in this work and in his present life. He not only told Creeley, "you see, you are here," but that, having recently lost others, "now you and Ann and the kids are the closest things I have." The intimacy and human quality he appreciated in glyphs are conspicuous in his letters, and it is clear, in this as in other work, that he could not carry on without co-respondents. The very number of letters he wrote shows how much he needed to share his immediate life, that is, almost *instanter* reenact it in writing, in the verbal space that had to make good the absent *polis,* the "missing community," as Paul Goodman said in lamenting its loss. This is probably just as true of Creeley, who at this time was at a standstill, involved in the depressing business of closing out his life at Littleton in preparation for the move to France. Lacking movement, which Olson said Creeley needed more than he did to "[give him] back echo," he wholeheartedly joined in Olson's, even sent him money to keep him going. "I damn well don't want to miss any of this," he said. "It is, too much."

The letters begin with Olson's report of a migraine headache and almost immediately provide a clue to what he is looking for: *a usage of life,* "precisely what usage they put life to," where *use,* always of importance to him, defines a way of employing one's life, the very vital energy whose temporal limitation, he tells Creeley, deeply troubles him. He would, he says, turn time into space by filling the moment as fully as he can; live as intensely and alertly as he learned from the glyphs the Maya did, "these Maya [who were] worth remembering because they were hot for the world they lived in & hot to get it down by way of . . . language." As he is, and as the next letter (Creeley used it to begin *Mayan Letters*) shows him to be—the letter on the chii-mi, whose indomitable spirit figures his own, or, subsequently, the letter of 23 April on his voyage to Jaina, from which this sample:

> The run was lovely: 4 hrs, with a strong following wind, so strong the cayuco, in the hour before the sun came, was heeled over so, her gunwhale was taking water! And by god if Con wasn't way the hell of in front of me, taking it! And it her first time in a fisherman! Tho I shld say, she knows sailing boats, I, never, previously, having been

> undersail except in schooners. Wonderful rich sea. And after, with the wind losing that first freshness, under double sail, going like hell across the gulf, straight run, almost due north fr here: a fine lad, 24, 10 yrs fisherman, without grace, but handling his boat confidently.

This passage probably came to mind because I was thinking that what Olson, in a pedagogic letter on Bérard's *Les Phéniciens et l'Odyssée,* says of *periploi* characterizes his own methodology, or, technically speaking, lack of one. His accuracies ("Love that, accuracy") are "sailor's accuracies," simply what "quick eyes" take in when men, in this instance, attend geography, "[go] by COASTS, . . . their shapes . . . remarkable features." Accuracies of this kind of attention—"the tremendous levy on all objects as they present themselves to human sense"—attract him to the Mayan "glyph-world," and this letter, now printed in full, restores the connection. As against professional archeologists, whom he finds stupid, lazy, and intellectually careless, Olson calls himself an "aestheticist," which doesn't mean that he is interested in beauty so much as the cultural testimony of art, "the total life of a people as what cargo art discharges." This may account for his coming to Yucatan so ill-prepared, without any Spanish, without dictionaries and maps, with only his typewriter (which soon broke down). "We are learning archeology," he admits, "without instruction, or tools!" This is to say that he goes about learning from the ground up (or down) and that he prefers to begin from scratch, wide-eyed, as it were. Such nakedness—"nakedness," he says in *Maximus,* "is what one means / / that all start up / to the eye and soul / as though it had never / happened before"—such nakedness is the *sine qua non* because, as he explains in reference to being caught naked in a tidal river, he associates it with *beginning*. As much as Williams, whose *Paterson* he discusses, his concern is with how "to begin to begin again"; and for him this means above all the recovery of a human universe, human sense, and human business, always humanly centered and sensuously known, whether the near ("snakes / ticks / vultures") or the far ("sun / moon / venus"), because whatever is known in this way is close at hand, or, better, eye ("the eye takes up life"). So now astronomy interests him not for the learned reason that the Maya were astronomers, but because he finds that "the life of [the] night sky is very thick & close"; his experience confirms theirs.

Olson was quick to learn, amazingly so, and demonstrates here what he later told Ed Dorn about the value of digging in one place. He was also quick to speculate and propose research. He entered the field with the assurance of a politician-general, much in the way he undertook the rectorship of Black Mountain College. I don't know—and it would be interesting to know—what the Mayan experts make of these letters. Have his primary insights, that the Maya were a sea-people and that Kukulkán (Quetzalcoatl) was related to the sea, been seriously considered? Should we take these speculations—properly so, since they follow from what he sees and examines—merely as ways in to the still more exciting and certainly more applicable matter of glyphs? And what do the experts say about his speculations concerning them?

From the literary side, Butterick wonders why Olson, who used Fenollosa in "Projective Verse," doesn't consider glyphs in terms of the Chinese ideogram. As a matter of fact, he does, but only to go beyond it: "Here is ideogram in a state much more available than Chinese." More available because "ours," of "this geography," and more important to him, he says, because the glyphs are a "more important order of language." When he notes that glyphs are "both ideographic & phonetic," he is thinking of Fenollosa, who, as sinologists keep reminding us, overlooked the phonetic element of the Chinese character; thinking, too, of how much the spoken language matters to him in undoing the abstracting and generalizing uses of language fostered by Logos. (When he wrote "Human Universe," the essay that reports the essential findings of the Mayan experience, Olson began with discovery and language; for its summary value and exemplification of how Olson took up his experience, it should be consulted.) The Chinese character, of course, is not "LANGUAGE by way of DESIGN," but, as Fenollosa insisted, visible etymology, function, verb. In "Projective Verse," Olson stressed this verbal character and criticized Hart Crane for "the push to the nominative." But now he finds the nominative the distinguishing feature of glyphs and even composes a poem wholly of nouns to demonstrate that "noun as graphic [is] 1st, allowing for narration afterwards . . . man makes noun, then makes verb." This isn't so much the volte-face it seems to be as an instance of Olson's keeping up with what had been discussed in the previous letters.

The glyphs might be said to be his luckiest find because their spatial organization is an art of *conjecture*. In them are represented both the poetics and the enabling stance of open poetry that had been treated separately in "Projective Verse": "the stance toward reality that is primary because it is requisite to poetry, is, as in the glyphs, a disposition to poetry"; or, as he says in "Human Universe," the glyphs, by virtue of the identity of definition and discovery, of language and act, are "language as the act of the instant." "Christ, these hieroglyphs," he exclaims in recognition. "Here is the most abstract and formal deal of all the things this people dealt out—and yet, to my taste, it is precisely as intimate as verse is. . . . Is their verse. And comes into existence, obeys the same laws that . . . verse does." *These hieroglyphs!* They taught Olson, as he announced in "Human Universe," that "there are laws, that is to say, the human universe is as discoverable as that other." They were evidence of a disposition of self that for both Olson and Creeley was the basis of a redefined humanism. In the large perspective of their work, this is the business of most significance in these letters.

III

Of course, the value of this edition of the letters is its fullness: the restoration of omissions and chronology, Creeley's letters, the excellent photographs of Olson's house on the beach and of Ann and her sons, and Butterick's extensive notes. (I miss only a map of the ruins.) Certainly, when Creeley said, in *Mayan Letters,* that he "was witness to one of the most incisive experiences ever recorded," he didn't think that his cutting had improved the occasion. To have followed the correspondence to this point is to find, happily, that it doesn't abate, and that for both writers it registers what Olson here calls *tropisms,* the swingings of attention by which, he says, "you can mark a man." Such tropisms reveal a human universe ("the making of our own lives & references") as well as an all-too-human universe ("I feel as though I'd never care a fuck if I never saw or heard of Mayan things again!"). Could it have been otherwise, Olson having made the trip on the windfall of "a couple of hundred [dollars]" and with the letters to remind him that he had only distanced but not eliminated the problems of the literary life? Everything continues: considerations of work-in-progress, frustration over delay in publication, concern for *Origin,* and the anticipation of the Guggenheim fellowship awards (the failure of Creeley's bid, incidentally, knocked Olson out, sent him to bed).

Where Olson closely comments on Creeley's "Helas," Creeley comments on "This," Olson's bullfight poem. And where Olson now sounds off about Corman, Creeley, still grudging and angry over the rejection of Paul Blackburn's work, reminds Olson that Corman, in the soon-to-be-published *Origin,* has stolen the march on the ever-delaying Richard Wirtz Emerson and "is worth, a good many Emersons." In the ongoing intellectual discussion, it is interesting to note that Creeley first introduces Whitehead. Olson, who had gone to dinner on Beacon Hill with this "decidedly priestly" man, puts him down as "only a metaphysical totalizer." He claims that he could never read Whitehead, yet in keeping with his tropisms, or, better, his way of "let[ting] what issues, issue," he seizes on the sentence I cited earlier and thanks Creeley for spotting Whitehead for him. In exchange, he writes about the nineteenth-century non-Euclidean geometers, Riemann, Lobachevsky, Bolyai Farkas (they "set out to figure the *disposition* of matter in space" and "broke the whole thing open"). He writes, of course, out of his usual (unusual) pedagogic generosity, but always with poetic use in mind, as, earlier, in a letter on Rimbaud in which he says, "Why, finally, I like him more than the apocalypts, DH [Lawrence], & Blake, say, is, that, I can't see that he'd buy the idea, let me rest my elbows out, on nature [the allusion is to Whitman]. Strikes me he was that stubborn deal, it's gotta be me, this substance, without reference outward, or, no dice." Among other valuable testimony in these letters is that of Olson's hostility to mechanization and Americanization, which, again, bears on his poetics because the consequent loss of "all intimate & human preoccupations" is what he wants to restore; he knew, as Wendell Berry has been teaching us, that in some places a pointed stick is superior to a tractor.

Now all of this, because it comes to us in letters, is eminently "human business," the very thing Olson has gone to Yucatan to find. These letters, like those of the earlier installments, have the virtue Olson missed in Pound's *Cantos* and Williams' *Paterson.* They give over the ego-position of the old anthropocentric humanism ("EGO AS BEAK," as Olson says of Pound's methodology) and "bring any time so abreast of us that we are in this present air, going straight out, of ourselves, into it." As before, there is also the human business of *writing* and the humanity it reveals. I am thinking of such things as Olson's description of posting letters ("always a pleasure, for, there is no box, one seeks out Carlos and together we weigh it, he or i gums the stamp, we talk, I look at his shells, or his new Brownie . . . dole out the centavos"), which reminds him that in his letter-carrying days this was the way he played post office ("much human businesses abt same, gab, etc: the maids on my route always found my mouth ready for their cake") and was the reason he was monitored for efficiency. And I am thinking of another instance of pre-occupation, this one Creeley's story of delivering chickens over muddy roads to an isolated, solitary farmer, which is just as good.

Arriving

I

Volume six, and only a little more than a year has passed! And for all that has happened, surely one of the most important things is this very correspondence. Both writers recognize this and realize, as Olson says when troubled in Lerma by "how it is unsitting with us," "christ, we've been one hell of a tandem a year now, without looking each other square in the eye (the physical eye, however, otherwise, eh?). . . ."

By means of letters they pull together and are pulled together. Nothing seems to cause desperation quite so much as lack of mail (Olson: "no new mail . . . i go nuts when nothing comes in fresh, to, ride me") or to give so much pleasure as its receipt ("damn wonderful . . . sitting down to, you"). Life and letters, or is it letters and life? Either way the connection is intimate, essential, a veritable transfer of energy, *that* gift exchange, and for these writers, who spend so much time in correspondence, as much the practice of their poetics and as important as any other writing.

The correspondence now seems to belong to their work in the way the *Journals* belong to Thoreau's. It provides a record of work and days, the proving ground of subsequently published writing and, accordingly, indispensable commentary. But, in addition, it is itself a *work*, a rich, full, and close expression of engagement with life, particularly that intensely serious, intently focused part of it sometimes romanticized as *the literary life*. In several senses, it is *quick*, and to enter it again after a two-year interval in publication is to find oneself immediately engaged, swept up by and at the very pitch of the lives it enacts.

These letters of 28 April–27 July 1951 are full of movement, the desideratum of the previous volumes. They catch Olson midway in his Mayan adventure, resolved to stay in Yucatan but forced by lack of professional affiliation and funding to move on to Black Mountain College where (to suggest the monetary gauge of this literary life) he worked for room and board—supplemented, fortunately, by a kitty got up by the students. As for Creeley, they catch the move from Littleton, New Hampshire, to Fontrousse, Aix-en-Provence, where not having French kept him unsettled and almost immediately prompted search for a place in England. Creeley welcomed movement—"that gain, just of movement"—and Olson, once put into motion, made mobile, he suggests, by Creeley's concept of motion, was eager to go on to Iran, to dig there ("Imagine, Arabs, after Indians. What better, eh?"). These moves coincide with other kinds, that of publication, notably the first and second numbers of *Origin,* which featured Olson and Creeley, respectively, and that of Con's baby, coming to term in October.

This volume marks a transition by including the second half of Olson's Mayan letters, most of them new, not published in *Mayan Letters,* and the subsequent letters of his first month at Black Mountain College. This disposition is admirable because it respects the continuity of Olson's experience and the carry-over of his most generative occasion. It is admirable also because it allows Creeley more prominence than he had in the previous volume. Olson remains the larger presence, but George Butterick has wisely given Creeley his place by including three hitherto unpublished works, a chapter of the novel Creeley then had in hand, a short story, and some brief notes on the theater. These have intrinsic value, fill out the record, and serve well here, the fiction as exemplification and the notes as elaboration of theoretical concerns. Juxtaposing Creeley's fiction to his letters also provides a measure of the difference in modes. Somehow the prose fiction is more direct in its flow and closer to the tension and movement of daily life, giving us its deep ground, not merely the background provided by the letters. And the fiction makes place here for Ann's presence: "Because there was, very certainly, no time to be lost and that she knew, and held to, that there was even a crime to considering more than the immediacies of the situation. And so it was she lived, and had lived, and perhaps would go on living with, no matter, the sureness of his continued opposition." At one point in the letters Creeley reports: "(Sd Ann to me/last nite: (pausing . . .) I like yr poems here [*Origin* #2], but OLSON. . . !)." And, later, in a postscript, she appears in propria persona, her straight-out prose directed to immediate maternal and domestic matters: "Has Con got any maternity dresses? . . . have you got names picked out. . . . I'm glad to hear you don't like Black Mountain either. . . . They all seem to take the COLLEGE so seriously and bypass the teaching. Like what might happen if Cid [Corman] decided to write the whole magazine [*Origin*] himself."

The literary life has life for its occasion. Inevitably, the letters make the literary aspect preemptive, and undoubtedly it was, since being "on" or "off" depended on place and people, others as well as intimates, on writing and receiving letters, on writing itself and the satisfaction of publication, and, in Olson's case, on talking—on lecturing and, afterward, "repeating to Con what I had got to." (In this instance, his first appearance at Black Mountain College, he talked for three hours "like an angel before 50 of em.") This second take, as much as the give and take of letters, "knocked [him] ahead." It was necessary to his way of working and involved Con in it. She, too, is now conspicuously present, and sometimes knocked him back. Writing from Lerma, Olson reports: "goddamned jumpy, anything (mainly Con) spills it out. And I'm wrecked for the day." Later, writing from Black Mountain, he is overwhelmed by Con's melancholy, proof, he says, of how the "evil greeding environment" of the college attacks "my life, my center, my things" (recall the final line of *The Maximus Poems:* "my wife   my car   my color   and   myself") and begins to wash away "all which is any of our own."

All which is any of our own points back, to Yucatan, to the last months there, when Olson decided to make the most of the remaining time by writing, with the consequence of altering his response to the place ("the fact that I have got some of my own work done always shifts a place"). There is considerable evidence of this, remarks such as "the place has sprung up, for both of us: we are very damned happy, excited, going, out" and "God, but we shall miss what we have wrought here—damndest thing, how I have come all the way over, and do not care for anything but this day of work precisely here. . . ." The letters from Black Mountain, when placed against those from Yucatan, bear out Olson's observation on returning to Pensacola: "I saw the old dirty American anxieties come back." (*Dirty* is a death-laden word. See "The Moon Is the Number 18.")

He says this of Con, but it also applies to him, and has for measure their life together in Lerma.

> Christ, it was beautiful, that last month: the two of us, alone, very solid and close, she sure of herself and her baby and of her mind, and of her speech, and helping me every day because she was: in fact, the HU [the essay, "Human Universe," the "base for anything I do now," the testimony of what he learned in Yucatan], and all that verse, and my letters to you, were because we were, each day, sitting around after breakfast, and when I was working I felt, as it is hard, because of her shyness, how thoroughly she was herself engaged, somewhere, and when it was over, how alert she was to what I had to show.

(The vignette is worthy of Creeley.)

The point, of course, is that if Black Mountain is "paradise" ("the goddamndest removed business in existence" where "one cannot talk so that anything keeps its weight"), Yucatan is a "human universe." It provided the vantage of his reply to Rainer Gerhardt ("there among Europe's things") as well as the agenda for his leadership of Black Mountain College, its transformation, for example, by his introduction of the new sciences of man (see *Olson #10*). For Yucatan, as Olson explained in the letter Creeley used to close *Mayan Letters,* was one of "the last remnants of the older life—that life which had been man's way all that time until our generation." This gave it "resonance," as it also gave Gloucester resonance—Gloucester evoked here by "the Birdseye freezing plant's generators" in a list of "American noises," all of them of motors whose "horrible regular [metronomic] beat" deeply offended Olson. Living "precisely at [this] watershed" was the special advantage—"we damn have the advantage of our elders"—and made the younger men "the legitimate bearers of value." And again Yucatan brought Gloucester into focus because it put Olson "almost exactly where things were, in the States, when I was [young]." The inclusive *we* tells us that this watershed moment is generational, the historical fact of greatest significance to the emerging (so-called Beat) generation.

There is no better index of what Yucatan had come to mean to Olson than his "attentions," the register, to use Creeley's phrases, of his "stance of immediate position. . . . the confronting, & its insistences." What should be distinguished here—*Mayan* names it—is the fact of *place,* of being placed as against being displaced. In Yucatan, Olson was in place, at home, more so than he was in the Gloucester of the early *Maximus Poems,* the mythological dimension, what mattered most in Yucatan, absent until he made good his absence by coming to Gloucester to live—coming *to live* there, and having the direct experience of it. The instance I cite is one of several of a similar kind, but in addition to being the first letter of this installment, it is especially good as representative of how the Olsons lived in Lerma. Olson begins by telling Creeley of the "delicious pleasure" he and Con had in talking about Creeley's poem "Hart Crane" (in *Origin #1*) as they walked through the nearby town of Quila. But before he scrutinizes the poem he tells of place and reenacts the previous day's experience:

> this town, five minutes away . . . has come to have the damndest meaning for us, for its fruits (it is the orchard town as Lerma is the fishtown), for its damned little girls who wake us, pester us, every morning, with their mean little cries, comprar huevos, naranjas, chile dolche, high & wicked, like a pin into a king's head, would wake, anyone, and, above all, because that is where Vasquez's farm is, which is where the lovely little CUYO is, which a long time, i have not mentioned, but, lately, we have been going back to, to, dig. And yesterday, after having a go at ORIGIN . . . we went again—and, for a celebration, found under a stone, perfect, the leg of a pot, with the clay worked into the twist of a rope, for design; plus a platter with a spiral in red paint at center. It was good (better than, a ball!). And going there, we both suddenly sd, how, yr poem, was so fine.

Creeley counterpoints Olson's high with the low of his displacement. His immediate response to France is very American, both his sense of being American and of being lost without his language. Least typical is his dislike of Paris, "not at all good, sd city," too rigid and contained, "freezing altogether." But, then, no city was his, "can never live in one again." He preferred the rural, and though Ann hated the dampness of Fontrousse and the domestic difficulties, he claimed that "the nearer to caves, the better." (The letter from which I cite is prefaced by a reading of Lawrence's *Etruscan Places*—Lawrence, one of the tutelary writers of both Creeley and Olson, teaching them the value of "the attentions" and to contest reality; Lawrence, who Olson said was the only elder writer who "stood there [at the watershed], getting it, as his own.") The Creeleys located at Fontrousse because Mitchell Goodman and Denise Levertov were there, Mitchell, especially, affording literary company. So: "Mitch is the gt/est. Damn truly—sometimes he bugs me (the care, & the caution) but myself, eh, who is the dull one. Anyhow, they are damn well cool—M/in particular. Rexroth thinks the wife is Dante's Beatrice returned, but I have my doubts. But she is good-humored, strong, British, & of no vices." *Cool*—nothing more approbative, the obsessive word in this installment.

II

Displacement did not interrupt Creeley's literary work, though it may account for his not completing the novel he had begun ("A slippery gig; one slide, & it's the end of it, & this attempt, to eat consciousness"). As before, the writing-in-hand tested theoretical matters, and these, as before, are the core of the correspondence, its common ground and essential work. The theoretical considerations are continuous; they build on what precedes them, and now might be called, from insistences that bring together Creeley's concern with narrative and Olson's with a "human universe," a poetics of attentions.

Olson puts the importance of attention when he says that "a poet (only now) goes by way of his attentions, even, in his poem, that is, that the medium has no other enforcement but, his choice of his, attentions." Read *choice of attentions* in two senses, as meaning what one chooses to attend as well as a selection of attentions. The first, one's stance toward reality, involves the "exploitation of, all realities"; it is a matter of inclusivity, of acknowledging "all mode and all areas," thereby restoring the "huge . . . material" Olson believed poets had left out. This huge material bears on Olson's notion of size, but only when a poet fronts reality can his poem be said to be big. The second, the selection of attentions, follows from the first and involves a processual focusing that respects the *weight, relation,* and *action* of things and does not diminish the fullness of reality. Both choices, clearly, belong to a poet whose vantage is within the world and whose acts of attention are themselves actions comparable to a dancer's movement (Olson considered dance the "forward art") or, in an image taken from Melville's *The Confidence Man,* a Drummond light: "a Drummond light (like the light of a lighthouse) which, as it moves illuminates objects in *their* place, its wake leaving small light on them, its promise lighting them ahead, and its illumination only full at the instant it is square with them." Language, then, may be an *act of the instant* and both *hew to experience* and *cover the real.* Olson's memorable phrases, italicized above, are probably the best summary of the matter.

Creeley's version of this acknowledges the difficulty: "a man cannot exist in any frame which is not declared, fresh, at each instant. . . . his acts come to comprise a complex of use & destruction, of taking up of one thing, & the destruction of, another. . . . this balance is, precisely, his tightrope." His chief concern, following from the earlier considerations of *conjecture,* involves an advance beyond the single point of view. This might be called multiple focus, the recognition of the fact that social reality is not singular but multiple and that the writer who truly represents it, as he already so notably does, does so by bringing several people together and "relat[ing] . . . the multiples of their actions." This is also to say that every thing has its *multiples* and that this must be respected, as Creeley explains in the following representative anecdote:

> As with Eleanor [Baron], we were sitting in the truck, abt 1 at night, parked just outside Copley Sq/, on a side street, back of that church, and quiet, I had wanted to make this *art* (if it comes to that) known to her, which is to say, open, as any man cd set out for it, & what hit, or what I hit on, even as quick as I cd think, just a spot, on the windshield, which, reaching, I cd put my finger on, to show her, to say then, *this!*, and then myself, against it, or with it, & that weaving, around it, to be, somehow, found, to find it, against its multiples, where *else,* making it *no* where else, & just *there,* which is my art, that embracing.

III

At last, with this installment, there is news of publication. The Olson and Creeley issues of *Origin* begin and end it, and in between there are *Fragmente, Golden Goose,* and the *Montevallo Review.* Though Olson wrote Corman that *Origin #1* gave him "the fullest satisfaction [he had] ever had from print," he told Creeley that he was dissatisfied with what was juxtaposed to his work and preferred to manage its disposition himself, in a book (prompting, probably, *In Cold Hell, In Thicket,* 1953). He was even dissatisfied with what he had written, but then he literally worried the issue. In a similar way he read and reread the Creeley issue, but only to praise, as gratified by it as Creeley was. Both must be cited because usually the trials rather than the pleasures of publication get reported, and *seeing oneself in print* is an important occasion. Creeley's elation includes Corman ("he is real joy") and is dramatized by being played off the Goodmans' "studied lack of enthusiasm": "Fuck 'em. THIS DAY IS MINE, eh? OK." A follow-up letter begins with "Still riding!" and explains the happier disposition of work in this issue in an extended account of Charlie Parker's "riding"—so, "altogether delighted / how a rides b rides c / in this one." Olson's enthusiasm, wonderfully generous and full, rides Creeley's, peaking with "christ, lad, who, is touching you—even Olson!" and (on rereading "Mr. Blue") "look, robt, the feeling was, and is, so strong, i cried out, to con, he, is a very great man, this, is what any of us crave to do. . . ." This must have salved Creeley's irritation with Robert Payne (of the *Montevallo Review*), who said that Creeley wrote "like it was thru the small end of a bottle."

Olson's irritation was of another kind, with misreadings of his work and attacks on his position. He did not trouble to reply to Kenneth Lash ("this bird Lash's notion that 'The Praises' is too much influenced by the 'New Criticism'!"), though, later on, his letter to Grover Smith appeared in Lash's *New Mexico Quarterly.* But being deeply troubled, he troubled to reply to Gerhardt, to his "Brief an Creeley und Olson." This poem, which he made out with a dictionary, had him "riding for a kill." He says this in a long letter, itself a valuable commentary on "To Gerhardt . . ." and an instructive example of the genesis of a poem and how correspondence furthered it. In fact, this letter, proposing to answer Gerhardt ("if it is as vital as I now read it, what i should most like to do is write back a verse to him"), is the proto-poem, stating the issues and throwing up some of its striking images. For example, "so pawed," with which the poem begins, initially figures in the context of Europe ("I was pawed by that Europe last night"), this context, moreover, including his realization of the value of Yucatan and his love of its people ("by god, why is there any question why i stand up to the kultur kads—Ez—on mixed bloods, and immigrants! That lie, the dream in the peasants' bent shoulders, what top-lofty shit"). *Peasant's bent shoulders,* from the *Pisan Cantos,* enters the poem, and the "kultur kads," named in the letter, are silently present.

There are other indispensable glosses, on *Apollonius at Tyana,* the dance-drama Olson composed and performed at Black Mountain College, and on "Human Universe," which was in one or another stage of composition during the period of this installment. Among other things, the dance-drama foregrounds movement-and-place, prompted, I suspect, by Olson's immediate experience. In the case of "Human Universe," of special interest is its shaping—how carefully Creeley read it, shortened it, and gave it striking power—and the long letter of June 24, which comments on many issues developed in the essay and on one merely enacted at the end in the telling of a myth. Reading this letter now, when we more deeply appreciate the importance of mythology, reminds us of the primacy of Olson's thought, in this instance his levy on Jung. Listen to the following with the work, say, of Joseph Campbell and James Hillman in mind: "we better be bold about it, and state, flatly, that man is his gods. . . . That gods are not at all inventions, but are disclosures of human possibilities, in other words, human necessities, that mythology is another word that has slipped, has been gobbled up by discourse, and has now the destroying connotation of fable or of a person existing only in imagination, as the dictionary would have it (thus making imagination itself a part of discourse! . . .). . . ." Or this: "I should like to restore dream to the place it has been deprived of."

IV

Indispensability is only one measure of interest. Creeley introduces Basil Bunting and Larry Eigner, and Olson writes at length about Ben Shahn and speculates, curiously, about Jews and blood. Nothing in this volume is of greater significance, I think, than Olson's realization that "will . . . is use": "for the first time, I am willing to understand that will is also kinetic, that it is not, as I have had to stand it off, for what it was, egotism, and thus a greed to rule any thing, to feed only, rather than create. . . ." And nothing quite gives me Olson as his remark on conversations ("they are difficult for me, simply, that what is talked about, I have so examined I go so fast I am far ahead what is there but, a monologue") or gives me

Creeley as this self-portraiture: "Yesterday walking along in Aix, with Ann & Dave, me trailing, holding the basket (& cannot, as did Lawrence in that picture, him & Frieda in the market, look: a m a n), & all those so damn *pure* w o m e n, looking, how they do, the eyes very deep, so fine—suffice it to say, all I needed was a collar, & a whistle every few feet."

(The) Going(s) On

The seventh volume of this remarkable correspondence advances the record by a little more than two months, from 25 July to 4 October 1951, and seems to me to be the most intense installment of the letters that began on 21 April 1950. At that time Creeley was living on a farm in Littleton, New Hampshire, and Olson was living in Washington, D.C. In the course of the year both moved, Olson to Yucatan (his Mayan letters comprise much of Volumes Five and Six) and then to Black Mountain College, where he has been in residence for only a few weeks, and Creeley to Fontrousse, Aix-en-Provence, where he has now lived for two months. Much was worked out in the correspondence, and by virtue of it, chiefly the projective or conjectural poetics of verse and prose as this poetics answered to the "contesting with reality" of work-in-progress and concern with a fundamental reorientation of civilization; and without the groundwork and momentum of the preceding volumes, Volume Seven would not have the large claim on our attention that I think it has.

It may be only that the two-year interval in publication, as this plays against what, when doleful, we call "the situation in poetry," accounts for my ready reception and high assessment of these letters. I think that what Creeley says of Olson in one of them still needs saying: "They [more of *them* later] have, thanks to you, as clean a set of statement as ever was made, on their craft, and damn well won't touch it, because they are 'afraid . . .' to." And I must confess that the letters often offer me just such "clarities" as the poems that Creeley, in *A Quick Graph,* says allow him to go on living. But other things also account for it.

Now the literary business of placement and publication is less prominent because, on Olson's part, the pressures at Black Mountain College have forced him to "squeeze out" much of it in order to give Creeley "speculations & conjectures rather than news—for the reason that, these things, are, I take it, substance between us in a permanent sense." The correspondence, accordingly, is unusually substantial, almost wholly unremitting in attention to primary matters, and essential in the deepest way to the on-going of both of them (*no:* all of them, since Ann and Con are involved in these goings-on). Its proceeding, moreover, is *instanter,* for mail delivery is quick ("you [Creeley] write Friday, and here it is Monday, and we have it! . . . Most exhilarating"). This sustains the dialogical character, the answering one to another of genuine correspondence, and this volume is notably so because, unlike earlier volumes, there is parity in the respective letters gathered here.

Inevitably, in the course of this correspondence, the co-*respondents* have come to rely on each other for "echo": for the closest scrutiny and measure of literary work, for intellectual community, and for the *literally* heartening and sustaining presence projective letters of this kind make possible. Olson and Creeley speak often of letters because of their daily dependence on them, especially now, when both are down. Olson: "I walked through the rain . . . to get the letter in [received] today—and what a difference it has made, in this black afternoon." Creeley: "Continue to ride on yr letter; very damn fine how that shook the works up, and let me get hold of things I hadn't really been able to, before."

The letters themselves exemplify the active concepts treated in them, both the ideas of conjecture and the single intelligence developed in earlier volumes and some new ideas that Olson considers now: that the Great Society doesn't matter to him, but rather the "society of our wives and friends," restored, as here, "*in the act of communicating to each other*" (yes, *to* not *with*); and that the correspondence itself may fulfill the function of *critique* for lack of which, he believes, we lose "the whole world of reality of which we are a part."

By *critique,* Olson means the intellectual clarification of the confusion that followed on the increase in "quantity" that characterizes the modern world. (*Clarity,* a conspicuous term in the work of Williams, Pound, Zukofsky, and Oppen, is a common aim in this tradition of poetry.) This is the very work of the single intelligence that *conjecture* does in respect to the *multiples* of experience. For this reason, the writing both are engaged in belongs with the large speculations about history and civilization for which Olson is notorious. This, too, is one of the reasons that both Olson and Creeley take writing as seriously as they do and that Olson believed the poet to be a pedagogue—the best pedagogue, he said, because he had in mind Homer. And foremost among others was Pound, whose *Cantos* he speaks of in these letters as "verse of critique." This phrase is worthy of currency because it names the intention and character of poems like *The Maximus Poems* (critique by clarity: attentions, perception). I note it here because it applies as well to the letters ("the function of critique . . . is even showing itself in the very form of our address to each other"). Olson thought that Creeley's letters exemplified the conjectural method and that this method, if followed in his novel, would facilitate the *passage* from one single intelligence to another. And if, as Olson complains at this time, "I am not, in print, or anywhere, sufficiently myself," it is only because he overlooks his own letters.

II

For Olson, these months at Black Mountain College were a dark time, relieved only toward the end of the correspondence by the kind of intellectual excitement it is often assumed he always enjoyed. In these letters, he is sufficiently himself, moving from dejection to what may be the excited equilibrium of his normal well-being. Much of the time he is both "hopped up" and "unhappy" ("Am quite unhappy. Tired. Puzzled . . ."; a "blackness" he hopes the letters will break).

Teaching, two long nights a week, does not contribute to this blackness, nor do the broken rib he got playing baseball and the bare subsistence and uncertain pay at the college. His troubles arise from self-questioning ("my attempt at an old answer, who am I & where do I belong") and insecurity ("I am not at all confident, except by moments. And the *real* . . . is *only* such moments"—hence, the value of writing which provides such moments and place to be, and his acknowledgment that by talking too much he has written too little). His troubles also arise from his dissatisfaction with the rewriting of "Human Universe," which he considers calling "The Laws." The new title is itself an indication of the aggression, and accompanying dogmatism, with which he responds when his fundamental thought is threatened, as it was on the "damnable Friday" that sets him off at the beginning of this installment. Touchy and erinaceous (he would have recognized the Erinys in the latter word), he is quick to take offense and fire back, as in response to Williams' letter, included in the notes, on Creeley's still "unformed" character and his own problematic "searching." He believes, he says, "by an act of aggression," and explains, "I honestly don't know *how* to *act,* toward any one, or any thing, except, to *shoot* myself—the only law I know is, that, energy, provokes, what I am interested in—what I *have to do.*" So he writes, as in the letters, "to give what, today, my mind is on," to empty his mind, to spill it, and "innocently," he claims, "straight out," with "no hidden cargo." Even so he knows his tone is "bad" and that only Creeley accepts it, knows how to "RIDE, without interference of, me." He himself, he says, doesn't "buy that fucking tone of mine (that tone which buggers me as much as I damn well know it drives everyone off me," and he'd be rid of it if he knew how. But he doesn't, and, as the letters show, his acts of aggression are necessary to him, serve him by setting thought in motion. For him, provocation both prompts writing and is its issue. He is the man of whom he said, in a letter to Ferrini, that he was his own muzzle and charge.

III

The balance of two statements in a letter of 14 August conveys Creeley's situation at Fontrousse: "All I can do to keep my chin off the ground"; "Well, here I am. The one fact I feel sure of. And not so damn bad, at that." He is not so far down as Olson. He is provoked by place, and probably provoked more by Olson's barrage at Williams than by the refusal of his novel by Morrow's. But he is not so deeply threatened. The solitary life enables him to avoid "the hopelessly lost neurotics" and, at the least or the most, to write, the one act, he says, in which he is "alive really," that is, is present in the real. For the real, a central fact of Olson's and Creeley's poetics, is the conjunction of self and world granted in verbal space by the literal activity of words, the meadow, as Duncan puts it, to which writing permits him to return. "The real / or this sense of it: to be that instant (any) when a thing (anything) coincides its presence (all aspects of that presence) with one's own." Writing, Creeley says, affords him this possibility and is the "only grip on the world I do have," the means by which he is true to the "exactness of his own living" and gets "peace," "passage to myself." So the fact that the writing of his novel doesn't prosper, is at impasse over the difficulty of *passage* or sequence, distresses him and is of most concern to him in these letters.

Creeley is less troubled than hitherto by the delays and uncertainties of publication ("We have too damn much steam up, to be backed off now"), troubled more by the "oddly dead summer," which takes its deadness, it seems, from his own stasis. George Butterick notes, in his introduction, that Creeley does not attend the immediate world of Provence, Cézanne's landscape, and that this "blind spot" belongs to his "essential nature"—to the need, in the writing at hand, to "make a *means* equal to anyplace, anytime, just from the angle of, myself." Creeley remarks on sitting too much at home—Ann seems always to be the one who goes to town—and on talking too little, and it is good to know that he finally gets a haircut and feels like a new man and has "real pleasure" in riding his bike along the ridge to Puyricard. Apart from the letters, he is excited most by meeting Ashley Bryan, an American painter, whom he immediately engages in the ongoing work; and he eagerly awaits the visits of Rainer Gerhardt and Richard Aldington, who, I suppose, will appear in the next installment, though not with the certainty of Con's baby.

Creeley doesn't attend the landscape because its historical and cultural weight oppresses him. Being in France contributes to the dead summer, and the impasse in writing becomes a trial of a poetics of the self-and-its occasions. France and writing are symbiotic, both characterized by lack of movement. France, he says, has "shook" him: "Past is here, is all around me, right now—and I am particularly sensitive to it, to the premises of authority, and custom, and the weight it supposes actual." The presence of the past is formidable and stirs fierce resistance. *This* provokes him, and in large measure, I think, because he sees his situation in terms of Olson's reply to Gerhardt's "Brief an Creeley und Olson," terms elaborated in these very letters in respect to American *Space* and European *Culture*. Finding himself in the situation that Gerhardt acknowledged but was too European to surmount, Creeley holds fast to the conjectural method of the single intelligence:

> It is, I see it, on the one hand: a man as the accumulation of acts which rise in a sort of priority . . . a heap from which can be taken, examples, or markers of worth, and the man never more present

> than in the past, because he has lived—I feel that European, or as much sense of their way as I now have: and for us, it is not that at all—is only, what is, now, on this one point, of whatever you call it, instant, present, or simply now. That is all we can have, and all I want. To be always here, and never a thing of all times, or places, etc. I can't stand that thought.

This division involves what Creeley, in *A Quick Graph,* speaks of as "a division of method": there are "those who make use of traditional forms, either for discipline or solution, and those who, as Olson, go 'by ear,' by, in effect, the complexly determined response to work literally in hand." Closed and open: no simple matter, but a poetics answering (back) to Culture and responsive to a culture (of immediate, particular references), turning on the need to be present in the ongoing reality of one's occasion. Williams, the focal figure in these letters, had already proposed some of the essential elements of this poetics—to turn the inside out, to live in the moment that one lives, in place, in a culture of immediate references, and so to the making of poems whose intrinsic movement is the measure of authenticity—and these elements are *issues* in the letters, in Olson's anger at the neoclassicists and in Creeley's selection of American poets for *Fragmente* and in his "Note on American Poetry: 1951." (Creeley chose Williams, Olson, Blackburn, Bronk, Samuel Morse, and Richard Wirtz Emerson—examples, he claims, of the fact that "there continues, in current American verse, some sense of that integrity which both Pound and Williams have gained for it." Olson wished to drop Bronk and Emerson and add Duncan, whom he considered part of the *push.*)

IV

The situation in poetry is clearly set out in these letters, and Olson might have written, as Creeley did, of the present weight of the past. The "damnable Friday" he speaks of was the occasion of a "damn conversation" in which he seems to have failed to push his views against the neoclassicists, whose presence at the college he may have little expected. The extent to which this situation "unheartens" him is easily measured by the exigency of his response, by his reconsideration of "Human Universe"—challenged, surely, by the neoclassicists—and by the composition, much of it in the letters, of "A Round & A Canon," which now, because we know the occasion, becomes as significant as "The Kingfishers," an earlier response to a similar situation. (*Apollonius of Tyana,* another later response to the present occasion and the triumph of the summer, gets some of his own back.) As for the situation in poetry, here is Olson's survey: "Bill Merwin [and] Larry Richardson's verse—those most able Neo-Classicists—who are more able than the Intermitters, Lowell (who is a bore), Berryman (who has a head like brilliant embroidered drawers), Jarrell (whose brains are all he has—peculiar how, all of these, get more like Karl Shapiro every year." He sees in them "the death of passion, or, the ignoring of same—the assumption, there is something else. . . ." They are not, as Olson says of the Maya at the end of "Human Universe," "hot for the world [the particulars of the world] they [live] in . . . hot to get it down the way . . . it is. . . ."

Olson is a reactive thinker, and his reactions are as large in anger as in generosity. If the neoclassicists prompt the wish to *destroy* the "humanistic un-universe," coming on Louis Martz's essay on *Paterson* prompts a flood (pages 63–80) of ideas, hypotheses, and learning that assumes familiarity and exists, chiefly, to forward his own thinking ("thank you, for having rizz me up like this"). Had Martz received this letter (in his fine fury Olson uses the entire page, the energy is visible, where elsewhere the format is conventional), he would have been shocked by this bolt from the blue. But the letter was never sent, only sent to Creeley with marginal comments that sometimes undercut his praise of Martz. The letter, itself an act of thought ("the ACT, always, more important than the MEANS or the END"), is a primary document. It focuses Olson's present thinking on Williams and Pound, Homer and the Sumerians, and situates a now explicit concern with the *archaic* in the context of his quarrel with the neoclassicists. In it, Olson fruitfully confuses *Pelagian,* used by Martz to characterize Williams, with *Pelasgian. Pelagian* was first used by Randall Jarrell to place Williams in terms of the Judeo-Christian-Classic tradition, that is, in respect to Eliot and the doctrines of the New Criticism. Olson recognizes the accuracy with which it calls up the neoclassical opposition, "the Original Sin Boys," those who "back-trail to [*added:* Xtian] classicism," subscribe to "Neo-Eliotism," turn to Dante, and never get out of the "Western Box" (500 B.C. to A.D. 1950). And he undertakes to do what he thinks Williams failed to do, "unshoulder" the O.S. Boys; to do this by discrediting their "sanction-system" and restoring the *"sanction-source"* of the Pelasgians (pre-Greeks, of Arcadia). Olson's push is back, to origin, to what is back of Homer, to what followed the "ICE" (the deglaciation of the Pleistocene), to place or space as primary, as force as much as Culture is force. For him *archaic* and *Arcadian* are cognate, and both inform the phrase "archaic-place truth." The archaic, he says, is not "a time archetype but a permanent and present dweller in anyone," the condition geography and nakedness restore and Culture frustrates, which is why he considers the Americans, possessed of space, "the last first people" and Arcadia an American's "home." This is Olson's (re)discovery of America. And what he says of Odysseus, that he had "to screw his oar in the earth in order to declare the place where planting may begin," applies to his own work of planting in *The Maximus Poems.*

These terms open the largest vistas of Olson's thought. At the same time they take their point from the immediate literary practice of Olson and Creeley. For the archaic ("the root from which a total creation is made possible") is realized in *nakedness*—

> nakedness
> is what one means
>
> that all start up
> to the eye and soul
> as though it had never
> happened before

Creeley cites these verses as the epigraph to Olson's *Selected Writings* and in his most personal essay explains that "'nakedness' is to stand manifestly in one's own condition, in that necessary *freshness,* however exposed, because all things are particular and reality itself is the specific content of an instant's possibility." Elsewhere, in an essay employing the distinctions of these letters, he cites John Wiener's

> Only . . . a man's
> struggle to stay with
> what is his own . . .

The archaic ("the personal, the passionate, the textural") is the primary ground of projective writing, and projective writing, so eminently physical, as Olson explains in the long concluding letter, recovers the "organic" that has been lost to the "mechanic"—that is, makes good what was lost with the "displacement of the oral," the "FIRST DIVISIVE ACT" when knowledge became visual at the expense of "ear and memory." Olson not only anticipates the argument of Eric Havelock's *Preface to Plato,* as Butterick points out, but, equally important, defines post-modern in terms of the archaic, as post-West. For, by way of the archaic, Olson proposes to overcome "world alienation" and restore "worlding" ("ancient confidence"). (*World alienation* and *worlding* are Richard Pevear's terms.) Recalling his quarrel with the neoclassicists, he says that "we are all . . . cripples of the West, hindered from the exercise of life by the divided & smothering air of the BOX. . . ." He would give us air to breathe, and have us dance; and for himself he would be the poet-culture-morphologist who shows us exactly "how daily life is informed," who is "at once archaic and culture-wise. . . ."

V

Creeley might have been thinking of these letters when he recalled that Olson's letters were "of such energy and calculation that they constituted a practical 'college' of stimulus and information." Perhaps he remembered the letter of 30 September, which marks an upswing ("The grand thing, is, that, I feel as you, that we are on, again"). In it, Olson tells Creeley that he has found, nearby in Asheville, a library that "can substitute for . . . the Lib of Cong" and is studying Greek, and exuberantly sets out what might be called "A Bibliography of 'the live ones' for Robert Creeley." Creeley, in his way, is equally useful to Olson because he stands up to Olson's attack on Williams ("Goddamn it, you slap this man too hard and too easily. . . . You jump too fast here—I feel them [at Black Mountain] pushing you") and moderates it with his own findings (he cites "Perpetuum Mobile," unrecognized by Olson, and wins his assent) and with a writer's deepest testimony ("I do love him for what he has written"). Olson, "brought up sharp," as he says, admits that he has been "pushing Bill around[,] a counter in some game of my own," and finally, since it takes him several letters to give over the "WCW biz," concludes that it's Williams' "concentration" (like Creeley's) that has always been "a kind of terror for me." The truth of the matter is that he doesn't want another father, and is willing to concede only that "Bill & I have a topography *different* from Virgil &, Dante. . . ."

Creeley stands fast because in defending Williams he defends himself, what he has found to be of use. His critical practice follows his injunction in "Note on American Poetry: 1951": "his attention to that [the poetry] of another must imply a search for what can be of *use* to his own." So it is with the notable example here, the poetry of Hart Crane (in low repute in 1951), which he proposes to Olson in the highest terms. Crane's poetry, he claims, "is as good, as good gets," his "sounds ["put into an incredible sense"] as incredible, as finely knit, caught, as any man ever wrote them." He believes that "we have no other poet of this kind; Americans do not reach this, easily," and he makes his case by diagramming the vowel and consonantal shadings of two lines of verse, by citing others that merit praise ("Is there anything finer in our poetry?"), and by listing seven poems from *White Buildings* and *Key West* that Olson should force "those people [at Black Mountain]" to hear. Within a week of Creeley's "push on Crane," Olson does this, "give[s] them, your lecture," convinced, but with "less clarity than you, & also less tenacity," that "[C]rane & Bill are more naturally of my predecession than some others. . . ."

The letters offer many instances of such exact and careful criticism, which raise Olson's spirits (the letter of 22 August calls to mind "Maximus, to Himself") and enable Creeley to work through the problem of *passage* in the stories, "The Grace" and "The Party." The peak, for both, may be represented by Creeley's response to *Apollonius of Tyana* (printed at the college printshop) and Fenollosa's *The Chinese Written Character as a Medium for Poetry,* which he has now read for the first time. *Apollonius,* he finds, is the "very best" that Olson has done, "the continuance" of his work, and the Fenollosa ("How it does LIGHT UP the works!") makes him realize that, even more than Pound, Olson has been the "continuance . . . on this matter," that Olson is "F/s son, i.e., this is the man behind you. . . ." The letters verify the fact that, as Creeley says, "it is impossible to contain this excitement," that now he can consider the "NEXT MOVE."

VI

There are other moves and continuances, the most important, Con's baby, coming to term. There is much comment on this prospect, clothing sent, names and naming pondered, and of most interest, Olson's acknowledgment of the ravages and beauty of lust and his recollection of first meeting Con at Rockport. Creeley, who early on lacked money for postage, helps out by sending $50, and the college pays Olson $61 for the month of September. Olson meanwhile concocts his own money-making scheme, the editing of many volumes in anticipation of the centenary of the Civil War, which may illuminate the now obsessive word *crazy.* Pound, whose "ukase" puts Aldington in motion, still lurks in the letters in the person of John Kasper, who, perhaps as a gesture of reconciliation, wants to do a selection of Olson's poems. We hear of Duncan and Bronk. Paul Goodman's encouragement is mentioned by Olson. Creeley gets together his first book of poems. "Crazy, isn't it, how it never stops, the 'concern.'"

And the superb editing of George Butterick continues, needing only the addition of page 119 to the references to "La Préface" in the index. I mention this because I would not like those people who read from the back to miss Olson's remark, in withholding the poem from *Fragmente,* that "the Buchenwald reference [is] too close" or his explanation, with Williams and Pound in mind, of the open parenthesis.[1]

Note

1. Readers of this and forthcoming volumes of *The Complete Correspondence* should consult Mary Emma Harris, *The Arts at Black Mountain College* (Cambridge and London: The MIT Press, 1987) for an excellent account of the significance of Black Mountain College and "Olson's University," for photographs of people mentioned in the letters, and for illustrations of relevant artwork, for example, Stan Vanderbeek's "Map of Moves" in *Apollonius of Tyana.*

This to Keep (You) On

The publication of this eighth installment of letters, of the period 4 October to 28 December 1951, follows so quickly on the previous volume that I thought to treat it under the same title, adding only a parenthetical *continued.* There is, of course, no break, much of the first four letters of Creeley answering the eighteen-page letter of Olson, entitled "The Law," that closed Volume Seven. But *keeping on,* a frequent signature now, is more exact. It measures, especially in Creeley's case, the desperation that overwhelms him as autumn moves towards winter and the three rooms the four of them occupy all but foreclose literary work. Not only does the house "shrink . . . [on] these wet cold days," as he says, but he must spend most of the day gathering and sawing wood, and this "kills everything else." This is not the kind of activity that he and Olson probably have in mind when they cite the touchstone from Whitehead: "the only endurances are structures of activity." How difficult it is to write when there is no place for a typewriter, and Creeley moves it upstairs and down to wherever it is momently convenient!

The glimpses we get of Creeley's outdoor activities attractively fill out our picture of him—he repairs a neighbor's well, uncertain of the proportions of sand, gravel, and cement, and he recalls planting, raising poultry ("I plan an old age with nothing but chickens"), and trapping in New Hampshire—but the farmer's recollections also measure despair. New Hampshire contrasts with France, an "impossible" place, where he has not yet come "to be *here*": "I hate their world here so much, so damn *completely;* I *do* loathe them 24 hours a day, and how can I make *anything* out of that? I have to, but *how;* what kills me at present." Surely, his own sense of "simply dying here" contributes to his belief that "this whole place (europe) is dead." Frequent bouts of flu and fever also bring him down, so low that Olson is distressed by his reaching "bottom," as he may be said to do when he "flip[s]" and kicks the landlord out the door, when "dirty" and "sick" with the deadness, he spends an afternoon looking out of the window, and when, exasperated with Corman, he gives over *Origin*.

Creeley's term for his condition is *dulled*, which declares the need for edge, tension, and motion. As he says in the context of the "clearness" of New Hampshire: "I want . . . only to be more simple, I mean, simply moved—somehow to get as clean as can be, to move on the most minimum means. All directions, that tension. You get so set, so particular in a dulled sense, sitting too long in the one world. . . . It sinks me very often, damn well into some kind of death, a feeling of simple chill & hate." We find him, then, driven to move. For much of this installment, he is intent on going to Lerma, in Yucatan, which Olson, weary of the incredible "drainage" of Black Mountain College, recognizes as the place of "our people, our home."

At such times, Creeley says, "letters can't make it at all," even though the testimony of the letters suggests otherwise, that the letters keep him on and relieve the chill and hate. They afford him an opportunity to comment (there is no better commentary) on all of the stories he has written, on what each achieves in respect to the poetics that has been, and remains, so central in the correspondence. This is an instance of what makes the correspondence both exciting and valuable: whatever the theoretical concerns, for both writers the focus is always, finally, particular, the work-in-hand, and, to cite a weighted word of Olson's, the *use* that can be made of ideas. The letters also afford Creeley a space for the recollection and vent he now needs, such recollections as the account of poultry-raising and the anecdote of the man who found ways to go to public events without paying, and such ventings as those against Corman (the most frequent and virulent) and those (sadder) involving the failed visit of Bud and Mary Ann Berlin and the failure to visit of Gerhardt. Most important are the occasions Olson provides him of keeping up with Olson's reading and thinking, his "IDEAS!," capitalized not because they are Platonic but because they are urgent and big. For Olson is reading now, not writing, "reading (which I always do when I am stupid"); reading *and* responding, the instant result long letters, primary documents, of irrepressible intellectual adventure. "I am on a beat again," he says.

"crazy with discoveries." These letters (preferred now to essays) are directed to Creeley, instances of the opportunity Olson finds in the correspondence to think things through, "to be clear," and they ask of Creeley the kind of scrutiny and assessment Olson gives here in working over Creeley's story, "Jardou." (George Butterick wisely includes this story, with Olson's interlinear comments, perhaps to show us how exact and close a reader Olson is—and how his large thought has this for base, as we shall see in what he says of Shakespeare.)

But first, the baby, to be named Kate, whose arrival on 23 October leavens this installment with the interest and humor of such occasions. Creeley matches Olson's exhilaration with his own sometimes sad response, and it may be that Olson's belated experience of parentage reminds Creeley to speak of such things as his son David's birthday and the preparations for Christmas, and the pleasure he actually has in family life. In reporting the natal event, Olson's immediate concern, it seems, is to calculate the place of conception (a *Begründer,* indeed) and, since it was Vera Cruz, derive a name from place. He mentions the usual things, noting his approval of the doctor ("none of that fat [capon fat] I abhor") and that when it was time to go to the hospital Con "washed her feet in the bowl (an old trick of mine, hating, baths!)." Able now to relax, he is possessed by the urge to talk—"crazy. so much. & always go wild: so many things loosen my tongue. can't stand to be silent long"—and he mentions later that Nick Cernovich dreamed (the fitting dream) that "Kate & I had already engaged in a big conversation!" The bill paid ($92) but lacking money for domestic help, Olson cooks and cleans, and soon reports the inevitable letdown ("in some terrible slump, grim & tired") and how much he misses the routine of "walk[ing] in, a coffee in my hand, on time, to set to a day." For, during this time, intellectual pressures remain; they break into, and sometimes over, these letters of nativity.

Nothing comes of the wish to leave Black Mountain, as he and Con hoped to do after the birth of the baby. He is not awarded a Wennergren grant and so cannot return to Yucatan, and the Fulbright for which he applies in order to get to Mesopotamia is, he knows, only a "slim" possibility. Using the Christmas vacation to go to Washington, New York, and Boston reminds him of the Chinese practice of living in the imperial city ("New York, the Beloved") and teaching in the provinces (Black Mountain) for a week each month, but this satisfactory solution is never worked out. His impatience sometimes takes the form of restlessness ("immense craving to be out [doors]"), and on one occasion he walks to the farms accompanied by the dog Paul Goodman left behind, an event of importance because it sets off an intellectual charge of the kind that followed his finding an adequate library in Asheville. Having told Creeley of his wish to leave Black Mountain, he tells of the "offerings, here":

> such wonderful things can be done: ex., yesterday, all afternoon: FARM. Just squatting & talking & watchin neighbor farmer take care of sick cow (afterbirth, calf-bed, 2 weeks, & torn tit, fr barbed wire); then, farm house, warm fire, talkin & readin Mrs. Jones' encyclopedia bought $120 for spastic son (13, Benny) Compton's—& impressed at what, such a thing offers, the folk: my father bought me the then lousy thing, "Everybody's," I believe it was—crap. But this one! Answer for me on CRUCIAL? [question] been kicking around:
> ANY TRACEABLE GRAPHIC or GLYPHIC
> PAST IN PHONETIC ALPHABET AMERICAN
> WORDS
> MADE UP OF?

The letter that frames this vignette is Olson's first in this installment. He prefaces it with his recognition of Creeley's need ("nor can i stand you shld look, each noon, for a letter") and immediately offers a characteristic notation of what is to be included in his grandiose concern ("i saw it fast") with "the ETYMOLOGY OF THINGS, of ALL T's":

> language :so, my wild craving for,
> alphabet a dictionary, an encyclopedia
> THE CITY history (OF SUMER, MAYA, etc)
> man as OMNIVORE the ICE, after it
> NARRATIVE PLATEAU
> art river valley
>
> NOW

The headings here will remain useful. They are keys to much of Olson's subsequent thought. But only "language" and "alphabet," tallied by his "wild craving," are treated in the letter. Olson boldly sets out the information he finds in the article on the alphabet in *Compton's Encyclopedia* and prepares a graph, adapted from the encyclopedia, to show the development of the alphabet from hieroglyphs to ancient Greek. The letter is especially lively, an enactment of (excited) thought made personal by parenthetical remarks ("thugs is short for bosses," "my old man used to say to me . . . 'what you need is a jaw-tackle'"), by the way Olson introduces Herodotus' anticipation of present scholarly findings ("kid sd, last night, 'Olson thinks there are two narrators worth . . . Creeley & Herodotus'"),[1] and by the announcement at the end that, in consequence, he is "going crazy, to buy books!" And the letter is *conjectural* because it gives the dimensions, the *multiples,* of this experience (consider it, for example, in terms of the usual school encyclopedia project). Coming when it does in the correspondence, it may be Olson's answer to Creeley's account of "the sudden way [in New Hampshire] one would buck into all kinds of reality. . . . Could never then tell, or anticipate, what next."

Where this letter is a follow-up of Olson's study of Mayan glyphs (Katherine Litz had danced "Glyph" during the summer), the subsequent letters, those before the letters on Shakespeare, are follow-ups of ideas proposed in "The Law" in answer to the question, "How did other men than the modern (or Western) ground the apprehension of life?" To summarize a long, complex argument, other men (read: archaic) didn't divide and thereby stop reality ("reality is this instant & me"); they didn't avoid the instant, the immensity, by adopting the stratagems of logic and classification, of discourse and description; they reenacted the reality of the instant in art, in mythology ("I guess," Olson remarks, "that is what is leading me, throughout"). In this discussion, the "act of rhythm" is the counter of the "act of logic" and secures the kind of form Olson considers moral ("content, as *'agitated material'* . . . is chaos, and immoral"). So, he says,

> it comes out quite simply that, art is the sole leader, simply, that act as rhythm is the only excusable one in the face of the going on, that all other acts of definition are discursive . . .
>
> > so, *system,* instead of action, & pride (which I now take to be the clue to humanism, that, man overrates himself once he lets his conceptual power escape the act of form he gets so pleased with his ability in discourse that he thinks himself mightier than his instant
> >
> > And so
> >
> > conceives himself as somehow separate from, & even, greater than, the "nature" of reality. Thus he is led subtly along to the idea that the splendor is his!

Reality is this instant & me. Nothing is more important to Olson and Creeley than a poetics that enables one to be true to this sense of things. This explains Creeley's concern with *sequence.* "The most basic thing I have ever felt about any continuity, of reality," he says, "is that it could not be anticipated . . . that reality somehow manages a continuity that is exact in every particular . . . [and that] nothing *else* could really have happened." Wanting an art of the same character, he finds his only reliance to be the poetics that they have already worked out: "that one is oneself the content, the SI [Single Intelligence], that form is the extension, that the conjectural method . . . is that one most useful for just this ordering." For this reason, he approves the art of Stendhal and dismisses Celine, who lacks, he says, the "'moral weights'" that, for a novelist, are the "most apprehensible characteristic" of "a world." And when he considers Pollock's art of drip painting, he insists on the need for control, on the necessary tension between man and nature ("when the man goes out . . . nature comes in"). In an art as gratuitous as Pollock's, he thinks that the "forces [are] too free of the man." His examples of control, taken from his own experience, are planting seeds and poultry-raising, the former done not by sowing broadcast but one by one, the latter done perfectly by his friend Ira, whose art depended on "constant *observation*" ("there were no accidents, or there were no accidents that weren't *noticed*"). He recalls that "the great pleasure from the poultry (poultry still seems to me the more or less 'perfect' attention to go along with writing, etc.) was that it cd all be deliberate. . . ."

The need for control is often overlooked in considering the openness (inclusivity is more to the point) of composition by field, but Olson did not overlook it in "Projective Verse" and responded to it enthusiastically as a desideratum of art. The difficulty, he knew, was "so to shape the energies that the form is accomplished"—not to impose (a) form but to allow the emergence of form in the course of attending the "several forces" whose "tensions," when "made to *hold,*" become the "high energy-construct" a poem is now said to be.[2] (The poem is a *tensegrity,* according to Hugh Kenner, whose models of such construction permit us to see the kinetic coherence of organic form.) Thus, when Olson discovers the prehistoric cave paintings, he sees an analogue of Creeley's art: "what really sends me . . . is, just this firmness of stoppage, this holding, and then (as you so often) the motion, inside, from, the personal act there as art, as so many lines and spaces, and each, only there, for, the relevant and elemental force they can be made to serve." When he takes up "Jardou," he tells

Creeley that "the secret of your art is the bearing, the constant sharpness to *all* inside any given go . . . *a* concentration, at all points. . . ." And when Creeley puts Duncan's "Song of the Border-Guard" against Olson's "An Ode on Nativity," this is the measure: "your ODE . . . the beauty of it, . . . the literal writing . . . is very firm, doesn't allow any looseness."

Form is a major focus (sexuality is another) of Olson's several letters on Shakespeare, to whom he returns at this time with obsessive intensity, and in whom, as his appreciation grows, he sees a practitioner of his and Creeley's art. *Antony and Cleopatra,* he realizes, is "the very text of objectism [see "Projective Verse," part 2] . . . here, life is held in its own hand, without intermissions of interpretations of same." This play, now paired with *The Odyssey* for its "lighted world," exemplifies, he says, "the act of composition [which] is to hold what holds itself as firmly & directly as though the maker was a hand holding each thing in such a way each thing & all the things together making a thing were free-wheeling, suspended as the earth in space, moving. . . ." Besides this instance of *grip* (to use Creeley's word), the play, among the others he studies, challenges the "verse of tightness" of his contemporaries ("All questions of tension, or the play allowable, or the leadings. These seem all bound now, or wrapped too surely, or tightly. One thing never leading to another . . ."). It challenges, too, the narrow lyricism that "sings the man as writer rather than the subject under hand."

Olson's close attention to language is notable and, in this instance, is sharpened by Paul Blackburn's criticism of his metaphors ("the only way a man of my order [one who knows confusion and therefore desires form] does know reality"). In *Antony and Cleopatra,* he is delighted with the image of candy in the verb *discandy* because it discloses "the solid-melting as the metaphysic" of the play. Again, in *King Lear,* he finds the clue to composition in the "image system" ("the play arose from ONE METAPHOR—the candy of A & C . . . the eye of LEAR") and begins to see that "verse is where his plays arose, not the verse as, the result of, his play." What has him "wild," he says, is that "you can't get out of it [the play]—you have to stay in—it is all like a hoop, a fine steel band, so porous, flexible, yet firm. . . ." Olson's critical discovery and practice here so closely approaches that of the New Critics that I wonder if he, always aware of the best scholarship, could have missed Robert Heilman's *This Great Stage: Image and Structure in King Lear* (1948), and I conclude that he did chiefly because he sees in Edmund more than I recall that

Heilman does. Olson is "tremendously caught, this run, by the cut of his figure" because Edmund does not fall back on the "passive humanistic" position that privileges "suffering" and "ripeness," and puts an end to "the shit of Nature's increase—of Contra Naturam." Shakespeare's Edmund answers Pound's "cheap half-truth" about the order of nature; moreover, adapting an earlier denunciation of Olson by Pound, "Edmund," Olson says, "is a Kike, an Olson, sure as hell. . . ."

The morality of form is also focal in another series of letters on the new learning (the New Sciences of Man, as an institute at Black Mountain will be called) that for Olson alters both our conception of reality and the tools with which to treat it. As he says in respect to *particularism,* the sine qua non of his poetics, "the push [is] *how* to stay as precise as New Learning has made us, & at the same time discover orderings more precise to *man's* peculiar life-system. . . ." He wants none of the "species shit," the generalization about human life that ends in the "lies" of progress and perfection, and here, again, he thinks of Pound and those who believe that ancient learning is more important than contemporary learning. (Pound is here, too, in what Olson says of the "bad science" of Remy de Gourmont's *The Natural Philosophy of Love.*) Now, so much involved with Shakespeare, Olson proposes metaphor, not biology, as "the human 'science' proper to human affairs & actions." For him, there is only "a single person's act" ("each of us by ourself figure out an ordering which is no more than our own"). That is, there is only the "human phenomenology" that image and metaphor serve—"the motion of . . . things in their relevances to each other," the motion that occurs "when the out & the in are both seen as one." Accordingly, he takes up Creeley's term *conjecture* ("life is anyone's or anything's just exactly to the degree that they move us") and concludes that "the *ordering of motion* is the only morality." In the briefest terms, "act is conjecture for order."

Pound is never out of mind. Creeley reports a dream in which Pound approves of Paul Blackburn's intelligence more than his own, and, admitting that he would be speechless and faint in Pound's presence, he tells Olson that Pound is "the only man . . . other than yrself, that I really want to meet. . . ." He especially values Pound's critical practice, his insistence on clarity, and is reminded by this of Harry Levin who, he says, is a "perfect example of a man who does *not know* what a *clear* statement IS." As for Olson, who is visited now by John Kasper, he reports his pleasure in playing with Pound's young publisher a cat-and-mouse game of the kind

Pound so adeptly plays. This neither ends in reconciliation with Pound nor in winning Kasper over, but aggrandizes Olson's awareness that he, as much as Pound, has a "conspiracy" and could use a publisher to bring out the texts of the new learning as well as his own work and that of Creeley and Duncan, "the three of us together, represent[ing] a push which needs just such swift publishing. . . ."

Publishing, as always, is a concern of the letters. Corman and Emerson, on whom Olson and Creeley have so far relied, take the brunt of their frustration. Emerson is the least swift of publishers as well as one of the most careless in keeping writers informed, but Creeley sends him his book of poems ("these first tweedles"). Corman, whom Creeley credits with the gain of *Origin 1* and *Origin 2*, embitters them as much for his letters and what they tell of future issues as for the slippage they find in *Origin 3*. Creeley's irritation is personal ("I don't really like the man") where Olson's is not, and he is conciliatory. Both look for new outlets, Creeley, by way of René Laubiès, in French publications, Olson in a series of broadsides to be published at Black Mountain. There is no end of busyness. Creeley remarks on the "Christly finagling"; Olson, down on all publication, says, "publishing smells."

This is not the place to leave them. Better to remember, as Creeley does, that "one picks up compatriots in the going-on" (among them, Blackburn, Eigner, Hawkes, Laubiès, Boulez, and Louis Dudek). Better to remember Olson at the farm, or "gabbin with Con," or celebrating the baby in Mrs. Mascari's food store in Asheville, and Creeley chanting Olson's "La Chute," which Ann dislikes for its "male will" and he can only chant when she is out of the house.

Notes

1. Olson shared Creeley's letters and stories with the wider audience at the college.

2. Albert Camus may be said to give the ontology of such composition: " . . . being consists of being able to do everything at the same time. In art, everything comes at once. . . ."

PART IX

Gary Snyder and Wendell Berry

Noble and Simple

To recapitulate:

I went into the Maverick Bar
In Farmington, New Mexico.
And drank double shots of bourbon
backed with beer.
My long hair was tucked up under a cap
I'd left the earring in the car.

Two cowboys did horseplay
by the pool tables,
A waitress asked us
where are you from?
a country-and-western band began to play
"We don't smoke Marijuana in Muskokie"
And with the next song,
a couple began to dance.

They held each other like in High School dances
in the fifties;
I recalled when I worked in the woods
and the bars of Madras, Oregon.
That short-haired joy and roughness—
America—your stupidity.
I could almost love you again.

We left—onto the freeway shoulders—
under the tough old stars—
In the shadows of bluffs
I came back to myself,

To the real work, to
"What is to be done."

"I Went into the Maverick Bar," one of the poems in *Turtle Island,* does for Gary Snyder some of the things "The Desert Music" does for Williams: it permits him to confront his present self as well as an earlier self and world, to acknowledge their continuing existence, and in its resolution to transcend them again and continue his work. The poem recounts a brief, determinative incident of entering/leaving, of coming "back to myself." The precipitance of its initial lines, especially of the double boilermakers, argues extremity, a need expressed only at the end of the poem, when the poet, coming back to his senses and to his true self, comes back to the "real work" he seems to have momentarily fled. "And drank double shots of bourbon / backed with beer": the self is lost in the haste of what the lines enact. Yet by this very gesture it is brought back to the world of "short-haired joy and roughness" so brilliantly evoked by the vividly registered details. It is a long-familiar world—yes, a world—and the emotions it awakens are of such depth and force that "I came back to myself" also speaks for its attraction as well as for the effort of rejecting it.

Though the poet of *Turtle Island* now has a "home country" (see "What's Meant by 'Here'"), he is still a wanderer, still on the Way, the "freeway" of this poem. And though many of the poems in this collection express equanimity and happiness, he is still, as here "under the tough old stars," aware of shadows and the night. Nevertheless, the Maverick Bar is not his clean, well-lighted place. In its familiar world he is now a critically observant stranger, and what he discovers by stopping and entering is an arrested world, the limited, stranded, unchanged, and unchanging (unchangeable) world he had known in his youth, the masculine world of the 1950s, when he was a logger, the world that *Riprap* (1959) and *Myths and Texts* (1960) both record and leave behind. Moreover, this bar in Farmington, near the Four Corners and the Navajo Indian Reservation ("Anasazi," the initial poem, and the book's title immediately summon the Indian whose "primitive" ways Snyder would restore), is America. It is an America he has loved and "could almost love . . . again"—his generation speaks in this reminiscently Ginsberg line—but cannot love now. For in this America longhairs enter at risk, cowboys (those Marlboro men to whom a critic once, mistakenly, likened Snyder) do "horseplay," friendly inquiry marks the stranger, marijuana is forbidden, and romantic love, figured in the dancing couple, is still the hang-up he knew it to be in "Nooksack Valley" (in *Riprap*), where in turning from it he chose long ago to follow another way.

"America—your stupidity." This judgment, coming as it does at the deepest and fondest moment of recognition, is mild. Even so it expresses the polarization felt throughout the poem and especially in the sharply juxtaposed departure and return-to-self of the closing stanza. Snyder polarizes, here and in eco-political poems, because, however much he celebrates in other poems the ecological harmony of his life and work, he knows the enemy that threatens it. He knows, as the title of Lenin's pamphlet ("What is to be done") reminds us, that to bring others back to themselves (to the deepest non-self Self), to the free way, and to the vast living and enduring natural universe of the "tough old stars," is a task of revolutionary magnitude and requires his leadership. In part, what is to be done is what he has already done and does again in this poem. It is also "the real work" he has accomplished by means of arduous education and meditation: "the real work / washing and sighing, / sliding by"—living in, moving with the flow, as the poem "The Real Work" tells us. And it draws strength, as the notable testimony of *Turtle Island* shows us he has learned to do, "from the realization that at the heart of things is some kind of serene and ecstatic process" and from knowing, therefore, as he says in "Four Changes," his most widely distributed proposals for ecological survival, that "nothing need be done." This is not, of course, counsel of passivity, for knowing this—that the universe will sustain us—"is where we begin to move from." The real work, then, respects and so sustains the earth. As he says in "Tomorrow's Song," it is *"in the service / of the wilderness / of life / of death / of the Mother's breasts!"*

Among the prose pieces, the "Plain Talk" that directly and indirectly comments on the poems is the following:

> The return to marginal farmland on the part of longhairs is not some nostalgic replay of the nineteenth century. Here is a generation of white people finally ready to learn from the Elders. How to live on the continent as though our children, and on down, for many ages, will still be here (not on the moon). Loving and protecting this soil, these trees, these wolves. Natives of Turtle Island.

Among the poems, in the section "For the Children," a legacy of lore and wisdom for them, is the following from "Tomorrow's Song":

Turtle Island returned.
my friend broke open a dried coyote-scat
removed a ground squirrel tooth
pierced it, hung it
from the gold ring
in his ear.

And from "What Happened Here Before," an earth-history from 300,000,000 years ago to the present that reminds us of our brief sovereignty:

Turtle Island swims
in the ocean-sky swirl-void
biting its tail while the worlds go
    on-and-off
        winking

In an introductory note Snyder glosses the title of the book. It is, he says, "the old / new name for the continent," old because "based on many creation myths of the people who have been living here for millennia," new because some of these people have recently "reapplied [it] . . . to 'North America.'" Its value lies in its accuracy, for it directs our attention not to arbitrary boundaries but to the land itself and the life-communities it sustains—not to the "map," as John Vernon would say, but to the "garden." And its value is also revolutionary because it speaks for a revolution in awareness—for the perception of relationship, interdependency, and process that informs ecological consciousness and conscience—and summon us to a new-old way of life that now more than ever before is a necessary means of survival. It rallies us to militancy, asks us to hear the voice of the land itself, of Black Mesa, for example, where strip-mining threatens its cancerous work. "To hear her voice," Snyder says, "is to give up the European word 'America' and accept the new-old name for the continent, 'Turtle Island.'" It is to repossess a new world by dispossessing ourselves of an old dream.

(Rape of the world: destructiveness of Western civilization. Those insane Spaniards in Central America—answering to abstractions of gold and religion. The nature, wildlife, Indian life, Mississippi, Grand Canyon, didn't move them. The whole Western hemisphere a gift to Spain from the Pope.)

This note in *Earth House Hold* (1969) tells an old story. It is familiar to our poets, and Snyder knows it well. And for him, loving the world as mother, speaking with her voice, "rape of the world" is not a metaphor but actual fact, the primal violation his work protests. It is now the primary theme of *Turtle Island* because now, *now,* as he says in "Front Lines," he must draw a line ("Our line") and stand against those who say to the land, "Spread your legs." Less than a decade ago he could say, in "Passage to More than India," that the dream of "ecological balance, classless society, social and economic freedom" was "one of the possible futures open to us." Now, with "Death himself, / (Liquid Metal Fast Breeder Reactor) / . . . grinning, beckoning," it is the only possible future. For the measure of crisis is that now every issue must take account of, even begin with, ecological considerations—that now human survival, as never before, depends on the survival of all the life that sustains it. This is the reason that, in *Turtle Island,* he has become the self-elected "voice" of the wilderness, of a constituency "not usually represented either in intellectual chambers or in the chambers of government."

now,

we sit here near the diggings
in the forest, by our fire, and watch
the moon and planets and the shooting stars—

my sons ask, who are we?
drying apples picked from homestead trees
drying berries, curing meat,
shooting arrows at a bale of straw.

military jets head northeast, roaring, every dawn.

my sons ask, who are they?

WE SHALL SEE
WHO KNOWS
HOW TO BE

Bluejay screeches from a pine.

These are the concluding verses of "What Happened Here Before."

The bluejay and the pine "came to live here" 3,000,000 years ago; the mountains, 80,000,000 years ago; the moon and planets were here before earth-history began. The apple orchards came 125 years ago, and the jet is *now.* The poet and his sons are also now, but living the open life of hunters and gatherers, living as the "human people" did 40,000 years ago, in the Pleistocene.

Other poems tell of "primitive," "archaic" ways, about bucking wood, hunting mushrooms and deer. One of them, "Two Fawns That Didn't See the Light this Spring," exemplifies the instruction in "Four Changes": "Don't shoot a deer if you don't know how to use all the meat and preserve that which you can't eat, to tan the hide and use the leather—to use it all, with gratitude. . . ." Another, "The Hudsonian Curlew," a ceremonial poem more complex perhaps but of the kind so characteristic in Snyder's work, follows the injunction, "*'Do you want to do it right? I'll tell you,'*" and describes the way to eviscerate the bird he has killed. Still another, "The Dead by the Side of the Road," tells of the use he will make of animals killed by "Log trucks run on fossil fuel": the Red-tailed Hawk ("Her wings for dance fans"), the Ringtail ("she will be a pouch for magic tools"), etc. Such poems are not incidental. They tell us how much of the outer and inner nature of wilderness upon which survival depends must be relearned; they remind us of how little, compared with the "human people," we know about "Turtle Island" and the ways of living there.

So Snyder sits in the forest with his sons. He is bringing them up, as he believes we must now bring up all children, "as part of the wildlife." All the necessary changes in respect to population, pollution, and consumption depend on the transformation that may follow from such education; and nothing less than such a revolution, he thinks, will do much good. We are, he reminds us, "the first members of a civilized society since the Neolithic to wish to look clearly into the eyes of the wild and see our selfhood, our family, there." Our work, the real work, he says, is to "master the archaic and primitive as models of basic nature-related cultures—as well as the most imaginative extensions of science—and build a community where these two vectors cross."

He is doing this.

In *Regarding Wave* (1970), his previous book, Snyder celebrated his marriage and the birth of his son Kai. He fulfilled an early wish ("having a wife and baby, / living close to the ocean, with skills for / gathering food") and after much wandering took up housekeeping on earth.

Since that time he has settled in the foothills of the Sierras, living in community with his family and friends. More than anything else this distinguishes this book, marks the spiritual autobiography of which it is a part. It accounts for two notable related things: his special secure sense of happiness in being at home in the world (compare this to the despair of Ginsberg's ecologues) and his militancy, his drawing the line, his fear that Coyote will be exterminated and his "sons will lose this / Music they have just started / To love." Snyder has dedicated the book to his mother, who for the first time enters the world of his poems ("my Mother's old / soft arm. walking / helping up the / path"). And he has given it to his children, who, with his wife, are lovingly present in it (see especially "The Bath" and "Gen"). The playful pictographs by Michael Corr recall the cave paintings to which Snyder often alludes and from which he sometimes dates his poems, and they recall the Pleistocene as well as invite us to read the book as a "children's" book.

The section titles, too, refer to this home country. *Manzanita:* a native bush that has survived for three million years—and whose hard green berries, like Snyder's poems, are "little apples": "The longer you look / The Bigger they seem. . . ." *Magpie's Song: "No need to fear / What's ahead / Snow up on the hills west / Will be there every year / be at rest." For the Children: "stay together / learn the flowers / go light."*

Some of the poems in *Turtle Island* are as good as any Snyder has written: "The Bath," "Night Herons," "The Uses of Light," "On San Gabriel Ridges," "By Frazier Creek Falls," "The Hudsonian Curlew," "Bedrock," "Toward Climax," "As for Poets." None marks any special "advance" in technique. All are swirls in the flow of his authentic experience, and their ideas, as Tu Fu said the ideas of a great poet should be, are "noble and simple."

Minds Like Compost

. . . a kind of composting / digesting . . .
and salvaging of nutrients. . . .
Gary Snyder, in a letter of 26 November 1983

I. Dwelling at Kitkitdizze

This handsome book (*Axe Handles*), a gift of Gary Snyder, came on the 24th of October, here, at Wolf Lake, near Cass Lake, Minnesota, where we are spending the fall and early winter. I read it through immediately in the intervals between getting in the wood and covering the drainfield with a blanket of straw, in the course of a soft, rainy afternoon, the lake gray and the sky gray, the only sounds the cry of loons and quack of ducks and startle of gunshot. It is a good book—a companion volume, we used to say—for someone, like me, who is inhabiting, or *reinhabiting,* to borrow Peter Berg's word for *going back* in order to make a *place.* There is much in it that anyone who knows, or is coming to know, rediscovering, rural life will find familiar, and this, to a considerable extent, accounts for the pleasure it gives. Familiarity, after all, derives from *familia,* family, household, which, even now, almost everyone is familiar with, and this book, more than any of Snyder's so far, is a book of the family, of Kitkitdizze, the home place, and its satisfactions.

I take the book up again now, in mid-November, and so appreciate, as one does the scent of wood smoke in crisp air, the exquisite serigraph by Mayumi Oda of the goddess of snow. She figures, as emblems have in *Earth House Hold* and *Regarding Wave,* as a reminder of the Great Goddess, whom, since these books, Snyder has served by founding a family and taking up householding on earth. She presides over the book because not only the title of the second part, "Little Songs for Gaia," but all of the section titles summon her. "Loops" (from ecology and cybernetics) and "Nets" (from Buddhism) name her, and the section titles, accordingly, do not divide the poems so much as note their interdependence, the reality represented in them.

We find the snow goddess in "Little Songs for Gaia," where Snyder dreams of himself as a god melting the winter snow with his breath. This reminds me of Hart Crane's evocation of the winter king and the glacier woman at the beginning of "The Dance," his fable of poetic vocation and of "manhood," of the vision quest and of the song with which the frozen earth is restored to life. In fact, Snyder's sequence of "Little Songs," with its dream of the Three Corn Maidens, depends, as Crane's poem does, on vegetative seasonal myth, on a processual cycle of succession and renewal (" . . . the world goes on"), and this "slow-paced system" is the "system of systems," the primary one, the totality of interdependent things on which Snyder has come to rely and by which he gauges the value of other systems. I also think of Crane because he saw the continent itself as the Goddess's body and would have readily appreciated Snyder's dedication to the San Juan Ridge. Even the book's title relates to the Goddess, as the epitaph from the *Shih Ching* informs us in the equations of axe handle to axe and wife to go-between and in what it affirms as important: "And here's a girl I know, / the wine and food in rows." So later we find among the "Little Songs" a summary verse of satisfaction:

> Snowflakes slip into the pond
> no regrets
> Thin shoots of new-sprouted grass,
> it grows.
> Two children learning Chinese checkers
> And grownups sipping whiskey,
> Spring evening snow.

The initial, titular poem also tells us that what Snyder has found in going back is the direct, "primitive" (preliterate) way of transmitting art and culture. (See David Antin, "the sociology of art," in *Talking at the Boundaries.*) In using an axe to shape an axe handle we have the model literally in hand and are able (enabled) to make things of genuine continuing use because others before us have provided the models and the ways of proceeding. This is not the way children in a literate culture are taught, and it evokes bitter comment:

> . . . the children will be taught:
> How to record their mother tongue
>   with written signs,
> Names to call the landscape of the continent
>   they live on
> Assigned it by the ruling people of the last
>   three hundred years,
> The games of numbers,
> What went before, as told by those who
>   think they know it. . . .

Nor is it the only thing to be taught. In a poem about repairing an old truck, he realizes what he didn't learn when, twenty-five years before, he had given himself to "Dharma-scholarship." Now he is taught what he needs to know "By friends who themselves spent / Youth with the Classics," where *spent* acknowledges, even as it discounts, the value of such devoted study. And now that the truck helps him haul the sawdust and sand he needs to lighten the clay in the garden, he notes that

> The garden gets better, I
> Laugh in the evening
> To pick up Chinese
> And read about farming.

The adversarial is less conspicuous in this book than it was in *Turtle Island,* where politically he drew the line and took his stand. Now it has chiefly to do, as parents often find on first sending their children to school, with education, a primary concern of political significance because it results in the "grasshopper man in his car driving through"—*straight* through the net of interdependencies—and the workers he sees in Alaska, like workers he had known in his logging days and finds everywhere, *universally,* doing "the work / of wrecking the world."

In Snyder's work, *loops* and *loopings* often go with *lore* and refer to the cultural feedback or recycling that for him goes back to the Pleistocene. Making an axe handle for his son is a representative instance of the "old way" by which one generation teaches another, transmits lore, "pass[es] it on," and thereby serves and nourishes; does so, it should be added, on the assumption that this way of life, and life on earth, will continue, that his founding of "a new kind of family—responsible, but more festive and relaxed," as he says in *Turtle Island,* is the beginning that makes it possible. In the poem immediately following "Axe Handles," Lew Welch returns from the dead to tell Snyder what is needed to overcome the "basic fear" of our culture: "teach the children about the cycles. / The life cycles. All the other cycles." In doing this Snyder is also teaching us that in the human life cycle, as Erik Erikson has it, teaching is the adults' work, a generative act of love. The book is a model of such teaching, concerned with cycling one's life on behalf of the greater life—this is what devotion to the Great Goddess means pragmatically—and one of the poems instructs us in composting, in how to have "a mind like compost." A father now instructs or "shapes" his sons ("I am an axe / And my son a handle"), and we should not overlook the fact that, though fathers are inevitably role models, this father is unusual in taking responsibility for his sons' education (he has no daughters), in extending his responsibilities to the essential cultural function of the family, which in many ways still belongs to the "system of systems." The most salutary thing in the book is this sense of generations. In Okinawa, Snyder drinks to the grandfathers and sings with his sons.

But, then, this is a book of *dwelling,* and his faith speaks for *being,* as do some of the poems, for example, "True Night" and "24: IV: 40075." I called it *satisfaction* earlier, having Whitman's usage in mind. *Dwelling,* of course, is a Heideggerian concept and best covers a record, poetic witness and testimony, of how, by our own activity, we have our being-in-the-world. According to Heidegger, *dwelling* depends on building, on *bauen,* which includes both raising a house and raising crops. I note in the pocket dictionary I have here that the word denotes a variety of constructive activities, among them making a nest, the primordial model of shelter and of structures, themselves round, that confer well-being (being is round, as Bachelard says); and I find the cognate words *Bauer,* farmer, *bäuerlich,* rural, *Baum,* tree. We have our being-in-the-world by being in the world, by taking in hand constructively and responsibly the things of the world and by doing this in awareness of manifold relationships. When Snyder sees the limestone ledges on Wendell Berry's farm he remembers the sea of another time—remembers that the earth has a history—and when he smells the foxes' den he recognizes it as "home." For him, a river calls up not only the watershed and the valley-section (the parallelism of "thousand-foot deep soils / thousand-acre orchards" conveys the jeopardy of intersecting histories) but all "flowing." When he pumps water to save the apple trees, he belongs to his surroundings, and this is why *menial* work (*menial* derives from household) need not be *mean*.

I think here of Hannah Arendt, who would have considered such household maintenance *labor,* that is, providing nothing durable, doing nothing more than keeping up with necessity, even demeaning, since for her it is without freedom. But my own labors of this kind, among them hauling and spreading manure, have taught me what Snyder teaches, and Heidegger, too, in associating building with cultivating: that in making soil one makes something durable, contributes to the endurance of the earth.

I'd like to call it *worlding,* appropriating a wonderful word used by Richard Pevear to distinguish poetic works that "belong to the world" and give it to us from "works that are alienating." Surely, Snyder's poetry is a poetry of worlding—in it we are not estranged from the familiar world—because on his journey to love he found the way to dwelling. In his search for the primitive he has found the feminine and some of the first (enduring and redemptive) things of family (tribal) life. When he goes to Australia, as told in "Uluru Wild Fig Song," he shares—learns from—the tribal life of the aborigines. George Oppen, whose work is Pevear's notable example of worlding, addresses the primitive in *Of Being Numerous* under a found philosophical statement, probably Whitehead's ("an experiencing subject is one occasion of a sensitive reaction to an actual world"):

> They made small objects
> Of wood and the bones of fish
> And of stone. They talked,
> Families talked,
> They gathered in council
> And spoke, carrying objects.
> They were credulous,
> Their things shone in the forest.

Families, here, comprise the *polis*—like the community of San Juan Ridge. This is not Arendt's *polis,* which frees us from family life and is the place of politics apart from it. But perhaps of greater importance:

> They were patient
> With the world.

This is the condition of renewal Oppen proposes against the most formidable odds.

If *Axe Handles* seems slight, considering that it is Snyder's only book of poems since the publication of *Turtle Island* nine years ago, it is because we are not mindful of the long transformative journey that preceded it and of the fact that dwelling takes time. Rural reconstruction at Kitkitdizze isn't exactly what we find in Blair & Ketchum's *Country Journal,* even though Wendell Berry, another exemplary inhabiter, writes instructive essays for it. The advance in this book is not notably prosodic but a matter of depth of life and of time, of memory. This is the book of a poet now in his fifties. The mind here is like compost: "All this new stuff goes on top." And the advance is a matter of laughter, which replaces the direct political opposition of the previous book.

Three poems now treat Snyder's work on the California Arts Council; two of them concern Governor Brown and the wearying weight of politics. In one of them the governor visits Kitkitdizze and naps all afternoon, while Snyder tends the chickens and sprays the apple trees. On the following day they read the newspapers and talk over ecological issues of political moment. Then, Snyder says, "we started laughing" and got the bow and shot arrows into bales of hay. We do not need the title from Lun Yü nor the allusion to Zen and archery in order to get the point of a poem in which the governor and the poet follow and find satisfaction in old models. I think also of Han-shan and Shih-te in Snyder's early work, the translation of *Cold Mountain Poems*—"purify our ears," in another poem, also reminds me of the T'ang poet. I think of him because Snyder, in repudiating Han-shan's reclusivity, has acquired his laughter, a sovereign remedy not necessarily for laughing-off but for confronting the ills of the world.

In the second poem, Snyder accompanies the governor from the capitol, past midnight, "tired of the effort / Of thinking about 'the People.'" Out-of-doors he observes the moon and the stars—the system of systems—and thinks of home. But, again, he does so not as a refuge from but as a matter of politics, for what he does at Kitkitdizze is as political as what he does at the capitol: direct action, in which, as his teacher taught him, he has become one with the knot itself, with the suburban household, its goods filling a double-spread in *Life* magazine, that Wendell Berry saw as the personal nexus sustaining the unsettlement of America. I say this also on the evidence of a short humorous poem, "Changing Diapers," in which Snyder refers to "a giant poster of Geronimo / with a Sharp's repeating rifle on his knee." Having done the necessary "woman's" work of cleaning his son, Snyder says,

No trouble, friend,
  you and me and Geronimo
  are men.

Not "men," as he had once defined them, but as he now exemplifies them: a man of the family, familiar with all of its tasks, willing, like Geronimo, to defend what he feels to be as endangered as once the Apaches were.

II. Placing Berry

It is now December, but even snow removal after five successive storms and the endless business of making- and getting-in wood doesn't take all one's time—is only part of a rhythm that includes books, makes them welcome. And now another North Point Press book has come, Wendell Berry's *Standing by Words,* and I am beginning to wonder if this press, in its name, isn't insisting on giving us cardinal directions. Though I am sure that others besides myself have thought of Wendell Berry and Gary Snyder together, North Point Press has brought them together, consolidated them in the substantial way of books, as publishers standing by words. Here, so to speak, they enter the list. Berry's book, moreover, is dedicated to Snyder, and the Chinese character on its dust jacket, literally representing a man standing by his word, is the work of Masa Snyder. Ezra Pound first called attention to this Chinese character for literary character, and Snyder, who acknowledges his debt to Pound in *Axe Handles,* is clearly meant by Berry to exemplify it. In fact, Snyder figures as the most conspicuous and important of the contemporary poets mentioned by Berry, the others mentioned chiefly by way of disapproval.

Much connects Snyder and Berry now, after interestingly divergent lives, but perhaps their association benefits us most by enabling us to see how much discipline matters to Snyder and how much tolerance Berry allows his categorical thinking. They join now chiefly as *inhabiters*. For both, the real work, as Berry defines it, "consists of the accumulation of local knowledge *in place,* generation after generation, children learning the visions and failures, stories and songs, names, ways, and skills of their elders, so that the costs of individual trial-and-error learning can be lived with and repaid, and the community thus enabled to preserve both itself and its natural place and neighborhood." Among the poets, they are probably our most prominent ecological spokesmen and householders-on-earth, "domestic" poets, according to Berry, teaching us the "old ways," reintegrative ways of healing and wholing because they restore the harmony of the "system of systems." Their poetry is the witness of this and of their *dwelling* and *worlding,* of what Berry speaks of as *descent* and *homecoming,* a return to "earthly vision," to the "very world," to the work and action of common everyday life, in place and of place. From this ground ("you can lose your soul or your soil"), they address us as didactic essayists or neo-functional critics, to use Paul and Percival Goodman's term for what, essentially, is "old-fashioned" moralism, for neo-functional critics see beyond mere fitness, the efficiency of means and ends, and take the trouble to trouble us by questioning the value of both.

To stand by one's word involves all this, and more. Berry is as much a critic of "tyrannese" as George Orwell, but his concern with how we use language is broader than Orwell's in "Politics and the English Language." He demands not only fidelity of word to thing, the necessary honesty of discourse, but fidelity of word and deed, word and people. He asks us to make words good by standing responsibly and actively on earth and, ultimately, by standing by the whole, the system of systems, and his admonition to poets is prompted by the fact that he believes they do neither, that, like most of us, they are alienated from the one and specialized beyond awareness of the other. Poets, here, are as representative of a "satanic" industrial economy, which is to say the diminished and destructive technological civilization of the industrial revolution, as agribusiness is in

The Unsettling of America. The present argument, moreover, follows the form of this notable book—Berry is moved by words and things he finds false, is moved to confront them, a debater given to polarizing, to extremity of statement that belies his sense of propriety and weakens his authority. I say notable because *The Unsettling of America* is better informed, better sustained, and more eloquent. Berry knows agribusiness and his cause, as Edmund Wilson said of the South's, has become the cause of all of us. But he doesn't know the situation in poetry in a comparable way.

"The Specialization of Poetry," the initial essay in *Standing by Words,* was originally published in the *Hudson Review* in 1974. This is to be noted because Richard Pevear's "Poetry and Worldlessness," an informed and cogent essay on the same subject, was published in the same magazine in 1976, and is the essay with which to compare Berry's. Pevear knows right off that the specialized poetry of "mind" of which Berry complains is simply "academic" and represents the situation of poetry (and poets) in universities and not the situation-at-large, which involves an avant-garde, poets, in fact, who are doing the kind of work, the joining of art and life, Berry asks for. David Antin, one of these poets who restores the story or narrative mode, considers this New Critical-derived poetry, the autonomous poem so much deplored by Berry and likened by him in value and use to chewing gum, as merely "trivial," that is, not in the current of serious artistic endeavor and not worth our attention. As for the interviews which Berry considers symptomatic of specialization—isn't everyone aware that the cause is not specialization so much as the cult of celebrity in our culture, just plain downright interest in literary gossip, and the self-advertising necessity of our prestige system? And who can wholly avoid this system (the work of Berry and Snyder was featured recently on National Public Radio), or, for that matter, avoid the university, which is not quite as evil as Berry considers it, indeed in our time is a major sustainer of poetry, even avant-garde poetry, and of the literary tradition to which Berry wants poets to return? Is Snyder, whose *The Real Work* includes several interviews, somehow exempt? Are all interviews as bad as Berry makes out? Can the New Critical poem, whose formal control Berry finds "totalitarian," be condemned along with formlessness; the New Criticism mentioned in ignorance of one's own indebtedness to its assumptions; Pound later approved, his call for responsibility acknowledged, his Usura Canto cited, without realizing that his formal legacy, the ideogram, broke the conventions of narrative at the same time as it provided another means of doing the epic communal work of telling the tale of the tribe?

Confused as it is, this essay is not without its point: that the worldlessness of academic poetry belongs to the self-aggrandizing mind, a mind alienated from the world but assimilating it to itself, as, for example, in Emerson's dream of being offered the apple of the world and eating it. To turn the whole world into mind is the dream of Idealism and the work of Symbolism; the aestheticism that Berry deplores accompanies them. This has been recognized for some time, long enough for poets not noticed by Berry to have established a countertradition. Pevear treats two of these poets, Louis Zukofsky and George Oppen, because he has their work under review, and Laszlo Géfin, in *Ideogram: History of a Poetic Method* (1982), treats them as part of a tradition beginning with Pound and Fenollosa that includes William Carlos Williams, Charles Reznikoff, Charles Olson, Robert Creeley, Robert Duncan, Allen Ginsberg, and Gary Snyder—Snyder, incidentally, being ranked highest for formally representing and taking a selfless place within the world of interdependent, interpenetrating things the Buddhists call the "Totality." These poets would surely appreciate Berry's touchstone-characterization of the offending arrogant mind, Satan's boast in *Paradise Lost* that "the mind is its own place," and, like him, they would put the mind in its place by restoring it to a place in the world; but they would not for these reasons dismiss, as Berry seems to do, the deep excursions into mind that, as in Snyder's case, have their warrant as enabling self-discipline in shamanist practice and meditation as well as in modern psychology. It is important to note that mind or consciousness, for Snyder, is one of the six constitutive elements of the world, that mind, as he says, is the only place where we are both in and outside the world at once. It is even more important to note that for him and the other poets mentioned above, the tradition that Berry sets out as redeeming the world from mind would seem to be fearfully like the tradition they oppose.

Readers of Berry will find in the six essays that compose this book—one is a gathering of notes, thematic seed-germs—much that is familiar: the way of arguing and the staples of the argument and admonition. This is as it should be, the inevitable result of integrity of thought; and of course we return to a writer because we wish to stand (with him) by his words, that is, enter again and understand from his point of view. All of the essays ring changes on Berry's established themes and some of them carry on the analogizing of poetry, marriage, and farming, the cherished concerns of his life, that characterizes his work. What distinguishes this volume is the focus on poetry, Berry's attempt to recall miscreant poets to a tradition that is of interest, finally, for what he makes of it and it makes of him—the way it grounds his own work. "Poetry and Place," an essay comprising nearly half of the book and one of the most recent, is devoted to explaining the Great Chain of Being, a concept of Western thought consonant with Idealism and almost as durable; explaining, I should say, by reinterpreting this concept and the poetry it informs in terms of his own profound ecological awareness and "domestic" interests. Nothing speaks so eloquently in this book for Berry's intransigent conservatism than this brave attempt to make do with a concept that no longer, as Wittgenstein would say, represents reality.

I mention Wittgenstein because Berry reminds me of him when he says, "The structure of a poem ultimately involves the structure of the life around it." Devotion to that structure or order, an "order that is not poetical," Berry believes "prevents the specialization of poetry." Now the Great Chain of Being figures for him this order or structure of life and serves to discipline the "winged" or "specialized imagination." Consequently, the "unspecialized imagination" is a "disciplined imagination"—that is, "a formal imagination . . . concerned with relation, dependence, propriety, proportion, balance" and, one should add, obedience, which Berry says is now obsolete, though it is of central importance in the poetics of, among others, Charles Olson and Robert Duncan. This melodrama of imaginations is reminiscent of New Humanist argument and values—of Southern Agrarian and New Critical thought as well—and puts one to the task of composting Berry's composting for the nutrients, of retrieving what is useful from a shapeless, ill-sorted, and often petulant essay.

Who would deny that the whole is greater than the part and that harmony or balance is preferable to the disintegration and destruction that Berry claims follow from partial or specialized interests? The issue is not the "system of systems"—Berry and Snyder join in using this phrase—but the model chosen to represent it, to represent reality. Where Snyder chooses the not-easily-schematized Buddhist "Totality" (recall the vectoral universe Fenollosa recognized in the Chinese language), Berry chooses the hierarchically ordered Chain of Being. He does this because the poets of "his" tradition have worked within this conceptual scheme and because with it he can press the claims of Christian doctrine in terms of "ecological intelligence," that is, get us to see the propriety of place within an order where place becomes a place, a farm, for example, that enforces discipline and responsibility. Propriety or decorum, living obediently within "an order of dependence and obligation," is what matters most to him, as it did to the Southern Agrarians. It is the lesson he reads in Dante, Spenser, Shakespeare, Milton, Dryden, and Pope—the lesson denied by Shelley and Wordsworth, Romantic egoists it was once fashionable for New Critics to despise.

Other than Dante, whose great work Berry reads as a "drama of decorum," Pope is the most highly esteemed poet in this tradition, both for his appreciation of the Great Chain of Being and for his achievement as a "domestic" poet. In his "Notes," Berry says: "I am endlessly in need of the work of poets who have been concerned with living in place, the life of a place, long-term attention and devotion to a settled home and its natural household. . . ." *Place,* in "Poetry and Place," refers to this as well as the ordered world, and Pope exemplifies both, and *Poetry,* too. So does Snyder, according to Berry, who enrolls him in this tradition as the only poet worth mentioning since Pope.

This generous placing is not supported by examples and commentary, and if Berry has any misgivings perhaps he expresses them in taking issue with Robert Bly who, it may be granted, does not read Pope as attentively as Berry does, but nevertheless recognizes hierarchical thought when he sees it. Berry defends hierarchy as a necessary, inescapable principle of order: "The ideal has always been a *just* hierarchy, not *no* hierarchy." He would agree with Kenneth Burke that the hierarchical is as much an element of our language as the negative, but forget, I suspect, the inevitable victimage involved. Were all men as just and good as he is! true husbandmen and nurturers, not patriarchs! Then they might read Genesis 1:28 as he does—read *subdue* as *bring under cultivation* and in consonance with *replenish.* But this has not been the case, as Snyder told us as early as *Myths and Texts.* In fact, having denounced the ecological consequences of the Judeo-Christian tradition, Snyder is one of the "'ecological' condemners of Western culture" of whom Berry disapproves, a member of the "ecology movement" dismissed pejoratively in the quotation marks because it does not subscribe to hierarchy.

For Berry the Great Chain of Being and *tradition* serve the same purpose as conventional poetic forms. They are "*set* forms," defined by him as prescriptive forms that precede content. Decorum is an ultimate issue because he needs the restraint of such forms; their obstruction he finds fruitful. Poetry, farming, and marriage are set forms, each an undertaking demanding discipline, the last involving a "sexual discipline" that dispenses, he says, with the "chemicals, devices, and procedures of 'birth control.'" Here, he differs most from Snyder, who has profoundly searched out both order and eros in his search for the primitive. Snyder's old ways are older than Berry's. He has gone back and outside what Olson, speaking of Pound, called the "Western box," and has found some of the nutrients of the Great Subculture that has kept alive our reverence for Gaia, Great Goddess, Earth. He has also learned an *inner* discipline of mind and, as Berry's humorlessness reminds me, the redemptive spirituality of laughter. Like Berry, he has acquired the sense of time that allows both to be patient with the earth, to work with her as well as *let be*. And again like Berry, who wins respect because of his fidelity to "atoning and renewing," Snyder has done in his different way "the atoning [at-one-ing] and renewing work" that Berry, following Faulkner, says "each person must do."

Snyder's Politics

Charles Molesworth's *Gary Snyder's Vision: Poetry and the Real Work* is about poetry and politics because "the real work," a phrase of Lenin's, reminds us of politics as we sometimes think of it and as Molesworth is mostly concerned with it. Snyder uses "the real work" in several contexts and insists on a range of meanings in choosing it as the title of a recent collection of talks and interviews. Even in *Turtle Island* (1974), his most obviously political book of verse *and* position papers, the conjunction of "the real work" with Lenin's "What is to be done" is qualified by the antecedent fact of coming back to himself, to the real self, where the real work he has in mind—much of it the work of mind, as in the third section of *Myths and Texts*—is done. What is to be done may be no more revolutionary than that or, as he learned in Zen training, than attending the immediate task, watering the apple trees, for example, as we find him doing in *Axe Handles,* his most recent book of poems.

The political force of *Turtle Island* is generated, among other things, by a sense of urgency: by the fact that what's to be done *now* in the very real work of inhabiting Kitkitdizze, the home place in California where he *reinhabits* Turtle Island, confronts the destructive elements of civilization he recognized and resisted from the beginning of his long, world-circling journey to place. Now, having begun to dwell, he draws the line—much as Paul Goodman had in *Drawing the Line* in 1946—and during the decade Molesworth considers quiescent ("the relative quietism and retreat from political activity that have been part of Snyder's career since 1970") does the needed community work in Nevada City, the needed work on the Arts Council of his home state, and the needed work (needed because his awareness of ecological diversity and "climax" demands it) of speaking up for what George Oppen calls the "unacknowledged world," the world of plants and animals and primitive peoples whose loss is ultimate diminishment. To adopt and modify the motto William Carlos Williams took from John Dewey—"the local is the only universal"—it is because Snyder *inhabits* the local that he realizes so profoundly the threat of universal monoculture and biospheric imperialism.

Molesworth is accepting and generously responsive to Snyder's political vision, a syncretic vision he variously characterizes as chiliastic-socialist, Buddhist Marxist, and American (Jeffersonian and Transcendentalist). Yet, as have others critical of it, he finds it lacking where they do. "Legislative representation for deers and Douglas firs is not an immediate prospect," he says, having said earlier that "this is Snyder's most challenging, most 'untraditional' notion." If this is so it is because Snyder has chosen to do a shaman's work and, in Ponge's words, has become an "ambassador of the silent world." As early as the second section of *Myths and Texts* he wrote songs for deer, bear, and birds, and to a considerable extent ever since has fulfilled not the prospect of legislative representation but the actual work of getting a hearing for the voiceless. "I wish to bring a voice from the wilderness, my constituency," Snyder said in addressing the Center for the Study of Democratic Institutions. "I wish to be a spokesman for a realm that is not usually represented in intellectual chambers or in the chambers of government." Acknowledged or unacknowledged, hasn't he become a legislator, and hasn't he, with others, begun the needed work of creating an ecological conscience, the immediate effects of which can be seen in intellectual and governmental chambers—in lobbies, too?

The supposition of much political criticism is that a political vision must become the controlling metaphor in the thought of vast populations and prove itself pragmatically in *realpolitik*—change the world, as we say. Little allowance is made for the *politics of vision* or what Edmund Wilson, in another time of political concern, said was the long-term indirect way in which literature actually does political work. Nor is the visionary (the word itself arouses suspicion) accorded much merit for acting on his vision, for being responsible for it, as Snyder is in his commitment to the direct action of small groups ("tribes," *garbha*), to a decentralized rural life that respects the ecosystem. The political value of being exemplary is not sufficiently appreciated.

Charles Altieri, whose criticism of Snyder's politics in *Turtle Island* Molesworth says he is answering, distinguishes between the work of the seer (visionary) and the prophet (promulgator of the vision) and finds especially lacking in Snyder the latter's work of implementation. But then, with commendable honesty, Altieri admits that he reads Snyder's poems aesthetically (as "pure" poetry, to recall New Critical doctrine) and in this way resists their moral and political appeal. In reading in this limited way, Altieri himself is exemplary: of the generations of readers who were trained *not* to look to poems for politics and who, as readers, may be said to fail Snyder.

In choosing the shamanic model of the poet—as have other poets of Snyder's generation unmentioned by Molesworth—Snyder joins poetry and politics in a single vocation. He knows that the vision quest he has undertaken on his arduous journey, that this way of poetry (not confessional), respects the tribe. If only because it restores the communal function of poetry, his poetry may be said to be political (recall the meaning of *polis,* as set out by Hannah Arendt and as used by Charles Olson). Of course, ever since the counterculture of the 1960s, if not earlier in the emergence of postmodern poetics after World War II, this has been the case. In our time, poetry has become "impure" and we do not know quite how to read it, only know that we must recognize its politics. This accounts for the significance of Molesworth's book as well as for what I find unsatisfactory in it—which is not to claim confidence in a "better" method but to indicate my sense of the critical situation.

Perhaps I can address both the significance and unsatisfactoriness of Molesworth's book by noting that concern for the politics of literature has become academically acceptable (fashionable?) and may only have replaced aesthetics as a privileged point of view. "Contexts," the title of the first chapter of the book, reminds us of contextualism, that a poem is not autotelic, and the epigraph from Walter Benjamin's "Conversations with Brecht" tells us that the exclusive context is political, not, say, inclusive of the other contexts referred to in Creeley's *Contexts of Poetry,* such contexts as personal life, fellow associates, literary situation, and so on. Moreover, having acknowledged context, the critic may, as I think Molesworth does, read the work in terms of this framework, that is, *understand* it in the sense of *Understanding Poetry:* assign meaning to it rather than let it predicate its several meanings, treat its themes rather than recognize its insistences. Frameworks are shortcuts, and the critical work often becomes speculative and theoretical, rich in references to the critic's other reading but distanced from the immediate complex experience of reading the poems.

Molesworth is a good reader when he chooses to be. He is especially attentive to "Through the Smoke Hole" and some of the poems of *Re-*

garding Wave. But he prefers to *characterize* Snyder's work, to play it off at considerable length against Adrienne Rich's poetry or locate it in terms of the intellectual schemes of Mannheim's *Ideology and Utopia,* Ellwood's *Alternative Altars,* and Arendt's *The Human Condition.* He would rather have us consider *Earth House Hold* in terms of references to *Walden, Life on the Mississippi, In the American Grain* (Goodman's *Utopian Essays and Practical Proposals* is qualified by *perhaps* and parentheses), and such epics as *Paterson* and the *Cantos* than closely engage the book itself. In deferring to a critic's authority, we assume that the work has been entered (read, as it were, from the inside out) and read *locally* (to use Molesworth's word), but in this instance there is too much evidence to the contrary.

For example, there is no indication that Molesworth appreciates the importance of the *Cold Mountain* poems and how Snyder's translations, disciplined and skilled in Chinese prosody, enabled the poems of *Riprap.* He seems to be unaware of the Reed College poems and the considerable influence that Eliot and Pound had on a fledgling poet who, in *Myths and Texts,* remained in their debt even as he challenged their epic work. The provenance of poems seems not to concern him: that the first edition of *The Back Country* was significantly altered by a second, enlarged edition and that a second edition of *Regarding Wave* filled out the story of the original text and modified its formal character go unnoticed. His scholarly debts seem needlessly light, and a reader unfamiliar with what has already been done would never know that Bob Steuding's *Gary Snyder,* so rich in groundwork, so fundamental, is something more than a bibliographical resource, a useful tool on a par with McCord's brief notes to *Myths and Texts.*

More disturbing, I find, is an insufficient awareness of the fact that the figure in the carpet, as Snyder himself speaks of it, is the journey and that its heaviest burden is eros, a difficult journey to love on which he transformed himself and, as we see in his *inhabiting,* aligned his thought and behavior with the matrifocal values to which he committed himself in his college reading of Graves's *The White Goddess.* He says in *The Old Ways* that defending the groves is the work of poetry, and his *Songs for Gaia* (1979), unmentioned by Molesworth, does that work, real work because what is crucial is overcoming the world alienation of the patriarchal mind. For the most part Molesworth's reading of texts is limited and skewed. None of them is put within the grasp of the reader, not even *Mountains and Rivers Without End,* with which he ends his account and predicts the high importance of Snyder's achievement. In addition, his sense of the trajectory of Snyder's work is questionable: "the curve of Snyder's career has been from the factlike density of perceptual intensity to the harmonious pattern of immanently mythic imagination." These characteristics of his work are better seen as constants—both appear in his early work, and the formal point of noting them is that for Snyder the book is always more than the poem. What is missing here is the remarkable life history, the story of life tracking life and of self-making that constitutes Snyder's journey-work and provides the essential ground for studying it. Such self-transformation may not be sufficiently political to be considered a political vision—in Snyder's case I think it is—but even so, it is because he has done this real work that his political vision has authority. Finally, and it does not detract from Snyder's achievement, his vision, in its essentials, is not unique and takes strength from the political concern of many people, not only the ecologists but the poets and anthropologists whose common interests unite in *ethnopoetics*, an undertaking of political moment named in this way by Jerome Rothenberg in 1968.

PART X
Barry Lopez

Making the Turn: Rereading Barry Lopez

21 May 1988

We are back (yes, *back*) at Wolf Lake—have been for ten days, long laboring days of settling in and setting things to rights. Spring is advanced this year; there is mowing and brushing to do and the gardens to be got ready (they wait on the Deere, which for the second time refuses to run at the beginning of the season). We have already dragged away huge piles of branches, the crowns of trees cut last fall. We have stacked some of the wood, leaving the larger logs to be split and stacked later. Making wood involves so much labor I am inclined to garner every last twig, but we already have enough wood for three years. So I was not reluctant to give a truckload to the young man who had come to help—willing, in this instance, to sacrifice economy to beauty, though in a proper *ecos* they are not separate but correlative.

I write this not so much for the record—such chores are customary—but in order to make a start here, in the little cabin in which I am now free to spend my mornings. It is salutary to divide the day between the work of the mind and the work of the body—the *vita contemplativa* and the *vita activa,* the latter, as I practice it, *menial,* according to Hannah Arendt—and it is necessary. The work of the body, outdoor work, is *out:* to do such work is a primary way of being-in-the-world, of finding oneself in the cosmos, in touch with things, physically "at home." The work of the mind, indoor work, is *in,* doubly interior: to do such work is too often a way of withdrawing from the world, of living with its images. I use the spatial distinctions (*in/out*) that accord with the dualisms of *mind/body, subject/object, self/world,* but these are the dualisms I wish to overcome:

when *out,* by a participatory activity of mind and, when *in,* by a meditative activity that seeks in words to hew to experience.

This may account for my interest in "nature writing." Not most of it, which doesn't challenge dualism so much as exploit it by giving the mind sovereign play, sometimes in sentiment and sentimental spirituality, and most often by a show of literary sensibility. Nature writers—I'm thinking of many of the contemporary writers represented in the *Antaeus* collection edited by Daniel Halpern and in *Words from the Land: Encounters with Natural History Writing,* edited by Stephen Trimble—are "fine" writers. As Trimble says, those he has selected "see themselves as writers first." They are personal essayists, often of distinction, who find some of their material in nature, and many of them, as in the Charles Addams cartoon I've posted here, sit for their own portrait when they go there. Seldom are they naturalists like Thoreau, Muir, and Leopold, who articulated a profound, lifelong engagement with nature, more often wrote to live than to make a living, and preferred advocacy to pacification. Taken together, the *Antaeus* collection and *Words from the Land* give us a canon and establish "nature writing" as fashionable, a genre ready-to-hand for writers' workshops.

I have spent an hour this morning looking for a few pages I had written several years ago on this entry in John Muir's journal: "Not like taking the veil—no solemn abjuration of the world. I only went out for a walk, and finally concluded to stay out till sundown, for going out, I found, was really going in." I cannot recall my exegesis now (the absence is palpable and disturbs me) but only that it provided the ground of my concern with *out/in,* about which I have been making notes, knowing that this insistence has proposed itself for writing. I have not lost the quotation: I know it by heart, and have it here, tacked on the wall. And I probably have the exegesis (for some reason I do not think I can now engage Muir's sentences as I did then in the readiness of the occasion) and will find it in the cluttered study in Iowa City. When I do I will fill this morning's gap by appending it.

The thought thought me because I was thinking about Barry Lopez, whose *Crossing Open Ground* I had just read by way of making the transition to what is now best defined as sub-rural. (*Sub* for *suburban* and *beneath*. The narrow sand road to our place has recently been named and we have been given a house number.) This collection of fourteen essays written over the last ten years is coherent and substantial, a wise selection from many journalistic pieces, and it seemed to me to be an entrance (because *entranced*?), a place to begin. The title, for which Lopez offers no explanation, imposes itself by virtue of three resonant words: *crossing*, which calls up Whitman's great poem on the intrinsic value of experience, one that the landscape permits us to share with the author, in this instance the experience of open ground and the ongoing process; *open*, which plays on the full range of the unbounded and modifies *ground*, a substantive of fundamental importance, by giving it sky and thus defining a spacious landscape. All told, I think of Olson's "In Cold Hell, In Thicket," where the resolution on change involves crossing:

> he will cross
>
> (there is always a field,
> for the strong there is always
> an alternative)

I also think of Olson because nature-writing, as Lopez exemplifies it, belongs to the project proposed by the new poetics—by an *open* poetics (*field* poetics, *compo*-sition) and ethnopoetics. Both writers situate us in the field, *world* us.

And both are concerned with landscape(s) and practice the cultural geography so notably represented in the work of Carl Sauer, whom both acknowledge. Sauer notes that Friedrich Ratzel said that "the geographer is naturalist." Yes, and the naturalist and the poet are geographers. Olson gives us Gloucester; Lopez, in *Arctic Dreams*, gives us the Arctic, and more often than not the essays in *Crossing Open Ground* present landscapes. For both, incidentally, birds are eminent examples of being-in-the-world. They figure in the opening and closing essays of Lopez's book and may be said to provide its measure by enclosing it in the wisdom he attributes to them.

A central essay in *Crossing Open Ground* treats landscape in relation to narrative (a focal issue also of *Arctic Dreams*) and seems to me to serve better as an introduction to Lopez's stories—*Desert Notes, River Notes, Winter Count*—than to his essays, though all he writes is characterized by intimacy, the indispensable element, he believes, of the storyteller's art. This quality, in his case unguarded but discreet, derives, he says, "from the listener's trust and a storyteller's certain knowledge of his subject and regard for his audience"; and it "deepens if the storyteller tempers his authority with humility" and the landscape ("the physical setting") is shared.

This meditation on the art he aspires to practice turns on an experience of listening to hunting stories in a village in the Brooks Range in Alaska. The original title, "Story at Anaktuvuk Pass," situates the essay in a landscape, which is carefully described, and the essay itself demonstrates the concordance of visual and verbal landscapes with which Lopez is concerned. Lopez employs some elements of the new journalism and as a storyteller assimilates the fantastic realism of recent Spanish American writers, but his primary model is an oral, "primitive" art. An early book, *Giving Birth to Thunder, Sleeping with His Daughter,* is a collection of retellings of stories about Coyote, and when he gets to the heart of the matter of landscape and narrative, his example is the Navajo. He says of his experience of stories that "the landscape seemed alive because of the stories" and that they "renewed in me a sense of the purpose of my life." This reminds me of Leslie Silko, whose *Ceremony* enacts these very things in the way myth (what is said: story) is made to work against the realistic prose of contemporary fiction, and whose essay "Landscape, History, and the Pueblo Imagination" is essential commentary on her art and Lopez's essay.

Aldo Leopold, who claims that in learning how to read the land we will learn (at last) how to live with it, would have appreciated Lopez's ability to study out the land, its idioms and its men (Whitman's phrase). To see relationships is the fundamental lesson. One of the personal essays, "Children in the Woods," is about just such ecological initiation and the way it "nurtures the heart." "Landscape and Narrative" also insists on this ("One learns a landscape . . . by perceiving the relations in it"), and many of the essays recount brief journeys in and out of landscapes during which perceiving relationships is the necessary work, the most intense activity. Perhaps the title of the collection is intended to suggest the movement of this journey-work, for nothing here tells of inhabitation, and what is lacking (to be found in *Desert Notes* and *River Notes* and the extensive regional journeys of *Arctic Dreams*) are, in Silko's words for the Hopi way, "interaction [participation] and interrelationship." The landscapes here are seen, not lived in, and, though Lopez is better able to see them because he enters the field with humility, he is still too much an observer, a reporter not yet wholly within them. *Landscape,* as Silko notes, is a visual term, speaking for the power of the eye (and *I*) to compose the scene (seen): "a portion of the territory the eye can comprehend in a single view." Landscape art—and sometimes the similar work of nature writers—is a Romantic art founded on philosophical idealism; yet *landscape,* used in an areal sense by Sauer and Olson, remains a serviceable word, much in the way *ground* does in the title of Lopez's book.

"I think of two landscapes—one outside the self, the other within." This is the way in which Lopez poses the problem of *out/in.* Presumably these landscapes correspond. In the efficacious storytelling of "aboriginal peoples," they are brought together, or, better, as with the Navajo, the "sacred order" of the exterior landscape, "the perceived natural order of the universe," grounds the interior order, that is, every aspect of the "indigenous philosophy." This wholeness (holiness, health) is the gauge of what is wanting as a result of the very Western mind that predicates *out/in,* the MIND, which I capitalize because Ed Dorn, in *Recollections of Gran Apachería,* sees it as "the highest mutation of force," the power that overcame the Apaches' holistic, mythic way of thinking ("I am Thinking Earth").

Dorn says that the Apaches' leading ideas came "directly from the landform." This puts ideas in their place, much in the way that Williams' "no ideas but in things" does. Lopez, too, thinks that this is the proper order. When he speaks of the *authority* of the landscape, he has this priority in mind, and an ethical measure comparable to Leopold's *integrity* of the land. He believes that the "relationships in the interior landscape," arranged as they are "according to the thread of one's moral, intellectual, and spiritual development," answer to the exterior landscape. "The interior landscape," he insists, "responds to the character and subtlety of an exterior landscape; the shape of the individual mind is affected by land as it is by genes." I agree that we are "deeply influenced" in this way but that rather than "draw[ing] on relationships in the exterior landscape and project[ing] them onto the interior landscape," we too often project—impose—our ideas on the world.

It is just because for us these landscapes do not correspond and we do not project the order of the exterior onto the interior landscape that we need storytellers to do this healing work for us, to do what Lopez wishes to do in nonfictional as well as fictional forms: "reorder a state of psychological confusion through contact with the pervasive truth of those relationships we call 'the land.'" This healing work is ultimately religious:

> . . . if you can really see the land . . . lose your sense of wishing it to be what you want it to be . . . strip yourself of the desire to order and to name and see the land entirely for itself, you see in the relationship of all its elements the face of God.

I cite from an interview with Jim Aton, where Lopez recalls Laurens van der Post's phrase, "the pattern we call God," and goes on to say that the landscape has authority "because its order is, at least in some places, still innate." By *still innate* I think he means *still undisturbed.* In some of the far places to which he goes God still authorizes the landscape—it is still, as he says, "creation"—because we have not yet done the Devil's work.

The critical question is the extent to which language may be made to answer to such complex representation of reality, and there is the moral question of the truth or honesty of *our* relationships that the functionalists, for example, put in terms of function and form and of the necessity of building from the ground up. Lopez says directly that "lying is the opposite of story" and adds that for the writer "truth reveals itself . . . not in dogma but in the paradox, irony, and contradictions that distinguish compelling narratives." What must be resisted are "reductionism in science, fundamentalism in religion, fascism in politics."

Lopez also considers national literature in terms of storytelling, as a literature that respects the land (the "source") and our relation to it. This is why he thinks that nature writing, so conspicuous now, "will one day produce a major and lasting body of American literature . . . [and] provide the foundation for a reorganization of American political thought."

Reorder, repair, restore, rediscover, reclaim, rethink. I haven't clustered all the words with this prefix (*re:back*), just a few that come to mind, enough to suggest the work of literature to which Lopez *recalls* us. "To repair a spirit in disarray"—such art, as with other contemporary writers, especially the poets, *recovers* the shaman's work, the primary work of *poesis*. "Landscape," Silko says, "has similarities with dreams."

Even in the frantic effort to control the blaze, I thought of Thoreau, whose notoriety in Concord came of having set fire to the woods. Given wind enough and time, I would have. Maybe the interval in writing—easily explained in terms of *maintenance* (from Old French, *maintenir,* to which I add *now* from *maintenant*)—is better explained by the sour-burnt-plastic smell that fills this cabin. The wreck is only a few yards away, up against the white oak that stopped the truck's forward motion and that didn't burn, no more than the oaks of the oak openings of the prairie. So much for moving a truck to make room for a bulldozer; so much for two inches of rotten neoprene tubing. Nothing unusual, the insurance adjuster said. What's unusual is the speed with which the volunteer firemen from Cass Lake got here—eight miles in ten minutes. And the efficiency of volunteers, our butcher, and others whom we recognized, among them.

When I read "The Stone Horse" in *Antaeus,* I found it artful, maybe because it seemed so in that context, and I was annoyed by such exact yet literary sentences as "The dark mouths of gold, talc, and tin mines yawned from the bony flanks of desert ranges" and "Wood smoke hung like a lens in the trees." Reading the essay now I am happier with the moral bearing of its deliberate art and appreciate its moral exemplarity, the reason, perhaps, that Lopez opens the collection with it.

The incident recalled is simple—and paradigmatic, as we now say. Having been given directions by an archaeologist with the Bureau of Land Management (the expert), Lopez enters the desert to inspect an artifact, a stone horse, an intaglio made by a Quechan three hundred years ago. The immediate context is the wholesale vandalizing of aboriginal sites, the destruction of evidence of human occupancy now believed to go back more than two hundred thousand years. Lopez tells of post-World War II occupancy and the more recent story of vandalizing (as also told in Tony Hillerman's *A Thief of Time*) that "devour[s] history."

He is, of course, a privileged observer, granted permission to see the intaglio because, as the essay shows, he is a pilgrim. Journey, for him, is pilgrimage, as in other essays, and involves withdrawal from and return to "civilization." (The fullest example is the next essay, "A Reflection on White Geese.") The occasion is meditative, never rushed, ritualized in the telling by the careful prose and the reenactment of formal art. His search for the primitive—the very search itself—is sacred, for landscape is sacred space to be entered reverently in expectation of realizations intense enough to be called epiphanic.

He approaches the stone horse at dawn, observes it during sunrise, in process, animated as it were, not in the frozen moment of an aerial photograph. He is not above the object, recording it, mapping it; he is present with the horse, as its maker was, seeing it from various perspectives and in various lights, and summoning as a necessary part of the experience of wonder all that the essay tells of geography, cultural history, and personal recollection. The stone horse, to cite Kerouac, is the jewel-center of the associations awakened by the occasion.

Lopez, a learned writer, is an intellectual historian as well as nature writer. Culture as much as nature concerns him. He does not leave out of account the fact that on the way to Tule Lake to see the geese he listens to Bach; in another essay he speaks of his pleasure in bibliography. In "A Stone Horse" he tries to earn respect for the plundered landscape by reminding us of the Dordogne and by suggesting its value as archive. For the history it holds is "a kind of medicine": it nullifies our belief in the sovereignty of the self and of the present. By permitting "the great breadth of human expression to reverberate," history of this kind clarifies and encourages, and reproves the vandals whose scorn and disrespect "create the awful atmosphere"—it is felt as menace—"in which totalitarianism thrives."

"With a slight bow I paid my respects to the horse, its maker, and the history of us all. . . ."

"The Stone Horse," belongs with "Searching for Ancestors" and "The Passing Wisdom of Birds," for these essays also treat the "original wisdom" to be found in "tribal America." The ancestors for whom Lopez searches are people like the Anasazi who were "intimate with the landscape, a successful people": they "responded resourcefully and decisively to the earth and the weather that together made their land"; the land was their "arbiter," and they lived with it with "utter honesty." Thinking of them (and the Peabody Coal Company now ravishing their land), he proposes what is surely his—and our—work: *"to find some place between the extremes of nature and civilization where it is possible to live without regret"* (my italics). The diversity and impenetrability of ways of life, witnessed in this instance by archaeological search for the Anasazi, humbles him, a requisite condition for what he experiences on their land, under the open sky:

> The slow inhalation of light that is the fall of dusk is now complete. The stars are very bright. I lie [here] recalling the land as if the Anasazi were something that had once bloomed in it.

(Flowering, the moral-aesthetic measure of contact with the environment in *In the American Grain;* a sentiment of being, deeply nostalgic, matched by the recollection of dusk in *A Walker in the City.*)

"The Passing Wisdom of Birds," the concluding essay, mentions Leopold and, like the essays at the end of *A Sand County Almanac,* makes the strongest, most direct statement of Lopez's case. Where Leopold uses the killing of Odysseus's handmaidens to inform our sense of ethical evolution, Lopez uses Cortez's destruction of Tenochtitlán (as Williams had) to mark an enormity we must now repair. In Leopold we look forward to a "land ethic," and in Lopez we find it by going back to what Dennis and Barbara Tedlock, in the title of their book on Native American lore, call *Teachings from the American Earth.*

Cortez's destruction of the city he had described as "the most beautiful city in the world" was completed in the most gratuitous act, the burning of the aviaries. Lopez finds this act so grotesque and unmitigated that even the recognition of the "dark side" of human culture fails to account for it. For him it images more than the "destructive madness . . . of imperial conquest"; it images "a long-term failure of Western Civilization to recognize the intrinsic worth of the American landscape, and its potential value to human societies that have since come to be at odds with the natural world." The measure of Cortez's enormity is that it "flies widely in the face of a desire to find a *dignified* and honorable relationship with nature" (I italicize *dignified,* a moral term repeated elsewhere). And the measure of our need is that we long to "find our way back to a more equitable set of relationships with all we have subjugated," a way that involves "rethinking [thinking back] our relationships with the natural world (i.e., in figuring out how to get ourselves back *into* it)," a way that aboriginal peoples may teach us.

Lopez's proposals for our difficult reeducation are exemplified to a large extent in his own attitudes and practice. Like Eiseley and Leopold he respects science but knows its limitations, appreciates field work and the "indispensable element of personal experience." Like Wendell Berry, he knows that the necessary transformation in attitudes is private and comes of individual effort and that each of us must "cultivate . . . a sense of mystery." To this end, he would preserve the still undisturbed landscapes and the learning of aboriginal peoples (the diverse ecosystems and nature-related cultures from which we have much to learn), give greater support to field biology and more attention to our libraries and the education in natural sciences and natural history of the next generation.

I am struck by his hopefulness. We are, it seems, still Nature's Nation. In his rethinking, this nineteenth-century characterization of America is given new currency:

> The philosophy of nature we set aside eight thousand years ago in the Fertile Crescent we can . . . locate again and greatly refine in North America. The New World is a landscape still overwhelming in the vigor of its animals and plants, resonant with mystery. It encourages, still, an enlightened response toward indigenous cultures that differ from our own. . . .

Perhaps he placed "Grown Men" between "Searching for Ancestors" and "The Passing Wisdom of Birds" because it speaks for his faith and hope. This personal essay pays tribute to three men ("grown," that is, mature men), the "grandfathers," tutelary figures, whose behavior furthered Lopez's moral and spiritual education. One of them, he says, "introduced me to a perception of America's indigenous people more complex than anything I was later to read about them. . . ." All of them had "integrity" and "implacable conviction," and when faced with trouble "act[ed] to help . . . rather than to assign blame. . . ."

This—as well as a sense of complexity—may explain why Lopez is never strident. In "Yukon-Charley," where he argues most fully in behalf of wilderness, he simply notes that "the Reagan administration regards such arguments from science [the gene pool] and ethics [animal rights] as frivolous." Measuring riches in the way Leopold does, he considers a limited economic understanding of wilderness "impoverished." In "A Reflection on White Geese," he comments on the Reagan administration in parentheses as if to suggest how out of place it is in the rich experience reported there. His appeal to a sense of beauty grants us the freedom to choose to foster the richer way: "We grasp what is beautiful in a flight of snow geese . . . as easily as we grasp the beauty in a cello suite; and [because we do,] intuit . . . that if we allow these things to be destroyed or degraded for economic or frivolous reasons we will become deeply and strangely impoverished."

I am reminded again of Leopold in reading "A Reflection on White Geese" because the crane, whose bugling is as old as the Pleistocene, awakened his sense of beauty and mystery and filled him with bitter regret for the economic expedience that drained their wetlands. Wildlife management is very much an issue in Lopez's essay. That we seem to be able to preserve the geese only by allowing them to be hunted is as paradoxical for him as it was for Leopold and Muir.

Lopez does not neglect crucial political issues of this environmental/ecological kind. He does so quietly (without rancor) and perhaps with more point because they are part of the personal experience that sets them off, questions them, and makes us realize the reversible equation of public issues and private woes. So in "Yukon-Charley," where Lopez's claims for the wilderness are verified in the experience of canoeing the Charley River, he challenges federal policy by defending resident subsistent hunters, like the Moores, who belong in the Yukon-Charley Rivers National Preserve because "they have a manifestly spiritual relationship with the landscape." On the one hand, legislation is often too simple and, on the other hand, the issues are often complicated. In "Borders," the rewarding experience of a day spent searching for the unmarked boundary between Alaska and Canada, raises the question of the arbitrary and the abstract and provides a measure of the frantic-oppressive emotion Lopez feels when, on return, he is confronted by legislation he has not had time enough to examine but nevertheless must decide on.

And morally. "A Presentation of Whales," the longest essay, considers the complications and cross-purposes of scientists, police, bureaucrats, press corps, and curious and concerned onlookers when whales, stranded on a beach in Oregon, create an opportunity for scientific research, a media event, and a health hazard. Lopez studies human beings—attitudes and angles of vision—as well as (other large) animals, and this essay, like one on cowboys who work the rodeos and another on people rafting the Colorado River in the Grand Canyon, is a presentation of humans, of "the worst and the best human behavior." Scientific research, questioned here, is more thoroughly taken up in "The Lives of Seals," a by-product of *Arctic Dreams*. The gathering of ecological data involves killing seals (the perspective is that of the Esquimos, who, in visiting the Tule Lake refuge, had been appalled by the wasteful hunting that jeopardized their lives), data that will be used "to guide oil and mineral development." Lopez's sentiments are clear enough: he would like this immemorial hunting and fishing land to remain inviolate. But he also respects knowledge, the scientific inquiry that seems always to be used to alter old ways and stable ecosystems. So he does not settle the matter "as if there were no seals" but uncomfortably stands "in the middle of the question" in the way he stands between the scientists and a crew that abhors the killing. As a writer accompanying marine biologists, his work, figured in gathering shells for the crew and represented by the essay itself, is to create the atmosphere of tolerance in which profoundly difficult questions of the propriety of human acts may at least be considered. His work, suggested in "A Presentation of Whales," is not to settle fundamental questions but to add the witness of a point of view too often omitted: "No novelist, no historian, no moral philosopher, no scholar of Melville, no painter, no theologian had been on that beach."

This determination on truth, I recall Warner Berthoff saying, is the hallmark of American literature.

I think that Lopez's distinctive work is in the three slim volumes of *Desert Notes: Reflections in the Eye of a Raven* (1976), *River Notes: The Dance of Herons* (1979), and *Winter Count* (1981). Slim volumes, like volumes of poems, and in their imaginative range, care for language, and formal shape, poetic. To read them requires the concentrated attention we give to poetry, though we also attend because they treat (and are) a discipline of being upon which our lives depend. As with all literary work that claims our attention, they engage us in *ta 'wil,* the exegesis of the soul. These books involve sacred space: not just the landscape of desert, river, or plains but the deep interior landscapes of self and imagination, landscapes at times undifferentiated, surreal. These landscapes are places of quest, of vision quest and shamanic flight. Lopez's desert is not Edward Abbey's or Gary Nabhan's; it has other dimensions and is as much out of space and time as it is out of mind, a place of mystery, disorientation, and self-transformation, where one goes crazy and comes to oneself, though a certain craziness—despair of the world—is needed to go there in the first place. Fancy hardly covers what is found there.

Notes, in the title, belongs to the humility that comes of uncertainty and incompleteness—to a book that questions itself. Telling of entrance to initiation ("the way inside"), *Desert Notes* is no farther along at its close than at its beginning. It is framed by a concern with spatial and spiritual directions which have as their measure the totality of the cosmic medicine wheel ("where everything is coming from") of the stories "Perimeter" and "Coyote and Rattlesnake." Native American lore, with the desert, grounds the book, belongs to the landscape Lopez has come in search of ("everything I'd come here to find out was hidden inside"); and at the end, in "Directions," where he "hear[s] a map . . . well spoken" from a man named Leon, he acknowledges the need for help from someone (a grandfather?) who has been tested by primary experience and has learned sufficiency.

Desert Notes is a guidebook without a map—maps, we are told, are "too thin." It is a spoken guide, its mode often oral, often dialogic, intimately addressed to the reader. "I would like to show you what lies before us," the narrator says at the outset, and, as with Prufrock, we go with him and, as with Whitman, we assume what he assumes, the ultimate seriousness of the quest. For, in coming to the desert he is making, as Thomas Merton says of the Desert Fathers, "a clean break with a conventional, accepted social context." He does this not only for reasons of psychic health but in order to save a civilization he has been told is approaching its end. "We are here . . . to change things," he says. "It is why I came to the desert."

The representative anecdote of the book, "Coyote and Rattlesnake," fables this cultural role. In this story the desert figures as the last outpost of nature facing an advancing civilization that is destroying the habitat and the old ways. This is adumbrated in "The School," where a woman tells of white occupancy as temporary as the mining that occasioned it. (See Lopez's update, "California Desert, a Worldly Wilderness," *National Geographic Magazine,* January 1987.) "The Shisa," Coyote realizes, "will take even the desert," and so, instructed by otter to purify and prepare himself, he goes to see Akasitah "about a new way of life." Coyote has a vision such as Black Elk had ("They had broken the circle and made it straight like a stick"), but Akasitah assures him that the Shisa, whom he himself had set free, will now—is there a better word?—self-destruct. This story is not in Lopez's or any other collection of stories about Coyote I've read. I suspect that he created it just as Silko, in *Ceremony,* created the more ferocious story of white Europeans and witchery, a story of world-alienation, one of the great eco-fables of our time. (Unerringly, Jerome Rothenberg includes it in the revised edition of *Shaking the Pumpkin.)*

Lopez acknowledges his debt to Native Americans in "Twilight," where, juxtaposing two prose modes, he tells the sometimes sordid history of a Navajo rug that had become an article of exchange and that now is used by the narrator for its original sacred purpose. Spreading the rug on the desert floor, he is both in and on the world of the rug; their landscapes have become one. *Raven,* in the subtitle, also indicates the extent to which Lopez assimilates the Native American vision. Prominent in the mythology of the tribes of the Northwest and sub-Arctic, Raven belongs in the desert because of the spiritual power attributed to him. Raven, purged of the qualities of crow, is not unlike a benign Coyote—and the story Lopez tells has some of the anecdotal character of Coyote stories. For him, Coyote and Raven are interchangeable, and in *Giving Birth to Thunder* he sometimes substitutes Coyote for Raven, a liberty, incidentally, not granted anthropologists. Even so, he understands their scruple, has relied on their work and mastered the scholarship, and given good reasons for wanting the tales more accessible in every way. The seriousness of his concern is unquestionable; he dedicates the collection "To the Native Peoples of North America." See also "The American Indian Mind," edited by him for *Quest,* September–October 1978, another effort at better understanding.

In reading, "The Blue Mound People," I thought of *The Narrative of Arthur Gordon Pym*—the prototype of fantastic realism? The Blue Mound People are "entirely out of the order of things"; sophisticated methods of archaeological inquiry cannot *explain* them. Notable for their "unusual [close] relationship with the desert," they remain a "mystery." Imaginary or not, they are the ancestors the narrator searches for.

The cover photograph of the paperback edition is by Lopez: a sharply defined desert landscape empty except for an empty rocking chair. The chair is anomalous if not surreal. It is not mordantly ironic in the fashion, say, of Michael Meyers' drawings in *Recollections of Gran Apachería*. It invites us to sit and wait, for as much as anything learning to wait is our business. First we must abandon civilization and give over the ego, as the narrator does in stepping out of his moving van. Then we must strip ourselves. (The discipline is universal, but the instance that comes to mind is Ike's initiation in "The Bear.") There is also the need to purify ourselves in the hot spring (told in a story less portentous than the narrator's first-person admonitions in "Desert Notes," which, stylistically, signals a break with convention). Finally, there is a correlative story of nakedness, of the repossession of the body and the anima. In this story of a white woman who comes into intimate relationship with the land, the play of mind and light enacts a cosmic eros that is salutary as against the perhaps more explicitly sexual *and* miniaturized instance of the ant (a male) with the seed.

To wait, and to be alert. As the old man says in "Conversation," you stay in one place and "you wait for yourself." You also wait "until you see for yourself." This passivity belongs to egolessness, but it is a wise passivity, as in Thoreau, alert. As for alertness, Ortega says it well in *Meditations on Hunting:* we are alert when, like the animals, we live "from within [the] environment." Hunting is the initial discipline of alertness in the "absolute *outside* of the countryside." But meditation, as in Ortega's book, is the hunt of the hunt, a discipline of alertness in the "absolute *inside* of ideas."

To answer Thoreau: Lopez hears the fishes when they cry. More than a century later, only now in the West, he responds once more to the manifest destiny of spoliation, the destruction of nature and Native Americans that Thoreau elegized in *A Week on the Concord and Merrimack Rivers.*

(The *re* cluster, I see, is matched by the *de* cluster. *Destroy,* and its cognates, is obsessive. We are a culture, Lopez says, that "devours the earth."

Forward motion or *progress,* too often destructive, calls up the necessity of return.)

Lopez has acquired the "Indian wisdom" Thoreau claimed for himself. By participant activity, by "direct intercourse and sympathy" and with the "finer organization" of his senses, he has come to know his immediate world. (He lives in Finn Rock, Oregon, a logging village on the McKenzie River.) *River Notes,* even more than *Desert Notes,* proves that Lopez is one of the aspirants to nature study who, Thoreau said, "will smell, taste, see, hear, feel better than other men." He has especially learned to listen. "I have trained myself to listen to the river," the narrator says, the river, with all of its extensions, its watershed, an *ecos;* and in the river's notes he has heard Gaia weeping: "The running . . . of rivers is the weeping of the earth for what is lost." We are told this at the beginning of the book, at the ocean, before he undertakes the spiritual journey, the return "up-river . . . [to] begin again." But even when he finds the "springs of celebration," he knows that the tears of ravens are the source of the river: "it is from *them* that the river actually flows, for at night they break down and weep; the universal anguish of creatures, their waiting in desolation, the wrenching anger of betrayals—this seizes them and passes out of them and in that weeping the river takes its shape." This is as true of him as of these tutelary birds (the Native Americans also weep), and as true of the book as of the river that runs through it. Hence the sadness of this unique book and its inimitable tone, its burden (as with all of Lopez's work) being to bring the desolate human spirit in "the last days" into concord with the desolated but still vital spirit of the world and so make good a double loss.

We go to nature, we say, to heal ourselves *(natura sanat),* but this now requires that we heal nature, learn to practice healing ways. This spiritual need joins *Desert Notes* and *River Notes,* makes them companion books. The first, in order of time and experience, involves the waiting, the vigil that has exhausted the distraught narrator at the beginning of *River Notes;* the second involves doing, the activity, ultimately, of dancing, the joining-with of at-one-ment. At the beginning, where the heron is wonderfully evoked, the narrator says that "I believe we will dance together someday [when he acquires the understanding and discipline the book records]. . . . I cannot believe it is so far between knowing what must be done and doing it." Though the raven is still present, the narrator addresses the heron as *thou,* and "expect[s] the wisdom of the desert out of you." Now the vision-quest, proposed in "The Search for the Heron," has become explicitly ecological, that is, of *ecos* and itself ecological in being instrumental in restoring *ecos*. The narrator may be said to have an eco-imagination, one that is profoundly imaginal (of the psyche, as treated by James Hillman) and profoundly resonant (awakening Bachelardian reverie). "The images are irrefutable, requiring only patience to perceive," the narrator says; and the story of what he perceives is myth, if myth, as Olson claims, reenacts our primary perceptions of self-and-world.

The unity of outer and inner landscapes accounts for the visionary power of the book. These landscapes interpenetrate or, in a book so fluvial, may be said to flow together. The stories, modulated by first- and third-person narration, are essentially oral and performative. Their slow dance—I think of the sarabande of Crane's "Repose of Rivers"—is as much a sacred gesture as the dance of the herons in which the narrator finally participates. In the overwhelming fable of eco-loss and recovery that closes the book, the narrator's sacred (selfless, gratuitous) gestures are acknowledged by the animals, in the "old way" of Native American stories. Blue Heron says:

> We were the first people here. We gave away all the ways of living. Now no one remembers how to live anymore, so the river is drying up. Before we could ask for rain there had to be someone to do something completely selfless, with no hope of success. You went after that fish, and then at the end you were trying to dance. A person cannot be afraid of being foolish. For everything, every gesture, is sacred.

Because he has done these things, the narrator enters the ever-present reality of Native American myth. He had been told by Hanner, in the story of how the river (in a way comparable to drought) taught the salmon and the bear, that everyone lives by "agreements and courtesies." These "obligations" remain unchanged. "Time has nothing to do with it," Hanner explains. "When you feel the river shuddering against your legs, you are feeling the presence of all these agreements."

The true feeling of worlding is aesthetic and moral: the harmony of nature is the result of (ecological) agreements. The terms of Hanner's eco-fable are moral, and just as significant is the fact that Hanner tells it as a medicine man had told it to him. This confirms the storyteller's shamanic role (when Hanner's voice changes, the narrator's hair rises and he feels threatened by "something in the dark": he has entered what Eiseley calls the night country) and it confirms that the healing, which always tried to restore harmony with nature, is now the essential ecological work. *No one remembers how to live anymore.* Lopez tells stories in order to teach us to see in the old ways (see Snyder's *The Old Ways*) and to behave accordingly: he would restore our ecological sense. And he tells stories because in them, to the extent that he may be identified with the narrator, he, too, must learn these hard lessons from those whose experience gives them moral authority.

Hanner's story, an apologue that supports his account of the disappearance of a utopian community, stands against the "rubbish" of popular history. So, too, the narrator's stories stand against, and are measured by, "The Rapids," which renders a reporter's search for what he thinks the public considers "human interest" wholly in the direct (often deadly) speech of his respondents. The narrator himself gathers stories, some of which remind me of Anderson's *Winesburg, Ohio:* "The Log Jam," for example, not only for the story of Rebecca Grayson but because all of its stories, of a logging village, comprise a community of suffering. And, as often as not, Lopez's "grotesques" are afflicted in the spirit. There is the man who "pondered gentleness" and made the stone fish in "The Salmon"; and there are Rebecca Grayson and the nameless woman of "Dawn," whose burdens of erotic loss (appropriately so in an eco-imagination) are spiritual rather than simply sexual. These anima-figures are unacknowledged or hidden presences whose recourse to the river recalls Chopin's *The Awakening,* even though they do not enact the Ophelia-death treated so well by Bachelard in *Water and Dreams.* The polarized world of "Dawn" as well as the use of two voices anticipates Susan Griffin's *Woman and Nature;* repetitive phrasing recalls Stein. The unseeing fishermen have a counterpart in the absent fisherman in Snyder's "The Elwah River," a poem of the grieved anima.

These analogues are not important except to show that Lopez draws on literate as well as preliterate sources and shares the deep concerns of our time. In fact, the book closest to his own is Snyder's *Myths and Texts,* which belongs to the same logging country, employs modernist and archaic techniques toward shamanic ends, and treats the initial stages of the arduous journey back to love that is at the heart of all eco-fables.

(Toward shamanic ends. "The initiation / of another kind of nation"—Olson, in the last volume of *The Maximus Poems.*)

The narrator performs gratuitous acts (of atonement, for childhood guilt, among other things) and dances with the herons because he has been enabled by another dance, which, in turn, seems to be the reward of careful attention (without "arrogance or presumption") to the natural relationships of the little-travelled upriver country. He studies this part of the river in the hope of "a larger vision," meaning by this both ecological understanding of the watershed and something truly visionary, befitting a return to source. A single sentence makes the transition and explains how the one occasions the other: "In this way [Way?] I came to a bend in the river . . . from which I could see a house. . . ." He has undertaken an archetypal journey, a quest of the kind that distinguishes our literature. *The springs of celebration:* how often we have sought them in childhood and a world elsewhere; how seldom in the heart of darkness. Yet, isn't the significant aspect in this instance the extent to which the narrator has made ecological study serve this end? the extent to which he has gone *out* in order to come *in*? With him, it may be said, the discipline of ecology heals the psyche and the healed psyche serves the unhealed world.

So the journey doesn't end in the deep interior space (the landscapes fuse) of the homecoming of "Upriver." Here he finds the anima and dances with her (the book is dedicated to Lopez's wife). This is told, appropriately, in the clairvoyant manner of dream or fairy tale, and it is recognized as such, as a mysterious occurrence whose moral meaning is nevertheless clear. *He dances and tells stories:* with these sacred gestures he celebrates the springs. He has been called as artist to restore the springs, and the springs themselves, as in Duncan's dream of Olson, are the source of myths. And he knows that he must do this in the realization that art, like rivers, is born of anguish and that the hope vouchsafed in dreams must, on return, encounter the terrors of the fallen world. Thoreau knew this too, when on the return from source in *A Week,* he left summer behind and entered the autumn of adult work. (I should have mentioned "The Forest Path to the Spring," the patently autobiographical story of how Malcolm Lowry learned from his wife to appreciate the feminine in the nature of the world. This fable of gratitude to the anima is surely cognate.)

The spiritual counsel of *River Notes* and *Desert Notes* belongs to the religious manuals of other times. There are chapters of explicit instruction: "The Bend," in which the ego yields its search for correspondences and becomes part of nature; "The Shallows," in which the narrator takes us by the hand and teaches us how to read things; "The Falls," in which a man, to be distinguished from the narrator, remains true to the vision-quest of his youth, follows the old (rough) ways and disciplines of nature. Stories of egoism, presumption, ambition, violation, trespass, and irreverence are foils for the virtues of guilelessness, compassion, forgiveness, and humility. And it may be, in a book so much indebted to the archaic, that it brings this to our attention in order to provide, as Charles Bernstein says of the archaic, a "chastening lesson . . . of our own ignorance and the value in acknowledging it."

When the river begins to dry up, the realtors move in. "Men with an intolerable air of condolence have appeared, as though drawn by the smell of death, dressed comfortably, speaking a manipulated tongue, terminally evil. They have inquired into the purchase of our homes." What would an eco-fable be without realtors and developers?

Even so, the beaver return (as on the river here) and a pair of osprey build their nest (as here). They live, the narrator says in one of the few ironies he allows himself, "as well as [may] be expected in that country."

Winter Count lacks an introduction, a feature of the previous books, probably because the narrator is no longer desperately troubled by the need for self-transformation and the stories he tells do not have the resolution of quest. The narrator now teaches at a university, and his familiarity with a wide range of books and with high culture defines him. Where the narrative fabric of *River Notes* is fittingly woven of references to raven, salmon, and heron, it is now (as with good academics) fittingly woven of bibliographical references.

A winter count, as a note informs us and the titular story exemplifies, is a personal history, a sequence of memorable events and determinative encounters. (*His story,* to cite Olson's special view of history, the record of an individual life tracking itself?) The narrator's stories are just such personal history and match those of the Plains Indians, recounted in "Buffalo" and "Winter Count 1973," in telling of foreboding, loss, and "fundamental anguish." His predicament is not as extreme as theirs—what it portends for our "tribe" may be—but it is comparable. For his allegiance is double, to both civilization and nature (Europe and America)—to define the issue as American writers in the nineteenth century did. He finds himself *between,* compelled by nature and native cultures (*nature, native,* and *nation* have the same root) but unable to dismiss the claims of civilization represented by European Culture. Story after story treats this dilemma, the condition in which Lopez also finds himself. This accounts for the resonance of his statement in *Crossing Open Ground:* "One of the great dreams of man [and woman] must be to find some place between the extremes of nature and civilization where it is possible to live without regret."

Restoration seems to be a way of mediating the extremes. The above statement, from "Searching for Ancestors," concludes a paragraph commenting on the zeal with which we now search out, record, and preserve the archaic past—"We worry over what is lost." And *Winter Count,* the title declaring an historical motive, names the work of the narrator and, more explicitly, of the exemplar in the initial story, "Restoration." Edward Seraut, a European book-restorer, practices his art with surgical aestheticism. He is not especially concerned with what the books in René de Crenir's library tell of de Crenir's intellectual life, although his recognition of this use prompts the narrator's investigation. Since the narrator is familiar with many of these old books on exploration, travel, and the natural history of North America, it is clear that de Crenir, a Frenchman who lived on the family cattle land in North Dakota, is an "ancestor."

His intermediate situation and intellectual interests survive in the narrator. The first is evoked when the narrator says in the course of an elegant dinner at the local hotel, "I was now deeply affected by the atmosphere of ideas and history that emanated from Seraut, and periodically stunned by the sight of young, ferine men cruising in slow-moving pickups on the other side of the window, or distracted by the . . . ranchers' voices and the din of country-and-western music in an adjoining bar." (See Snyder's "I Went into the Maverick Bar" and Williams' "The Desert Music.") The second plays off the first because it involves the almost insuperable difficulty of coming to know what is alien to one's ideas—the difficulty, that is, of altering perspective and perception. De Crenir had understood this ("a cultural and philosophic bias had prevented nineteenth-century European naturalists from comprehending much of the plant and animal life they saw in North America"). He had even understood that "les bêtes sont les propriétaires," that, as the narrator explains, "in North America the indigenous philosophy [Native American lore] grew out of the lives of animals." This insight, so singular then, disturbs the narrator who wonders, "Whom might he have spoken with about it?" It is a question of present moment for him (and the author of *Of Wolves and Men*) because the issue now is animal rights.

In this story multiple perspectives and inclusivity of perception accommodate the very dilemma they present. For this reason, the concluding paragraph has the power of revelation. Far and near, out and in, past and present—everything, however anomalous, is sharply seen synchronistically, as belonging together.

> Out of the window we could see several miles across the rolling brown hills. In a draw below the house there suddenly appeared six antelope, frozen so still they seemed to shimmer in the dry grass. I saw sunlight glinting on the surface of their huge eyes, their hearts beating against soft, cream-white throats, their slender legs. Surprised by the house, or by us in the window, they were as suddenly gone. At the end of the room, beyond a blue velvet rope strung between polished brass stanchions, a line of tourists passed. They stared at us and then looked away nervously into the shelves of books. A girl in yellow shorts was eating ice cream. In a shaft of window light I could see the wheat paste dried to granules under Seraut's fingernails and the excessive neatness of my own notes, the black ink like a skittering of shore birds over the white sheets.

("Only the copied text," Walter Benjamin says in a lesson on reading, " . . . commands the soul of him who is occupied with it. . . .")

The copied text in this instance is preceded by an example of accommodation. Seraut, in talking of Montaigne's misgivings, "spoke in a genial way, as though misgivings were a part of everything."

This may be the wisdom of Europe, steeped in history and evil, as we have been taught to believe by Henry James and other American writers. "The Tapestry" is a Jamesian story of a passionate pilgrim ("I was awed by European culture") whose European legacy involves knowledge of the evil in the world and presentiment of catastrophic end. This is the vision bequeathed him by the fifteenth-century Flemish tapestry that his Spanish grandfather had purchased—the end of a vision-quest that takes place in a museum, in the Prado, where the tapestry is stored. The tapestry, of course, represents the grandfather with whom the narrator is said to be in temperamental accord. Thus the "innocent brooding" that characterizes the arrested world of the tapestry belongs as well to grandfather and grandson, brooding, however, that allows the grandfather but not the American grandson to accept uncertainty without being tyrannized by it. In telling of a search for the past, the culture (Culture) of Europe, this story also tells of rejection, especially of a tradition so heavy (so institutionalized and protected by museums, curators, and documents) it makes for stasis and hopelessness. At the end, in a gesture that recalls Columbus, who belonged to but opened the world of the tapestry, the narrator sails for home.

Europe is not the way back. (Remember what Olson said of Pound and the "Western box.") But neither is America, except in a diminishing number of places where sometimes are to be found people further back. (And remember Lopez's injunction to take better care of "the repositories of our own long-term cultural wisdom.")

Yet the narrator sails for open ground. "Winter Herons" puts the dilemma in terms of East and West, New York City and Montana—in terms of *Les Sylphides* and the dance of cranes, and of a ballet dancer whom the narrator tries to initiate in the ways of the "north" but finally fails to win. (" . . . she stood at the river's edge with her arms folded across her bare chest looking down the river with a chin line hard enough for that country. She had tied a flicker's feathers in her hair.") His solace, perhaps, is the recollection of a snowy evening when, having been left by a friend, he sees a flock of great blue herons descend into the canyon of the city street.

(Is this Lopez's addition to the myths of swan maiden? Had he read Snyder's study of a Haida myth, published in 1974?)

In this book of stories Lopez is more than usually concerned with actual and spiritual fathers and with a correlative reverie toward childhood.

(Bachelard supplies the calculus: the well-being recovered in such imaginative work often belongs to the recovery of our cultural "childhood" in the natural world.) A notable instance is "The Orrery." Set in the desert country Lopez had known as a child, it tells of returning to find a man whose "grip seemed sure, as though whatever it was he was doing was as good as one might hope to do." With artful artlessness and liberating discipline this solitary man joins self-sufficient practical arts (baking bread, gardening, even the art of native medicine) with high culture (he plays Bach and Satie on a clavichord). He belongs with the woman in "The Woman Who Had Shells," for she, too, joins the worlds the narrator finds himself between. The narrator says of this conspicuous anima figure who enables him to imagine that "it was possible to let go of a fundamental anguish" what may also be said of the man: that "we carry such people with us in an imaginary way, proof against some undefined but irrefutable darkness in the world." To this desert father, whose eighteenth-century orrery is the model of the celestial world he has set out in stones on the desert floor, the narrator owes an experience of cosmicity that restores the well-being of childhood. (No prayer rugs here, no sand paintings.) And to him, he owes good counsel. "With enough care," he is told, "almost anything would keep. It was only a matter of choosing what to take care of." And this, in conclusion: "If one is patient, if you are careful, . . . there is probably nothing that cannot be retrieved." (*Re*trieved.)

"The Lover of Words" glosses this fantastic story. In this instance another solitary man, a Mexican gardener in Los Angeles, an autodidact whose self-making is in the chrysalis stage, is destroyed by self-awareness and loss of innocence. The acute account of his anguish and self-destruction is Andersonian and may be read as a critique of individualism, the norm of most of the stories. For Lopez is very much an American writer in seeking to solve within the self the social, cultural, and moral problems that must also be confronted outside the self, concertedly, in community. The gardener's dilemma is also the writers's: it is not enough to appreciate "how words healed" (even now as I write them), the refuge to be found in them.

The character closest to the narrator is Roger Callahan, the anthropologist in the titular story, "Winter Count 1973: Geese, They Flew Over the Storm." Callahan teaches at Nebraska State College and has spent his life studying the Native Americans of the high plains north of the Platte River. Is he intended to call up Loren Eiseley, a Nebraskan who worked this country—and, incidentally, was as skeptical of science as Callahan and expressed the kind of weariness he feels at a professional meeting? ("The Woman Who Had Shells" also calls up Eiseley, his essay "The Star Thrower," where a gratuitous act suggests the dance in Lopez's "Drought." And shells are important for the association with Venus established by the woman who gathers them but no longer keeps them, this goddess-figure to whom the narrator gives the single small shell he had chipped from the ice of an Arctic beach. Consider, then, the significance of Lopez's gathering shells in "The Lives of Seals.")

To anyone who has been to professional meetings the story of Roger Callahan is doubly pointed in not being as parodic as it seems. Such meetings are sometimes extreme situations, as this one is for Callahan, who has not attended for years and feels himself to be marginal if not a Native American clown, wholly outside. It is also extreme for the narrator, a younger man, for whom Callahan's crisis raises the question of whether entering the profession and seeking advancement denies the necessary spirit and so precludes entering another culture. What Kenneth Burke calls the scene/act ratio makes the issue vividly clear: the meeting, in a hotel, is suffocatingly enclosed, an interior world shut off from the weather, the storm that enters the room when Callahan, finally, decisively, opens the window. There is no better resolution of the dilemma of *out* and *in,* which is why the subtitle records it as a winter count. The world is permitted to enter; its wet air fills the lungs; and "in the deepest distance," Callahan hears "the barking-dog sounds of geese, running like horses before a prairie thunderstorm." (In Callahan's winter count this is associated with childhood, with having gone with his father to see the flight of whooping cranes, an experience "crucial in the unfolding of his own life." It is to be associated with the presence of birds in other stories, for example, "the pounding of wings overhead" in "The Woman Who Had Shells.")

"He remembered a friend's poem about a snowy owl dead behind glass in a museum, no more to soar, to hunch and spread his wings and tail and fall silent as moonlight."

Callahan remembers Lafcadio Hearn because he entered another culture and became an informant. The insignia of Callahan's membership is a medicine bundle; the winter counts that punctuate his memory like found material in a poem ("1891 Medicine bundles, police tore them open") have become a living part of his personal history and enable him to defend the dead from professional inquisition. His own paper on winter counts is a defense of personal, even divergent, histories; it exemplifies his belief that history is story, to be told, "unpacked," "unfolded." No longer concerned with theory and proving himself right, he urges the professionals to tell "the story as it was given to you" and to tolerate "the individual view, the poetic view, which is as close to the truth as the consensus."

"His own count would be personal, more personal, as though he were the only one." This story is Lopez's apologia—and serves as well for a generation of writers, who, as Creeley said of Whitman, believe that "the authenticity of the personal" is warrant enough. Lopez claims no expertise. He is only a "writer." Even his reporting is storytelling, always personal, and confirms his belief, expressed by Callahan as the deepest Native American wisdom, that "everything is held together with stories. . . ." That is all that is holding us together, stories and compassion.

> "I will tell you something about stories,
> [he said]
> They aren't just entertainment.
> Don't be fooled.
> They are all we have, you see,
> all we have to fight off
> illness and death."
> —Leslie Silko, *Ceremony*

Remembering (Hannah Arendt). Re-memberment.

1847 White buffalo, Dusk Killed it. This winter count, remembered by Callahan, confirms the mysterious event told (recounted) in "Buffalo." Method is the issue here, for the disappearance of the great herds of buffalo upon which the Native Americans depended is not in question, but rather the truth of its visionary correlative, the story of white buffalo who ascended a mountain. The Native Americans acknowledge the event but at the time and for most of the nineteenth century are unable to fathom its meaning. White people, at a meeting in 1911, remain skeptical of its factual truth and do not recognize its poetic truth—they do not "understand the purpose of such a story." The narrator, whose research begins when he finds factual evidence of buffalo at that unusual height in the *Journal of Mammology* (see vol. 36, p. 470), follows the advice of a Native American to seek another truth. This, of the poetic kind, is, as the Arapaho have come to believe, that the buffalo, reported to have sung a death song, "tried to show them how to climb out through the sky," or, as the narrator rephrases it, how "to get away from what was coming."

This puts the deep rationale of Lopez's storytelling, which is made urgent by the ever-presence of myth, shown here by the *fact* that the narrator, who has gone into these mountains, awakes (in a double sense) to find his legs broken.

The concluding story, "The Location of the River," is also about method and may be read as a prolegomenon to *Of Wolves and Men* and *Arctic Dreams*. Like the story of the buffalo, this story involves an unusual event—the disappearance of the upper Niobrara River for a period of several months. This is not disputed by Benjamin Foster, an historian who had spent much of his life with Native Americans. Still, it is a phenomenon he tries to verify, first with "traditional methods" (scientific) that fail, then with "less conventional" (Native American) that succeed. After a long vigil, he reads the disappearance of the river in the shapes of the clouds. Nevertheless, as the narrator comments, "This must have been slightly disquieting for Foster living in two worlds as he did . . . thinking what he did not know, could and could not prove."

Methodological doubt comes of being between, and the narrator shares it. To some extent he identifies with Foster, whose biography preoccupies him. Yet he believes that the river never disappeared—that Foster, "troubled by the destruction of native cultures," went mad. On the evidence of Foster's essay, "Studying the Indian," this seems to have been the outcome of having been told that he "learn[ed] everything wrong." An illustration depicts a fragment of this manuscript with "I got everything wrong," inscribed in Foster's hand, situated between land and cloud-filled sky. It is a cautionary motto for historians, among them the narrator, who, in turn, finds the flooding Niobrara at night but loses it in the morning.

Of Wolves and Men belongs to an occasion: Lopez signed a copy for us when we happened into Prairie Lights Books during his visit to Iowa City.

He did this in a fashion wholly his own, having first established, in conversation, a personal relationship. He recognized us as attentive listeners at his lecture and reading, and this facilitated gift exchange. It might be said that this is the way he does business. The dedication of *Winter Count* is "For Friends, Their Uncommon Grace"; that of *Crossing Open Ground* acknowledges the men and women with whom he traveled and worked; and that of *Of Wolves and Men* is "For Wolves," in their behalf, an "effort at understanding," and in gratitude for their "company."

The only wolf that I have seen is Lobo, the stuffed animal in a glass cage at the entrance of Morell's Trading Post in Bemidji. He is as much a part of the folklore here as the statues of Paul Bunyan and the Blue Ox in the amusement park across the street. What I know of wolves I have learned mostly from Farley Mowat and Lopez, and witnessed, at second hand as it were, in the behavior of two of our dogs, Flash, a female Siberian Husky, and Mukwa (Black Bear), a male German shepherd-black Labrador, both, incidentally, acquired from Native Americans, here on Wolf Lake. (Having initially to fend for themselves, they remain good hunters, whose presence now outside my cabin reminds me of the skunk they killed on this morning's walk.) My appreciation of the crushing pressure of a wolf's jaws derives from a recent experience of the 750 pounds per inch exerted by a German shepherd, an enactment (almost) of the myth of Fenris and Tyr.

Of Wolves and Men follows *Desert Notes* and the collection of stories about Coyote. It is Lopez's first "big" book, a work of travel and research (landscape and library) like *Arctic Dreams*. It brought him recognition and the John Burroughs Medal for natural history writing. It did this, I think, because it exemplifies his belief that "a viable natural philosophy, one that places us again within the elements of our natural history," may be found in the study of wild animals. Such study, he says, may draw us back "into an older, more intimate and less rational association with the local landscape"—it is one of the ways of familiarization—and it may prompt us to question the "objectivity" and "troublesome lack of heart" of "Western Science."

An epigraph from John Rodman's "The Dolphin Papers" leads us to discover there another instance of the anti-Cartesianism of recent thought, especially the anti-theriophobia that characterizes Lopez's work; and Lopez's work gains power by its concurrence with and contribution to a main current of revisionist thinking. The epigraph from Rodman, noting the aversion to "a Heraclitan world," names the patron philosopher of many avant-garde poets and philosophers, and with other epigraphs from Henry Beston and Montaigne announces the moral concern that as much as anything is the moving force of Lopez's work.

More than most writers of natural history—or more conspicuously—Lopez is a moralist who has taken to heart Montaigne's remarks on presumption and Beston's belief that animals are not to be "measured by man." He does not so much admonish us as figure his own thought. His moral stance (and stand) is attractive because it does not overlook the claims of (and moralistically deny) what it opposes.

A notable instance is the conclusion of the section on wolf-killing in nineteenth-century America, an enormity he likens to a pogrom, even to the Holocaust. Here he recalls the old wolfers he had interviewed and says, "You could not blame these men, at least I could not, for what they had done, as though it had all happened in a vacuum." He does not blame them because *we,* as much as they, had been moved by a complex of motives and actions called Manifest Destiny: "We killed hundreds of thousands of wolves. Sometimes with cause, sometimes with none." This obliges us to do what he has done, "go back and look at the stories we made up when we had no reason to kill"—that is, look to ourselves, to our imaginings, to our psychological projections, to what moves us when we literally have no reason. His natural history has the distinction of including (I borrow an Emersonian title) both the natural history of intellect and the history of intellect, its errors and follies, in its encounter with nature. To recover a more natural, more hospitable and humble relation between self and world is the overriding intent of his work.

(I associate Lopez with Terrence Des Pres. He, too, is a moralist, his *The Survivor: An Anatomy of Life in the Death Camps* one of the essential moral investigations of this generation of writers. *Of Wolves and Men* also treats survival, not only the survival of wolves but of endangered Native Americans whose lifeways involved them. "By 1900," Lopez notes, "there wasn't much point in being either a wolf or an Indian in the United

States"—the Indian who might have asked the Great Spirit, "Help me to fit, to be valuable in the world, like the wolf.")

I am not as pleased on this rereading as I was initially because I am not as much aware of Lopez's presence (his entry into my life) as I am of youthful earnestness and nostalgia for the primitive. I also notice the popular character of the book and its pedestrian style. Lopez achieves the clarity but not the elegance he seeks, the latter compromised by colloquialism ("you may think I'm pulling your leg"), patronizing identification ("the English philosopher Alfred North Whitehead"), and expositional signal ("I would like to close this chapter . . ."). The data he has collected is simply set out in workmanlike fashion. (The book, he told an interviewer, was written "in longhand," in twenty days, "at the rate of about 5000 words per day.") Where possible he employs anecdotes and stories; accounts of his own experience are few—he tells what he learned by raising two red-wolf pups, and he tells more about his work in the Pierpont Morgan Library than in the field. He admits that he is not "an authority on wolves," and how to incorporate his experience with that of the experts is a fundamental problem better solved in *Arctic Dreams* and *Crossing Open Ground.*

My present reading of Richard Nelson's *Make Prayers to the Raven* undoubtedly contributes to the above criticism. Lopez brought this book to my attention ("a non-Cartesian field guide, grounded in historical research, on lengthy interviews, and the author's own experience") and narrated the TV documentary based on it. Nelson's use of Koyukon oral material and his own journal, set out as "found" material in a collagist way, distinguishes this scientific study, already distinguished by its respect for the ecological wisdom of indigenous natural history. Nelson's journal entries are especially fine, sensitive, and well-written—expressive of much that scientific discourse does not admit.

The four-part structure of *Of Wolves and Men* makes the argument of the book. The scientific findings of Part 1—Adolf Murie published the first ecological study only as recently as 1944—give us an essentially unbiased but limited view of wolves (their sociality requires the plural) and acquaints us with these remarkable animals, one of the "other nations," Beston says, "caught with ourselves in the net of life and time." It provides objective knowledge, the kind of knowledge we respect, and invites our partisanship by giving us the truths that make us privy, as it were, to the inside narrative.

Part 2 both implements and corrects the (modern) scientific view by juxtaposing to it the ancient "vision" of the Esquimo and other hunting peoples whose lifeways "correspond" with those of wolves. Lopez begins this section of the book by noting the distrust of science already evident in Part 1 in his comments on the methodological risk of typicality and unconscious biases of perception ("The male hunter—male leader image of the wolf pack is . . . perpetuated by males, who dominate this field of study"). He would open the closed (assumption-bound) ways of field biologists by introducing them to the open ways and intimate knowledge (and oral culture) of hunters. He proposes a participatory mode of scientific study based on the practice of the Nunamiut as well as the kind of widening of concern represented by his own work. "What I am saying is this," he editorializes in a passage I cite also for its style: "We do not know very much at all about animals. . . . to approach them solely in terms of the Western imagination is, really, to deny the animal. It behooves us to visit with a people with whom we share a planet and an interest in wolves but who themselves come from a different time-space and who, as far as we know, are very much closer to the wolf than we will ever be."

Lopez asks biologists to enter the field in the way poets have, responsively, attentive to the particulars of each occasion, in intimate relation to the landscape of experience. He would have them hunt for facts in the way peoples whose lives depend upon it hunt for animals. This means that he would have them (and all of us) recognize a metaphysics in which animals and humans do not live in separate realms but have life in common. He talks at the boundaries of the modern and the archaic, and the title of his book, in its double meaning, suggests their collision. For *Of Wolves and Men,* which in its totality is about the many ways men throughout history have viewed wolves, is at heart about the similar ways of wolves and men—those people who live in the same landscape and depend on the same ecology as wolves and, accordingly, have learned from them. Lopez's fundamental assumption is that the social organization of these hunting animals and hunting people is alike. We may question this and still acknowledge that he celebrates the primitive because he values social interdependence, the virtues of hard survival, intimacy with the immediate world, and a way of life made sacred, ultimately, by what he calls "the conversation of death."

Parts 1 and 2 set off the enormities described in Parts 3 and 4. "The Beast of Waste and Desolation" in the title of Part 3 is not the wolf but man himself, who exterminated the wolves of America. Lopez's sense of moral outrage is both explicit and expressed by the data that saturates the exposition, and he thinks we should "answer to ourselves for all this":

> As I have tried to make clear, the motive for wiping out wolves (as opposed to controlling them) proceeded from misunderstanding, from illusions of what constituted sport, from strident attachment to private property, from ignorance and irrational hatred. But the scope, the casual irresponsibility, and the cruelty of wolf killing is something else. I do not think it comes from some base, atavistic urge. . . . I think it is that we simply do not understand our place in the universe and have not the courage to admit it.

In Part 4, Lopez searches in history for the imaginary wolf. He focuses on the demonology of the Middle Ages and extends the study of human ferocity. There may be too much about such things as werewolves and the Inquisition, but this serves as a foil for what is of most interest here, Lopez's "alternative gospel." In this gospel the "new wolf" he claims we are now ready to look for is the wolf-mother, the benevolent wolf, as in the legend of Romulus and Remus, who "nurtures." Lopez does not spell out this essentially feminist insight nor connect it with his own fictive search for the anima. But this good news is the soul of the book. *Of Wolves and Women*, then, for *animal*, in an etymological sense that goes to the root of things, depends on *anima*.

I first read *Arctic Dreams* during the winter of a sabbatical we spent here at the lower edge of the boreal forest, where the frozen expanse of the lake and the sub-zero weather and the diminished things (the abstraction of that season) provided enough similitude for valuing an earned account of the Arctic world. It was, as much of my reading had become, the pleasure of the evening and the snug warmth of a down comforter, and it soon became the subject of long breakfast conversations before the fire.

Now, even in a summer of extreme heat and drought, I respond to it with as much enthusiasm and with a critical (more exacting and exact) sense of its remarkable achievement. It is one of the best books about landscape I know—of a different kind, say, than Ronald Blythe's *Characters and Their Landscapes,* which comes to mind because it is informed by a similar unassuming disposition (gentleness, as Jim Summerville says of Lopez in a recent letter) and is written with equal clarity and elegance. Here is (a) man *in* the landscape (Paul Shepard's title) who, as Shepard's subtitle has it, appreciates the "Esthetics of Nature" and exemplifies a practice favorable to it. Favorable to it, and in favor of it, because *aesthetics* in his understanding, as in Aldo Leopold's, refers to the beauty and harmony of the world realized by us in an ecological awareness of its interrelationships and interdependencies and in recognition of its ultimate mysterious reality. *Aesthetics,* which hitherto involved the visual appreciation of nature (or Nature), the spectatorial viewing of its scenery, is now a cover-word for depth of ecological understanding, for "living as if nature mattered," to cite the subtitle of *Deep Ecology,* by Bill Devall and George Sessions, which appeared before the publication of *Arctic Dreams* and, accordingly, does not list Lopez in its bibliography. From the writers listed there—among them, Leopold, Berry, and Snyder—we have been learning what it means to have a living world and *to world,* to live within its complex web. To live as the animals, plants, and native people of the Arctic have done in order to survive. For the Arctic, the vast panorama of challenging landscapes in Lopez's account, dramatizes urgent global problems and conflicts of ideas. The simplest formulation—too melodramatic perhaps, insisting too much on good vs. evil—puts *ecos,* in its wide and deep understanding, against *econ,* the narrow determination on utility and development with which it is often confused.

Arctic Dreams treats the desire to live with(in) the *ecos* and give over its exploitation, the desire, in a word, to resanctify life. It is the work of a master, where *Of Wolves and Men* is the work of an apprentice, work of the order of a doctoral dissertation. *Of Wolves and Men* is also indebted to the Arctic and—this holds for most "serious" writers—comes from the same generative center. In the chapter entitled "Migrations" in *Arctic Dreams,* Lopez tells of having observed wolves on Ilingnorak Ridge and of having thought much about hunting. He says that eventually he came to experience this primary human activity and understand it better as a "dialogue" with the land. This is to say, as Buber's word for what occurs *between* tells us, that he recognized that the Esquimo hunters had an I-Thou relationship with the landscape, a relationship of utmost eco-

moral significance, and that this primitive subsistence lifeway challenged the I-It relationship, the objectification and depersonalization, that characterizes modern Western culture. For Lopez, as for Richard Nelson, the native hunters of the North possess a deep ecological understanding. Ecology is their preeminent science as well as theology—a *paideia* transmitted by story.

The recovery of the primitive is central for Lopez because it involves the being-in-the-world to which he aspires, the worlding that puts an end to world alienation. He would like to be "fully *incorporated* into the landscape"—I italicize to stress the bodily as well as communal nature of having "the land around you like clothing." The sacrality and sociality of hunting move him, the moral discipline imposed by the first ("most men understood how to behave") as well as the shared endeavor of the second ("In no hunting society could a man hunt successfully alone"). He admires the ability to closely attend the always shifting patterns of *what is*—"a frame of mind that redefines patience, endurance, and expectation"—and the fear that acknowledges ignorance of "perfect harmony" and contributes to *nuannaarpog,* the "quality . . . of taking extravagant pleasure in being alive." In sum, he values the "*struggle* . . . to live with dignity and understanding, with perspicacity or grace." The Esquimo hunters, he says, "know something about surviving," and, he adds, "they are a good people to know . . . facing as we do our various Armageddons. . . ."

Survival. This is the ecological measure of success, and learning to live in harsh environments, as both the animals and humans he describes have done, teaches us to respect an adaptiveness of incomprehensible complexity and defines a kind of heroism (of sufficiency) we seldom consider. There are many accounts of heroism in *Arctic Dreams*—discovery and exploration necessarily involve this—but none seems so much to the point as the brief story of an Esquimo. We appreciate the story of Comock's competence (the pragmatism of *what is*) just as we recognize the often arrogant ignorance of explorers because Lopez has already given us a scientifically grounded sense of Arctic landscapes (eco-scapes), a strategy like that of *Of Wolves and Men,* where knowledge precedes lore. Faced with starvation, Comock and his family undertook a journey over sea ice to an island, and on the way, when the ice opened beneath their camp, they lost most of their possessions. With what remained, Comock "reconstructed his entire material culture, almost from scratch, by improvising and, where necessary, inventing." For Lopez, this is not the story of an Esquimo Robinson Crusoe but a parable of "people who lived resolutely in the heart of every moment they found themselves in, disastrous and sublime." *And who survived:* "He survived. His family survived. His dogs survived and multiplied."

In reading *Make Prayers to the Raven,* I noted by way of summary that to live in the world you have to get your living there. This is why a market economy jeopardizes the subsistence lifeway of Esquimos and why most of us are beyond the possibility of recovering a primitive (primary) way of being. Lopez admits this in the epilogue, where he tells of participating in a walrus hunt and of "brood[ing] about hunting" and the paradox of life sustained by death ("the horror inherent in all life"). He understands how a sacral sense of life allows one to live with this contradiction and how "making your life a worthy expression of a leaning into the light" may help one do this. Even so, the butchery and blood on the snow trouble him. He himself is not a hunter, and he does not know how to bridge the "gap [in lifeways] between civilized man [estranged from the land] and the society of the hunter." He can do only what he does in this book—use imagination to transform desire—and, in the end, he can only (literally) bow to the landscape, to whose smaller mysteries of living things it has become his habit to pay respect. Like the man who dances with the herons, his is a "gesture of reverence." I borrow Richard Nelson's term, used by him in speaking of the Koyukon Indians: "Because spiritual power is everywhere in nature, gestures of reverence are nearly constant as people interact with their environment, as they carry out the necessary activities of subsistence and survival." *Arctic Dreams* is such a dance, the action Lopez takes because he knows what the dancer in the story knew, "that without such an act of self-assertion no act of humility had meaning."

Perhaps it is inevitable that hunting, as with Ortega, becomes a metaphor that enables Lopez to speak of the requisite alertness of another kind of experience, that represented by the arduous tracking of (and in) the landscapes of this book. "By hunting," Lopez says, "I simply mean being out on the land." This also means—and not so simply, for the discipline is demanding—having a "state of mind" or stance (to use Olson's word) that allows us to be receptive to and engage in conversation with the land.

Conversation with the land. Lopez acquired this phrase from Maurice Haycock, a Canadian landscape painter associated with the Group of Seven. Haycock used the phrase to describe his work of painting the subtleties of the land and air of Cornwallis Island—subtleties that Lopez also attends throughout his book and especially in the chapter "Ice and Light." A painter in the Arctic—not Rockwell Kent, whose stance was heroic and whose "imagination worked against [the land]"—Haycock, found by Lopez among the scientists of a research station, is one of the grandfathers. He is one of "the estimable rather than famous people," someone whose previous work as a geologist increases rather than cancels his appreciation of the aesthetics of nature. His singular presence among scientists, who for the most part are on Cornwallis Island as the advance-guard of development, points up what is lacking in our "swift and efficient possession of places"; and the fact that Lopez treats him in relation to the Luminist painters, who, like the Group of Seven, were not especially indebted to European tradition, suggests the extent to which "leaning into the light" may be learned in encounters with American landscapes. ("The European culture from which the ancestors of many of us came has yet to make this turn ["of unknown meaning before coming home"]. . . . It has yet to understand the wisdom, preserved in North America, that lies in the richness [not riches] and sanctity of a wild landscape. . . .") Haycock, then, is the kind of hero Lopez wishes to become and whose own conversation with the land proposes. At the end of the book, where he speaks of landscapes as "crucibles of mystery," he says that they "are not solely arenas for human invention": "To have no elevated conversation with the land, no sense of reciprocity with it . . . shows a certain lack of courage, too strong a preference for human devising." The hero stands with the land; his "especial province," as Olson said of the Sumerian kings, "is the guardianship of the earth."

I have often thought of Olson when reading *Arctic Dreams* because he is a preeminent poet of landscape (he, too, admired the Luminists and leans into the light in *Maximus* III) and because the stance he defines in "Projective Verse" is essentially the stance Lopez has adopted. Olson pushes harder than Lopez, is didactic and dogmatic and sometimes bellicose—

and more explicit in his attack on Western culture (the tradition of philosophical idealism), the threat of which he especially felt after World War II in the Old World's attempt to retain hegemony. But his project, the work now of the two generations of poets, is also Lopez's, not derived directly from Olson but from sources and concerns common to both. And, for all of his disclaimer, Lopez is a poet because of his care for language and his subscription to the shamanic role (the communal, healing art) set out in ethnopoetics.

Olson's fundamental demand, like Lopez's, is personal: that we yield the ego (the agent of heroism) in obedience to something larger than self, that we give over the "will to power" that moves us to possess things instead of living openly and responsively (and responsibly) with them. Olson presents this radically new (and archaic) stance in the figure of Maximus, who comes home to the landscape of Gloucester, his native place, by carefully and closely attending the particular things that compose it and by the equally necessary searching out of its past, the history of its geology, discovery, and settlement. Lopez does comparable work in *Arctic Dreams,* where the use of personal experience to frame each chapter is the significant literary advance on *Of Wolves and Men* and the propriety of its management a measure of his achievement. He speaks not of himself but of a narrator who is "a refinement of something that's inside of me that I found useful technically"—useful, clearly, in moderating the "enormous act of ego" always involved in writing. Yet, even though he claims that the narrator is "the number two guy . . . [and] never intrude[s] on the reader's ability to enter the environment," Lopez himself is present and his way of entering the environment is a notable and instructive aspect of the book. He enacts the way to perceive about which he also writes—has *humilitas,* "an humilitas sufficient," as Olson says, "to make him of use."

Lopez travels the vast spaces of the Arctic by ship, airplane, truck, and snow machine, but he relates to the landscape, as nature writers always have, by walking. (Is there any other way to approach a plover's nest to see the eggs glowing "with a soft, pure light, like the window light in a Vermeer painting"?) He is, as Olson said of himself, a walker (from "the last walking period of man") for whom walking is a mode of attention and meditation, a participant activity in which outer and inner come together. "The Country of the Mind" may be the most abstract chapter, as he claims, but it is also the most personal, half of it devoted to a walk on Pingok Island. This "circumambulation," to borrow again from Olson, is a winter's walk, like Thoreau's excursion, and serves as the representative anecdote of Lopez's proceeding. And it has instructions for ours.

"The Country of the Mind"—the chapter title itself is a metaphor for the metaphoric relationship of the terms contained in it, and much of the chapter is devoted to fundamental categories, that is, to how we imagine time and space. The issue for Lopez is not metaphor itself but the way in which we use it to privilege the mind and give it sovereignty over things. Yet metaphor in our literary tradition is, as Stephen Owen argues in *Traditional Chinese Poetry and Poetics,* a "substitution trope" in which one term displaces another, that is, in which the world is displaced by mind; we have not been prepared by "Western theories of literature" (derived from Plato) to read poems, as the Chinese have, as "omens of the world." Metaphor, for us, seems inescapable: "Man is an analogist," Emerson says in the chapter entitled "Language" in *Nature,* and cannot "be understood without these objects, nor these objects without [him]." Lopez acknowledges the incredible power of the mind by employing *imagination,* the arch-Romantic word, in the subtitle and by describing the imaginings (and their often disastrous consequences) of the many explorers who, it may be said, tested themselves in this Romantic way against the ice. Closer to his own experience—cautionary—is what he says of the artist's exploration: "Relationships with the land that are intensely metaphorical, like [Rockwell] Kent's, are a lofty achievement of the human mind . . . a sophisticated response, like the creation of maps. . . . The mind can imagine beauty and conjure intimacy. It can find solace where literal analysis finds only trees and rocks and grass."

That this projective power may be anthropomorphic does not trouble him. Anthropomorphism, a "very old human tradition," is not *sophisticated;* it respects mystery, has none of the arrogation conveyed by *intensely* and *lofty,* and does not mislead us in the way mistaking the map for the territory does. For the risk, he knows, is in "finding our final authority in the metaphor rather than in the land," in imposing "mental maps" (and two-dimensional grids) on a landscape that others, the Esquimo, experience in three dimensions and know as a "country of the mind": the landscape evident to the senses, as it is retained in human memory and arises in the oral tradition . . . as a repository of mythological and 'real-time' history. . . ." Where "mental maps" are abstract, the "country of the mind" is particular, belonging to the local culture, depicting its reality in the way its language does. For this understanding of language and culture, Lopez, like Olson, turns to Benjamin Whorf, but reads him differently. He claims that, for Whorf, language is created by man and imposed on the landscape, instead, as Lopez would have it, of evolving from a conversation with the land.

Whatever the truth (I don't have my Whorf here), the point, as with metaphor, is clear: imposition must yield to "gentle interrogations" and conversation; to I-Thou. The Esquimos with whom Lopez talks about their land-claims wonder at the men who make land-use surveys, "the men who owned the maps"—wonder at their indifference to the corroborative details of Esquimo history. This disregard of what native people know is what *Arctic Dreams* redresses at a time when what they know about "a good way of life is disintegrating" and "the sophisticated, ironic voice of civilization insists that their insights are only trivial. . . ."

Lopez's narrative art is a practice of humilitas. He speaks, in an interview, of cultivating "a sense of yourself as the one who doesn't know"—and he presents himself as an inquirer, never as an expert. He usually thinks of *expert* in respect to scientists and always associates the word with authority. (His own authority is moral, the result of the "shaman-light" of his storytelling, and his expertise is that of an artist who is not as deferential as he was in *Of Wolves and Men* to the scientists whose findings he now uses to compose a more inclusive ecology of the Arctic world.) The authority, he says, "will always be with the subject," in this instance, the largest subject, the landscape itself.

Lopez's conversation with the land begins with three progressively larger essays. In these prefatorial installments Lopez situates himself (and us) and establishes the themes of this well-orchestrated book. I think of Chapter One ("Arktikós") as prefatory because, with the preface and the prologue, it does the initial work of familiarization. It gets us beyond Greek myth and the notions of early European culture and alters as well our temperate-zone perspective. By following the sun's course through the tropical, temperate, and boreal zones we learn about three major ecosystems, how each adapts to the solar radiation on which all life depends; and we come to appreciate the light that for Lopez is the primary phenomenon, a wonderful fact that flowers into a wonderful truth. (The essentials of the phrase are Thoreau's for the attending that eventuates in wonder.) This solar journey brings us to "the final landscape," a realm of two seasons, of limited flora and fauna, of little diversity and stability.

Because it is "inherently vulnerable," the Arctic (also a last frontier) serves admirably the purposes of eco-fable. The significance of the central episode of the prologue—the destruction of the ecosystem and the native people in the nineteenth century by the whalers at Pond's Bay—is now footnoted in regard to the "stress" brought about by industrial and other developments: "arctic animals are apparently unable to tolerate both the inherent stress to which, in an evolutionary sense, they are accustomed and new stresses of man-made origin—oil blowouts, pollution from mine tailings, noise from arctic shipping, and the unnatural patterns of sea-ice disruption associated with icebreakers." Since the stability and well-being of the *ecos* is the standard, economic development is an "intrusion" and the Esquimos, who think of us as "the people who change nature," become the guardians of the *ecos*. They have the wisdom of restraint—*restraint*, one of the most important moral qualities that Lopez thinks we can acquire in a search for the primitive.

In the first half of the book, Lopez treats animals in the spirit of his own counsel: "to try to understand the animal apart from its background . . . is to risk the collapse of both." Musk-oxen, polar bear, and narwhal—he considers each of these large animals in terms of a different place, a different *ecos*, and all of them, like the Esquimos who hunt them, are truly wonderful examples of adaptation and survival, both animals and people threatened now by economic development. Each chapter is a smaller but equally rich *Of Wolves and Men* and fulfills the literary task, proposed by Neruda, of taking animals off the shelf and bringing them to life. And bringing us "off the edge [of the land], into the ice and sea," where "Migrations," the culminating chapter in this sequence, puts us into the air with the birds as well as into the sea with the fish and marine animals. Brilliantly, in surging prose, Lopez gives us an entire *ecos* in motion over geologic time, an intricate dance to the rhythms of life in all the spaces of the Arctic world, searching always for new niches. (Darwin's "tangled bank," though in this adventurous book the Darwin of *The Voyage of the Beagle* more often comes to mind.)

"Migrations" also gathers earlier thought into a meditation on hunting that establishes the norm of primitive lifeways and makes the transition to the other imaginations and desires (the Western human presence) treated in the rest of the book. Here, as Lopez says, "I deal with ice, with icebergs and the behavior of sea ice; with the behavior of light—arctic sunlight, cathedral architecture, landscape painting, and so on. . . . I deal with how mind imagines place, and time and space . . . [and] with history—who went up there, why they went, and what they were looking for. I . . . show historically what conceptions of time and space have done to *our culture*" (my italics).

Neither his summary nor my previous use does justice to these remarkably rich and learned chapters. Much of what is canvassed here is the historical analogue of present exploitation—set off, it should be noted, by the fullest descriptions of the sublimity of Arctic ice and light, the fearful beauty of "the floor of creation." I have stressed economic developments, but Lopez doesn't; in his narrative they are a subtext. His accounts of traveling with scientists does not belabor this aspect of their work, and only briefly, and in this instance in the manner of the new journalism, does he report on industrial development.

What he writes of two excursions, one by truck and one by air, to the oil fields at Prudhoe Bay follows immediately on an extensive treatment of early polar exploration in which he points out that our ideas do not necessarily fit the land and that the land cannot be possessed, only manipulated by technology. So the road to Prudhoe Bay and the pipeline it parallels are manicured, the roadside planted to blue grass—the road that Leopold knew divided and conquered the wilderness and Benton MacKaye said was the spearhead of the metropolitan invasion of the indigenous environment.

At Prudhoe Bay the road (the way to wealth) ends, Lopez says, in a "landscape more austere than any I had ever seen in the Arctic." It has been made so by "muscular equipment" and "muscular engineering," the former "sitting idle like . . . [clenched] fists in [the] oil-stained yards" near a wretched bungalow camp of desperate workers, the latter part of the immaculate and luxurious controlled environment of the well-secured base of operations. He thinks of Cape Canaveral, and the revulsion expressed by leaden prose and what he says of lack of dignity ("Without dignity . . . people are powerless . . . you can direct any scheme you wish against them") reminds me of concentration camps, though he is reminded of state prisons and "factory life in America, [the] ugly way the country has arranged itself. . . ." He notes the colonial sensibility and economic vocabulary of the supervisors, and he is disturbed most by the misogyny of an all-male society, by men who think of women and treat them in the brutal way they treat the land. (They are not likely to see, as he does, an "image of vulnerability" in the genitalia of a female polar bear.) To their "what else is it good for?" his book answers, and he writes it as much to save them (us) as the native people and land their (our) technology "mangles."

Not Prudhoe Bay but what follows—the exalted sense of beauty he experiences at Axel Heiberg Island—is the Northern Passage and homecoming he seeks. This prompts him to say:

> In approaching the land with an attitude of obligation, willing to observe courtesies difficult to articulate—perhaps only a gesture of the hands—one establishes a regard from which dignity can emerge. From that dignified relationship with the land, it is possible to imagine an extension of dignified relationships throughout one's life. Each relationship is formed of the same integrity, which makes the mind say: the things in the land fit together perfectly, even though they are always changing. I wish the order of my life to be arranged in the same way I find the light, the slight movement of the wind, the voice of a bird, the heading of a seed pod I see before me. This impeccable and indisputable integrity I want in myself.
>
> One of the oldest dreams of mankind is to find a dignity that might include all living things. And one of the greatest of human longings must be to bring such dignity to one's own dreams, for each to find his or her own life exemplary in some way. . . . A way to do this is to pay attention to what occurs in a land not touched by human schemes, where an original order prevails.

The moral exploration of this original order ("the pattern that we call God," to recall Laurens van der Post's phrase) and the love of light ("the *relationship* between God and man was light," he says in discussing cathedral architecture)—these seem to me to warrant thinking of Lopez as a legatee of the transcendentalists. To subscribe to the original order of nature is to accept, as they did, the organic mandate and to think of relationship as light—Emerson spoke of "ray[s] of relation"—is to grant ecology the depth that allows for "numinous events" and, as Lopez says of the Arctic ecosystem, "a forgiving benediction of light." The question that he asks now and answers in revisionist terms in *Arctic Dreams* was once asked and answered by the transcendentalists: "What does the nature of the heroic become, once the landscape is threatened?"

20 August 1988

Previous Publications

I am pleased to acknowledge the editors who generously opened their journals to me and sustained my critical endeavor: Roy Skodnick (*All Area*), William Spanos (*Boundary 2*), Arthur Marotti (*Criticism*), David Hamilton (*The Iowa Review*), Jack Stillinger and Dale Kramer (*Journal of English and Germanic Philology*), Robert W. Lewis (*North Dakota Quarterly*), and Herbert Leibowitz (*Parnassus*). I am grateful to them and to the Louisiana State University Press for permission to republish, and so forward again, the materials of this book.

"Open(ing) Criticism": *North Dakota Quarterly*, L (1982), 9–18.
"Clinging to the Advance": *North Dakota Quarterly*, XLVII (1979), 7–14.
"Tory Formalists and New York Intellectuals": *Journal of English and Germanic Philology*, LXXX (1981), 273–277.
"Poetry and Old Age": *Journal of English and Germanic Philology*, LXXXI (1982), 282–285.
"Serial Poems from Canada": *North Dakota Quarterly*, L (1982) 108–118.
"Ideogram": *Journal of English and Germanic Philology*, LXXXIII (1984), 104–107.
"Eros and Logos": *The Iowa Review*, XIV (1984), 200–204.
"Ethnopoetics: An 'Other' Tradition": *North Dakota Quarterly*, LIII (1985), 37–44.
"Canon-Making": *Journal of English and Germanic Philology*, LXXXV (1986), 602–605.
"Nature and Poetry": *Journal of English and Germanic Philology*, LXXXVI (1987), 152–154.
"Emerson's Poetic Legacy": *Criticism*, XXI (1979), 175–179.
"A Sketchbook of the Artist": in *The Shaken Realist*, ed. M. J. Friedman and J. B. Vickery. Baton Rouge: The Louisiana State University Press, 1970, pp. 21–44.
"Stieglitz, Williams, and Cubism": *Journal of English and Germanic Philology*, LXIX (1970), 548–550.

"Williams' Background": *Journal of English and Germanic Philology,* LXXI (1972), 555–558.
"The Later Poems": *Journal of English and Germanic Philology,* LXXII (1973), 580–581.
"*The Embodiment of Knowledge*": *Journal of English and Germanic Philology,* LXXV (1976), 307–310.
"The Early Poems": *Journal of English and Germanic Philology,* LXXV (1976), 310–312.
"Coles on Williams": *Journal of English and Germanic Philology,* LXXV (1976), 617.
"Whittemore's Biography": *Journal of English and Germanic Philology,* LXXV (1976), 617–619.
"Williams and the Other Arts": *Journal of English and Germanic Philology,* LXXVIII (1979), 576–579.
"A Revisionist Study": *Journal of English and Germanic Philology,* LXXXIII (1984), 580–583.
"Romantic Idealist?": *Journal of English and Germanic Philology,* LXXXIV (1985), 583–585.
"A Modern Master": *Journal of English and Germanic Philology,* LXXXII (1983), 149–152.
"R. W. B. Lewis on Crane": *Journal of English and Germanic Philology,* LXVII (1969), 329–332.
"Crane's Prosody": *Journal of English and Germanic Philology,* LXVIII (1969), 324–326.
"An Inside Biography": *Journal of English and Germanic Philology,* LXIX (1970), 325–331.
"A Personal Biography": *Journal of English and Germanic Philology,* LXIX (1970), 684–686.
"Family Letters": *Journal of English and Germanic Philology,* LXXIV (1976), 151.
"Crane and Winters": *Journal of English and Germanic Philology,* LXXVIII (1979), 284–286.
"*Maximus:* Volume 3": *Boundary 2,* V (1977), 557–571.
"Olson and Pound": *Journal of English and Germanic Philology,* LXXVI (1977), 283–285.
"Dancing the Man": *Boundary 2,* VI (1978), 622–627.
"Birds, Landscape, Place, Cosmicity": *The Iowa Review,* XI (1980), 45–61.
"A Letter on Olson and Burke": *All Area,* no. 2 (1982), 64–65.
"An Olson Primer": *Journal of English and Germanic Philology,* LXXXIII (1984), 146–148.
"A Letter on Rosenthal's 'Problems of Robert Creeley'": *Boundary 2,* III (1975), 747–760.

"Understanding Creeley": *Journal of English and Germanic Philology,* LXXVIII (1979), 579–581.
"Gripping, Pushing, Moving": *Parnassus,* IX (1981), 269–276.
"Holding": *North Dakota Quarterly,* L (1982), 119–126.
"Entering": *North Dakota Quarterly,* LI (1983), 144–151.
"Arriving": *North Dakota Quarterly,* LIV (1986), 51–58.
"(The) Going(s) On": *North Dakota Quarterly,* LVI (1988), 109–118.
"This to Keep (You) On": *North Dakota Quarterly,* LVI (1988), 21–29.
"Noble and Simple": *Parnassus,* III (1975), 217–225.
"Minds Like Compost": *North Dakota Quarterly,* LI (1983), 142–153.
"Snyder's Politics": *Journal of English and Germanic Philology,* LXXXIV (1985), 294–297.